LIVING
DOWNTOWN

LIVING
DOWNTOWN

THE HISTORY OF

RESIDENTIAL HOTELS

IN THE

UNITED STATES

PAUL GROTH

University of California Press

Berkeley   Los Angeles   London

Portions of chapter 4 are excerpted from
"'Marketplace' Vernacular Design: The
Case of Downtown Rooming Houses,"
pp. 179–191 in *Perspectives in Vernacular
Architecture* 2 (Columbia: University of
Missouri Press), edited by Camille Wells.
Copyright © 1986 Vernacular Architecture
Forum. Reprinted by permission. Portions
of chapter 9 are excerpted from "Non
People: A Case Study of Public Architects
and Impaired Social Vision," pp. 213–237
in *Architects' People*, edited by Russell Ellis
and Dana Cuff. Copyright © 1989 by
Oxford University Press, Inc. Reprinted
by permission.

University of California Press
Berkeley and Los Angeles, California

University of California Press
London, England

Library of Congress Cataloging-in-
Publication Data
Groth, Paul Erling.
    Living downtown : the history of resi-
    dential hotels in the United States /
    Paul Groth.
            p.   cm.
    Includes bibliographical references
    and index.
    ISBN 0-520-06876-9 (alk. paper)
    1. Single-room occupancy hotels—
United States—History.   2. Architecture
and society—United States.   3. City and
town life—United States.   4. Housing—
United States—Sociological aspects.
    5. Single people—Housing—History.
    I. Title.
    HD7288.U4G76   1994
    647.9473'01—dc20   93-39896
                                     CIP

Printed in the United States of America

1 2 3 4 5 6 7 8 9

The paper used in this publication meets the
minimum requirements of American National Standard for Information Sciences—
Permanence of Paper for Printed Library
Materials, ANSI Z39.48-1984 ∞

There is nothing more frightening than active ignorance.

GOETHE

CONTENTS

IN DOWNTOWN SAN FRANCISCO, JUST ONE BLOCK from the Transamerica pyramid, is the large relict basement of the International Hotel. The lot has stood empty since 1977. In the Western Addition, one and a half miles to the west, there stretched until recently a vast tract of bulldozed basements; many of the former buildings had been rooming houses. While I have worked on this book, these two empty sites have haunted me. Before demolition, both had been commercially developed as single-room housing. Yet both sites—undeveloped land in the middle of a densely built and prosperous city—seem to have been sown with salt.

These lots represent important aspects of the American single-room housing crisis: first, the seemingly irrational destruction of millions of private low-rent housing units that are still desperately needed, and second, the near total misunderstanding of life in such places. This book charts the social and cultural history of this residential life and how Americans have arrived at today's hotel housing crisis. For two hundred years, hotels have served a series of domestic roles in urban vernacular environments and subcultures; for at least one hundred years, the keepers of official culture have aimed at eliminating these roles. The hotel housing crisis has resulted from the clash between these two histories.

My overarching purpose in this work is to expand the notion of "home" in the United States. I have arrived at this goal slowly. When I began, I was a critic of living in hotels. In 1977, when thousands of demonstrators were protesting the evictions and demolition at the International Hotel, I asked, "Why such a fuss? Why would anyone want to live in a hotel?" Then a 1980 study presented this startling fact: half the hotel rooms in San Francisco were residential, and most were in small thirty-room buildings. "Where were all these hotels?" I asked. "Who were they built for?" In answering these questions, the positive potentials of hotel life became apparent. There are major problems in some hotels, but I am now convinced that where hotels are properly managed and maintained, they deserve a place in the range of American housing.

Although this study is chronological, the sections of the book do not follow a single chronological line. In each chapter, the chronology is typically broken and begun again. The outer edges of the years studied are 1800 and 1980, but the greatest historical detail dates from between 1880 and 1930, the period when downtown hotel life was most vigorous. The majority of the remaining residential hotel buildings in the United States date from this period. These fifty years also marked the widest viable range of housing diversity in American urban history.

The methods used in this work depend on the conviction that studying the interweaving of buildings and social groups can provide important historical insights. Explaining the tensions between the vernacular and the official, as well as the social and the architectural, has required close study of the physical fabric of ordinary buildings and streets that are rarely photographed or described by experts. In the absence of systematic social surveys or verbal accounts for all types of hotel life, the buildings themselves (or records of those buildings) have been essential documents, and I have studied them with methods borrowed from quantitative social history. To discover what constituted the architectural average of everyday hotel living required a sample of several hundred buildings randomly selected from city directory listings for San Francisco hotels (more precisely, a 12 percent sample of all businesses listed under the categories of hotels, boardinghouses, rooming houses, lodgings, lodging houses, and rooms for the years 1880, 1910, and 1930). Each sampled hotel was then carefully described using data interpolated from Sanborn insurance maps, city tax records, building permit and inspection records, and water company records (which often recorded plans and plumbing fixture lists). This process provided a fairly reliable answer to what types of buildings and locations were in fact most common (table 1, Appendix). Thus, when I refer to a "typical" building—particularly between 1880 and 1930—I can do so with confidence. As with manuscript sources, what is erased often proves to be as culturally telling as what remains. In demolition records (where they survived), the nature of the struggle between the official and the ordinary became most clear.

This focus on the ordinary locates *Living Downtown* as an urban example of cultural landscape studies—where *landscape* means not scenery or open space but the spatial and cultural relationships between groups of people and their everyday surroundings. As such, this study is also within the overlapping realms of cultural and urban history, architectural history, and human geography. However, the work does not develop a traditional aesthetic history of hotel architecture. Nor does it provide a detailed history of San Francisco or suggest specific policies for the future of hotel living. These aspects have been studied by others cited in the notes. Also, most attention goes not to the elegant palace hotels but to rooming houses and cheap lodging houses, because of their larger populations. Where it is used, the slippery term "center city" refers to the retail and office downtown together with the industrial districts and older residential neighborhoods within reasonable walking radius (one or two miles) from the downtown. I have touched only lightly on hotel labor issues, which are well documented elsewhere, but I place a strong emphasis on employment and property capital as integral aspects of American culture. This study critiques downtown landowners, Progressive Era reformers, architects, and city planning officials, but many of the book's heroes are also from these groups. My targets are not any particular people or profession but narrow thinking and the insidious power of both inadvertent and deliberate ignorance. I hope that *Living Downtown* will be a point of departure for further study and a step toward preventing more empty sites like those of the International Hotel and the Western Addition.

I dedicate this work to the memory of my father, Erling Groth, and to my mother, Evelyn Groth. The book is also dedicated to the people who want to live in hotels. Ultimately, this book is for them.

ACKNOWLEDGMENTS

THIS BOOK HAS BEEN MANY YEARS IN THE MAKING, and a great number of people have been essential catalysts in the process. My initial introduction to both the problems and the possibilities of hotel living came from Richard Livingston in San Francisco's Cadillac Hotel. James Vance and Allan Pred agreed that hotel life could be a dissertation topic in historical geography. Gunther Barth rightly saw the topic as cultural history and generously aided the early phases of the work. Pierce Lewis's enthusiasm for the built environment kept the buildings themselves at the center of the study. Clarence Glacken's encouragement in studying ideas helped to link the physical and human elements of the story. Dell Upton set admirable standards and has been a good friend both to me and to the project. By his example and advice, John Brinckerhoff Jackson has shown that the cultural meaning of the environment must be studied in terms of its inhabitants.

Deserving special mention are other readers who have slogged through the entire manuscript in one of its preliminary forms: James Borchert, Barrie Greenbie, Jaime Kooser, Richard Longstreth, Judy Metro, Bradford Paul, and Richard Walker. At critical points, the ideas and encouragement of Christine Rosen, Tamara Hareven, Donald Meinig, and my editor, Stanley Holwitz, kept the project afloat. Others who read parts of the manuscript and injected timely suggestions include Kenneth Ames, Catherine Bishir, Betsy Blackmar, Jim Buckley, Lizabeth Cohen, Michael Conzen, Elizabeth Cromley, Robin Einhorn, Cliff Ellis, James Gregory, Neil Harris, Tom Harvey, Frederick Hertz, Thomas S. Hines, Deryck Holdsworth, Gary Kulik, Margaretta Lovell, Larry McDonald, Michael Laurie, Earl Lewis, Clare Cooper Marcus, Michael Smith, Jean Spraker, Kim Voss, Christopher Yip, and Wilbur Zelinsky. Dorothée Imbert converted my rough sketches into elegant drawings; Marc Treib lent valuable design advice. Roger Montgomery good-naturedly combined intellectual challenges with dire deadline warnings.

Specialists in housing history and hotel activism have also donated essential help. Robert Slayton and Charles Hoch graciously agreed to exchange early drafts of their manuscript for *New Homeless and Old: Community and the Skid Row Hotel.* Karen Franck, Joanne Meyerowitz, and Paul Rollinson also shared early drafts of their work. Michael Pyatok, Ron Sillimon, and Mike Estrada have challenged me with news from the hotel activists' trenches. Richard Penner of the Cornell School of Hotel Management advised me on palace hotels. In New York City, I owe thanks to Carroll Kowal, a pioneer in the fight to preserve hotel housing, and also to three people in the city's Department of Housing Preservation and Development, Colleen Myers, Robert Trobe, and Steve Norman, who literally opened doors in the Bowery.

For the time to draft the book manuscript in 1985–86, I owe thanks for a National Endowment for the Arts Museum Fellowship from the Office of Advanced Study at the Henry Francis du Pont Winterthur Museum and Gardens and a postdoctoral fellowship in the Smithsonian Institution's National Museum of American History. At the University of California, Berkeley, the Committee on Research supported graduate research assistants who were willing to find the answer to any question. Some worked for a few weeks, others for a semester. They are Bob Adams, Jim Buckley, George Henderson, Greg Hise, Douglas MacDonald, Louise Mozingo, Mark O'Malley, Adriana Petryna, Liz Vasile, Diane Shaw, and Lesley Watson. Other key assists came from Travis Amos, Anne Bloomfield, Frances Butler, Douglas Brookes, Don Coppock, Miriam Dobkin, Scott Dowdee, Claudia Farnswick, Brian Godfrey, Daniel Gregory, Kate Hutchins, Karen Kevorkian, Daniel Krummes, Dave Larson, Ellen Liebman, Bonnie Loyd, Patrick Macey,

Arthur Morris, Lucille Oberlander, Louise Quenneville, Gail Radford, William Savidge, Sylvia Shive, and Scott Wirth.

The keepers of photo collections were gracious and helpful: Linda Ziemer at the Chicago Historical Society, Patricia Paladines at the New York Historical Society, and particularly Marguerite Lavin at the Museum of the City of New York and Patricia Akre of the San Francisco History Room, San Francisco Public Library. For their help with other document collections, my thanks to Estelle Rebec of the Manuscripts Division, Bancroft Library, University of California, Berkeley; Eleanor McD. Thompson, Winterthur Library; Samuel Duca, Assessor of the City and County of San Francisco, and his staff; Robert C. Levy and Peter Burns of the San Francisco Bureau of Building Inspection; Robert Vasconcellos, Denise Davilla, and the staff at the San Francisco Water Department; Mary Catherine Haug-Boone and Peter Theodor of the San Francisco Redevelopment Agency; Michael Corbett and Eric Sandweiss of the Foundation for San Francisco's Architectural Heritage; and Mary Smyth at the Alice Statler Hotel Management Library, City College of San Francisco.

If this book serves to fight public misunderstanding, it is because all these people have helped to counteract my own.

ABBREVIATIONS

BL	Bancroft Library, University of California, Berkeley
FSA-LC	Farm Security Administration Collection, Library of Congress
MCNY	Museum of the City of New York
NMM	National Maritime Museum, San Francisco
NYHS	The New York Historical Society, New York City
NYPL	New York Public Library
SFR-SFPL	Photo Collection of the San Francisco Room, San Francisco Public Library

Full citations for illustrations from early published works, if not given here, are in the bibliography.

1.1.   Underhill Collection, MCNY.

1.2.   Author.

1.3.   Author.

1.4.   Jack Delano, FSA-LC. Negative no. LC-USF 34-42608-D.

1.5.   Photograph by R. R. Earle in Breckinridge and Abbott, "Furnished Rooms," *American Journal of Sociology* (1910): 303,

1.6.   Wilson, "Chicago Families in Furnished Rooms," 75, courtesy of Regenstein Library, University of Chicago.

1.7.   James Motlow.

1.8.   Author.

1.9.   Dorothée Imbert.

1.10.   Jacob A. Riis Collection, MCNY.

1.11.   Author.

1.12.   Byron Collection, MCNY.

1.13.   Courtesy of Mosser Victorian Hotel, San Francisco.

1.14.   Dorothée Imbert.

2.1.   Byron Collection, MCNY.

2.2.   Roy D. Graves Collection, BL.

2.3.   Henry Morrison Flagler Museum, Palm Beach, Florida.

2.4.   Photo postcard. Collection of Larry McDonald.

2.5.   Society of California Pioneers.

2.6.   Dorsey and Devine, *Fare Thee Well*, 139.

2.7.   Photograph by G. P. Hall and Son, NYHS.

2.8.   Roy D. Graves Collection, BL.

2.9.   Arthur Siegal, FSA-LC. Negative no. LC-USF 34-110165-C.

2.10.   Byron Collection, MCNY.

2.11.   Henry Morrison Flagler Museum, Palm Beach, Florida.

2.12.   Henry Morrison Flagler Museum, Palm Beach, Florida.

2.13.   Byron Collection, MCNY.

2.14.   SFR-SFPL.

3.1.   Oakland History Room, Oakland Public Library.

3.2.   *Harper's Weekly*, August 12, 1871, 744–745.

3.3.   *Harper's Weekly*, August 12, 1871, 744–745.

3.4.   Gilman, "The Passing of the Home," 141.

3.5.   Byron Collection, MCNY.

3.6.   *Hotel Red Book*, 1936 ed., 167.

3.7.   From a photo postcard, Chicago Historical Society.

3.8.   Michael Koop.

3.9.   Michael Koop.

3.10.   Dorothée Imbert.

3.11.   George B. Corsa Hotel Collection, NYHS.

3.12.   Photo postcard. Collection of Larry McDonald.

3.13. SFR-SFPL.

3.14. George B. Corsa Hotel Collection, NYHS.

3.15. *Architectural Forum* 41 (November 1924): 261.

3.16. Photo postcard. Collection of Larry McDonald.

3.17. Dorothée Imbert.

3.18. Courtesy of Claremont Hotel.

3.19. George B. Corsa Hotel Collection, NYHS. Brochure was hand-dated "June 8, 1939."

3.20. *Architectural Forum* 41 (November 1924): 253.

4.1. Byron Collection, MCNY.

4.2. Dorothée Imbert. Original 1840 pattern book plan from Mary Ellen Hayward, "Urban Vernacular Architecture in Nineteenth-Century Baltimore," *Winterthur Portfolio* 16 (1981): 33–63, on 53.

4.3. Arthur Rothstein, FSA-LC. Negative no. LC-USF 33-3528-M.

4.4. Dorothée Imbert.

4.5. Author.

4.6. Author.

4.7. Dorothée Imbert.

4.8. Dorothée Imbert.

4.9. Author.

4.10. Dorothée Imbert.

4.11. Byron Collection, MCNY.

4.12. Jack Delano, FSA-LC. Negative no. LC-USW 3-14108-D.

4.13. Collection of Larry McDonald.

4.14. Dorothée Imbert.

4.15. SFR-SFPL.

4.16. SFR-SFPL.

4.17. SFR-SFPL.

4.18. SFR-SFPL.

4.19. George B. Corsa Hotel Collection, NYHS.

4.20. Byron Collection, MCNY.

4.21. Photo postcard. Collection of Larry McDonald.

4.22. Roy D. Graves Collection, BL.

4.23. Lewis W. Hine Collection, NYPL.

4.24. Roy D. Graves Collection, BL.

4.25. Edwin Rosskam, FSA-LC. Negative no. LC-USF 33-5168-M4.

4.26. From Wilson, "Chicago Families in Furnished Rooms," courtesy of Regenstein Library, University of Chicago.

4.27. Dorothée Imbert.

5.1. Jacob A. Riis Collection, MCNY.

5.2. Arthur Rothstein, FSA-LC. Negative no. LC-USF 33-3033-M1.

5.3. John W. Proctor Collection, NMM.

5.4. Jacob A. Riis Collection, MCNY.

5.5. Marion Post Wolcott, FSA-LC. Negative no. LC-USF 33-30637-M3.

5.6. Adapted from Roderick Duncan McKensie, *The Metropolitan Community* (New York: McGraw-Hill, 1933): 246.

5.7. John Vachon, FSA-LC. Negative no. LC-USF 34-62539-D.

5.8. Author.

5.9. California Commission of Immigration and Housing, *Ninth Annual Report*, 1923.

5.10. Reconstructed from a drawing found on site. Dorothée Imbert.

5.11. Dorothée Imbert.

5.12. Jacob A. Riis Collection, MCNY.

5.13. John Lloyd Thomas, *Municipal Affairs* 111 (1907): 72.

5.14. John Vachon, FSA-LC. Negative no. LC-USF 33-1709-M4.

5.15. Dorothée Imbert.

5.16. SFR-SFPL.

5.17. Lewis W. Hine Collection, NYPL.

5.18. Photo postcard. Collection of Larry McDonald.

5.19. John Vachon, FSA-LC. Negative no. LC-USF 34-60518-D.

5.20. Dorothée Imbert.

5.21. Chicago Historical Society.

5.22. NMM, courtesy of Bethlehem Steel, Inc.

5.23. Ira Nowinski.

5.24. Author.

5.25. Lil and Al Bloom, Chicago Historical Society.

6.1. NYHS.

6.2. SFR-SFPL.

6.3. Author.

6.4. SFR-SFPL.

6.5. Courtesy of Mark Hopkins Inter-Continental Hotel.

6.6.   John Vachon, FSA-LC. Negative no. LC-USF 34-60531-D.

6.7.   Russell Lee, FSA-LC. Negative no. LC-USF 34-32895-D.

6.8.   Dorothée Imbert.

6.9.   John Vachon, FSA-LC. Negative no. LC-USF 33-1615-M2.

6.10.   Panel from the 1878 Eadweard Muybridge panorama, BL.

6.11.   Dorothée Imbert.

6.12.   Author.

6.13.   SFR-SFPL.

6.14.   SFR-SFPL.

6.15.   Courtesy of Belmont-Buckingham Apartments.

6.16.   Author.

7.1.   SFR-SFPL.

7.2.   Ehrenreich and English, *Complaints and Disorders*, 71.

7.3.   Byron Collection, MCNY.

7.4.   *Harper's Weekly*, August 12, 1871, 744.

7.5.   *Harper's Weekly*, August 12, 1871, 745.

7.6.   *Harper's Weekly*, December 26, 1857, 825.

7.7.   The Bettmann Archive.

7.8.   Deforest and Veiller, *The Tenement House Problem*, 313a.

7.9.   *National Police Gazette*, July 26, 1879.

7.10.   Arthur Rothstein, FSA-LC. Negative no. LC-USF 34-4213-E.

7.11.   Photo postcard. Collection of Larry McDonald.

7.12.   California Commission of Immigration and Housing, *Fifth Annual Report*, 1919, 36.

7.13.   *Architectural Record*, January 1903, 90.

7.14.   Lewis W. Hine Collection, NYPL.

7.15.   Ehrenreich and English, *Complaints and Disorders*, 64.

7.16.   Ben Shahn, FSA-LC. Negative no. LC-USF 33-6416-M5.

8.1.   John Vachon, FSA-LC. Negative no. LC-USF 1868-M1.

8.2.   Courtesy of California State Library.

8.3.   Roy D. Graves Collection, BL.

8.4.   Jacob A. Riis Collection, MCNY.

8.5.   John Vachon, FSA-LC. Negative no. LC-USF 34-60530-D.

8.6.   Author.

8.7.   Author.

8.8.   Dorothée Imbert.

8.9.   Author.

8.10.   Author.

8.11.   SFR-SFPL.

8.12.   "Zone Plan for SF," *Architect and Engineer* 62, 3 (September 1920): 70.

8.13.   Alameda Community Hotel Corporation, *Alameda's Transient and Apartment Hotel* (Alameda, Calif.: Chamber of Commerce Promotional Booklet, 1926): 1. Collection of the author.

8.14.   Arthur Rothstein, FSA-LC. Negative no. LC-USF 342-RA 3073-A.

8.15.   SFR-SFPL.

8.16.   Author.

9.1.   SFR-SFPL.

9.2.   Author.

9.3.   SFR-SFPL.

9.4.   Dorothée Imbert.

9.5.   John Vachon, FSA-LC. Negative no. LC-USF 34-8946-D.

9.6.   SFR-SFPL.

9.7.   SFR-SFPL.

9.8.   San Francisco City Planning Commission, *The Master Plan of San Francisco*, 24a.

9.9.   Scott, "Western Addition District," pl. 6.

9.10.   Scott, "Western Addition District," pl. 1.

9.11.   Scott, "Western Addition District," pl. 9.

9.12.   SFR-SFPL.

9.13.   Ira Nowinski.

9.14.   Ira Nowinski.

9.15.   Author.

9.16.   Courtesy Rob Wellington Quigley, Architect.

9.17.   Photo by David Hewitt and Anne Garrison, courtesy Rob Wellington Quigley, Architect.

9.18.   Courtesy David Baker, Architects.

CONFLICTING IDEAS
ABOUT HOTEL LIFE

PEOPLE LIVE IN HOTELS, FULL-TIME, throughout the United States. Americans have done so for over two hundred years, often choosing hotel life over other housing options. Hotel rooms have provided indispensable housing units, sheltered important social groups, supported essential industries and businesses, and represented cosmopolitan diversity in American society. Hotel homes have also revealed deep conflicts in urban life, helped industrialists exploit workers, generated fortunes in downtown real estate, and challenged the dominant cultural values of how homes should shape American culture.

Most American hotels are now run exclusively for either tourist use or residential use. Until about 1960, however, a majority of hotel keepers not only offered travelers rooms for the night but also provided rooms or suites for permanent residents who rented by the month. Although residential hotels have moved into the shadows, they still provide a significant share of America's urban homes. In 1990, hotel residents numbered between one million and two million people. More people lived in hotels than in all of America's public housing.[1]

In 1980, San Francisco's permanent hotel residents numbered three times the population in the city's public housing projects. Permanent residents occupied over half of the city's 51,000 hotel rooms, and those

27,000 hotel homes comprised 10 percent of the city's total housing units. Other cities have reported similarly significant figures. In New York in 1986, the largest study of inexpensive hotel homes ever undertaken by an American city found that 87,000 New Yorkers lived in hotels. Citizens in small towns and small cities also rely on hotel housing; for example, planners estimate that one-third of California's residential hotel rooms are in cities with populations under 50,000.[2]

HOTEL HOMES AND COSMOPOLITAN DIVERSITY

Commercialized hotel life and private household life occupy different positions in regard to several cultural issues: the proper type of household, who should cook the food, how close Americans should live to their neighbors, who (if anyone) should have control and surveillance over an individual's activities, how mixed the land uses adjacent to American homes should be, and how committed Americans should be to private material possessions. These issues cut through all of the several types of hotel life.

Defining the wide range of hotel life. The diversity of hotel life stems from the diversity of hotel residents, the relative stability of their work, and their income. Recent hotel residents have included people like San Francisco's Cyril Magnin, the wealthy owner of a chain of clothing stores, three-time president of the Chamber of Commerce, and San Francisco's chief of protocol for over twenty years. From 1960 until his death in 1988, Magnin lived in a multiroom suite that occupied the fifteenth floor of a city landmark, the Mark Hopkins Hotel.[3] In Washington, D.C., Lawrence Spivak, longtime moderator of NBC's "Meet the Press," has lived for over thirty years in the Wardman Tower of the Sheraton Washington complex, a large hotel in a single-family neighborhood near Rock Creek Park. Spivak's hotel neighbors have included Dwight Eisenhower, Lyndon Johnson, Perle Mesta, Clare Booth Luce, and Herbert Hoover (who also maintained a hotel suite in the Astor Towers of New York's Waldorf-Astoria).[4]

Prestigious addresses, time saved in traveling to work, snob appeal, spectacular views, and having unctuous service without supervising servants are conveniences that keep busy and wealthy residents at exclusive hotels. All this has led Paul Goldberger, the architecture critic

FIGURE 1.1. The Ritz Tower in New York City in 1926, one year after its completion. The Ritz has long been a favorite for permanent guests.

for the *New York Times,* to write that "the perfect apartment, at least in New York, is probably in a residential hotel" (fig. 1.1).[5] In an expensive hotel, permanent residents usually rent two to seven large rooms, including a kitchen, and in many ways live as they would in an apartment.[6]

Only a tiny fraction of hotel life is so elegant. Dorothy Johnson, a sprightly sixty-five-year-old widow, lives in a single room in a Minneapolis hotel. Like a great number of middle-income people who rent one or two rooms in a decent hotel on a good street, she cooks simple meals on a hot plate in her room and enjoys daily room service, a moderately priced dining room, and several cheap coffee shops close by. "I've sold my car because everything is within walking distance," Dorothy says. "My friends in the hotel and I can look forward to an outing arranged by the staff, or on the spur of the moment we can go shopping, take in a movie, or see a play—all without driving."[7] A significant notch lower on the price scale was the hotel living experience of playwright Jane Wagner. In 1958, she moved to New York City as a young woman "absolutely alone," as she puts it. For three years Wagner lived in a room at the YWCA. For her it was "the college dormitory she had never stayed in." Wagner's experience is hardly unique. In terms of the number of rooms rented in the 1980s, the YMCAs and YWCAs were the third-largest hotel chain in the world.[8]

As residential hotel prices edge toward the lowest range, the streets and neighborhoods are less safe and less desirable, but the locations are still central. In 1982, a veterans' center poster in San Francisco advertised such a hotel like this:

Rooms for rent. Family atmosphere; clean, freshly painted rooms. Community kitchens; clean sheets once a week. Close to the subway. Only $195.00/month rent.

The advertised building is old; built in 1906, it has forty-nine rooms. The bathrooms are down the hall.[9] In hotels of this price range it is not uncommon to look into a room and see a group of friends and four plates on the bed: a dinner party for four, the host cooking (almost legally) on a camp stove, his spice and pot racks on shelves above. Plants crowd some rooms; books, a television set, and cast-off easy chairs crowd others. On occasion a pet kitten scampers down the hall (fig. 1.2).[10] In 1977, Felix Ayson, a Filipino field worker, explained to reporters that he had lived in such a hotel in San Francisco on and off from 1926 to 1977. "Whenever there was no work in the country, I have come to find a job in the city, and I have lived here. Most of the time in America I have spent in this hotel, so it is my home."[11]

Although their homes are very different, Cyril Magnin, Dorothy Johnson, Jane Wagner, and Felix Ayson all have enjoyed what the law defines as a hotel. Legally, a hotel provides multiunit commercial housing, usually without a private kitchen. More precise definitions are complicated since local ordinances, state statutes, and federal programs

FIGURE 1.2. A hallway in San Francisco's National Hotel, a large inexpensive residential hotel which mixes permanent and transient guests.

set different criteria. Most state codes define a hotel as a commercial operation renting sleeping rooms by the day, week, or month. California's legal definition of 1917, still in force, stipulates that a hotel is "any house or building, or portion thereof, containing six or more guest rooms which are let or hired out to be occupied or are occupied by six or more guests."[12] Depending on the state, the minimum number of rooms in a hotel can vary from three to thirty. Hotel definitions exclude group quarters such as hospitals, jails, and military barracks.

The definition of permanent residence in a hotel (as opposed to being a transient guest) has to do with the length of time one stays. In most states, if a tenant lives in a hotel room for more than a month, that room is then a residential hotel unit, and the person is legally considered a permanent resident of the city. The one-month residency often

FIGURE 1.3. Two nineteenth-century houses converted to rooming houses, photographed in 1985. In most states these Lexington, Kentucky, structures would legally qualify as hotels.

applies to apartment dwellers as well and has been a typical residence requirement since the time of the Civil War.[13]

The phrase "boardinghouse reach" comes from an important variant of hotel life. In *boardinghouses,* tenants rent rooms and the proprietor provides family-style breakfasts and evening dinners in a common dining room. Traditionally, the food was put on the table, and everyone scrambled for the best dishes. Those with a long, fast reach ate best. The term "residential hotel" includes other variations. In *private rooming houses* (called private *lodging* houses in some cities), tenants simply rent a room and buy their meals elsewhere. If tenants eat their meals with the family, they are called boarders; if tenants eat elsewhere, they are called roomers or lodgers.[14] If a family rents out many rooms (more than six in California), their boardinghouse crosses over into the definition of a commercial hotel. Commercial boardinghouses and lodging houses are technically open to taxation and inspection as hotels (fig. 1.3).[15] Residential motels, particularly common in resort areas and along bypassed highway routes, operate under the same legal definitions as residential hotels.

The absence of a private kitchen separates hotels from apartments. By 1900, lawyers used the cooking area *and* the presence of a private bathroom for each unit to distinguish the more socially proper apartment from the less proper tenement. The terms usually stipulate that "families living independently of one another and doing their own cooking" in buildings for three or more households are living in apartments and not in hotels.[16]

Cultural challenges of hotel life.   People living in hotels of all types create and support alternatives to traditional household culture.[17] Foremost traits among the distinctions of hotel life are unsupervised individual independence, cosmopolitan mixture, and a life unfettered by place and possessions.

Hotel life offers more individual freedom than any other housing option. Residents in 1870, 1920, and 1980 have all appreciated this characteristic. Without telling anyone in advance, they can dine one night at 8:00 and the next at 5:00 and yet inconvenience no one. In hotels, people on unusual schedules can sleep when tired, awaken when refreshed, eat when hungry, and drink when thirsty.[18] Those few services not available in the hotel can be found within walking distance. Hotel freedoms, however, have never been complete. As in most apartment houses, complete acoustical privacy can be difficult to obtain. One's comings and goings are less controlled than in a family house, but hotel desk clerks take careful note of everyone who passes.[19] However, hotel clerks rarely question the personal life of any guest whose bills are paid and who is not annoying neighbors. In short, hotel life can be virtually untouched by the social contracts and tacit supervision of life found in a family house or apartment unit shared with a group.

Another general ingredient of downtown hotel life is neighborhood mixture—a composite of retail and office activities, production and consumption spheres, many types of recreation, and people who are rich and poor, famous and infamous, married and single, young and old, transient and resident.[20] The term "cosmopolitan" certainly fits these juxtapositions. Active hotel people can feed on the 24-hour stimulation and spontaneity that their choice of residence offers. "You know," one happy hotel dweller affirmed, "I just love to be where there's life and city lights."[21] Downtown hotel life has the promise to be not just urban but urbane.

In another major departure from the typical household culture of the United States, residents of hotels keep themselves freer of material possessions than their suburban counterparts. The absence of household property makes hotel people more obviously mobile than other Americans who move often. Most hotel residents share typical American values, but they do not (or cannot afford to) fasten their identities to the anchor of private property. Even for wealthy hotel residents, a month or a season's lease is the longest financial commitment and tie to their home. They rent their furniture, dishes, and all other aspects of shelter.

Underlying the personal freedom, mixture, and unfettered nature of hotel life is the reality that hotels are blatantly commercial, not in a realm separate from business or manufacturing. Nor has hotel life, especially at the cheaper levels, always been chosen. Within the logic of industrial capitalism—particularly as it matured about the turn of the twentieth century—some employers have relied on a large force of temporary and marginally paid workers. Hotel living helps to make this labor force viable (fig. 1.4). Yet hotels are not always housing of last resort. Studies consistently show that many Americans prefer hotel life over other available and affordable options. Some residents cling to hotel life rather than live with relatives, share an apartment, or (for the elderly) live in a nursing home.[22] Because of public policy and new economic forces, this preference is in a precarious position.

BARRIERS TO UNDERSTANDING HOTEL LIVING

For over twenty years, the supply of residential hotel rooms has not met demand. In about 1970, reporters began to write about a situation they called the "SRO crisis," which highlights long-standing themes in the history of hotels. For city planners and housing experts, "SRO" does not mean standing room only. It means single room occupancy and refers either to an entire hotel or to a room within such a hotel. SROs are the most inexpensive types of residential hotels. They are almost entirely residential, offering few, if any, tourist rooms. For social workers, the term "SRO" means single room occupants—not the buildings but the residents.[23] If the rebuilding of our cities continues in its current path, the acronym SRO may indeed soon mean "standing room only." As the supply of residential hotel rooms rapidly dwindles, former hotel residents join the homeless on American streets and in city shelters. In

part, the present crisis results from misconceptions about who currently lives in hotels and has its roots in a cultural amnesia about this alternative downtown housing style.

FIGURE 1.4. World War II shipyard workers photographed outside their hotel in Bath, Maine, 1940.

The SRO crisis as a subset of today's hotel life.   SRO hotels are a subset of hotel life but its most important subset, both historically and in the present. Inexpensive hotels have pushed the traditional patterns of hotel life to social and practical limits. Statistics from most cities show that since World War II the United States has been losing affordable hotel homes at staggering rates and not replacing them. Downtown hotel owners, to improve their income or to eliminate management problems, have converted SROs to tourist rooms or other uses, torn the buildings down and built office towers, or simply closed the buildings. Between 1975 and 1980, San Francisco landowners eliminated 6,085 units, almost a fifth of the city's entire stock of residential hotel units. Chicago lost almost 23,000 units between 1973 and 1984.[24] A typical public housing project has about 250 units; thus, Chicago's loss—in units—is equivalent to the loss of 92 housing projects. Some observers see these losses as positive developments—the removal of substandard housing and unwanted neighbors. To others, this whole-sale closing and destruction of residential hotels is a major tragedy and a root cause of homelessness in the United States. These opposing views are not new; they have existed at least since the 1860s. Essential re-source or public nuisance? How can one housing type be called both for more than one hundred years? How can the question remain open when the homes of as many as two million Americans depend on the outcome?

The lives of SRO residents inextricably intertwine with downtown hotel buildings; some residents literally cannot exist without them. Few, if any, housing alternatives for these residents exist. When owners close a building, tenants are lucky if they can find a worse hotel at higher rents. As the hotel stock dwindles, the option of moving evapo-rates, and tenants move to the streets. The street option has become increasingly evident in the numbers of America's homeless and street people. Even officials who dislike hotel life become alarmed as they re-alize that the closing of a 100-room hotel means that perhaps 150 more people may be living on the streets.[25]

In part because of the SRO crisis, myths about today's hotel residents abound. Hotel people are supposedly all friendless, isolated, needy, and disabled; all elderly; all on welfare; all elderly men; or all welfare moth-ers with three young children. All are presumably socially marginal, all mildly psychotic, all alcoholics or drug addicts, all drifters and tran-sients who never live anywhere more than a few months; they are thought to be people whose homes cost taxpayers millions of dollars because of political corruption and bureaucratic waste. In spite of resi-dents like Cyril Magnin and Dorothy Johnson, the most pervasive mis-conception about today's hotel residents is that they are all poor.[26] Journalists have made "welfare hotel" a synonym for all hotel life. In New York and other American cities, inexpensive hotels have become, in Jonathan Kozol's phrase, refugee camps for the American poor.[27] Each of these characteristics is sadly true of conditions in particular SRO buildings. However, not all SROs and certainly not all residential hotels with higher rents reflect such conditions.

Several recent studies dispel the stereotypes. For instance, fewer hotel tenants live on welfare than newspaper headlines suggest. Workers living in hotels are still important to the urban economy. The authors of a San Diego study found that over half of the residents (and often more) were "independent, self-reliant individuals who were not dependent on public or private social services, nor had they been in the past." The older tenants often had fixed incomes, and the average tenure at the longest-held job was about twenty-one years. At the cheapest price range, a 1985 study of the SRO residents in Chicago found "a small prosperous minority, a majority barely earning enough to make ends meet, and a large minority of impoverished workers."[28] Where racial and ethnic minorities have low incomes, there hotels are also typically an important housing resource. In New York, a third of all SRO residents are black; a quarter are Hispanic. In San Francisco and Los Angeles, newly arrived families from Southeast Asia make up an increasing proportion of hotel residents. In San Francisco's Clayton Hotel, half of the residents are retired Filipino or Chinese laborers who, like Felix Ayson, have lived in one hotel seasonally for twenty to forty years.[29]

Not all single room occupants are single people. In New York, one-half of the SRO occupants are single; they occupy about three-fourths of the city's SRO units. Nor are all hotel residents transients. Some do move frequently, but the majority of America's hotel tenants move no more often—in many cases less often—than apartment renters.[30] Visiting nurses in the 1970s used to joke that "you could tell how long someone had lived in their hotel room by counting the layers of nicotine on the walls."[31] Their joke described both long residence and poor building maintenance. Nor are all SRO tenants elderly. The average elderly population in a city's hotels is about one-half of the total number of SRO occupants. In New York City in 1985, 43 percent of all SRO residents were under forty years old, and an additional 32 percent were between forty and sixty. Also contrary to popular opinion, the demand for hotel life among the elderly is not dwindling.[32]

More than other types of hotels, today's SROs have fueled a fierce debate about the history and the future of hotel life. Hotels are often the cheapest private housing available close to downtown. Many housing professionals and social workers today insist that hotel living is not only viable but essential to urban economy and urban society. Hotels, the apologists argue, are a valuable civic resource and respectable housing. The hotel defenders say that the people who choose hotel life do so

FIGURE 1.5.   A hotel family
of Eastern European immi-
grants in Chicago, 1910.

FIGURE 1.6.   A hotel family
of recent migrants to
Chicago, 1929.

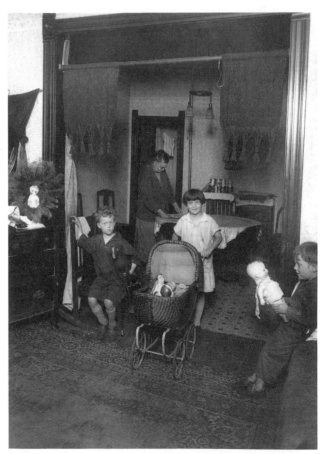

for good reasons. The promoters propose (against loud clamors from the other side) that cities should be building *more* residential hotels.

Although the term "SRO" is relatively new, for at least one hundred years other commentators have railed against the real and implied dangers of single-room housing. In 1916, Walter Krumwilde, a Protestant minister, saw the rooming house or boardinghouse system "spreading its web like a spider, stretching out its arms like an octopus to catch the unwary soul."[33] Early social workers abhorred the idea of commercialized, retail housing for the poor. Generations of hotel critics have used photographs of families living in single rooms to shock Americans into recognition of SRO problems and to prompt ameliorative action. These different eras of hotel family portraits have a haunting similarity (figs. 1.5, 1.6, 1.7). Today many city health officials, architects, city planners, and politicians still argue that no one should live in hotels. Hotels, they say, exhibit severe social and physical maladjustment. Eliminating the hotel stock, the critics argue, will eliminate a public nuisance. One of the recurring complaints from people who are fighting *for* hotel residents is that no one seems to know very much about hotel people or the buildings they live in. This ignorance is not an accident.

FIGURE 1.7. A hotel family of Southeast Asian immigrants in San Francisco, 1980.

Cultural invisibility.   Hotel residents and buildings are real enough, but they stubbornly remain outside of public awareness. Not surprisingly, two of the path-breaking books of the 1970s on SROs have the words "unseen" and "invisible" in their titles.[34] Early in the fight to make hotel life better understood, a St. Louis observer, Ira Ehrlich, summarized the problem in direct terms:

Single room occupants are omitted in the language of housing legislation, written off in the minds of communities, ignored and rejected in urban development plans, and pushed from one area to another on the waves of fluctuating real estate markets.[35]

More recently a San Francisco architect and scholar, John Liu, has written that "the Single Room Occupancy (SRO) residential hotel is perhaps the most controversial, the most neglected, and the least understood of all housing types."[36]

Hotel lives are culturally invisible in part because the public is disinterested and ignorant about *any* housing needs of the poor. Cushing Dolbeare, a founder and longtime executive director of the National Coalition for Low-Income Housing, complains, "As a problem, housing often eludes our grasp. It does not gain the political constituency it deserves. Other than homelessness, housing needs are simply not visible to most Americans."[37] Another barrier to understanding hotel life is based on the fact that so many hotel people are single and have developed social orders strongly differing from those in traditional American family units. Housing needs for single people—twenty-five years of age or fifty-five years of age—are rarely discussed even by housing experts. One of the path-breaking New York hotel activists, Carroll Kowal, writes that "federal housing policy deals with the population it is comfortable with: the family. Housing authorities have no understanding of non-family persons," let alone living units with no kitchens and a bath down the hall.[38] The numbers of single people tend to be underestimated throughout our society, even though they have always been an important share of the American adult population. In 1980, America had about 50 million married households and 21 million people living alone.[39]

Small hotels, which can make up half of a city's residential hotel stock, are easy to miss because the hotel rooms are usually on second and third floors above retail shops. Signs left from the 1920s feebly

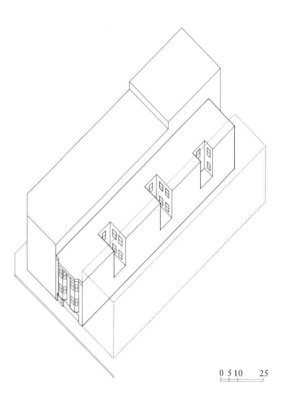

0 5 10   25

announce the upstairs hotel functions while public attention is dis-
tracted by the signs and show windows of stores, restaurants, and
nightclubs. In San Francisco's North Beach entertainment district,
Carol Doda's sign and club at Broadway and Columbus were well-
known landmarks to tourists and residents (fig. 1.8). Yet within three
hundred feet of that sign, on the second and third floors of the buildings, are over three hundred hotel homes (fig. 1.9).[40] Virtually no one
passing on Broadway thinks about those seventy-year-old dwellings, or
who lives in them.

More expensive hotel life is hard to see as well. Travelers in expensive
hotels assume everyone else is a transient guest, too. Old buildings with
names like the Barrington prompt the belief that they have always been
apartment buildings when, in fact, they were originally hotels. At a
public meeting in 1981, Melvin Carriere, a vice president in San Francisco's Wells Fargo Bank, confessed that he had never *heard* of a residential hotel or the notion of living in one until a community group
asked for a hotel loan. He had been passing residential hotels every day

FIGURE 1.8. The corner of
Broadway and Columbus
Avenue in San Francisco's
North Beach neighborhood
in 1985. Between Big Al's and
the Condor Club is the small
street entrance to the residential hotel above Big Al's.

FIGURE 1.9. Isometric
drawing of the Sierra House,
the rooming house above Big
Al's North Beach nightclub.

FIGURE 1.10. The unfinished city. Jacob Riis's photograph of small wooden shacks next to a brick tenement in Hell's Kitchen in New York City emphasized the problems of old city rules.

on his way to work but had never noticed them. "I couldn't believe people *wanted* to live in a hotel," he added.[41]

Another barrier to understanding hotels is revealed when writers persist in labeling all people who live in hotels or motels as "homeless." The horrors of New York's welfare hotels or the squalor of a Los Angeles residential motel frequently matches the worst of homeless conditions. But if not overcrowded, a good hotel room of 150 square feet—dry space, perhaps with a bath or a room sink, cold and sometimes hot water, enough electric service to run a 60-watt bulb and a television, central heat, and access to telephones and other services—constitutes a living unit mechanically more luxuriant than those lived in by a third to a half of the population of the earth. As Dolores Hayden reminds us, many of the world's people would consider an American two-car garage an excellent dwelling in its own right.[42] The urban Americans living in hotels are not homeless. They are living in admittedly minimal and unusual dwelling units, often in hideous repair and under woefully inadequate management but dwelling units nonetheless. Calling SRO people homeless reinvokes the cultural bias against hotel life. In the long run, the ecologically and culturally aberrant idea about housing may prove to be the huge single-family house on an open lot, not the more social way of living downtown in a hotel.

Other barriers to appreciating hotels have to do with the different notions people have about the ideal city. Supporters of hotels and those who see them as perverse ghettos hold deeply rooted and opposing conceptions about the proper rules for building urban space. The old city view stems from centuries-old European mercantile cities that had an urbane, densely congregated way of living with mixed income groups, adjacencies of housing, commerce, and workshops, all in buildings that crowded their lots and the street, with very little guarantee of permanence or a finished state (fig. 1.10). Downtown American hotel districts are a holdover of old city life.

After 1880, visionary experts and commercial leaders in America worked feverishly on building a new kind of city. Faced with the social and physical problems of industrialization in cities, directed by the needs and values of business elites, and reinforced by discoveries in public health, reformers consciously rejected the building and land-use rules of the old city. Beginning in large new suburbs, in vast industrial works, and in monumental architectural projects downtown, reformers and property developers embraced a modern set of architectural rules built around separation and specialization. The new rules promised each function in an area by itself, uniformity within areas, less mixture of social classes, maximum privacy for each family, much lower density for many activities, buildings set back from the street, and a permanently built order (fig. 1.11). By the 1890s, new city ideas had begun to be popular, particularly among the middle and upper class. Promoters of the new city planned for hotel living to be a deliberate casualty of the transition between the old city and the new city. Thus, as early as the 1890s, hotels had begun to be forbidden housing; their residents, forbidden citizens. These tensions between ideals were particularly clear in rapidly growing new cities.

SAN FRANCISCO'S HOTELS AS EXEMPLARS

This study draws on a national literature but focuses especially on the hotel history of San Francisco. San Francisco rarely led national trends

FIGURE 1.11. Workers' houses near the Santa Fe railroad yards, Topeka, Kansas, built ca. 1915. New neighborhoods like these stressed the uniformity, single use, and visually coherent organization of new city rules.

in hotel life; instead, its experience after the Civil War epitomizes experiences repeated, with minor variations, in hundreds of other American cities. What was ordinary in San Francisco proved similar to what was ordinary in Chicago, New York, or St. Louis. Thus, in the chapters that follow, examples from San Francisco will predominate with corroborating asides and illustrations drawn from elsewhere.

A case study city.   Compared to cities on the East Coast, San Francisco's evolution began late and eccentrically with the gold rush of 1849. From 1849 to 1870, San Francisco was notoriously unlike other cities: it had many more men than women, more Chinese immigrants than anywhere else in the United States, a notoriously unconventional population, and very tenuous transportation links to the East. However, by 1870, San Francisco's manufacturing and downtown office employment was burgeoning; by 1880, its population profile looked roughly similar to that of other large U.S. cities. Some differences remained. Tourism was a greater part of the urban economy than in other American cities. The housing of San Francisco—wooden row houses instead of wooden open-lot houses—was also more like that of the East Coast or older midwestern cities than like other cities of the West or the South. But with those exceptions, San Francisco's industries and housing roughly reflected national patterns. By 1900, San Francisco ranked eighth in the nation for industrial production, and it was also the predominant wholesaling and financial center for much of the West. The earthquake and fire of 1906 leveled all of downtown but merely hastened the rebuilding of obsolete structures. By 1915, the land uses and buildings of rebuilt San Francisco were not strikingly different from those in cities that had no great fire.[43]

More than was true in any other city, the citizens of San Francisco tested the validity of hotel living. Nineteenth-century tourists noted that "vast numbers" of residents lived in hotels and ate exclusively in restaurants. In both 1880 and 1900, the ratio of boardinghouse and rooming house keepers in proportion to the total population was higher in San Francisco (and other new West Coast cities) than in many of the older American cities.[44] Surely if hotel housing were to have bested its critics anywhere, it would have been in San Francisco. In the late 1950s, Alfred Hitchcock's *Vertigo* portrayed downtown hotels as natural homes for the city's young secretaries. In the 1970s, some of the most bitter struggles over hotel living—the destruction of hotels in the South of Market and the fight over the International Hotel—showed an unusual public awareness of hotel housing.

While *more* of a hotel city than other cities, San Francisco was not an anomaly. It was simply the most highly developed example of hotel housing. Because so much of the city's economy and population appeared after 1865 on a relatively empty stage, San Francisco's architectural and social history exhibited national post-Civil War industrialization and trade with little competition from previous eras. Bursts in hotel construction in San Francisco were also matched in other West Coast cities, in the Midwest, and on the East Coast.[45] Based on both written and architectural evidence, San Francisco had about 15,000 hotel rooms of all types in 1880, or about one hotel room for every 16 people in the population. In 1910, those figures had grown to 65,000 total rooms, or one hotel room for every 10 people (table 1, Appendix). That ratio remained roughly the same through 1980.[46]

From the early 1800s up to the 1960s, managers in hotels of all types mixed permanent and transient guests, often with seasonal variations. A 1930 survey of the more expensive American hotels showed that about a third were mainly transient and about a sixth were mainly permanent. Managers of the remainder called their businesses "mixed transient and permanent."[47] The mixture of transient and permanent guests also varied by the type of hotel. It appears that permanent residents lived in an average of 20 percent of the rooms in the most expensive third of American hotels and at least 75 percent of the rooms in the remaining cheaper hotels.[48] This was likely the case for at least several months of the year (if not year-round) and in most American cities. Applying these ratios to San Francisco indicates that a consistent 60 percent of all of the city's hotel rooms between 1880 and 1930 were permanent residences for at least one or two seasons of the year. This is slightly more than the precise 52 percent reported for San Francisco in 1980, with the city's much expanded tourist industry and reduced use of hotels as residences.[49] A San Francisco sample also revealed four very distinctly stratified sets of building types that are found in most American cities.

Hotel ranks, social class, and the plan of the book.　The four types of average hotels in San Francisco can be characterized as palace hotels, midpriced hotels, rooming houses, and cheap lodging houses. These four ranks of building types, arrived at strictly by architectural evidence, closely match social stratification suggested in written records. In 1903, for instance, the New York hotel keeper Simeon Ford amused a banquet of hotel managers with this characterization of hotel life:

We have fine hotels for fine people,
good hotels for good people,
plain hotels for plain people,
and some bum hotels for bums.[50]

The original construction details of these four types of hotels—especially their plumbing and air wells—were surprisingly reliable counterparts to the social stratification and class differences of their intended original clients as summarized by Ford. By the end of the nineteenth century, city residents easily recognized the four types of hotels and the social status of their residents (these are discussed in detail in chaps. 2–5).

At the social pinnacle were the buildings of a price range best called the *palace hotel rank* (fig. 1.12). Like Cyril Magnin, the people who lived in such hotels were generally from the nation's wealthiest families. When people at this rarified social and economic level chose their homes, cost mattered little. Their hotel suite was often one of several

FIGURE 1.12. The original Waldorf-Astoria, a quintessential palace hotel. In 1907, it became the largest hotel in the world when the Astoria section was added to the 1893 Waldorf.

residences. If they lived in an apartment, it was also palatial; if they had a house, it could be a mansion or an estate.

Hotels of the next cheaper type, the *midpriced hotel rank,* were intended for overnight guests and permanent residents who had a comfortable income and intermediate social status (fig. 1.1). In their basic values, politics, museum or church activities, education, and recreation, these people often emulated the truly wealthy. With their best clothes and manners they could infiltrate the palace hotel dining room for a memorable meal, but they could not live like that every day. Their incomes forced compromise, but as chapter 3 shows, it was socially respectable compromise. If they had not lived in a hotel, they might

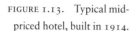

FIGURE 1.13. Typical mid-priced hotel, built in 1914.

have chosen a substantial private house or flat with one to three servants or an apartment hotel.

Americans informally called these two social strata the upper class and the middle class. However, between these two groups there was little of the social or cultural opposition that theorists require for a true division between classes.[51] The palace and midpriced hotel groups were two levels within a single class; they were the "middle and upper class," with "class" in the singular. The material culture evidence of their hotel housing, like other social and cultural indicators, showed that their differences were matters of degree rather than proof of sharply divergent and opposing realms. For people in the middle and upper class, hotel life was a choice; they could afford to live in other ways and encountered few barriers in doing so. However, the people in the middle and upper class were in clear cultural and often political opposition to the residents of the two less expensive hotel types, whose residents had much less choice in housing. In their work, ownership of property, and access to cultural and economic power, the people of the upper two hotel ranks differed markedly from those of the two lower hotel ranks. Here was a true class division with both cultural and economic formations. Their material culture was an important reinforcement—not merely a reflection—of position and power. Both sides displayed in their material life a decided class consciousness, as was particularly clear with rooming house residents.

Ford called the *rooming house rank* of hotels "plain hotels for plain people." Such places were home for people in skilled trades who earned a steady but relatively low income, especially before the 1930s. For the single teacher, stenographer, and machinist, their rooms, their financial instability, and often their personal lives were evidence of the sharp division that stood between them and the upper and middle class. However, chapter 4 shows that rooming house residents relied on their rooms for a minimum of material respectability, a tool to mask their differences from the middle and upper class. If roomers wished to live outside of a family or live alone, they had few other affordable housing choices. Roomers also had the choice of boarding or lodging with a family, with the consequence of again living under household surveillance.

Finally, at the *cheap lodging house rank,* hoboes and day laborers hung precariously on to shelter with the marginal incomes they obtained when work was available. While the cultural opposition of rooming house residents was subtle, lodging house residents lived and worked in flagrant opposition to the rules of the middle and upper class. The lodging house residents' poverty, backgrounds, political beliefs, family life, speech, and education all set them utterly apart from the polite society of the middle and upper class. If they wished to live in the city, lodging house residents had virtually no other choice but to live in some version of a cheap downtown hotel (fig. 1.14).

The cultural and social opposition of rooming houses and cheap lodging houses to middle and upper class norms did the most to bring official condemnation on hotel housing of all four ranks. The first half of this work analyzes hotel life and downtown cosmopolitanism as valuable public resources, while the second half traces the idea of hotel life as a public nuisance. Chapter 6 examines the segmentation of hotel

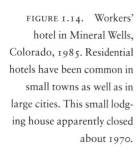

FIGURE 1.14. Workers' hotel in Mineral Wells, Colorado, 1985. Residential hotels have been common in small towns as well as in large cities. This small lodging house apparently closed about 1970.

owners and how their increasing specialization of the city intensified downtown as a zone of residential opposition. Chapter 7 looks in detail at the critiques of hotel life and the gradual ways that residential hotels became defined as an aberration. The last two chapters follow the expert reformers of the Progressive Era and the post-World War II period as they worked to build the long-desired new city and to eliminate hotels and cosmopolitan diversity. No matter what position one takes on hotels as homes, their rapidly dwindling inventory cannot be seen simply as an accident of supply and demand in a free market. The crisis in the residential hotel supply is a planned event—a function of local, state, and federal government policies that have encouraged housing for some types of people and reduced supplies of housing for others.[52]

The mistrust of cheaper hotels is more understandable in light of their historical dominance in downtown hotel life (fig. 1.15). The residential proportion of hotels was heavily weighted toward the inexpensive hotel types. Indeed, the architectural evidence in San Francisco reveals that cheap lodging-house rooms made up half of the city's hotel homes. Rooming houses provided a third of the residential hotel rooms. Rooms likely to be used as permanent residences in palace and midpriced hotels, combined, made up only the remaining sixth of the residential hotel stock. These proportions remained roughly the same between 1880 and 1930 (table 1, Appendix).[53]

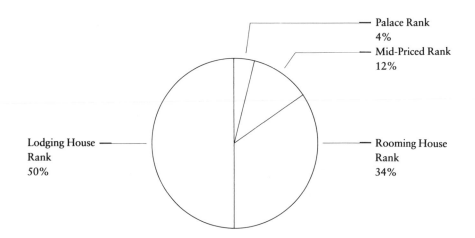

Palace Rank
4%

Mid-Priced Rank
12%

Lodging House —
Rank
50%

Rooming House
Rank
34%

The issues of hotel life still reverberate in the lives of recent hotel residents—from Cyril Magnin in his palace hotel and Dorothy Johnson in her midpriced hotel to people like Jane Wagner in rooming houses and the Filipino laborer Felix Ayson in his cheap lodging house. The history of hotel living shows the dangers of too rigidly enforcing a single ideal for the American home. Nonetheless, the people who felt most immune from the criticism of hotels were those in palace hotels. More than any other types of hotel residents, they had all the advantages of living downtown.

FIGURE 1.15. Proportional diagram of residential hotel rooms, by rank, in San Francisco in 1930. Surveys in 1880 and 1910 revealed similar distributions.

PALACE HOTELS AND
SOCIAL OPULENCE

IN HER 1913 NOVEL, *The Custom of the Country,* Edith Wharton created the Spragg family of the Hotel Stentorian. The Spraggs—a wealthy midwestern industrialist, his wife, and their spoiled daughter, Undine—had moved to New York City to find Undine an eligible mate. For Wharton, the Spraggs were the typical "rich helpless family, stranded in lonely splendor" in sumptuous West Side hotels with names like the Olympian, the Incandescent, and the Ormolu.[1] In time Wharton allows the Spraggs to accomplish their matrimonial goal, helped by the social position and the acquaintances made possible by their hotel home. Up until the 1950s, people like the Spraggs and homes like their expensive New York hotel were common to the writers of popular fiction and society columns. Although both cheap and expensive hotels were tools for creating class distinction and social stratification, palace hotels displayed that role most blatantly (fig. 2.1).

PERSONAL EASE AND INSTANT SOCIAL POSITION

In 1836, just before the famous Astor House opened in New York, Horace Greeley's *New Yorker* said, "We hear that half the rooms are already engaged by families who give up housekeeping on account of the present enormous rents of the city."[2] In 1926, when the Mark

FIGURE 2.1. The Plaza Hotel, New York City, opened in 1907 on a dramatic site overlooking Fifth Avenue mansions and the corner of Central Park. It epitomized the social and practical advantages of palace-rank hotel life.

Hopkins opened in San Francisco, high rents for private houses and the social prestige of hotel life were still attracting permanent hotel guests in high numbers. On opening, half of the Mark Hopkins rooms had been leased by permanent guests. At palace hotels the truly wealthy enjoyed perfected personal service, superior dining, sociability as well as privacy, physical luxury, and instant status—all at a cost lower than keeping a mansion or large house. Through palace hotel life, nouveaux riches could buy reliable entry to high society; similarly, through hotel life those already at social pinnacles could maintain their position.

Convenient luxury. At the most practical level, wealthy people loved hotel life because it eliminated the routine responsibilities of managing a large house and garden, devising details for the constant round of dinner parties and elaborate family meals, and supervising an often un-

FIGURE 2.2. The dining room of the Lick House in San Francisco, built in 1861. Until the 1940s, dining areas remained the chief social vortex of palace hotel life.

ruly staff of servants. Beginning in the 1870s, middle and upper class Americans in private houses (especially the women of the houses) complained regularly about the "servant problem." The available servants were ill-trained, prone to move often, expensive, and not nearly so docile as servants in England. From the 1890s to 1920, the problems increased as immigration brought fewer domestic workers from northern Europe. In the face of these problems, hotels promised perfected service 24 hours a day, 365 days a year. "A suite at the luxurious Westward Ho! will solve all your housekeeping problems," chirped a typical hotel advertisement in the decade before World War I. "We're glad to do your hiring and firing."[3]

Hotel life also offered a gregarious existence not possible in private houses. Grand hotels were built for crowds, and hotel life was spectacularly and notoriously public. In an expensive hotel, barrooms concentrated political and business life; dining rooms, social life.[4] San Francisco's Lick House featured a dining room one hundred feet on a side; the long tables could seat four hundred people amid decor modeled after the dining hall of Versailles (fig. 2.2). The dining room of a palace hotel usually outshone all the other public spaces except the lobby. Before the Civil War, servants sounded great gongs to announce

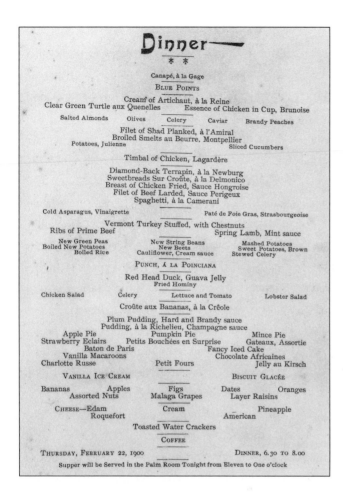

Dinner ——

✱ ✱

Canapé, à la Gage

BLUE POINTS

Cream of Artichaut, à la Reine
Clear Green Turtle aux Quenelles   Essence of Chicken in Cup, Brunoise

Salted Almonds   Olives   Celery   Caviar   Brandy Peaches

Filet of Shad Planked, à l'Amiral
Broiled Smelts au Beurre, Montpellier
Potatoes, Julienne   Sliced Cucumbers

Timbal of Chicken, Lagardère

Diamond-Back Terrapin, à la Newburg
Sweetbreads Sur Croûte, à la Delmonico
Breast of Chicken Fried, Sauce Hongroise
Filet of Beef Larded, Sauce Perigeux
Spaghetti, à la Camerani

Cold Asparagus, Vinaigrette   Paté de Foie Gras, Strasbourgeoise

Vermont Turkey Stuffed, with Chestnuts
Ribs of Prime Beef   Spring Lamb, Mint sauce

New Green Peas   New String Beans   Mashed Potatoes
Boiled New Potatoes   New Beets   Sweet Potatoes, Brown
Boiled Rice   Cauliflower, Cream sauce   Stewed Celery

PUNCH, À LA POINCIANA

Red Head Duck, Guava Jelly
Fried Hominy

Chicken Salad   Celery   Lettuce and Tomato   Lobster Salad

Croûte aux Bananas, à la Créole

Plum Pudding, Hard and Brandy sauce
Pudding, à la Richelieu, Champagne sauce
Apple Pie   Pumpkin Pie   Mince Pie
Strawberry Eclairs   Petits Bouchées en Surprise   Gateaux, Assortie
Baton de Paris   Fancy Iced Cake
Vanilla Macaroons   Chocolate Africaines
Charlotte Russe   Petit Fours   Jelly au Kirsch

VANILLA ICE CREAM   BISCUIT GLACÉE

Bananas   Apples   Figs   Dates   Oranges
Assorted Nuts   Malaga Grapes   Layer Raisins

CHEESE—Edam   Cream   Pineapple
Roquefort   American

Toasted Water Crackers

COFFEE

THURSDAY, FEBRUARY 22, 1900   DINNER, 6.30 TO 8.00

Supper will be Served in the Palm Room Tonight from Eleven to One o'clock

FIGURE 2.3. Dinner menu from the exclusive Royal Poinciana Hotel in Palm Beach, Florida, 1900.

the beginning of the serving hours, which extended for several hours for each meal. Guests walked in during the first half hour, sat down with other people at unreserved tables, and ordered dishes from the day's long bill of fare (fig. 2.3). The American plan of hotel pricing combined room costs and four meals a day into a single daily price. As late as 1910, most of the best hotels were strictly on the American plan.[5]

Astute observers explained the popularity of hotel dining—and hotel living in general—as a manifestation of a peculiarly sociable and gregarious American spirit. In England during the mid-nineteenth century, upper-class hotel guests usually ate alone in private hotel dining rooms. In 1844, when a New York hotel offered this service for the first time in the United States, a local editor objected to the idea as "directly opposed to American ideals of democracy." The public experiences in hotel dining rooms and drawing rooms, he continued, were the "tangible republic"; "going to the Astor and dining with two hundred well-dressed people and sitting in a splendid drawing room with plenty of company" were major charms of urban life. He warned that private dining in hotels "engendered the spread of dangerous blue-blood habits."[6]

The convenience and sociability of hotel dining aside, pre-Civil War cooking in palace hotels was not always inviting. After spending most of 1862 in America's elegant hotels, the English writer Anthony Trollope praised the vast quantities and types of food served but dreaded the sight of the "horrid little oval dishes" in which all the food swam in grease.[7] After the Civil War, palace hotel managers increased the use of fine cooking to distinguish their hostelries. They imported the best chefs, offered elaborate and exotic menus, and initiated more socially stratified seating procedures in their dining rooms. After 1870, new guests had to know the maître d' (or buy his attention) to get a prominent table, and the tables were no longer of mixed parties. In most cities by 1900, three of the top five restaurants were sure to be in palace hotels, and the creative cookery and inventive bar drinks of the era often emanated from hotel chefs or hotel barkeepers. Parker House rolls, Waldorf salad, Maxwell House coffee, and the Manhattan cocktail all gained their names from hotels. The importance of dining in the company of an elegant crowd and fine food continued into the twentieth century, although elite Americans were building more privacy and class separation into their environments (fig. 2.4). In the 1930s, for instance, a group of New York millionaire investors wanted to have residential suites in a hotel whose restaurant would match the quality of chef Charles Pierre's Park Avenue restaurant. They backed the chef in building the forty-two-story Hotel Pierre.[8]

As Wharton's Spragg family found, palace hotels offered their greatest advantage in the commercialized and nearly instant social position they conferred on their residents. Tenants at palace hotels bought status rather than waiting for it to accrue. Hotel life did not require the slow building and furnishing of an expensive house in the correct neighborhood, the gradual building up of a reputation, or the laborious wheedling of one's way into the proper social clubs and dinner circuits. Immediately after moving into a palace hotel, newcomers could begin to observe (and be observed by) the local elite. The revelry of upper-class dances, banquets, and weddings provided still more social stimu-

FIGURE 2.4. The Old Poodle Dog Restaurant in San Francisco, an elegant restaurant that competed with palace hotel dining before 1920.

lation and opportunity. "The pleasantest parties in the world are given at the Lick House," wrote Mark Twain in 1864, further noting that scarcely any save the guests of the establishment were invited.[9] For over a hundred years, hotel advertisers reminded readers that their ballrooms were the scene of particular "invitational dances of the inner circle of society," or they featured photographs of their entertaining rooms to emphasize the hotel's central position in society rituals.[10]

Although the public rooms of a hotel harbored a gregarious life, once residents left the ground floor they could arrange for absolute privacy. As one guest put it, "One of the great joys of being in a hotel" was "to be alone and to be left alone."[11] Desk clerks screened visitors, salesmen, community fund solicitors, and journalists. The service hallways allowed politicians or stage personalities to evade public contact. The better the hotel, the heavier were its walls and draperies and the better the acoustical isolation of its rooms. The *selectivity* of hotel privacy was its advantage over other private realms. One could intersperse days or hours of seclusion with the conviviality of the dining room, lobby, bar, or downtown theater, gymnasium, or club. "A distinguished literary person can be as isolated in a hotel room as in a cabin in the north woods," wrote one observer, "and yet meet and talk with people at will." At some points in their careers, he added, many prominent business people, scientists, artists, writers, and editors relied on hotel seclusion to meet deadlines in their work.[12]

For the very wealthy, a handsome suite in the best hotel cost only a fraction of the price for maintaining a mansion or large private house with comparable amenities. In 1870 in one of San Francisco's five best hotels, a suite of rooms and food cost about $1,000 a year, or $19 a week.[13] By the 1920s, the peak decade for living in hotels, a single room and bath cost from $100 to $230 a month for rent only. Special service and food were available for additional fees. (The usual palace resident rented at least a two-room suite; the single-room price is given here for comparison with other hotel types.)[14] These prices, too, were considerably less than the cost of keeping up a large house with servants (See table 2, Appendix).[15] The generally expanding and volatile business climate of the United States generated both the incomes that paid these costs and also the people who chose hotel life.

Wealthy hotel dwellers.   In palace hotel life, one most often met first- or second-generation wealth—newly successful entrepreneurs in retail, investment, industrial, or mining enterprises. In Chicago's Sherman House in the 1850s lived Marshall Field's partner Levi Z. Leiter and Potter Palmer. Two prominent tenants in an 1869 apartment hotel in Boston were Major and Mrs. Henry Lee Higginson. Major Higginson was a prominent banker as well as the founder of the Boston Symphony Orchestra. In 1874, he moved to his own apartment hotel, the Hotel Agassiz.[16] The families of many of the 1870s leaders of San Francisco's Merchant's Exchange lived in hotels; the exchange was the center of western America's business life.

Predictably, the social groups living at different hotels developed distinct reputations. The eccentric San Francisco philanthropist James Lick, a piano manufacturer who made a fortune in real estate, built the Lick House that later intrigued Twain. In the 1860s, Lick declined to decorate his hotel with the usual buxom female nudes and instead displayed cartloads of tranquil mountain scenes by Albert Bierstadt and Thomas Hill. Thereby, he helped establish the Lick House as the city's preeminently proper family hotel, the home of the "Lick House set." Lick lived out his years at his own elegant hotel, adding his personal reputation and presence to attract others of his economic rank.[17] By the 1890s, the highest prestige in San Francisco had shifted from the Lick

FIGURE 2.5. Lloyd Tevis, president of Wells Fargo Bank, with friends and servants on the top floor of the Palace Hotel in San Francisco, ca. 1880.

House to the Palace Hotel. Dozens of California's leading families filled the suites on the top two floors of the hotel, including former Governor Leland Stanford, the president of Wells Fargo Bank, and the editor of one of the city's foremost newspapers and his wife (fig. 2.5). After 1910, the residents of the St. Francis Hotel developed a reputation for being the fashion setters and high rollers, while the Palace residents became known as the more traditional and respectable group.[18]

So many business leaders lived in hotels that some developed appropriate corporate legends. In New York City, John W. Gates hammered together the organization of U.S. Steel in his suite at the old Waldorf-Astoria, where he was one of the first permanent guests. James R. Keene, Charles M. Schwab, and other top Carnegie associates also lived at the old Waldorf. When the new Plaza Hotel opened in 1907, the *New York Times* printed a cutaway diagram of the hotel, revealing the corner suites of the most prominent residents, representing among them many of America's most famous fortunes (fig. 2.6). John Gates

FIGURE 2.6. Newspaper diagram of the Plaza Hotel, 1907. Published just before the hotel opened, this cutaway view shows where the wealthiest families were to live.

PLAZA HOTEL TO BE HOME OF N. Y. BLUE BLOOD AND RICHES

A. G. Vanderbilt, George J. Gould and Oliver Harriman Have Apartments.

WILL OPEN ON OCTOBER 1

Appointments of $12,500,000 Hostelry Costliest of Any in the World.

Photograph of the new Plaza Hotel, and diagram sketch showing location of choice corner apartments facing Central Park South and the Plaza leased by well-known millionaires.

With the assured distinction of shelter-ing as permanent guests the largest milli-onaire colony in this city, or, as a matter of fact, in the entire world, the new $12,-500,000 Plaza Hotel will be viewed by offi-cial invitation for the first time to-day. All is complete with the exception of a few finishing touches in arranging furniture

and his wife were on the list, along with Mr. and Mrs. George J. Gould, Mr. and Mrs. Alfred G. Vanderbilt, and Mrs. Oliver Harriman.[19]

These most famous and wealthy hotel tenants probably moved to hotels largely for convenience. However, every famous and influential hotel resident attracted a dozen other people like the Spraggs, people who needed to know and be seen with the dominant social group of the city and nation. Indeed, the palace hotel was an important residential counterpart to the increasingly national and closely linked social group leading American business. The rapidly expanding size of corporations and the sheer number of large business organizations after 1900 meant a marked expansion in the number of highly paid and fairly mobile white-collar employees. Developers made ample provisions in the new palace hotels for this infusion of investors, lawyers, bankers, brokers, financial analysts, and other professionals looking for expensive residential hotel rooms. In 1910, for instance, Tessie Fair Oelrichs, the daughter of the mining king James Fair, completed the Fairmont Hotel in San Francisco. On opening, half of the rooms were reserved for permanent guests who needed a downtown pied-à-terre. This level of demand was repeated sixteen years later when the Mark Hopkins opened directly across the street from the Fairmont.[20]

Hotel children.   Since married couples (particularly young married couples) often lived in palace hotels, children were a prominent part of residential hotel life, especially in the nineteenth century. The wealthier the young family (with either one parent or both parents present), the more likely they were to have children with them. In 1880, 114 out of the 225 permanent guests in the Lick House were families: 15 married couples with no children, 12 couples with one child, and 9 families with two or more children. One family had five children.[21] When Twain lived at the Lick House, he learned to detest the younger children there, and he explained his judgment by describing a typical afternoon as he tried to work in his room:

Here come those young savages again—those noisy and inevitable children. God be with them!—or they with him, rather, if it be not asking too much. . . . I know there are not more than 30 or 40 of them, yet they are under no sort of discipline, and they make noise enough for a thousand. . . . They assault my works [the door to his room]—they try to carry my position by storm—they finally draw off with boisterous cheers, to harass a handful of skirmishes thrown out by the enemy—a bevy of chambermaids.[22]

In Twain's account, the chambermaids abandon their brooms. The children, still without supervision, ride the brooms as horses and return to taunt the author. Next they attack a Chinese laundryman, steal his basket, and pull his queue. Finally, the children's nurses arrive and drag them off, to Twain's relief.

Twain was hardly alone in his exasperation. "Close and frequent acquaintance with small juveniles in an American hotel," wrote the London journalist George Augustus Sala in 1879, "is apt to induce the conviction that, all things considered, you would like the American child best in a pie."[23] Victorian hotel rules expressly prohibited the conversion of corridors into playgrounds, but besides the children's dining room, youngsters had few other places to go. In the 1890s, in keeping with new attitudes about children's spaces in American homes, the managers of large hotels began to install kindergartens, playrooms, special classes, and other organized children's programs. The huge McAlpin Hotel in New York had an entire floor set aside for women and children—for both transient and permanent guests.[24]

By the late 1920s, with the greater expansion of apartment living and suburban housing options, the demand for raising children in hotels declined. Only a few palace hotels had so many young children, and some allowed no young children at all. In 1929, for instance, all the 160 permanent residents of San Francisco's Canterbury Hotel were listed in the social register. There were 94 single people (single women outnumbering single men by about 4 to 1), 27 couples with no children, and only 6 families with children.[25] Yet in 1955, Kay Thompson could still choose New York's Plaza Hotel as the setting for a children's book with a rambunctious heroine named Eloise who terrorizes the lobby, elevators, empty meeting rooms, and corridors. Eloise epitomizes the pampered, privileged, upper-class hotel child: she is six years old, with a tutor who goes to Andover, a full-time English nanny, and precocious knowledge of how to order anything she wants from room service. She also divulges that her mother is thirty years old, has a charge account at Bergdorf's, knows the hotel owner ("and Coco Chanel and a dean at Andover, too"), and travels a great deal.[26] At age six, Eloise is well entrained in an upper-class trajectory, and her mother is apparently maintaining her own class status as well.

Edmund White gives a less glowing account of growing up in a "luxury hotel, sedate and respectable," at about the same time as Eloise. White's mother apparently chose the best possible hotel to meet the kind of new husband who could improve her shaky financial status. She could afford only one room with twin beds; White and his sister took turns sleeping on the floor. His mother was gone most of the time, and on cold days the children morosely hung around the hotel, picking fights with each other and eating at different times to avoid each other in the dining room. White discovered an accessible parapet off the empty ballroom and spent hours there, reading.[27]

Especially after 1930, hotel children like Eloise and White had few playmates because outside children were afraid of hotels. For adventure and companionship hotel children often tagged along with the chambermaids and bellboys on their rounds, learning all the inside gossip about the guests. Conscientious mothers complained that they had more child-care responsibilities in hotels compared to houses, because in hotels it was harder to keep children happy.[28] Indeed, the hotel emphasized adult social needs, in contrast to the child-centered suburban environment.

The children in hotels may not have cared much about architectural opulence, but adult hotel residents certainly did. Like the commercial sociability and other personal advantages of hotel life, architectural luxury and geographic prominence of palace hotels were important attributes for the class formation aspects of expensive hotel life.

INCUBATORS FOR A MOBILE HIGH SOCIETY

Multiple architectural advantages favored public hotels over private houses as social incubators. Few private houses could guarantee more than a fashionable address or a local architectural prominence. Palace hotel life, however, enveloped residents in an international network of architectural distinction. By definition, a palace hotel required a building of world prominence and a series of interior public locations—the lobby, the bar, the dining room, the ballroom, the terrace—that were known to virtually everyone in the city (at least everyone in polite society) and that were generally accessible only to the truly elite. Palace hotel opulence—no matter who the architect, owner, or manager—was not only an individual achievement, but also a social fact. Until their prominence was replaced by office buildings in the 1890s, hotels were often the city's most important landmarks. And unlike city halls or office buildings, one could *live* in these landmarks. The development of these architectural realms paralleled the historical development of the palace hotel as a social institution.

Early developments: The first-class hotel. The architectural development of the palace hotel was a story of ever-increasing specialization and separation. Wealthy members of the business elite, very much like the fictional Spraggs, began to live permanently in hotels in about 1800, at the same time that the best hotel buildings began to be more than mere inns. American inns and taverns in the 1700s looked much like large single-family houses. Not until the late 1700s did grand architecture or elegance grace travelers' lodgings in Europe or America; simultaneously, the word *hotel* (in English) came to denote inns of a superior kind.[29] Between 1790 and 1820, associations of wealthy businessmen in the United States improved on English hotels by building structures with elaborate public spaces as well as a totally new scale of 70 to 300 very simple sleeping rooms. In Boston's 300-room Exchange Hotel, opened in 1809, putting numbers on the room doors was enough of a novelty to merit mention in travelers' accounts.[30] After 1820, American hotel investors outbuilt structures like the Exchange Hotel and essentially invented the world model for the large modern hotel. Simultaneously, they added a new level of luxury and a more private life in personal rooms. Providing each room with an individual washbowl, water pitcher, and soap at first distinguished these hotels. Significantly, it was in this generation of expensive hotels that permanent guests first gained a high profile. English travelers in America frequently complained that they could not get the good rooms they wanted because the best accommodations were occupied by permanent boarders—judges, lawyers, merchants, and others who brought their families to live in the hotel.[31]

Most American inns and hotels before the 1820s had mixed people from somewhat disparate backgrounds, to the chagrin of those European travelers who were both fastidious and wealthy. The opening of Boston's Tremont House in 1829 signaled new and more socially restrictive management ideas for the United States. The Tremont had only one room rate—a high one for its time—of $2 a day for room and board. For permanent residents, it offered elegantly furnished private parlors attached to suites of rooms. As part of their rent, Tremont tenants enjoyed lavish hotel service that included the first bellboys and the first hotel dining room in the United States to feature French cuisine. The managers and the architect of the Tremont also analyzed functions that had been crowded into earlier hotel rotundas and separated them into four spaces—lobby, desk or office, baggage room, and bar. The Tremont was thus one of the first hotels where guests went into a lobby

to register instead of going into the bar. It was also one of the first hotels with truly private rooms: each room had a separate key, and strangers were not sent to share rooms. (As late as the 1860s, in cheaper hotels rooms were still shared by strangers when necessary.)[32] By 1840, urban Americans were using the term "first-class hotel" to distinguish the very best hotels. With at least one hundred rooms, imposing architectural style, luxurious service and food, and often a famous manager, first-class hotels became an urban social center for the elite, a place to do business, and—for some—a place to live (fig. 2.7). High prices kept out most middle-income residents, except those who stayed for a few days as transient guests.

Like the shift represented by the Tremont House and its followers, shifts in hotel sizes and styles coincided with periods of national economic development. The big inns like the Exchange Hotel came to life in the 1790s with the beginnings of a distinctly American economy and a more reliable system of stagecoach travel. The first-class hotels of the 1820s and 1830s followed another surge of business expansion, land sales, urban population growth, shipping, canal building, and turnpike construction. An imposing hotel became an essential ingredient for any aspiring city in the battle to attract new capital investors and professionals. Emulating the chartered companies of wealthy merchants in established cities, boosters on the urban frontier built ever-larger and more imposing hotels in each generation.[33] Boosters often overbuilt; to fill the rooms, the managers of grand new hotels often had to offer attractive rates to permanent residents. By the 1860s, the transformation

FIGURE 2.7. An 1895 view of the Astor House in New York, built in 1836. This panoramic view shows the venerable hotel and St. Paul's Chapel at the corner of Broadway and Vesey Street. The fire escapes were a late addition.

of the economy, availability of larger capital investments, perfection of new management practices, and use of passenger elevators and steel frame construction made even larger hotels feasible. These changes also made necessary a more distinctive architectural and social category of hotel.

Palace hotels.   After the Civil War, new hotels—some of them with only middle-income dining and service—jumped to a size of 500 and 700 rooms. By the 1880s, dozens of hotels in any large city could boast "first-class" amenities; the term had come to mean merely a good hotel rather than a socially exclusive hostelry. To distinguish the one to five most elite hotels in the region, citizens began to speak of *palace* hotels—hostelries that maintained the pinnacles of price, luxury, fine food, social prominence, and architectural landmark status.[34] The heyday of residential life in palace hotels occurred between 1880 and 1945. In name as well as in experience, the Palace Hotel of San Francisco exemplified the type for the Victorian era. The $5 million hotel opened in 1875 and covered an entire city block. Its two prominent owners—the state's most audacious capitalist and a wealthy U.S. senator—set its social status. It had 755 rooms in seven stories arranged around a large central courtyard with a skylight and two additional very large air wells. For the next thirty years, the Palace reigned as a landmark. Its massive seven-story volume loomed over the city, and its hundreds of bay windows dominated downtown vistas (fig. 2.8).[35]

The sumptuousness of a palace hotel suite was recorded in 1879, when Sala enthusiastically listed the furnishings of his $4-a-day "alcove bedroom" at the 400-room Grand Pacific in Chicago:

Height at least 15 feet; two immense plate-glass windows; beautifully frescoed ceiling; couch, easy chairs, rocking chairs, foot stools in profusion, covered with crimson velvet; large writing table for gentlemen, pretty *escritoire* for lady; *two* towering cheval glasses; handsomely carved wardrobe and dressing table; commanding pier-glass over mantelpiece; adjoining bath-room beautifully fitted; rich carpet; and finally the bed, in a deep alcove, impenetrably screened from the visitor's gaze by elegant lace curtains.[36]

Sala concluded that there was no more splendid hotel in the world than the Grand, although he said something similar about almost every pal-

ace hotel he visited. From 1820 through the 1940s, suites of two or more rooms remained part of the standard plan of all large hotels. Many were typically occupied by permanent guests.[37]

FIGURE 2.8. San Francisco's Palace Hotel, as seen from the South of Market district, ca. 1890. The hotel, at rear left, was a Victorian era landmark in every sense of the term.

The elegance, comfort, and convenience of palace hotel life relied not only on food and architecture but also on the level of human and mechanical service. Like ocean liners, some palace hotels employed as many as four or five staff for each guest; ratios of one employee to one guest, or three to two, were the minimum for a palace hotel. In 1990, the twenty to thirty most expensive hotels in the United States were still distinguished by lavish hospitality and an extremely high level of personalized service.[38] Only a small fraction of the hotel personnel were publicly visible as clerks, bellboys, elevator operators, or waitresses. The rest worked in what Sinclair Lewis called (in 1935) "the world behind the green baize doors at the ends of the corridors." There one found industrial-scale machinery that could heat and air-condition thousands of rooms, provide instant hot water, and launder thousands of napkins and sheets. There were large shops for upholsterers, carpenters, and plumbers, along with tailors, printers, florists, and a dozen other trades and specialties.[39] Indeed, in any period after 1880, the gen-

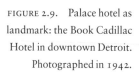

FIGURE 2.9. Palace hotel as landmark: the Book Cadillac Hotel in downtown Detroit. Photographed in 1942.

eral manager of a palace hotel hired, trained, and supervised a staff of thousands. At peak seasons and for special events, the manager routinely employed by the day hundreds of additional helpers.

In 1893, when the owners joined the 10-story Waldorf Hotel and its adjoining 16-story Astoria Hotel to create the original Waldorf-Astoria, they set a 1,000-room pace for the new post-Victorian generation of palace hotels. In 1907, the 18-story Plaza Hotel at the corner of Fifth Avenue and Central Park South easily surpassed the Waldorf-Astoria as New York's leading palace hotel.[40] In the next fifteen years, palace hotels elsewhere—for instance, the Book Cadillac in Detroit and the 500-room Drake Hotel on Chicago's Lake Shore Drive—set sparer architectural styles but changed little else (fig. 2.9). On the upper floors of such hotels a few wealthy families often built 10- to 30-room penthouse suites. A case in point is a 1913 hotel home built by a shipping and lumber baron at the top of San Francisco's St. Francis Hotel. He leased two entire floors, one for his family and one for the servants. The entertaining rooms of the family's suite survive today as part of San Francisco's City Club.

Builders of the next generation of palace hotels, beginning in the mid-1920s, added parking garages and true skyscraper towers but offered smaller guest rooms. Hotels like San Francisco's Sir Francis Drake prominently advertised their built-in garage, with elevator service direct from the garage to guest room floors. The typical bedrooms in late Victorian palace hotels had been 20 feet by 20 feet, offering twice the floor area of rooms in fine hotels built in the 1920s. The palace hotel rooms of the 1920s were still elegantly furnished—but no longer with brocades, fringes, and ornamental brass.[41] Outside, a tower of 18 to 30 stories, in Art Deco architectural style, was almost essential. Managers experimented with penthouse dining rooms; with the end of Prohibition, they added flamboyant bars to the tops of their hotels. Radio stations or at least radio programs originating in palace hotels became another way for hotels to retain their prominence.[42] In 1930, the *new* Waldorf-Astoria leapfrogged the Plaza in size but never regained its social hegemony because the Waldorf was simply too large. Three hundred of the new 2,253 guest rooms had parlors, but true palace hotel status accrued only to the Waldorf Towers section, which had its own entrance and 500 deluxe suites with 18-foot ceilings, open fireplaces, 45-foot by 25-foot drawing rooms, and 14-foot by 18-foot bath-dressing rooms. In the 1980s, rents for such a suite could range from $5,000 to $8,000 a month. The Waldorf Towers attracted many world-famous people as residents, including Herbert Hoover (who lived there from 1934 to 1964), General Douglas MacArthur (1951–1964), Henry Kissinger, and former President Gerald Ford.[43]

Permanent residents retained a prominent part in palace hotels up to the early 1960s, and some palace hotels still had permanent residents in 1990.[44] A San Francisco journalist's survey in 1983 found fifteen residents, including Cyril Magnin at the Mark Hopkins, living in three of the city's palace hotels, still echoing the advantages listed by generations of palace hotel dwellers. Ruth Fennimore, at ninety-one years of age, had worked hard to return to hotel life. She and her husband had lived in a palace hotel for a year after their marriage in 1912. In 1973, some time after her husband died (he had been a prominent optician and president of the Retail Merchants Association), Mrs. Fennimore moved back into a hotel. For her one-bedroom apartment, the rent was

FIGURE 2.10. The University Club in New York. A classic example of an elite residential club, it contrasts sharply with the houses to the left.

more than $3,000 a month, but that included what she called "perfected service." She and the other residents visited back and forth just as suburban neighbors did. Another resident confessed, "You know, when you're 86, most of your friends are in the cemetery. The Huntington is my family, from the lowest housekeeper to the manager."[45] San Francisco's permanent palace hotel residents were mostly elderly, although the families of three corporation presidents also kept suites at the Huntington. In other cities, hotel life at the palace level has depended more on the whim of hotel managers than on the demand; only a few managers are willing to take permanent residents. New York City remains the capital of palace hotel living.

If single men or single women were of upper-class social status but did not want to live the relatively public life of a palace hotel, they might have chosen life in an elite private club (fig. 2.10). Each city had its own top clubs, but usually an expensive club's exclusivity, its quiet and dignified buildings, reasonably good food, and social contacts made residence there a substitute for palace hotel life. For many, clubs were an improvement on hotel life. Because club members carefully chose their companions, life in a club was guaranteed to be more exclusive than life in a hotel, which accepted almost anyone who could pay. Living at a private club was also a prime option for elderly men and women of high status but lowered spending capacity, since living in elite clubs could often cost less than living in posh commercial hostelries.

Cycles of life at palace hotels.   On a day-to-day basis, the visible signs of achieving and maintaining membership in upper-class hotel life seemed to consist of wearing stylish clothes and following other avenues of conspicuous consumption as social competition strategies. One hotel resident of the 1920s, disgruntled with the system of buying one's status, complained to an interviewer about the hidden expenses of hotel life:

In order to be recognized as an admirable person, you need a constant shower of money to the help, expensive and very up-to-date clothes, and one must entertain at dinner, play cards, order motors [motorcars], and rush about to theaters and parties.[46]

Another guest, who could afford the expenses and enjoyed hotel life, admitted that the only possible drawback in comparison to life in a private house or apartment was that one had to "constantly be dressed up."[47] Extravagant and stylish clothes did mean a great deal in the palace hotel world. The vast marble-columned lobbies and dining rooms set suitable stages for the daily parade of wealth. Society columnists regularly reserved space to cover hotel visitors and entertainments. Hotel residents helped to redefine a city's social ranks by showing the new canons of consumption and its essential public display; such people had money to spend and the need to display it, as Thorstein Veblen explained. In 1875, Countess Maria Yelverton presaged Veblen as she rather jaundicedly noted that palace hotels permitted the wealthy "to display their riches to the greatest advantage, and make as much show as possible for their money."[48] In 1920, a Chicago society reporter observed the continuity of tradition as she reported that women could give inexpensive parties, "amounting to no more than afternoon tea," followed by a grand announcement in the newspaper that "Mrs. So-and-So entertained 50 guests at luncheon at the Plaza Hotel, the company afterwards playing bridge."[49]

The displays of wealth and the system of "social-position-for-cash-and-appearance" also had unwanted side effects. The instant status conferred by proper clothes, manners, and spending money meant that intelligent thieves could efficiently establish an assumed identity at a hotel, deftly meet officers and employees of large firms, and then extract precise tips about their payrolls and company deliveries. The rich, feeling that they were in a protected environment, inadvertently advertised their enticing jewelry in the lobbies and dining rooms. Hotel people of high social standing were also easy targets for blackmail.[50]

Outnumbering the outright thieves in hotel life were the professional gamblers. Porters quite rightfully described palace and midpriced hotels as the "worst gambling places in the world"; in the 1920s, staff reported that when they took men's bags to a room, one of the more frequent inquiries was, "Say, can you lead me to a little game?"[51] San Francisco's Palace Hotel had many small "committee rooms" devoted largely to card games for large stakes. Women, too, joined the hotel ranks of professional cardsharpers and gamblers. At one palace hotel in the 1920s, an attractive and well-mannered woman met three other women residents. Over a period of days she invited them to her suite for competitive games of bridge and a week later, made off with $9,000 from her victims, who were obviously fond of playing cards for high stakes.[52]

Prostitutes—both men and women but most commonly women—were another socially marginal group who lived and worked in all ranks of hotels, including palace hotels. Hotels were also notoriously convenient places for men to keep mistresses or for women to keep paramours. As late as the 1890s, hotel managers barred single women from registering and staying alone for fear they would be prostitutes and damage the respectability of a proper hotel.[53] Into the 1950s, comments about and images of "loose women" continued to mix with hotel life. The fact that the phrase "loose men" was not common indicates a cultural double standard more than a more abstinent male population. The presence of thieves, professional gamblers, and prostitutes continually proved that even the exclusivity of palace hotels was not absolute.

If palace hotel residents were looking for a gaming or sexual or retail venue not available at the hotel, they could avail themselves of the full diversions of the surrounding city. That was true for other services as well. Yet, technically, palace hotels needed their neighborhoods only for a labor supply and deliveries. Hotels of such scale and complexity could conceivably exist with minimal reliance on outside services or independent shops on the surrounding streets. With four or five restaurants, three bars, dozens of shops, and several promenade hallways in the interior of their hotel, palace residents were not forced to walk outside.

The locations of palace hotels, more scattered than midpriced hotels, attested both to their insularity and to the fact that only in a few places of the city could people assemble a single plot of land socially appropriate and large enough for a palace hotel. In San Francisco, these locational directives indicated Union Square (established very early as the retail shopping center of the city) or Nob Hill. At the end of the nineteenth century, Nob Hill was the most prestigious address in the western United States; it was famous as the home of several of California's and the world's richest families. New downtown mansions were still being built not far away. Flamboyant Victorian piles, like the multitowered mansion of Mark Hopkins, were looking like haunted houses; their owners had died or moved, and the children wanted to live elsewhere. Not surprisingly, between 1900 and 1920 (just before and after the great fire of San Francisco), landowners on Nob Hill transformed their properties from an exclusive private neighborhood to the quintessential palace hotel neighborhood, with several parallels to areas like Fifth Avenue in New York and the Gold Coast of Chicago. Nob Hill's real estate developers, often children of the famous families, could see that their sites offered all the necessary neighborhood elements for fashionable hotels, apartments, clubs, and restaurants. In a sense, in replacing the individual private opulence of the Nob Hill mansions, the new palace hotels and clubs helped to create and reinforce elite class position with a more conspicuously *social* opulence. The optimum stage to display social opulence was at the center of the city, not buried behind shrubbery and trees on a private estate road twenty miles from town.

Nob Hill's location was central, and its transportation was excellent. The best office and retail blocks were within walking distance but not so close as to bring hoi polloi right to the doors of the hotel. The hill's elevation gave commanding views of the rest of the city and beyond to San Francisco Bay. Several of the city's most expensive boutiques were either inside the hotels or around the block; fine restaurants were close by; the opera house and elite museums were a short cab ride away. The site of the Crocker mansion had become the city's new Episcopal cathedral. (A preponderant share of California's pioneer business families were at least socially Episcopalian). At the top of the hill, a small park gave an urbane and European focus to the district; next to the park was the one remaining prefire mansion in the area, converted into an exclusive men's club. By the 1920s, three palace hotels (the Mark Hopkins, the Fairmont, and the Huntington) and several lavish apartment blocks surrounded the park and club. Although there was no public coercion, virtually no retail stores were visible from the sidewalk. The mixture of residential and commercial activity occurred but in hidden and guarded interiors. The only outwardly visible signs for the restaurants were tiny brass plaques; insiders already knew their locations. In the early 1920s, polite hotel districts like these were so accepted and growing so rapidly that utility engineers made plans for 1940 assuming other zones fully occupied by high-class residential hotels. Hotel keepers, too, expected a "Nob Hill/Gold Coast/Fifth Avenue" future for urban residential life.[54]

For social status, leaving a palace hotel and its neighborhood could be as important as being there. Elite downtown living figured as only one phase in an annual cycle of different residences. A hotel suite served as a center city pied-à-terre complementing homes in the country and world tours or business expeditions. So few palace hotel guests stayed at one hotel for the entire year that they were well known among the staff. Wealthy hotel residents moved heavily and ostentatiously from place to place with servants, piles of trunks, valets, and governesses for their children. Some of these shifts of residence were for health reasons: to a resort hotel in Florida, in California, or in the Southwest to avoid the winter; perhaps a trip in the fall to a family house in rural New England; then back to a major city for the opera season, shopping, or business.[55]

Important stops in the annual rounds of residences were a handful of exclusive resort hotels. Compared to downtown palace hotels, upper-class resort hotels were more likely to be sheathed in wood rather

than marble and horizontally impressive rather than vertically imposing (fig. 2.11). However, the best resort hotels matched the downtown
opulence of food, service, and furnishings and added spectacularly
beautiful and healthful rural settings and multiple outdoor amusements. The Hotel Del Monte, built in 1880 on a 7,000-acre site at the
edge of Monterey, California, offered the requisite amenities: scenic
vistas, elegant public rooms, 26 acres of landscaped gardens, a golf
course, a polo field, a racetrack, tennis courts, and a 17-mile private
carriage road through the Del Monte forests to Pebble Beach and
Carmel. Wherever possible, the sites of palace resort hotels included
prominent sidings and landings for the conspicuous arrivals of private
railroad cars and yachts (fig. 2.12). As Robert Louis Stevenson said in
reference to the Del Monte, there one would be sure to find "the millionaire vulgarians of the Big Bonanza."[56]

Like downtown palace hotels, upper-class resort hotels offered a constant round of social entertainments but with a more closed set of participants. Of the vast Royal Poinciana in Palm Beach, which flourished
from 1893 to the 1920s, Henry James wrote that "there, as nowhere

FIGURE 2.11. Aerial view of
the Royal Poinciana Hotel,
Palm Beach, Florida. Briefly,
the Poinciana was a winter
pinnacle of society.

FIGURE 2.12. Group leaving on a private railroad excursion from the Royal Poinciana, March 1896. The group includes Mr. and Mrs. Cornelius Vanderbilt, Henry Whitney, Gladys Vanderbilt, and Gertrude Vanderbilt.

else in America, one would find Vanity Fair in full blast . . . compressed under one vast cover." Both men and women had to bring trunkloads of different outfits appropriate for a daily cycle of events that might consist of breakfast, a morning stroll, swimming or boating, lunch, bicycling or carriage riding, golf, tea, an afternoon stroll, a very formal dinner, an evening promenade, and dancing. One dared not repeat an outfit too often during the summer's stay. Because theaters and clubs were not immediately adjacent, the summer resort had to offer lavish entertainment as part of the program.[57] Palace resorts were as expensive as downtown palace hotels. One account cites the cost during the 1890s at Mohonk Mountain House in the Catskills at $125 a week for two parents, a daughter, a maid, and two horses versus $6 to $12 a week per person for modest boardinghouses in the valley for middle-income vacationers.[58]

At palace resorts, dress codes and high prices screened out most people who were economically undesirable, as in downtown palace hotels. But exclusive resorts screened out undesired guests much more overtly than the downtown hostelries. The code word *restricted,* sometimes seen in advertisements or road signs, meant that Jews, blacks, Asians, or blatantly practicing Catholics (Italians and Irish, especially) would be accepted as servants but not as guests. A few resort hotels advertised all-white kitchen staffs. These restrictions lasted in some resort hotels until World War II.[59] The tightly drawn social circle pointed to a major role for the best resort hotels: because they were so much more insular than downtown hotels, they were the perfect place for the young people of America's elite to meet strictly appropriate people of the opposite sex. Resort hotels also played a recruiting role for hotel residence in the city. While on holiday, summer guests could have their initial conversion experience to the comforts and convenience of more extended hotel life.

Summer vacations notwithstanding, other downtown living options away from a mansion were also appealing to wealthy Americans.

Apartment alternatives.   From the 1880s to the 1930s, neighborhoods like Nob Hill were ideal for expensive apartments as well as palace hotels. Yet even when they stood on the same street corners, hotels retained some advantages over apartments. At best, an exclusive apartment building gave its residents a good address on a fashionable street and perhaps a well-known name. A hotel or apartment hotel, however, could add the reputation of its ballroom, the popularity of its chef, and the notoriously high price of its dining room. Hotels also gave nouveau riche residents more opportunities to show off clothing or packages from expensive stores. In apartment lobbies, no one saw these things.[60] In the 1920s, when most of present-day Nob Hill was completed, a luxury apartment of five to seven rooms might have cost $250—about the same price as a multiroom suite in the Mark Hopkins or the Fairmont but not including the food (see table 2, Appendix).

It is hardly surprising that expensive apartments and expensive hotels like the Mark Hopkins would stand on opposite corners, since the two building types had closely intertwining histories. The fashionable apartment's role in reinforcing social class, its architectural form, its facade styles, and especially its mechanical accoutrements before 1900 owed far more to the American residential hotel than to the distant Parisian flat (fig. 2.13). Nineteenth-century apartments in France mixed people of different economic classes; the higher the floor, the cheaper the rent. In America, the availability of the elevator and the

FIGURE 2.13. The Hotel Majestic and the Dakota Apartments seen from Central Park in 1894. In their early development, elegant apartments and residential hotels often shared location, clientele, and building types.

relative insecurity of social position reinforced the desire to build apartment buildings as class-specific as were new hotels.[61] To keep good tenants happy, apartment promoters had to offer a series of features that tenants had come to expect from their stays in palace hotels: wider air shafts, fast and quiet elevators, "the hottest radiators and the most gleaming plumbing in the world," electricity in all rooms, twenty-four-hour telephone service, and all-night elevator service.[62] The intertwining evolution of hotels and apartments also meant that Americans interchanged *words* for them as well. The earliest American apartment buildings, aimed at wealthy tenants, usually had "hotel" in their title. Before World War I, journalists interchangeably applied terms such as "French flat," "decker," "hotel," "apartment," "apartment hotel," and "family hotel" in articles about a single building that could have been either a hotel or an apartment building. Not until 1930 did some city directories show a heading of simply "Apartment Buildings" and not a listing of "Apartment Houses (see also Hotels)," linking hotels and apartments.[63]

CONVERSION EXPERIENCES FOR THE NEW CITY

Upper-class apartments were like palace hotels in that they were not backdrops for a society already formed, not passive stages for human action. Palace hotels played an active role in shaping the flow of life through them. Restaurants, polo grounds, barrooms, and ballrooms channeled daily lives and structured social interactions; they helped to form and revise social groups as well as to reinforce them. Simultaneously, hotel spaces helped to shape the social consciousness derived from daily life and were spatial tools often consciously wielded by members (and would-be members) of the elite.[64]

Palace hotels played more civic roles as well, influencing the acceptance of new ideas about the arrangements of domestic and urban space.[65] As architects and hotel managers hammered out the architecture and social relations of the first-class hotel and palace hotel, they showed people a possible future for the city. The jumbled, crowded, mixed-use city of the nineteenth century did relatively little to organize human life officially; downtown urban life remained a seemingly disorderly landscape of confusion, individual competition, and commercial greed. The experience of living in and frequenting palace hotels helped to prepare the urban elite to make decisions about more organized, articulated, and stratified urban space (fig. 2.14). The palace hotel was only one place among several where urban elites from the 1820s to the 1890s experimented with the new organization of space; other venues included the commercial arcade, prison, school, campus, and eventually the great pleasure garden park.[66] However, the palace hotel was especially apt as a scale model of a successful future city. Throughout the nineteenth century, palace hotels were increasingly efficient machines for keeping people of different strata and classes in their place, in a total scheme coordinated by centralized planning and direction. Like the city, hotel life brought several groups of strangers together in large numbers and in close juxtaposition. The hotel was overtly commercial, but because it was a privately managed fiefdom, its public spaces presented a uniform and homogeneous arrangement of space and people. The lobbies, dining halls, and hallways of palace hotels were public only to those people in the upper and middle class whose clothing and decorum passed the unobtrusive inspection of a phalanx of hotel detectives and floor clerks who, if necessary, were ready to quietly interview and eject people who looked out of place.

The palace hotel was also a complete and total scheme for a diverse but centrally planned and coordinated set of activities and spaces. Hotel managers could control potentially competing activities. Architects and managers steadily specialized and separated spatial and social ar-

FIGURE 2.14. The old city and the new city, 1876. Temporary sheds in the foreground contrast with San Francisco's Palace Hotel in the background.

rangements. Each space and time, if possible, was increasingly organized for one activity and one social group. Palace hotel buildings provided multiple parlors and dining rooms—some for men, some for women, some for men and women together, some for children, some for transient guests, some for permanent residents. Designers and managers strove mightily to keep invisible the world of the hotel workers—servants' hallways, laundries, kitchens, the entire world beyond the green baize doors. Wherever possible, knowledge of the realms of work (production) was not to overlap with the realms of the residents' daily life (consumption). In hotels this became possible more quickly, more thoroughly, more socially, and at a much larger scale than in the large private houses or other elite environments of the same periods.

Long before the era of the push button, the commercialized community of the hotel was made to appear automatic, effortless, and socially seamless. No wonder, then, that Henry James wrote, "One is verily tempted to ask if the hotel-spirit may not just *be* the American spirit most seeking and most finding itself."[67] Many middle and upper class Americans agreed with James. However, most of them probably agreed because they thought he was referring not to a palace hotel but to a more common and more approachable type, hotels best known by people of middle incomes.

MIDPRICED MANSIONS
FOR MIDDLE INCOMES

RETAIL SALES MANAGERS DID NOT GENERATE headlines and society page gossip as did the heiresses and silver kings who lived in palace hotels. However, twice as many people of middle incomes lived in downtown hotels than wealthy people who lived in palace hotels.[1] These less-expensive hotels supplied housing needed for a mobile professional population that was expanding the American urban economy. Compared to their wealthier counterparts, middle-income hotel residents shared many values and advantages in hotel life, but they lived in hotels less for social reasons and more for personal and practical reasons. The midpriced hotel was an alternative choice of residence for people whose lives did not mesh with a six- to ten-room single-family suburban house.

CONVENIENCE FOR MOVABLE LIVES

Like palace hotel life, midpriced hotel life began in the early 1800s. In the young Chicago of 1844, about one person in six listed in the city directory lived in a hotel, and another one in four lived in a boardinghouse or with an employer.[2] Walt Whitman reported in 1856 that almost three-fourths of middle and upper class New Yorkers were either boarders or permanent hotel guests. When Whitman asked one little girl where her parents lived, she answered instructively, "They don't live; they BOARD."[3] Through the 1890s, visiting writers from London emphasized that (compared to the English) many more Americans could buy a modest house of their own but preferred to live in board-inghouses and hotels. American writers concurred. One remarked about the "temptation to live in hotels instead of in apartment houses." In 1919, the sociologist Arthur Calhoun explained that hotel life might begin in a couple's youth and continue through their mature years or be resumed after a period of housekeeping. He wrote that "almost any family, even the wealthiest, might at some time try this manner of life."[4]

Immediate places for new job holders. The occasional shortage of single-family houses in rapidly growing cities was one factor that sent middle-income families who were new to a city to a hotel. House prices and mortgage terms were high. Also, from 1870 to the 1920s, the building of new suburban houses did not consistently match demand. Families waiting for a house often lived in a hotel for a year or more. In 1880, the family of San Francisco stockbroker Daniel Stein (including his daughter Gertrude Stein) lived for over a year in a suite in a commodious wooden hotel in Oakland while they waited to move a dozen blocks away into a suburban house with a ten-acre garden (fig. 3.1).[5]

Temporary jobs created other middle-income hotel dwellers. From the Civil War through World War II, people in rapidly expanding business markets were often sojourners. The expansion of trade and rail-road links throughout the United States opened thousands of white-collar positions in manufacturing, marketing, and managing chain store and branch store businesses. Engineers, accountants, lawyers, and other professionals flocked to assist these new operations.[6] Many people very tentatively began their stay in a new company or city; they expected to live there only for a period of a few months to two or three years. Such sojourners made up a significant share of the permanent residents in midpriced hotels, and their initial visit often stretched into lifelong hotel residence.

Epitomizing the sojourner household were Mr. and Mrs. Walters, a couple interviewed in the 1920s. They had lived in hotels in small cities near Chicago for a succession of years. In each place, Mr. Walters spent

FIGURE 3.1. The Tubbs Hotel in suburban Oakland, soon after its opening in 1871. Gertrude Stein's family lived here while waiting for completion of their house two miles away.

four or five months establishing a branch sales department for electrical appliances; then he placed a sales person in charge and moved to another town.[7] Similarly, construction projects required experts who stayed for months or years of planning and building. Architects flocked to cities after major fires, then moved on a few years later. It was not unusual for sojourning architects to live in hotels; in a few cases, they also set up offices in the same building. Louis Sullivan's life was not as peripatetic as some of his lesser-known colleagues, but the famous architect lived in hotels much of his life.[8] Because of their centrality, hotels made ideal temporary office sites. In certain midpriced hotels, traveling sales people set up temporary offices in sample rooms purposely built and reserved for the display of wares. Some business people rented rooms in a residential hotel in the winter simply to avoid cold-weather commuting from their houses in distant suburbs. People serving on temporary government or business committees also relied on hotels in the midprice range.[9]

For sojourners in a new city, moving into a hotel simplified the housing search. Hotels required commitments of only a month (at most), rather than the long-term leases required of apartment and house renters. Another inherent advantage of hotel life was avoiding the packing and lugging of household goods and large pieces of furniture. As one hotel observer put it, when a family had to move frequently, "even a large wardrobe is a nuisance, and a collection of furniture would be as appropriate as a drove of elephants."[10]

Like palace hotel residents, residents in midpriced hotels were well positioned to weave themselves into the social groups they needed for their work or personal ambitions. Hotels combined central location, maximum information availability, and high potentials for human contact with influential people of the middle and upper class. Hotel lobbies and dining rooms—in the early nineteenth century the official stock exchanges in many cities (and official slave markets in the South)—were alive with business and gossip. In other hotels, informal and open-ended social groups formed around billiards, dice, and card tables. In the 1920s, one young hotel resident wrote that her businessman father fortuitously met many other men of affairs in the lobby and in the smoke-filled billiards room after dinner.[11] Not all social aspects of hotel life were positive, but for a distinct minority of households, the advantages outweighed the problems (figs. 3.2, 3.3).

FIGURES 3.2 AND 3.3. The problem of hotel noise, 1871. The *Harper's Weekly* cartoonist Thomas Nast emphasized the risks of hallway interruptions especially where permanent residents were not separated from tourist rooms.

Assists for politicians and young couples. Given these virtues of centrality, sojourning politicians naturally made up a significant hotel residence group. Through the 1800s, each urban political party patronized
a particular hotel, and politicians to this day often live in capital city
hotels while legislatures are in session. When owners tore down the old
Neil House in Columbus, Ohio, President Warren Harding wrote to the
managers saying that the hotel had been the "real capitol" of the state.
Huey Long maintained a suite at the elegant Fairmont Hotel in New
Orleans, spending so much time there that Louisiana lore suggests that
he built State Highway 61 from the state capitol directly to the door of
the hotel for his own convenience.[12] The most famous hotel-dwelling
politician was Calvin Coolidge. The thrifty Coolidge and his wife
were very long term hotel tenants. They lived many years in a dollar-a-
day room in the old Adams House of Boston (built in 1883). When
Coolidge was elected governor of Massachusetts in 1918, on the advice
of friends he moved into a $2-a-day room. In 1921, Vice President and
Mrs. Coolidge moved into the same modest fourth-floor corner suite in
the Willard Hotel that Vice President and Mrs. Thomas R. Marshall
had occupied throughout Marshall's second term in the Wilson administration. In 1922, a Washington hostess tried unsuccessfully to establish a pretentious vice-presidential house. Coolidge himself quelled the
move, saying that maintaining such a residence on a $12,000-a-year
salary was out of the question. The Coolidges remained in their Willard
Hotel suite.[13] More recently, Supreme Court Justices Felix Frankfurter
and Earl Warren have lived in hotels.[14] For most of 1931 to 1934, early
in his career in Congress, Lyndon Johnson lived at the Dodge Hotel in
Washington, D.C. During the early years of the Reagan administration, Attorney General William French Smith and Secretary of Defense
Caspar Weinberger settled at the Jefferson Hotel.[15]

Newlyweds often lived in hotels. In the last half of the 1800s, people
considered it unremarkable when a young couple lived the first two or
three years of their marriage in a good boardinghouse or hotel. Such a
life could be just as respectable as residence in a private house. In 1879,
Sala noted that American married couples lived in fine hotels "by the
half-dozen years together." Young married couples made up the main-
stay of the guests in many expensive hotels, and teenage wives became
the most numerous female residents.[16] At least until the 1890s, young
well-to-do and middle-income brides often relied heavily on hotel so-

ciability. In a time when the median age for women at marriage was twenty-two to twenty-four years, younger brides could move into a hotel and enjoy the familiar routine of courting days and the company of young friends. They could spend a major part of their days visiting one another in their rooms or in the public parlors, either mimicking the formal visiting of residential neighborhoods or merely gossiping. According to the social historian Robert Elno McGlone, the conviviality of hotel life relieved women's fears of "early fading" or being "laid upon the shelf," phenomena they saw in many hardworking young wives and mothers who toiled at keeping house. For wives whose husbands traveled a great deal, hotel sociability also made life less lonesome than life alone in a house or an apartment.[17]

Young couples or single people—especially those accustomed to a high standard of living in their parents' homes—could more easily match or improve those standards by living in a palace hotel or midpriced hotel than by buying the expensive furnishings for a private house. Up to the 1890s, there were apartments for the very rich but a less ready supply of socially respectable apartments geared to middle incomes. Hotel managers catered to these desires for an impressive domicile; the plush furnishings in a good midpriced hotel could cost about half as much as the building itself. A traveler in 1855 observed that the better boardinghouses and almost all hotels were "furnished in a far more costly manner than a majority of young men can afford"— in fact, a life-style that would have cost twice as much in an individual household. This continued to be true into the 1920s. In 1926, a conservative estimate for the cost of complete furnishings for a professional person's household, with no servant and only an upright piano as an extravagance, totaled $5,000.[18] Such an initial cost, spread out in monthly rentals, bought far more sumptuous surroundings in a hotel.

Monthly rental costs in a midpriced hotel were usually one-half to one-third the rates at palace hotels. A Chicago sociologist, Norman Hayner, compared costs in the mid-1920s and found that a single room with bath at a midpriced hotel usually ranged from $40 to $60 a month. Hotel managers almost never advertised or divulged monthly rents charged to tenants, since they were individually negotiated. For permanent guests, monthly rates were always less than four times the weekly rate; sometimes they were only two weeks' rent for a month of occupancy.[19] For single people who did not have a servant or a family

FIGURE 3.4. The core of co-operative housekeeping. A hotel's kitchen and serving staff pictured in *Cosmopolitan* in 1905.

member to perform food preparation and housework, these prices were a bargain. As late as 1909, social workers admitted that it "nearly always" cost more "time, effort, and money to live well in suburbs than in town." Three Chicago schoolteachers explained to Hayner that separately they had been paying $6 or more per week for rooms with individual families. By pooling their rent money for a large room in an elegant midpriced hotel, they each saved a dollar a week and lived far more conveniently and convivially.[20]

New household roles for women. Cooperative housekeeping was the hotel attraction appreciated most by middle-income people. None of the men in hotels had to fix the furnace, repair the windows, fertilize the garden, or mow the lawn. The most enthusiastic people being set free from housekeeping were women who wanted to take an active part in city life or whose employment left them too little time for house-work. In a hotel household, none of the women needed to shop for food, cook it, serve it, or wash the dishes (fig. 3.4). Laundry, house-cleaning, and decorating were also commercialized. Wealthy women avoided the "servant problem" of hiring, supervising, and firing their cooks, maids, and butlers; middle-income women avoided the supervising problems of one or two servants and also their own share of the housework. However, an early observer wrote that the convenience and amplitude of hotel meals were the "strongest attraction the hotel offered." Destroy the meal plan and the families would form private households, he added.[21] Before the 1920s brought revolutions in food processing and packaging, assembling the raw, unprocessed ingredients to feed even a small middle-income family demanded myriad errands and consumed many hours. Feminists like Charlotte Perkins Gilman and Christine Herrick looked forward to the days when housekeeping schools would train skilled, professional home labor and when hot dinners would be cooked at central kitchens by salaried employees. They wrote that such arrangements would give domestic service "dignity and independence, and a scientific quality"; such a business would be "a sort of Adamless Eden, run for and by women." In the meantime, hotel and apartment hotel life freed women from what the writers saw as the drudgery and humiliation of unpaid and undervalued cooking and housework and the waste of "a hundred fires being run to cook a meal instead of one, a hundred cooks, where six could do the work."[22]

By the 1920s, in part because hotel service freed them from housework, women often predominated as residents in midpriced hotels, although the proportions varied considerably with the district of the city. In the 1930 U.S. Census of Chicago, areas with large numbers of residential hotels showed about three women to every two men; in the larger, more transient hotels in the Loop, the proportions reversed. Of the married women in several fairly expensive midpriced hotels of the 1920s, only 2 to 10 percent worked for monetary return. The rest, according to one study, had "interests in charities and social reform or were simply 'mental rovers.'" In Seattle, two-thirds of the women in midpriced hotels lived alone, and most of them worked if they were below retirement age. The working women in the better hotels were predominantly teachers, buyers in department stores, executives in other businesses, writers, librarians, private secretaries, social workers, or women politicians. Showing the common social or professional congregation that occurred in residential hotel life, in one large downtown hotel in Seattle, 60 percent of the four hundred guests were women, and almost 25 percent of them were schoolteachers. Many of these women were *not* merely sojourners. Married or not, they were escaping female roles in traditional households and fully expected to live in hotels for at least several years. A journalist writing in 1930 characterized these people as the vanguard of the "new woman."[23]

Self-preserving associations.   Exclusion or discrimination also pushed some middle-income people to live in hotels. Jewish people figured prominently in some midpriced residential hotel markets. In *The Ghetto* (1928), Lewis Wirth stressed that predominantly Jewish hotels had become the latest avenue of escape from some Jewish neighborhoods. Wirth noted that in both Chicago's Hyde Park and North Shore districts, a "Jewish hotel row" had begun to spring up, inhabited by middle-income business people and their families. In the Chicago Beach Hotel, for instance, 80 percent of the tenants were Jewish. Wirth felt that housing in more Anglo-American hotels offered Jewish people a ready avenue for mixing with Gentile society, a residential proximity not then possible in most expensive suburbs.[24]

The mistrust of actors and artists as residents in other types of housing brought them, too, to hotels. "Born in a hotel and died in a hotel, Goddamn it!" were the dying words of Eugene O'Neill. Indeed, until automobile travel, radio, and movies restructured the American entertainment industry, sojourning theatrical troupes were often part of a hotel's residential composite. Unlike O'Neill (who lived in a house most of his life), star actors as well as bit-part players could spend most of their adult lives in hotels; headliners, in palace hotels. Sarah Bernhardt required an eight-room suite when she was performing in San Francisco (fig. 3.5). In less-expensive New York hotels have lived stars such as James Cagney, Tallulah Bankhead, Sammy Davis, Jr., Bill Cosby, and Cher.[25] Yet because of some actors' mobility, Bohemian moral codes, perpetual swing shift hours, and high divorce rate ("seven times the average for all occupations," clucked one newspaper reporter), actors and entertainers were not very welcome guests. Managers sometimes looked askance even at opera stars and symphony musicians. In cities with a population of more than 100,000, the less famous entertainers could find a budget-priced and slightly dilapidated "theatrical hotel." Chicago had six theatrical hotels in or near the Loop; hotel guides marked these hotels clearly, in part to warn other travelers.[26]

So many writers, editors, and composers made midpriced hotels their homes that they became another distinct client group. Artemus Ward

FIGURE 3.5. Sarah Bernhardt in her suite at the Hoffman House in New York City, 1896. Among theater people, only headliners could afford such expensive hotel homes.

lived in a hotel in New York's Greenwich Village when he came in the 1860s to edit the first *Vanity Fair*. Several writers made New York's Brevoort Hotel their home and through the 1880s mentioned life in the 100-room building in their novels. At New York's Majestic Hotel, at 72nd Street, another set of writers and artists congregated.[27] During two periods in her life, Willa Cather lived in a hotel: first, when she moved from Pittsburgh to New York City, and again in 1927, when building demolition forced Cather and Edith Lewis to move out of their apartment into the Grosvenor Hotel, at 35 Fifth Avenue. What they intended as a temporary refuge became their home for five years. Dylan Thomas and composer Virgil Thompson were only two out of many creative artists who made the Chelsea Hotel famous. Edna Ferber lived at the Sisson Hotel in Chicago. Nearer to the University of Chicago, Hannah Arendt and Thomas Mann each lived at the Windermere Hotel for part of their lives. Charlie Chaplin lived for a time in the Ambassador Hotel in Los Angeles, and for almost fifty years the Am-

FIGURE 3.6. Advertisements for residential hotel life, 1936. Special monthly rates, social activities, and good food were key promotional elements.

IN THE HEART OF THE LOOP

Always SOMETHING DOING AT THE Allerton

A social hotel, ideally located. Weekly dance, daily afternoon tea, concerts, lectures, theatricals, gymnasium and dance classes. A world of social activity, yet complete privacy for those who desire it. Fourteen floors for men and women, seven floors for women exclusively. Serving "Just Wonderful Food" sensibly priced in dining rooms and cocktail room.

$1.50 per day single; with bath, from $2.00 Special Monthly Rates

Real CLUB SPIRIT

FEATURING SMART RESIDENTIAL SUITES

Hotel Allerton
701 N. Michigan Ave.
CHICAGO

JOHN P. HARDING Hotel MANAGEMENT KEN. WILLIAMS Man. Dir.

Off THE BEATEN PATH YET CLOSE TO Everything

You're close to everything at The Seneca — shops, offices, theaters, all downtown activities. The smartly furnished, perfectly serviced two to seven room suites are tops in comfort. Popular one cost plan permits living in luxury at surprisingly reasonable rentals. Special monthly rates.

$3.00 per day single with bath
Kitchenette Suites from $5.00 per day

The SENECA
200 E. Chestnut St.
CHICAGO

bassador was Walter Winchell's home.[28] The famous Round Table at New York's Algonquin Hotel met in the hotel dining room, but for the most part the members were not hotel residents.

Like most other downtown hotel residents, all types of creative artists thrived on hotel locations. These artists relied on and helped to support nearby restaurants, nightclubs, theaters, and other entertainments. A Gramercy Park hotel brochure in 1927 promised that its fortunate residents would "find themselves at the heart of the best New York can give."[29] Libraries, medical buildings, legal offices, and churches added to the downtown's convenience (fig. 3.6).

Retired and elderly middle-income tenants were also attracted to midpriced hotel life by the central access to recreation and downtown services as well as the pedestrian independence hotels afforded. When the health of elderly hotel tenants waned, room service and hired nurses replaced their former independence. Throughout the history of inns and hotels, elderly people had been a proportion of the permanent residents.[30] Nonetheless, Sinclair Lewis's George Babbitt put retirement in a midpriced hotel in a dark light. Babbitt's in-laws had sold their house and moved to the Hotel Hatton in Zenith City, "that glorified boarding house filled with widows, red-plush furniture, and the sound of ice-water pitchers." After a sad and soggy Sunday dinner, the Babbitts had to sit, "polite and restrained, in the hotel lounge, while a young woman violinist played songs from the German via Broadway."[31] Hayner's Chicago study gives the more positive example of the retired Martin couple, who had lived for twenty-five years in their own house in a small Illinois city and then for twenty-one years in various Chicago apartments. When their daughter married, the Martins moved to a hotel where they had often dined. Both of the Martins enjoyed dancing at the hotel. Mrs. Martin, an active woman in her late sixties, loved to be in the center of things and reveled in a crowd. When she was not in her room sewing for her nieces she was out shopping in the Loop.[32]

Not all hotel keepers wanted elderly tenants, healthy or not. "A nice old lady is nice," Ford said about elderly guests in his large midpriced hotel in New York, "but the average old lady is a troublesome boarder." Ford did not mention elderly men, but he continued, "When old ladies come to stay I don't try hard to cater to them. They go away. There's one hotel in town where most of them land."[33] Indeed, each city had several midpriced hotels with derogatory nicknames like "The Old People's Home" and coffee shops called "wrinkle rooms," even though no more than half of the residents at those hotels may have been elderly. Not all hotel residents were in such places. Kate Smith, for several years before her death in 1986, particularly liked to watch the ocean liners from her three-bedroom suite at the top of the Sheraton Motor Inn near the Hudson River and 42nd Street in New York.[34]

For all types of people, personal safety was a hotel attraction that many downtown apartment buildings could not match. Hotel desk clerks watched entrances around the clock; at intervals during the night, watchmen patrolled the halls checking for fire problems or situations amiss. When tenants had an emergency, staff were always on duty. People away from home overnight or for long periods of time could leave with a sense that children, a spouse, or an elderly parent would be safer and have more readily available help than in a private home.[35]

Clearly, residents also came to live in midpriced hotels for emotional reasons as well as for practical and social advantages. The expanding local economies that helped to create jobs often meant an expanding supply of appropriate hotel buildings whose visual appeal, interior design, and gustatory delights helped to convince people to make the hotel their home.

MANSIONS FOR RENT

The palace hotels of the very rich were fabled realms, true palaces. Midpriced hotels were mere mansions, more common than palaces but several notches above the typical middle-income house. The builders and managers of midpriced hotels emulated palace hotels as much as their construction, decoration, and operation budgets allowed. Because they were building for less wealthy clients, midpriced hotel operators could develop many more hotels in many more places—from great cities of a million people to small towns with as few as 2,000 people—with the consistent theme of practical and affordable good taste.

The classic midpriced hotel.   In Victorian Chicago, the woman retailer who was a single parent or the enterprising New England mill representative and his wife might have chosen as their place of sojourn a building like Chicago's Hyde Park Hotel, built in 1887–88 (fig. 3.7). It had an open rectangle plan that left an ample light court for the inner rooms, a huge skylit lobby, and a first floor devoted to public rooms. Throughout the hotel were electric lights, telephone service, electric call and return bells, and steam heat for three hundred rooms arranged in two- and five-room suites. In the 1890s, many similar hotels labeled as "family hotels" or "private hotels" took few, if any, transient guests. Guests typically leased rooms by the year and decorated their rooms as they would a private house. Demand in San Francisco was such that applications for suites in new family hotels were often made six months before the building was finished. By the turn of the century, most large cities had rows of buildings with similar features on a few respectable streets or boulevards.[36]

FIGURE 3.7. The Hyde Park Hotel in Chicago, opened in 1887. It featured two-room to five-room suites and was located at Hyde Park Boulevard and Lake Park Avenue. Photographed ca. 1928–1930.

By the 1920s, the most common suite in a midpriced hotel was two rooms, and use of those rooms varied. One occupant interviewed at that time had a parlor with a western exposure facing a park. He had brought in his own table, lamps, chairs, bookcase, and pictures. Elsewhere, a woman and her adult daughter shared a two-room suite. A Murphy bed in the parlor meant that at night each of them had a private room.[37] S. J. Perelman gave this graphic description of a single room in New York's Hotel Sutton, a midpriced residential hotel intended primarily for single people. The description could double for the modal midpriced hotel room:

The decor of all the rooms was identical—fireproof early-American, impervious to the whim of guests who might succumb to euphoria, despair, or drunkenness. The furniture was rock maple, the rugs rock wool. In addition to a bureau, a stiff wing chair, and a lamp with a false pewter base and an end table, each chamber contained a bed narrow enough to discourage any thoughts of venery.[38]

Had Perelman given a more complete furnishings list, he would have noted that the interior designer had specified the wing chair and its floor lamp in *addition* to a desk, a desk chair, and a desk lamp.

Perelman's room was not large enough for a dining table, which some larger midpriced hotel rooms had, but in many such hotels the guests could give dinner parties in private dining rooms near the lounges and lobbies.[39]

Midpriced hotel buildings could be very small (figs. 3.8, 3.9). Some, for instance, contained only twelve rooms (several with fireplaces, perhaps), all tucked within a 25-foot-wide building on a narrow downtown lot. At the other end of the scale, midpriced hotels could be notable structures of three hundred rooms with meeting facilities.[40] By the turn of the century, in hotels intended to have a mixture of permanent and transient guests, architects often included, off the lobby, a mezzanine floor with a more private parlor, sometimes including a piano, for the use of residents. These spaces probably evolved from the special ladies' parlors that most large hotels furnished through the turn of the century. The mezzanine floor offered conviviality with less overt supervision from the ground floor desk. Some residents also preferred hotels with side corridors to the street or cafeteria so they could avoid the public lobby and the routine surveillance of the hotel desk clerks.[41] Due to a series of public spaces reserved for them, especially before the 1930s, women in polite hotels could also have an experience of hotel life largely separate from men. Some hotels had a separate women's entry, different lounges, separate women's coffee shops, and different house rules. Likewise, the billiard room, barroom, and some lobbies and reading rooms were largely men's turf and off-limits to respectable women.

Degree of personal service and amount of plumbing distinguished the social rank of a midpriced hotel just as surely as the size and furnishings of the guest rooms. While palace hotels employed from one to four servants for each guest, one employee for every two guests was the norm in midpriced hotels through the depression. People on tight budgets who lived in hotels noticed that chambermaids went first to the larger, expensive suites and cleaned better there because those tenants could afford higher tips.[42] Plumbing saved on servant expense and drudgery, and more plumbing per room was particularly notable at the turn of the century. In 1875, the Palace in San Francisco had a bath for every room, but not until 1907 did a midpriced hotel make the claim of every room with a bath.[43] By about 1910, in midpriced hotels virtu-

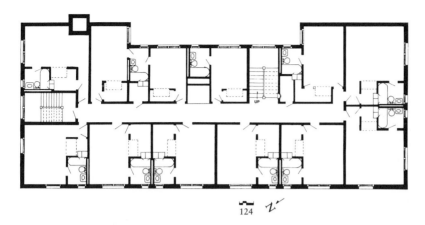

FIGURE 3.8. Typical upper floor plan of the Ogden Hotel, Minneapolis, built in 1910. Fairly large rooms, Murphy beds, and private baths helped to make this a socially correct hotel for middle-income tenants.

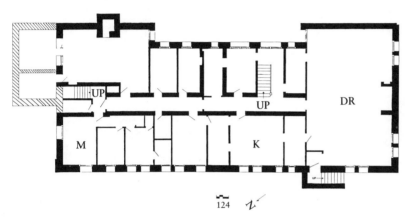

FIGURE 3.9. Basement floor plan, Ogden Hotel, Minneapolis. Note that the dining room (*DR*) has a separate entrance from the outside for nonhotel patrons. The kitchen (*K*), pantries and storage rooms, and an apartment for the manager (*M*) filled out the floor.

ally every bedroom offered at least a room sink with hot and cold water. This provision had become common in private houses and hotels for the same reason: carrying water to the bedrooms was one of the onerous repetitive tasks required of the servants. In hotels of 1910, however, providing a full bathroom for every room was not yet common. About half the rooms had a private bath, and the rest shared hall bathrooms. Only by about 1930 did new hotels of this rank offer a private bath for every room.[44]

In small cities one building often had to serve as the equivalent of the town's palace hotel as well as its best midpriced hotel. Design guidelines for such hotels in 1930 noted that if 20 percent of the rooms had private baths, that was sufficient. Another 50 percent of the rooms were to have half-baths (basins and toilets), and the remainder of the rooms were to have simply room sinks and shared baths down the hall.[45] The hotel's date of construction often determined its precise bath ratio as well as the relative size of light wells and other amenities (fig. 3.10).

FIGURE 3.10. Comparison of typical 1907 and 1927 light wells in San Francisco. Because the earlier building codes (right) had minimal requirements, the light wells of midpriced hotels built before World War I were much smaller than those of a typical hotel of the 1920s.

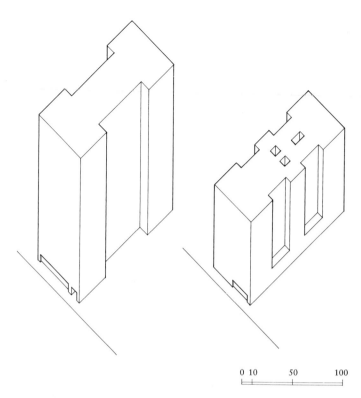

0 10   50   100

Together, these features set the hotel's intended socioeconomic strata for at least its first generation of clients.

The plumbing and heating in midpriced hotels were often better than their counterparts in most private houses. In the mid-1800s, public rooms and corridors in hotels had steam heat; hotel bedrooms had individual stoves and fireplaces long before the bedrooms in average houses. Europeans soon began the tradition of complaining that Americans overheated their buildings. In later hotels most Americans first experienced the luxuries of indoor plumbing, push buttons, and iced or hot water readily on tap.[46] In the 1920s, such material comforts still contrasted sharply with life in most private houses. Residents of midpriced hotels of the jazz age repeated litanies of service and comfort heard only in palace hotels the generation before:

Life is luxuriously comfortable. . . . The idleness, the heat, the comfort [are totally unlike a family house]. . . . I have four towels each day, fresh sheets several times a week, hot water at any hour, lots of light and heat and a private bath. In the hotel are a restaurant, laundry, dry-cleaning establishment, bootblack, and many mail deliveries a day.[47]

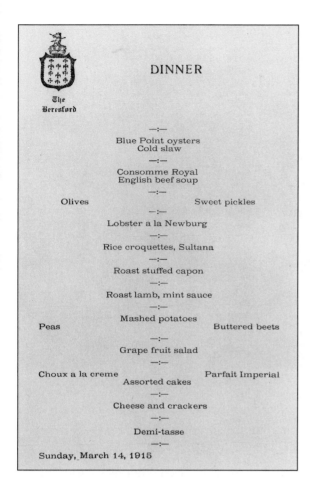

DINNER

The
Beresford

—:—
Blue Point oysters
Cold slaw
—:—
Consomme Royal
English beef soup
—:—
Olives   Sweet pickles
—:—
Lobster a la Newburg
—:—
Rice croquettes, Sultana
—:—
Roast stuffed capon
—:—
Roast lamb, mint sauce
—:—
Mashed potatoes
Peas   Buttered beets
—:—
Grape fruit salad
—:—
Choux a la creme   Parfait Imperial
Assorted cakes
—:—
Cheese and crackers
—:—
Demi-tasse
—:—
Sunday, March 14, 1915

FIGURE 3.11.   Sunday dinner menu from the Hotel Beresford in New York City, 1915.

Luxury, wrote one architect, was hotel living's outstanding characteristic and best drawing card; hence, attention to luxury was essential even in midpriced hotel design and especially in the public spaces.[48]

Large midpriced hotels always had an imposing lobby and a well-appointed dining room for full, leisurely, and fairly expensive meals (fig. 3.11). These spaces, along with the ballroom, bar, and breakfast room, were where the scale and social impressiveness of a public mansion could best be experienced. By the time of World War I, visitors could also expect to see the terms "café" or "coffee shop" used for casual lunchrooms in hotels. "The coffee shop idea," wrote a hotel kitchen expert in 1924, "seems to have completely uprooted the dairy lunch and cafeteria service of a few years back, and along with it the grill or grill range has replaced the long steam table."[49] Two residents on a tight budget told Hayner that they rarely used the elegant ground-

MAIN DINING ROOM OF THE
NEW DELMONICO, 362 GEARY ST., S. F.

FIGURE 3.12. Postcard view of the Delmonico Hotel dining room, in San Francisco. The tall ceiling and musicians' gallery set the tone for the room. European plan pricing allowed residents at midpriced hotels to sample the fare at other restaurants.

floor dining room in their hotel but ate instead in the basement café. With food smuggled in from the outside, they also routinely stretched a room service meal for one into a meal for two. The smell of food illegally cooking on alcohol lamps or electric hot plates was known even in very fashionable hotels.[50] Many hotel managers eventually gave up the battle against long-term tenants cooking in their rooms and installed permanent hot plates or kitchenettes in some suites (depending on prevailing building codes). In the forty-nine largest palace and midpriced hotels in Chicago in the early 1920s, about 8 percent of the units were full apartments with a kitchen.[51] Also, the managers of midpriced hotels were among the earliest hotel keepers to give up the American plan of combined board-and-room payment. Instead, they offered rooms on either the American or European plan (fig. 3.12).

Even with the cheaper European plan prices, to live with hotel advantages people with middle incomes had to give up space. If they had been renting a suburban house or a respectable five-room apartment, they had to accept either a very small suite in a good midpriced hotel or a larger suite in a less elegant hostelry. Hayner writes of a family of four, with children aged three and eight, who paid $650 a month for their large house in a Chicago neighborhood that had lost its cachet;

for $700 a month, they rented a small suite in a hotel on the fashion-able Lake Michigan shore. He concluded that for families with incomes of at least $8,000 a year, hotels were cheaper than houses or large apartments of comparable social status.[52]

Links to the tourist's and shopper's downtown.   If the palace hotel was usually surrounded by some of the city's most exclusive boutiques, the midpriced hotel was usually close to the city's best department stores and reasonably close to the financial district. After 1910 in San Francisco, sojourners could find the most densely clustered midpriced hotels along Bush and Sutter streets between Powell and Jones. Depending on one's point of view, this small area was called lower Nob Hill or upper Union Square. The area contained almost a third of the city's midpriced hotel rooms and a large number of coffee shops and gift emporiums. Most hotels advertised for tourists, but they also listed themselves as "a home in a hotel" or "a residential hotel on an ideal residential street" (fig. 3.13).[53]

Although the self-image of the residents and hotel managers of these blocks revolved around the elites on Nob Hill, their daily lives revolved around Union Square. The square itself was a place to sit and watch

FIGURE 3.13.   Bush Street near Grant, at the edge of a large midpriced hotel district in San Francisco, 1946. While automobile drivers were stalled in traffic, hotel dwellers could always walk to work.

urban life. Nearby theaters and evening shopping lent a respectable nightlife to the streets. Grills and restaurants ranged in price from the expensive to the very cheap, making dining out easy and varied. It was a pleasant neighborhood for the middle-income person who wanted to be in the middle of the city's action.

According to the local myth, the hotels of Bush and Sutter streets, along with the nearby streets of the Tenderloin area, were built for tourists coming to the city's Panama-Pacific International Exposition in 1915. Every large city has similar rumors about the role of special events, and the rumors require debunking. Indeed, for midpriced hotels (and for palace hotels, too), travelers were always the primary market. In San Francisco, tourism became a major industry early in the city's history, and convention trade boomed with the advent of reasonable railroad rates. In 1897, the Southern Pacific Railroad helped to lure over 20,000 people for the Christian Endeavor Society convention. In 1904, the Triennial Conclave of the Knights of Templar brought 19,000 participants. These spikes of tourist dollars boosted the profits of hotels and other businesses more obviously than the steady stream of other travelers. In 1910, members of San Francisco's Chamber of Commerce announced ambitious plans for the Panama-Pacific International Exposition, to be held in 1915. The exposition would celebrate the opening of the Panama Canal and prove that the city had fully recovered from its earthquake and fire of 1906.[54] As a direct result of the exposition announcement, many San Franciscans did build new hotels between 1910 and 1915. For the owner of a new hotel, the exposition guaranteed a year of total occupancy at maximum rates and enough profits to repay short-term construction loans. However, no one purposely built a sixty-year structure for only one year of business—not in San Francisco or any other city. In the long term, spurts of hotel construction like these were responses to downtown business growth. When the Panama-Pacific crowds went home, managers at the dozens of new 100-room hotels in San Francisco's Bush Street and Tenderloin neighborhoods knew they could rent rooms permanently to a combination of tourists and workers in the expanding downtown office sector. Floor plans of many downtown hotels show how their configurations could be shifted from one-room units to five-room units to match seasonal or occasional changes in the market (fig. 3.14). However, in San Francisco as in other cities, people of middle incomes who wanted

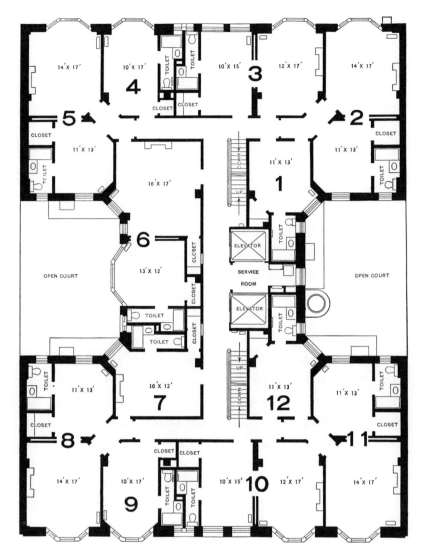

FIGURE 3.14. Plan of a typical floor in the Algonquin Hotel, New York City. Accommodations could range from one room to five-room corner suites.

to live downtown were not forced to accept life around Union Square in a classic midpriced hotel. By 1900, developers offered a range of other rental housing options in both hotels and apartments.

ALTERNATIVE QUARTERS

In addition to the classic example of a hotel purposely built as a midpriced hotel, middle-range hotel options came in at least four other modes: back halls of palace hotels, formerly grand hostelries, converted houses, and residence clubs. Apartment options at this price range, not readily available in 1880, became far more accessible both in number and in price between 1910 and 1930. The different types of midpriced hotels showed more variation than did palace hotel life, in part because midpriced hotels served a much larger and more scattered market. In most cases, however, the midpriced hotel matched the values and norms of the middle and upper class, albeit sometimes with difficulty.

Variations of the midpriced hotel. If a young business person of moderate means hoped to rub shoulders with upper-class investors, his or her most logical choice of a hotel home would not have been living in a midpriced enterprise at all but rather renting a back hall room at a palace hotel. Few palace hotels could be as imperious as Boston's old Tremont House, which charged only one high rate. Prices usually varied widely. Jefferson Williamson notes that before the Civil War the grandest hotels—those advertising prices of $2 a day for board and room—offered "in profusion" 50-cent or $1 accommodations for lesser rooms.[55] As hotel owners installed indoor plumbing, prices of rooms with a private bath could be two and a half times greater than rooms in the same hotel but with a shared bath down the hall. Hotel architects relegated such rooms to areas along alley walls, in noisy corners of the building where the only light came from narrow air shafts, or where the occupants would have no view (fig. 3.15). In the 1920s, managers at the Chicago Beach Hotel on Lake Michigan charged a middle-income rate of $56 a month for a room without bath in an old wing built in the 1890s; meanwhile, lakeview suites in the newest section started at a princely rate of $700 a month.[56] Even the lower-priced rooms at a palace hotel had the advantages of service, public rooms, and general prestige. But they betrayed themselves in social engagements. "No, don't bother to come by our rooms, we'll meet you in the lobby," was the refrain of back hall hotel residents. Middle-income residents could also locate their hotel home in a palace hotel that had fallen slightly from social grace, thanks to the real estate process known as filtering. If palace hotel tourists shifted to a more fashionable hotel, the rents in the older building usually dropped into a range affordable at middle-income levels.

Small hotels at the lower end of the midprice rank hung on to their social class respectability with difficulty, and their amenities sometimes ranged precariously close to their poor relatives, the rooming houses. To qualify socially for residents of middle income, even the smallest

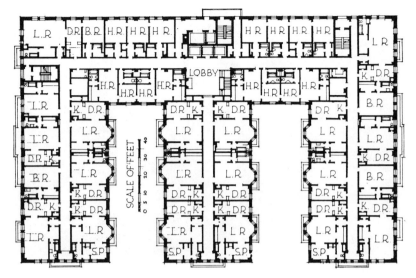

TYPICAL FLOOR PLAN

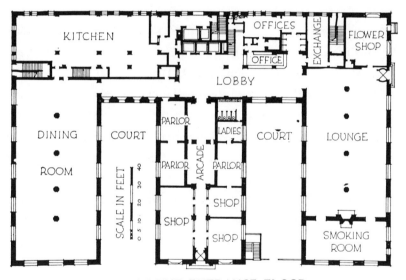

PLAN OF THE ENTRANCE FLOOR

FIGURE 3.15. Plans for the ground floor and a typical upper floor of the Hotel Pennsylvania, Philadelphia, published in 1924. Single hotel rooms are at the back, suites at the front. Unusual room labels include *H.R.* for single hotel rooms and *S.P.* for sleeping porches. Most living rooms have Murphy beds.

hotel had to have a lobby and a dining room on the ground floor (fig. 3.16). For the smallest midpriced hotels, architects tucked cafés or dining rooms into the back of the building, under skylights at the bottom of light wells, or into reasonably well lighted basements. Better room furnishings, more unctuous staff, and having an elevator also helped to distinguish small midpriced hotel buildings from mere rooming houses.[57]

FIGURE 3.16. The dining room of San Francisco's Hotel Cecil. With a fairly low ceiling and awkwardly placed columns, this dining room was architecturally a step down from the dining room of the Delmonico Hotel but still proper for middle-income patrons on a tight budget.

These smaller hotels descended from the long nineteenth-century tradition of respectable boardinghouses—single-family houses converted to commercial housing use. To attract people with polite middle-income pretensions, either the food offered or the architecture of the original house had to be quite grand. Two San Francisco houses in the lower Nob Hill area, both converted to boarding operations by the 1880s, show the edge of social propriety (fig. 3.17). Miss Mary J. Fox and Mrs. Robert McKee rented out rooms or suites of rooms in their modest houses on Post Street near Jones. They borrowed social sheen from the much larger houses a block uphill to the north, on Sutter Street. Behind Miss Fox's house loomed a new building, the Berkshire family hotel, a four-story brick building with an elevator (a luxury feature for a hotel of its size at that time). Early insurance records simply called the Berkshire a private hotel, but it was one of the city's best family hotels, the fourth largest one opened in the city. Like the small converted houses nearby, the Berkshire was managed by a woman. By 1900, because of the built-in amenities in structures like the Berkshire, only if a single-family house were very large and opulent, perhaps built by a well-known family, could the owners convert it and charge middle-income rates.[58]

Beginning in the 1880s and continuing through World War I, real estate speculators also experimented with midpriced hotels in the suburbs. In a large and proper suburban area, developers often included

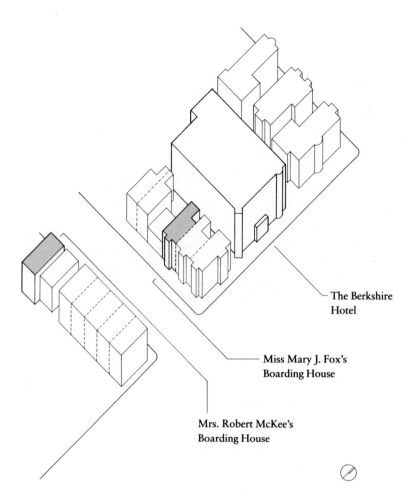

FIGURE 3.17. Axonometric drawing of a lower Nob Hill neighborhood in San Francisco, 1885. Single-family houses are mixed with boardinghouses (shaded) and the Berkshire, an expensive residential hotel with an elevator.

The Berkshire Hotel

Miss Mary J. Fox's Boarding House

Mrs. Robert McKee's Boarding House

a snowy hotel—part real estate office, part residential building, part country club. In the San Francisco region, the Claremont Hotel is a quintessential example (fig. 3.18). It opened in 1915 on a wooded site with a creek and sixteen acres of gardens at a prominent overlook at the end of a major interurban transit line. Naturally, the land development company itself developed the rail line and advertised their hotel as "five minutes from Berkeley, fifteen minutes from Oakland, a half-hour from San Francisco." Two hundred rooms, half with baths, were in a 700-foot-long wooden building with 500 linear feet of porches looking out over a spectacular view of the hills, the bay, and San Francisco. Streetcars and carriages entered on one side, where there were also large stables; automobiles had a separate porte cochere and garage on the other side.[59] Below the hotel on three sides were devel-

FIGURE 3.18. The Clare-
mont Hotel in Oakland, California, a classic example of a
suburban resort and residential hotel, opened in 1915. It
was located at the end of an
interurban line from San
Francisco and was sur-
rounded by expensive
house lots.

opments of substantial new suburban houses for the middle and upper
class. The residents of these houses were expected to be frequent diners
at the hotel.

Other suburban midpriced resort hotels were on beachfronts, lake-
sides, or hilly wooded lots along a stream. Some country clubs also
had sleeping rooms, eventually used permanently. Yet after 1920, as
a result of zoning restrictions and suburban market realities, further
developments of such outposts of urbane commercial life were to be
overwhelmed by garden apartments and rules prohibiting the mixture of uses that the Claremont Hotel meant for its surrounding
neighborhood.

Residence clubs. At the least expensive end of the midpriced hotel
social spectrum were residence clubs offering midprice hotel amenities
at a budget price. Like their plebeian cousins (the YMCA or YWCA)
and also their rich uncles (exclusive private clubs), commercial residence clubs usually were tailored for single men or single women. A
few clubs accommodated both single men and women by having them
live on separate floors—a policy rarely used in public hotels.[60] Allerton
Houses, Ltd., seems to have built the first large buildings of this type in
New York just after 1900; developers in other large cities followed suit.
Managers pared costs by providing very small rooms—almost exclu-

FIGURE 3.19. Room view from a 1939 brochure for the Barbizon Hotel, New York City. The text emphasizes a "home away from home" with "full-length mirror, no-draught ventilators, three-channel radio, convenient electrical outlets."

sively single rooms—with day beds that converted to couches. Typically, about three-fourths of the rooms had a private bath.

Life in the residence clubs was like life in a YMCA but without the "C." The clubs kept staff to a minimum, especially in food service. Typically each club had its own restaurant and cafeteria or a restaurant that ran on self-service lines for breakfast and lunch and provided table service for dinner.[61] Perelman remembered a rather upscale residence club with a ground-floor coffee shop with waitresses in peach-colored uniforms who served a thrifty club breakfast costing 65 cents. "You had a choice of juice—orange or tomato," he wrote, "but not of the glass it came in, which was a heavy green goblet. The coffee, it goes without saying, was unspeakable."[62] Compared to private boarding-houses, residence clubs offered more flexible dining hours in addition to lower costs; compared to the Ys, clubs were a hefty notch higher in cost but offered more privacy and less supervision. New York's twenty-two-story Barbizon Hotel, built in 1927 and operated as a women's hotel until 1981, stood at the top of the midprice residence club scale (fig. 3.19). The women who lived there had at their disposal musical evenings in the lobbies, a swimming pool, a gym, and a library. In hard times, a cherished tradition of the better clubs was a free daily teatime in the lobby. At one club, which tended toward a literary crowd, during teatime the lobby was said to take on the air of a book-and-author luncheon. At the Barbizon, girls on a tight budget frequently made their largest meal of the day out of the bite-size complimentary sandwiches.[63]

Apartment hotels and efficiency units. Furtively cooking in one's room or continually eating in restaurants could be major irritations and expenses of hotel life. Residents who liked other aspects of downtown life often welcomed the development of affordable downtown housing units that offered private kitchens. By the 1920s, apartment hotels and efficiency units, often rented complete with furniture and dishes, were the principal downtown competition for midpriced residential hotels.[64] The typical mix of services is shown in this advertising copy from a 1920s brochure:

Exclusive Apartments—Hotel Service: The Plaisance contains 126 apartments of one to four rooms, all beautifully furnished and completely equipped. All with private baths—the four-room apartments with two baths. A large lobby, parlor, ladies parlor, and general dining room are situated on the main floor. There are shops necessary to insure comfort and convenience for the guests of the hotel. . . . Every apartment has a breakfast room and buffet kitchen completely equipped.[65]

In apartment hotels, buffet kitchens or service pantries were small kitchens with a minimum of counter space but a full-sized sink, an icebox or refrigerator, and at least a double hot plate and a warming oven, if not a full cooking stove. Tenants in an apartment hotel could cook, take their meals in the public dining room, or (for an extra fee) have meals served in their own suite using their own silver, linen, and china if they chose. The staff of apartment hotels often took over window washing and making the beds along with periodically scouring the sink, icebox, and cupboards.[66]

Apartment hotels were often outside of downtown on parks or parkways, along major avenues and streetcar lines, adjoining new suburban apartments, or replacing former downtown mansions. In 1929, a nationwide survey revealed that apartment hotel buildings were typically large—100 units with an average of 2.7 rooms each—and most rooms

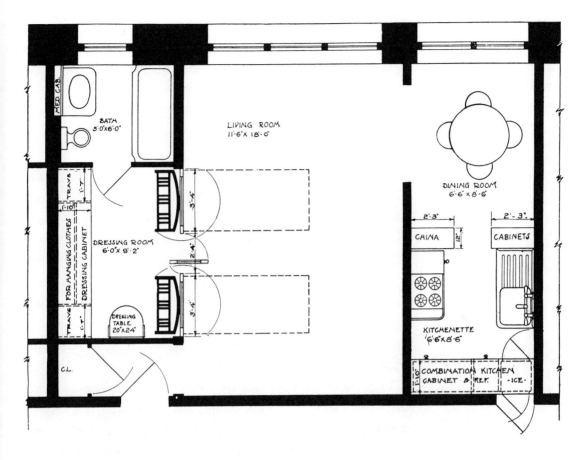

were rented furnished. About half of the buildings had separate maid's rooms and garage space available to tenants.[67] By the 1920s, design guides identified three distinct price ranges. Expensive examples offered full apartments with all the public rooms and services of midpriced hotels. Medium-priced examples had a lobby, desk staff, a ballroom, a billiard table or two, and a roof garden. The least expensive buildings had only switchboard service and porters for ice, groceries, garbage, and errands. These buildings more closely resembled average efficiency apartments.[68]

FIGURE 3.20. Plan of a typical efficiency apartment, published in 1924.

The minimum apartment for the middle-income household was the efficiency apartment, perfected between 1900 and 1930 (fig. 3.20). At about $25 a week (in 1920s prices) efficiency apartments were bargain versions of the apartment hotel, which started at about $50 a week (table 2, Appendix). The central innovations of efficiency apartment designs were folding beds—doors with attached, spring-loaded bed frames. These allowed tenants to turn the bed upright and pivot it into a closet or dressing room. The most common brand, the Murphy bed, was named after a San Francisco manufacturer. Rebuilding after the 1906 fire, together with the general population and building boom on the West Coast, created such a large initial market for Murphy's new folding beds (and for a host of early imitators) that journalists reported the efficiency apartment itself had originated in California. Like so many other apartment innovations, Murphy beds had been initially marketed primarily to hotels.[69]

By 1911, the tiny kitchen areas in efficiency apartments (originally called buffet kitchens) were common enough and socially correct enough in San Francisco apartments so that local housing reformers gave them special consideration in proposed housing laws. By the 1920s, similar six-foot by eight-foot rooms were popularly called kitchenettes. They epitomized the simplifications in cooking and reliance on packaged foods that also marked smaller kitchens in new single-family houses.[70] Unskilled women working in canneries and food processing plants were doing many of the food preparation steps formerly done in individual kitchens.

Compared to tenement flats, apartment hotels and efficiency apartments were expensive. To live cheaply and comfortably in a middle-income apartment, single people either had to have quite a high income or had to relinquish their independence and team up with roommates. Group living proffered certain benefits—among them, regular company at meals and better space. Not everyone, however, wanted a roommate, and few apartment landlords wanted to rent to nontraditional household groups. Edge-of-the-city apartment complexes of the time were not a strong alternative for single people. As late as 1942, Parkchester, with its 12,000 units in the Bronx, had fewer than a dozen single people living in their own apartment, and those residents were mostly retired. The adjacent Hillside Homes project had 1,410 families but only 14 unattached people.[71]

ROOM FOR EXCEPTIONS

Anecdotes give only scattered views of the people who lived in mid-priced hotels. The sociologist Day Monroe, using information from the 1920 census, left a thorough perspective of Chicago's hotel residents. Unfortunately, Monroe eliminated single people from her study, but her survey of Chicago's family groups revealed that 3.4 percent of the families lived in rooming houses and hotels. This proportion equaled only about one in thirty families, fewer families than were living with relatives. However, Monroe's total sample had included the burgeoning immigrant populations of Chicago; few immigrants, rich or poor, lived in hotels. Thus, only when Monroe looked at particular social groups did she find hotel families comprising a more significant fraction. According to her, the three family groups with the highest proportion of hotel dwellers were those headed by professional men and women, families of executives and officials, and the families of low- to medium-salaried employees.[72] She gave the following detailed figures:

Occupation of Breadwinner	Percent Lodging
Professional	8.0
Executives and officials	7.1
Low- and medium-salaried employees	5.1
No occupation listed	4.7
Employed in an independent business	2.3
Skilled wage earners	2.3
Unskilled and semiskilled wage earners	1.5

Eight percent of the professional households, one family in twelve, lived in hotels. The unemployed and unskilled listings in the table do not reflect the massive numbers of Chicago's single casual laborers living in hotels.

Monroe found other groups with reasonably high levels of hotel living, groups that overlapped the professional and skilled strata. Prominent among these were childless couples and young parents; almost 10 percent of Chicago's childless couples lived in hotels. The data showed young parents still figuring heavily in hotel families; many of the mothers were under twenty-five years old.[73] Monroe reported that one out of six of Chicago's single fathers with only one child under fourteen years old were living in hotel housing in 1920. However, Monroe found that single women with children were much less common in hotels; she believed this was because their income levels were so much lower.[74]

The 8 percent of Chicago's professional households that lived in hotels in 1920 were a telling minority. If a family could afford hotel life, they could afford an apartment. Virtually any of those households could also have paid for a private house—a small house on expensive land close to downtown or a larger house in more distant suburbs. We cannot precisely reconstruct why these families chose hotels. The important point is that one out of twelve of these households did choose hotel life. For at least part of their life, these households did not fit the dominant pattern for the middle-income American family, that is, living in a house or an apartment of their own. These families had made an eccentric choice of family *residence;* however, the one professional family in twelve living in hotels were not necessarily eccentric families. Their reasons for being downtown—waiting for a house to be built, holding nearby jobs, staying only for a year or two, caring for an elderly parent who needed some looking after during the day—were reasonable and practical. Suburban life did *not* work for them, at least during one part of their life cycle, and hotel life *did* work.

Hotel life left room for such exceptions without eliminating any other options. For a reasonable number of family people in the comfortable salaried strata, the commercialized option of cooperative housekeeping was viable and desirable. For a more complete picture of the role that midpriced hotels were playing in the metropolitan housing stock, we can only wish that we knew how many of Chicago's single professionals and single elderly were living in hotel housing in 1920.

Unfortunately, the people who gradually codified the single-family house ideal rarely allowed for exceptions or minority opinions. As early as the 1850s, one of Nathaniel Hawthorne's characters observed urban life from a hotel and objected to the "stifled element of cities," the "entangled life" of so many people together. People were "so much alike in their nature, that they grow intolerable unless varied by their circumstances." The alternatives Hawthorne's character had in mind were the individualized little farmhouses like those he had just left behind in rural New England.[75] This example is simply one among thousands of such well-meaning statements from the century of building, writing, and living that helped to confirm the monolithic ideals of the single-family American house. The rural and small town social experiences and values of opinion leaders like Hawthorne became sedimented in their actions and writing—particularly in their verbal support for the single-family home and abhorrence of any variation from that single ideal. Not all nineteenth- and early-twentieth-century writers excluded alternatives or exceptions in housing, but most did. In their values, neither Hawthorne nor his characters left room for those future people—

perhaps the one family in twelve in 1920—who could not or who did not want to fit into the norm of a private house or a private apartment with a private kitchen and a private dining room and a life untouched by neighbors. The repercussions of this kind of exclusion in housing would not become clear until almost a century after Hawthorne died.

If the pleasant hotel life of those with professional salaries was to some people a stifled and entangled life, then the life of the next cheaper type of hotel, the rooming house, was surely beyond the pale. Indeed, the downtown life in rooming houses that so often were only a block or two away from midpriced hotel zones frequently crossed the line from the realm of the middle and upper class to a realm of a very separate class.

ROOMING HOUSES
AND THE MARGINS
OF RESPECTABILITY

AT THE TURN OF THE CENTURY, AN EIGHTEEN-YEAR-OLD woman named
Dorothy Richardson left western Pennsylvania and moved to New York.
She had meager cash reserves but was determined to find city work and
a new life. "A waif and a stray, unskilled, friendless, almost penniless,"
she wrote of herself on her first day in the city. She found lodging in a
rooming house late in the evening and woke to find rain pouring down
on the skylight of the dreary, windowless little room that she hoped she
could afford while she looked for employment.[1] Richardson's story
typified the situation of many rooming house residents (fig. 4.1).

A century earlier and in much smaller cities, young male workers
would have left their families and learned a trade while being appren-
ticed to a master, often living under the master's roof. However, the
nature of the new industrial economy and its call for greater numbers of
unskilled and lower-paid workers had undermined and overwhelmed
the old apprenticeship system and loosened the direct residence ties between employers and workers. With the lure of new jobs downtown,
women like Richardson were also breaking free from traditional household bonds. By 1923, one out of five employed young women in
America lived away from a family home.[2] While the people who lived
in palace and midpriced hotels did so largely as a matter of choice,

people of lesser means found hotel housing one of their few options for living downtown, particularly if they wished to live outside of a family.

Single people living alone caused concern in some circles. In 1907, the social worker Robert Woods wrote of the "social danger of a great population made up of detached men and women" living apart from the "safeguards of a good home." As late as 1949, a sociologist described a Los Angeles rooming house district as a "universe of anonymous transients."[3] Indeed, in their home life, rooming house residents belonged neither to the middle and upper class nor to the working class; the domestic rules of both classes were largely based on family life and group households. Critics felt that rooming house residents were potentially eligible for membership in polite society but constantly in danger of losing that eligibility. Rooming house residents, too, knew they were on a social edge, but to them it was often a leading edge, one moving toward more independence. As new work roles within the large

FIGURE 4.1. A working girl eats breakfast by candlelight in her small room, New York City, 1890s. Behind her bed, old bedspreads conceal her clothes, probably hung on nails along the wall because the room had no closet.

industrial city threw individuals into a social and cultural limbo, the rooming house and its surrounding district helped them balance their marginal state of affairs.

PLAIN ROOMS

The precedents for commercial rooming houses were old-fashioned boardinghouses. Especially before the 1920s, the lines were hazy between a private family house and a commercial rooming house because so many people boarded or lodged with private families. *Boarders* slept in the house and also took their meals with a family; *lodgers* slept in the house but took their meals elsewhere. Entire families boarded—often parents or single mothers in their late twenties—but the most common boarders were young unmarried men or women with slim financial resources. Boarding and lodging so pervaded American family life (along with the presence of servants and live-in relatives) that throughout the nineteenth century and early twentieth century, use of the term "single-family house" is misleading. In a conservative estimate for those years, one-third to one-half of all urban Americans either boarded or took boarders at some time in their lives.[4]

Most private families took in one or two boarders at a time. Where more income was needed, a private boardinghouse could have six to ten tenants. Keeping a low profile helped the family avoid the technically required hotel licenses and annual taxes. In such a place, the landlady operated as surrogate mother and father. She wielded authority over parlor life and over curfews and guests. If the old house was a good structure in a decent neighborhood, the residence could be respectable for middle-income families.[5] After 1900, many people looked back nostalgically to these enterprises in comparison to their commercial counterparts.

Former-house rooming houses. The commercial rooming house of 1910 was run overtly and officially as an inexpensive hotel. Its manager often paid for a commercial license. The business was in a twenty-five- to forty-year-old house, three or four stories high, originally built for a middle-income family. The owners had moved to the edge of town and leased their downtown house to someone—inevitably a woman—who rented rooms as her chief source of income. The landlady of a commercial rooming house often advertised in her front window with a card reading ROOM TO RENT or FURNISHED ROOMS.[6] Like Richardson, rooming house residents often began their first solo encounter with downtown life as they lugged their suitcases down the streets in rooming house districts and searched for window cards.

The typical rooming house had earlier been a boardinghouse. After the Civil War, the number of commercial boardinghouses sharply declined. In 1875 in San Francisco, for instance, boardinghouses made up almost 40 percent of the commercial housing listings in the city directory. By 1900, boardinghouses had dwindled to fewer than 10 percent, and by 1910, they constituted less than 1 percent of those listings. Boston and Chicago saw similar declines.[7] During these declines, boardinghouse keepers were not quitting but getting out of food provision—shifting their businesses from boardinghouses to rooming houses. This shift considerably eased the landlady's life. She could rent out her dining room and parlor as additional bedrooms; she could fire the one or two servants she had needed to provide the meals. Eliminating meal service eliminated the most troublesome and costly parts of her business.[8] In a rooming house, the residents ate their meals with a family down the street or (as was most often the case) in commercial eateries.

Architecturally, the former-house rooming house was usually a fairly large row house with from sixteen to eighteen rooms, including the bath, the laundry, and the landlady's kitchen, if there was one (fig. 4.2). Owners or landladies created extra rooms by subdividing larger bedrooms and parlors and providing approaches to them with dark dead-end hallways. Like the attic room that Richardson found in her first week in New York, some rooms had only a transom window onto a hallway, a tiny dark air shaft, or a nonopening skylight. Until after World War I, few of these rooming houses offered central heating; small individual stoves or coal grates served to heat the rooms.[9] The high rents of undivided parlors and dining rooms required two residents to pay for them. The lowest-priced rooms were on the upper floors, with unheated attic and end-of-hallway rooms costing the least. On occasion, owners joined several houses together, creating a single rooming house with as many as forty rooms and seventy tenants.[10]

Chairs—their number, repair, and plushness—indicated any hotel room's social rank. In a good midpriced hotel, three chairs were the minimum; in rooming houses, two were the maximum. At the second

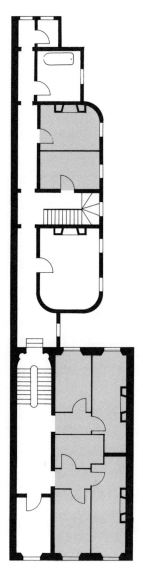

FIGURE 4.2. Second-floor plan for a conjectural conversion of a large single-family row house into a rooming house. Shaded areas indicate where thin walls have been added to cut up the large rooms of this 1840s house. The warren of five rooms at the front was constructed from the two former principal bedrooms and their closets.

of Richardson's many rooming houses, she listed the furniture in her room: a battered but cheering "tiny mite of a stove," an equally battered wooden bedstead that creaked and groaned at her every move on its thin mattress, a single chair with a mended leg, an evil-smelling lamp with a wick not quite long enough, and a tremulous kitchen table. She longed for simple comforts of more expensive quarters, complaining that there was "no bureau, only a waved bit of looking-glass over the sink in the corner. My wardrobe was strung along the row of nails behind the door."[11] Beneath the row of nails and her few pieces of clothing Richardson stored a wooden trunk, her only piece of luggage.

Most former-house rooming houses offered only the one bathroom built for the original family, whether the house had nine bedrooms or eighteen, six tenants or twenty. Usually the bathroom was on the second floor. To conserve the high cost of fuel, landladies tacked up signs that sternly limited residents to no more than one hot bath per week. The customary plan was to supply hot water once or twice a week, although during the summer, hot water could be unavailable for months at a time. Towels were often in short supply. Residents facing a week without hot water could resort to large public or commercial bathhouses where hot baths cost 10 or 15 cents in 1900. Tenants lucky enough to have a room with a washstand, a pitcher, and a bowl—a pitcher and bowl that were "inevitably cracked"—carried the water themselves.[12]

From one city to another, names and conditions in old-house rooming houses showed only minor variations, one of which was what people called the buildings. In Philadelphia, the common term was *furnished-room house;* in New York, Chicago, Cleveland, and St. Louis, *rooming house;* in Boston and San Francisco, *lodging house.*[13] Since blacks were excluded as guests in most hotels and rooming houses, in many cities, black rooming houses and boardinghouses had a greater mixture of transient and permanent guests than did rooming houses run for whites. Other special cases of converted buildings were converted apartments. Especially after the depression and World War II, entrepreneurs would lease old, eight-room to ten-room apartments and then sublet the rooms individually. All the tenants would share the bath and the kitchen. An entire multistory apartment building could be converted into such single-room units.[14]

Building owners also made rooming houses out of run-down palace or midpriced hotels. They eliminated service, repairs, and amenities until the rents matched rooming house levels (fig. 4.3). For example, San Francisco's Central Pacific Hotel was originally built as a midpriced hotel. By the 1880s and 1890s, it commanded only rooming house prices and was home to a wide range of residents. In 1880, behind the five ground-floor shops lived the shopkeepers and their families, 21 people in all. Also on the ground floor were the hotel dining room and lobby. Upstairs were transient guests, along with 42 permanent residents. Fifteen of the permanent residents were the hotel owners, the two servants, and their three families. Of the remaining 27 permanent lodgers, 26 were single adult males, overwhelmingly Irish (as were the owners of the hotel, the Farrells). The lodgers were mostly twenty-five to thirty-five years old, although the range was from a fifteen-year-old blacksmith to a sixty-three-year-old laborer. The depression of the late 1870s had hit these men hard; the average tenant at the Central Pacific Hotel had been out of work for over seven months in 1879–80.[15] Large hotels like the Central Pacific had the advantage of a night clerk, which eliminated the small rooming house's curfew. Instead of the landlady

FIGURE 4.3. A Victorian era booster hotel on a small town's Main Street and public square, 1940. By the time of the photograph, the clients of this Rockville, Indiana, hotel were likely paying rooming house rents.

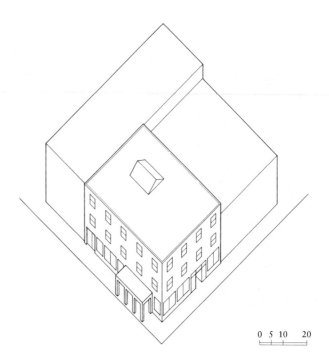

FIGURE 4.4. A generic-loft rooming house, built about 1880. The Frye Rooming House near Chinatown in San Francisco was adjacent to a cigar factory. The upper floors, with 16 rooms, could easily be converted to other uses. The fenestration is conjectural.

0 5 10 20

locking the front door at ten or eleven at night, the doors of a large hotel were open around the clock. Late tenants did not have to rouse an angry or inquisitive manager.[16]

In the relatively chaotic years of urban growth and experimentation between 1870 and about 1910, the most casual rooming houses were built inside adapted commercial buildings. Downtown landowners often built two- to four-story loft buildings, the ground floor being an open slot of space for a store, restaurant, or saloon. If the owners wanted to lease out the upper floors as a rooming house, they built in hallways and bedrooms but in such a way that they could easily be torn out to leave a clean, simple loft space for future offices, light manufacturing, or warehousing should those uses demand higher rents in the future. Sometimes the plumbing was only on the first floor (fig. 4.4).[17] Such *generic-loft structures* were meant for people with the smallest rooming house incomes. Loft buildings filled their entire plot, canceling out the chance for side windows. "Dark rooms" (rooms with no direct exterior light) had windows opening into daylit corridors or into interior stair halls that had skylights over them. Some dark rooms had no windows at all.

Whatever form the old rooming house had—row house or huge recycled apartment building—the owners were often waiting to sell their land or to lease their building at a higher price for retail or factory uses. They remodeled as little as they could. However, especially after 1900, other downtown property owners took a different tack: they built buildings with rooming houses specifically in mind.

Buildings purposely constructed as rooming houses. Living in a "used" building—one constructed for something other than multiple residences—was for tenants a bit like wearing hand-me-down clothing. The cultural fit was often less than perfect, the social appearance sometimes embarrassing and demeaning.[18] In the struggle to establish respectability, a room that was new and solely intended to be a rooming house room could be an asset for better self-respect and public status. For managers, a purpose-built structure was easier to manage than an ad hoc one. All rooms could be an equal size, with no oversized or difficult-to-rent rooms. When American landowners chose to provide permanent hotel accommodations for this price range, they did so in two different ways: small purpose-built rooming houses and huge downtown hotels.

A great many new rooming houses were built downtown after 1900 on house-sized lots but usually with an improved, specialized type of building: the *downtown rooming house.*[19] These buildings improved on the livability of the former-house and generic-loft buildings. The construction was not temporary; owners were confident that single-room living would bring in reliable rents for a long time. On the ground floor were store windows and commercial spaces that in their form, use, and lease income clearly said "downtown." The fifteen to forty rooms on the floors above said "residential" to those living in the structure. Relatively generous light wells illuminated and ventilated the upstairs rooms and reinforced the permanent commitment to residential use. San Francisco's Delta Hotel, built about 1910 and still in residential use in the 1990s, exemplifies the type (fig. 4.5).[20] On the street level next to the storefront is a small door, demurely marked, with a narrow interior stairway extending to the eighteen rooms on the second and third floors (fig. 4.6). Public space is at a minimum; the only lobby is a wide area in the second-floor hall near the room that serves as an office and part of the manager's unit (fig. 4.7).

Renters sometimes called their purpose-built rooming houses "upstairs hotels." The phrase is apt, since before 1910, elevators were rare

FIGURE 4.5.   Street view of a
typical small downtown
rooming house, 1992.
The former Delta Hotel
in San Francisco's South
of Market district.

FIGURE 4.6.   Entrance door
to the former Delta Hotel,
San Francisco.

FIGURE 4.7.   Plan of the second floor in San Francisco's
Delta Hotel. A room sink is
next to the case closet in
each room; the toilet room
and bathroom are off the
rear hall.

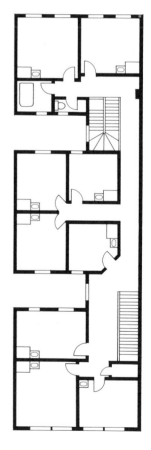

0 1   5   20

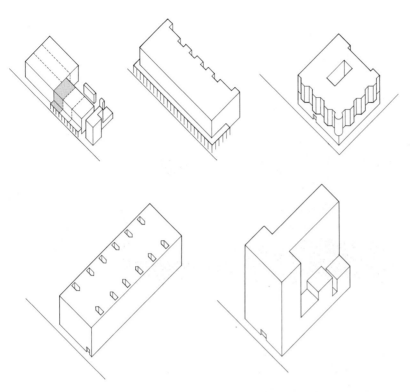

FIGURE 4.8. Typical rooming houses in San Francisco. *Top row,* from left to right: Isabel Cory's lodgings (shaded house), built ca. 1870; the Central Pacific Hotel, ca. 1880; the Oliver Hotel, 1906. *Bottom row:* National Hotel, ca. 1906; the Salvation Army's Evangeline Residence, 1923.

in hotels of this price range. Climbing one to four flights of narrow stairs was a modal and often reluctantly faced experience for residents.[21] Stairs figured in the letters written home by Will Kortum, an eighteen-year-old lumberyard clerk from a small California town. Kortum, who moved into a new hotel of the rooming house rank on his arrival in San Francisco in early 1906, wrote this to his mother after several weeks in the city:

I received your letter last night. It is always a feeling of great pleasure when the hotel clerk in answer to your inquiry for mail, dodges behind his desk and produces an envelope. And the long stairs seem a good deal easier to climb.[22]

Later designs for large rooming houses included elevators and floor plan arrangements that were variations on the plan for the Delta. By 1930, three-fourths of San Francisco's rooming house rooms were in taller, blockier buildings of five or six stories (fig. 4.8). Lobbies and dining rooms were small (if they existed), rooms were very simple, and there were rarely more than two chairs per room. Elevator or not, at this price range, most baths remained down the hall, at a ratio of about one bath to every five or six rooms. This far exceeded the one-to-fifteen

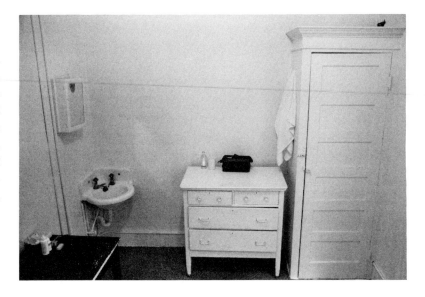

FIGURE 4.9. Room sink, dilapidated chest of drawers, and case closet in a large rooming house, the National Hotel, San Francisco. In rooming houses for men, sinks were often mounted lower than usual and informally doubled as urinals.

ratio available in converted houses.[23] Another upward step in plumbing was a small sink in every room, typically on the same wall as a case closet—a closet built like a large cabinet or wardrobe rather than being built into the walls (fig. 4.9). The sinks, along with smuggled-in hot plates, made light housekeeping easy for tenants. For a larger rooming house, San Francisco's National Hotel is typical of the cheapest sort: no lobby, no frills, but ninety very regular rooms opening off very small light wells (fig. 4.10).

Whether found in small or large rooming houses, new or old, the conditions of one's room depended on the hotel's market and management. Matrons from the middle and upper class of San Francisco conducted a rooming house survey in 1926 and were shocked at what they saw:

There were dark rooms where it was impossible to find the washstand without first turning on electric light; dingy rooms where the carpets had a musty smell, and the furniture was shabby and faded; sleeping rooms with lumpy double beds and dirty lace curtains. . . . Most of the rooms had such dim lights that no one could read in the evening.[24]

The matrons could recommend only one-fourth of the downtown rooms they inspected. Sinclair Lewis had given a similar description in 1905, adding that the gas light "neither illuminated the mirror nor enabled the guest to read in bed."[25]

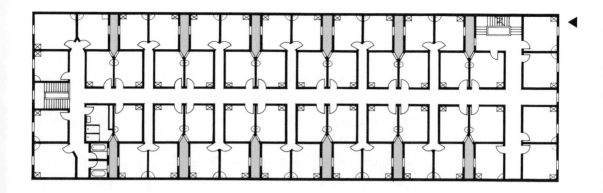

FIGURE 4.10. Floor plan of a large rooming house. The second floor of the National Hotel in San Francisco, built ca. 1906. The location of the street entry is marked by a black triangle; the first room at the head of the stairs is the office; toilets and baths are off the left rear hall. Shaded areas are light wells.

In a rooming house, one's room was never really isolated. Even for the very shy, life was indirectly social. After the third or fourth day, astute desk clerks would greet tenants by name. After two or three weeks, residents realized that they had begun to smell a bit like their hotel. At night, when the street noise died down, residents involuntarily monitored the activities and conversations in all the adjoining rooms. Coughing was a communal act; one always knew when one's neighbors had a cold. Carrying the sounds were light wells, floors, and walls built with minimal sound-deadening details; in hot weather or when the heating system overdid, hall doors and open transoms also carried sound. Personal affairs such as fights between couples could not necessarily be conducted privately behind closed doors.[26] For a guarantee of behavior better matching middle and upper class norms, some residents looked to rooming houses with more overt management.

YMCAs and other organization boardinghouses. As rooming houses and their residents proliferated downtown, religious and other philanthropic leaders worked to bring back old-fashioned boardinghouses at a larger scale and with more centralized administration. Providing vigilant supervision of the tenants and offering some sort of group parlor life (while at the same time prohibiting card playing and drinking) were seen by reformers—overwhelmingly Protestants—as minimal replacements for the safeguards and respectability of a private family house. Thousands of downtown residents seemingly agreed with these social and architectural guarantees of respectability (at least for short periods) as organization boardinghouses were built in great numbers and were almost always full.

The Young Men's Christian Association and the Young Women's Christian Association, transplanted from England to the United States in 1851 and 1866, respectively, pioneered in providing inexpensive, morally conservative homes for city residents who otherwise might have lived in a rooming house.[27] Historically, because of their sharp disadvantage in salaries, women relied more on institutionally subsidized rooms than did men. Although the founders of women's boarding institutions stereotyped women living apart from families as helpless and incapable of managing their own lives, both men and women knew the advantages of Ys and other subsidized rooming houses: they were generally clean, dependable, respectable, and cheap. The combined room and food costs were often less than just the price of a room at a commercial rooming house.[28]

Especially between 1890 and 1915, other charitable boardinghouse organizations joined the movement. These homes were often sponsored according to ethnicity, race, or religion, since not all Ys accepted everyone. In 1915, New York City had fifty-four organized, nonprofit lodgings for women; Chicago had thirty-four, not counting homes run for special groups such as immigrants or unmarried mothers. From 11 to 320 women lived in each home; managers wrote that 90 to 125 tenants constituted the optimal client group.[29] The YMCA opened its doors more widely in 1925, offering membership to Jews, Catholics, and people with no religious affiliation. Each city made its own rules regarding integration of black and white members; through World War II, the YMCA typically built separate facilities for blacks and Asians. More fully integrated chapters became more common in the 1940s and particularly after the beginning of national desegregation in 1954. In some chapters, blacks could stay as transient guests but not as permanent residents.[30]

Ys and other organization boardinghouses often occupied America's most specialized boardinghouse buildings. The eight-story, 211-room Evangeline Residence built by the Salvation Army in San Francisco opened in 1923 on a site just a block from the new Civic Center. The T-shaped plan imitated the best middle-income apartment buildings and hotels. The Evangeline, however, had very small rooms, no private baths, and very plain and economical interior construction. Its managers compensated for these with a sun deck on the roof and several social spaces in addition to the lobby, dining room, and reading room.

The managers of nonprofit lodgings often imposed curfews, lectured the tenants on morals, tightly enforced house rules, and required tenants to pay for meals whether they ate them or not. Together with the general air of charity and institutionality, these rules repulsed many people looking for long-term homes. The Ys became known as places for men and women to live only while looking for work.[31] Hearing the complaints, commercial entrepreneurs ventured successfully into the same market. The large Allerton Houses in several cities were physically very much like YMCAs and YWCAs. By 1915, Chicago had six Eleanor Clubs, a chain of commercial and self-supporting women's clubs with 60 to 150 residents each. This competition convinced the subsidized homes to reduce their restrictions.[32]

For many people, rooming houses were acceptable because of their similarities with college dormitories, fraternities and sororities, retirement homes of fraternal, ethnic, and benevolent societies (such as the Oddfellows' retirement homes), and orphanages, together with the monasteries and convents of religious orders. Institutions like these have been and still are providers of thousands of subsidized housing units in every large American city.[33]

ECONOMIC LIMBO

Like Dorothy Richardson, the vast majority of single-room residents in turn-of-the-century rooming houses were young men and women recently arrived in the city. In 1906, the sociologist Albert Wolfe characterized the rooming house residents of Boston's South End as a "great army of clerks, salesmen, bookkeepers, shop girls, stenographers, dressmakers, milliners, barbers, restaurant-keepers, black railroad porters and stewards, policemen, nurses, . . . journeymen carpenters, painters, machinists, and electricians" (fig. 4.11).[34] In more clinical terms, Wolfe had found an army of low-paid but skilled white-collar and blue-collar workers, rarely immigrants but usually American-born of northern European and most often Protestant stock.

These city recruits struggled with their uncertain standing: they often held strong family values but were living outside a family; they were capable of being well dressed but only in one or two outfits; they aspired to material comfort but had access to very little of it; they aimed for economic security but lived with uncertain incomes. Typically, work had lured rooming house residents to the city, and it was the realities of their work that kept them in an economic and residential limbo.

FIGURE 4.11. Course in typing and Dictaphone, 1906, at Bryant High School, New York City. Young people trained in these skills were often rooming house residents.

Rooming house women and men shared similar employments but had sharply differing incomes. The women's situation was the more acute. Women represented a third to a half of the people in American rooming houses.[35] In Wolfe's 1906 study, about one-sixth of the women were wives with no employment outside their homes. Single elderly women, or as Wolfe put it, "old ladies, most of them living on modest incomes, or supported by some relative or by charity," made up 8 percent of the women in his study. Stenographers, waitresses, dressmakers, saleswomen, and clerks roughly tied as the most common occupations among the working women, with 6 to 8 percent apiece.[36] The waitresses typically worked in small cafés within the rooming house district itself. The clerks worked in small shops, not in department stores where wages were too low to support even the cheapest rooming house rents. In San Francisco, women's average pay in similar jobs in 1920 was still typically too low for women to live alone in a rooming house as men did (table 3, Appendix). Thirty to 60 percent of San Francisco's working women could not afford a room alone, especially before 1920, and they doubled up with another woman to share the rent. The only lower pay rates in San Francisco were those of Chinese laborers and children.[37]

After 1920, new industrial and commercial jobs and the sudden rise of entry-level white-collar work helped more women migrate to the city and live outside a family. The U.S. Census showed an increase from 1,300 San Francisco stenographers and typists in 1900 to nearly 12,000 in 1930. In those same years, women's jobs as bookkeepers, cashiers, and accountants increased by a factor of six. The number of women working in more traditional retail clerk jobs doubled between 1900 and 1910 and again by 1920. Nationally, women were half of the total office force by 1920; clerical work made up a quarter of women's jobs and had surpassed manufacturing as the second largest employer of women.[38] These surges in women's office work were closely related to factory and wholesaling expansions. From 1890 to 1920, each two additional unskilled industrial workers added a new salaried overseer or skilled office worker.[39] These women, when they were single, increasingly looked to rooming houses for shelter.

Among the men in Wolfe's study, "clerk" and "salesmen" were the most common occupations, with 13 and 8 percent, respectively. Merchants and waiters were equal, with about 5 percent; the other significant groups were foremen, engineers, real estate and insurance workers, and cooks.[40]

Skilled workers did not figure prominently in Wolfe's study of Boston, but in many cities skilled workers were common in rooming houses (fig. 4.12). In San Francisco, for instance, a fourth of the city's carpenters in 1900 were boarders or lodgers, most of them living downtown. Students in colleges and business schools relied on rooming houses. Woodrow Wilson lived in Baltimore rooming houses in 1883–84 while he was a graduate student at Johns Hopkins University. After World War II, the employment of rooming house men shifted with the urban economy. In New York, people working in the merchant marine or night bus routes became as common as waiters had been before the war.[41]

For both men and women in rooming houses, frequent moves were common. Half the roomers in a city moved within a typical year, usually from one rooming house to another. Frequent moves were also part of the work life for machinists, cigar workers, and people in construction trades. Layoffs were another major factor in this rooming house

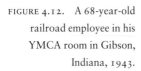

FIGURE 4.12. A 68-year-old railroad employee in his YMCA room in Gibson, Indiana, 1943.

mobility. Jobs at this income level were often erratic or seasonal. Particularly in the slow summer months, roomers were forced to desert the city and live elsewhere—often with their rural families. Frequent moves were easily accomplished because roomers owned few personal possessions and could pack them into one or two bags or at most a trunk. Two rooming house women joked that the word *home* for them meant "a place where we can unpack our trunk, anchor our electric iron and hang our other blouse over the chair."[42]

Although the number of roomers increased from 1870 to 1950, and their employment changed, the sex and age composition of rooming house areas remained relatively constant. Ages between twenty and forty-five were far more represented than in immigrant family neighborhoods or in the suburbs. Rooming house people rarely had children living with them, although social workers' interests in children meant that reports usually overemphasized them. The elderly men and women in rooming houses, although not generally prominent before World

War II, tended to live in the older and cheaper buildings. In the late 1920s, one committee reported that lack of proper heat was "one of the great privations of the elderly" in single-room housing.[43] Landladies said that they preferred men to women as tenants because men were more easygoing and long-suffering—and out of the house more. Women were "constantly waiting to use the laundry, wash in their rooms, or do light cooking." Men could also afford higher rents. From their side, women complained that the landladies required women tenants to do their own cleaning, while for the same rents, the men did not.[44]

Nineteenth-century rooming house residents also sorted themselves by ethnic, racial, and occupational considerations. Some housekeepers preferred Catholic or Protestant tenants, or mechanics over clerks. These distinctions became less common after 1900. When blacks moved into Chicago rooming house areas, the population pyramids and age-sex formations did not change, although racial discrimination meant that crowding was far worse inside black rooming houses.[45]

Not everyone in rooming houses was single or living alone. Couples, either married or unmarried, ranged from 7 to 38 percent of the roomers. White couples often rented two-room suites. Crowded conditions in black rooming houses largely precluded more than one room. After World War II, some rooming house districts had a higher proportion of couples (again, both married and unmarried) than those neighborhoods had seen in the 1920s. The life-style remained similar to the earlier period. For women, becoming a "charity girl" (that is, living with a man without marrying him) became one way to escape the binds of low wages. Being a charity girl was at least an alternative to working in the sexual service sector: prostitution, taxi-dance work, dancing in a chorus line, gold digging (that is, consorting with men primarily for expensive gifts or lucrative divorces), or in later years, cocktail waitressing.[46] Nominally appearing to be single, homosexual couples of men or women could also live together in rooming houses. They apparently provoked little suspicion or approbation, as adult pairs of men or women commonly lived together to share expenses. Some rooming house districts were known to be areas that gay men or lesbians lived in and frequented.[47]

Rooming houses also proved useful for families with a problem relative. Families could rid themselves of offending relatives by sending them to a distant city and supporting them with steady monthly payments as long as they stayed away. From wealthy families, such a remittance man or remittance woman could derive a comfortable life in a palace or midpriced hotel. For the vast majority, however, this situation meant a rooming house. Each remittance person had his or her reasons for being sent away; the common problems were drink, gambling, congenital brain defects, eccentricity, or being mildly crazy. "Every hotel has its crank boarders," hotel manager Ford told his peers at a convention speech in 1903. He continued with this example:

One of the good old New York hotels had a lady who stole a plate at every meal and kept them all in her room—for 30 years. She's not quite right in her mind, but she's unexceptional in regard to everything except plates.[48]

In surveys taken in the 1920s, college students complained that rooming house and residence club life forced them to associate with people who displayed personal peculiarities and maladjustment or who were "mentally or nervously upset."[49] The cheaper the hotel, the more likely would residents find this admixture to the population.

Low entry costs coupled with low and uncertain pay brought most people to the front desk of a rooming house. Unlike setting up an apartment, rooming house tenants did not have to buy linens, dishes, furniture, or cleaning equipment. In 1906, for their ready-to-live-in room, tenants paid from $1 to $7 a week (or its multiple by the month). Young Will Kortum in San Francisco found that the cheapest livable hotel rooms in the South of Market district were dark hall rooms at $2 a week or rooms with outside light for $2.50 a week. In Boston's South End, he would have found similar prices. The large rooms in an old house cost from $4.50 to $6.[50] After two decades of inflation, 1920s prices in former-house rooming houses had not gone up, while tenants in newer, purpose-built rooming houses paid from $4 to $10. The average rooming house tenants paid about the same per week for food as they did for rent.[51] Against these weekly costs, a woman salesclerk or sewing machine operator in San Francisco earned only $9 to $12 a week in 1910; unskilled confectionary workers or biscuit packers made only $6 to $9. Men operating sewing machines made $18 to $21, and other skilled men's incomes went to about $25 a week (table 4, Appendix).[52] The low prices in rooming houses kept an independent low-paid work force available to downtown industries and also helped young single Americans forge personal independence and a subculture separate from the city's family zones. The rooming house district became notable for both of these roles.

ROOMING HOUSE DISTRICTS: DIVERSITY AND MIXTURE

In addition to many rooms at low prices, rooming house residents needed at least two other features: easy access to work places, and a surrounding neighborhood with mixed land use including stores, bars, restaurants, and clubs for association with friends and commercial recreation. Few outsiders questioned the first of these two needs. However, the retail mixtures of rooming house neighborhoods caused concern within the dominant culture. They also reinforced the liminal status of rooming house residents.

The mixtures of rooming house streets.   Work places and rooming houses were inextricably linked. Especially during boom times, employers needed a ready supply of help on short notice, and workers could afford only so much time and money for their journey to work. Given the erratic availability of employment, they also needed to be within easy reach of many different companies. Roomers rarely owned cars. Thus, rooming house areas were usually within half a mile of varied jobs. For the greatest number of rooming house residents, work was downtown in the retail shopping district in the office core, or in a warehouse, shipping, or manufacturing zone very close to the center of the city. Higher-paid white-collar workers could afford to commute on streetcars to an outlying rooming house area (fig. 4.13). Streetcar transfer locations like these were exceptions to the dominant pattern, but made up between 5 and 10 percent of San Francisco's rooming house supply by 1930.[53]

Rooming houses might have seemed unnecessary to downtown, but they were just as essential for urban economic growth as the family tenements that stretched next to factories and just as basic as the new downtown skyscrapers and loft buildings. At the turn of the century, urban Americans knew at least two different types of rooming house areas: districts of old-house rooming houses, and newer purpose-built rooming house districts.

FIGURE 4.13. A large out-lying rooming house in San Francisco, photographed ca. 1912. Streetcars to downtown ran directly past the building. Note entrance to hotel under the small gable roof in the center of the storefronts.

A large central area of San Francisco known as the Western Addition was a quintessential old-house rooming district. Fillmore Street was its commercial and entertainment spine (fig. 4.14).[54] The Western Addition was a twenty-minute walk west of downtown. Between downtown and the Western Addition was a neighborhood of newer flats and houses with higher rents, an area rebuilt after the fire of 1906. Several major streetcar lines crossed the Western Addition on their way farther west to single-family neighborhoods. By the 1920s, Fillmore Street's vaudeville houses, dance halls, and inexpensive restaurants were well known in San Francisco. After the fire, many downtown entrepreneurs had relocated along the street. From the public experience of this main artery, the whole Western Addition was most commonly known as "the Fillmore," although the street itself was off-center, near the edge of the neighborhood (fig. 4.15). Most of the area was filled with former middle-income houses and flats, most built in wood between 1870 and 1900, the later ones using wildly exuberant Victorian ornamentation. Commercial land-use mixture in the Western Addition was common. Owners had built long rows of storefronts into the base of houses or flats and leased them to corner grocery stores, tobacconists, bars, mil-linery shops, secondhand stores, and antique shops. On the side streets were auto dealers, repair shops, and commercial laundries that stood next to housing and were important employers in the neighborhood (fig. 4.16). Along the major avenues were other employers. At the southeastern corner of the district, the postfire city hall and civic center office complex offered nearby white-collar employment.[55]

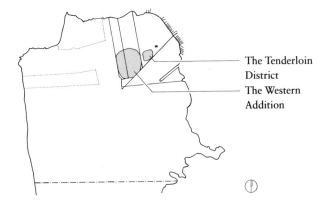

The Tenderloin
District
The Western
Addition

FIGURE 4.14. Map of two
principal rooming house districts in San Francisco. Streets
running north and south
(vertically) are, from left to
right, Divisadero, Fillmore,
and Van Ness. The diagonal
is Market Street.

FIGURE 4.15. Residential section of Fillmore Street
in 1944. Seen looking north from Grove Street, this
view was typical of the southern edge of the Western
Addition.

FIGURE 4.16. Side street in the Western Addition in the 1920s. Laundries and industrial shops mixed with older flats, many rented as rooming houses.

To people from the newer, richer family districts of San Francisco, the streets of the Western Addition epitomized mixture, crude commercialism, and unskilled employment. Many of the commercial building fronts were jerry-built. The housing and commercial spaces were built of wood and rarely faced with masonry, as were the areas closer to downtown. The district represented reuse, the filtering of blocks to new tenants. In the late 1950s, when Alfred Hitchcock looked for an old rooming house setting for a mysterious transitional character in *Vertigo*, he found what he needed on the southern edge of the Western Addition.[56]

The Western Addition was also known for its social, ethnic, and racial diversity. After the fire, inexpensive rooms of the Western Addition became home for a growing number of German, Russian, and Eastern European Jewish immigrants, along with more consolidated settlement patterns of Japanese and African-American families who had been living in dispersed patterns before the fire.[57] At the end of the depression, San Francisco's Real Property Survey documented race on a unit-by-unit basis, showing that at the eastern edge of the Western Addition African-American families were mixed with Japanese, Filipino, and European families. The 1940 census showed that the city's 5,000 blacks

made up less than 1 percent of the city's population; in the Western Addition, African-Americans comprised 5 percent and by 1960 would comprise half the residents in the area.[58] Most cities had a zone of converted houses with a succession similar to the Western Addition. In Boston, it was the South End; in New York, Chelsea came to be a zone of converted houses; in Chicago, it was the Near North Side.

An adjacent San Francisco area, the Tenderloin district, exemplified another type of rooming precinct—a rebuilt rooming house area that was overwhelmingly white as late as 1970.[59] The Tenderloin is essentially bounded on the west by the Western Addition and on the north by Nob Hill, and it is immediately west of the department stores around Union Square. By the 1920s, most cities had two or three such areas, some of them only a few blocks in extent. Such areas were not composed of old converted houses but new urbane buildings expressly intended as rooming houses, often next to middle-income apartments and midpriced hotels (fig. 4.17). If a single 100-room hotel had represented the social stratification of the hotels in the Tenderloin in 1930, 52 of the rooms would have been of the rooming house type; 26, midpriced; and 22, the cheap lodging house type. The Tenderloin typified a rebuilt rooming house area also in that along one side (the Nob Hill

FIGURE 4.17. Ellis Street in the Tenderloin district, San Francisco, in the early 1940s. Buildings of one-room and two-room apartments are interspersed next to tall residential hotels.

FIGURE 4.18. The bright light district on Fillmore Street in the 1920s. After the fire of 1906, Fillmore became one of the substitutes for the burned Market Street. The corner light fixtures added a festival air to the street year-round.

side), it had expensive apartments and houses; and on the opposite side (the South of Market) was a huge district of working-class housing. The newness of the Tenderloin in the 1920s was a result of the rebuilding required after San Francisco's 1906 fire. Even without such a stimulus, however, landowners in other cities had found the same rebuilding necessary and profitable. In 1930, the Tenderloin had 59 percent of San Francisco's rooming house units. All of the new rooming house districts, together, had a third of the city's residential hotel rooms.[60]

For roomers in any type of rooming house district, a short journey to play was as important as a short journey to work. Rooming house areas relied on thoroughfares with heavy streetcar or bus service and commercial businesses that catered to people from throughout the city. In San Francisco, prime examples were Fillmore and Market streets. Like the thoroughfares that cut through the bright light districts of other cities, Market and Fillmore were busy at night with people going out to eat and be entertained at the theaters, vaudeville houses, movie halls, and large dance halls—the latter being prominent and often on the second floor above retail stores.[61] Inexpensive restaurants, cafeterias, bars or lounges, and variety stores filled the interstices (fig. 4.18).

Above the larger men's clothing stores were often pool halls. As one commentator put it, in such an area the clothing store signs always advertised for "gents," never for "men" or "gentlemen."[62] These bright light entertainments and retail bargains depended more on people from outside the rooming house zone than from inside it. Local residents relied more on smaller stores scattered throughout the zone: small bakeries, tailor shops, laundries, drugstores, shoe repair shops, and also (depending on the decade and local state law) corner liquor stores that also sold convenience food and snacks at exorbitant prices.[63] Nearest the workers' cottage or tenement districts were usually a few good-sized public bathhouses so essential for tenants who had hot water only once a week.[64] At the sleaziest or least expensive side of the rooming house area, but never far from the main thoroughfare, one would see astrologers' parlors, saloons, and fairly obvious houses of prostitution. No matter where one traveled in the rooming house zone, however, there were restaurants of all descriptions. Their role was central to the residents of the area.

Simple food. On a day-to-day basis, the most important provision of the rooming house district was inexpensive food (fig. 4.19). Individualized dining was a major advantage of rooming houses over old-style boardinghouses. Boarders complained about eating at preset times, paying for meals whether they were there or not, not getting enough food, not having food they liked, and enduring very repetitious fare. While living in a rooming house, tenants could choose from a variety of places to eat, at varied prices, and over a much wider range of hours—provided payday was not too far away.[65]

The cheapest eateries were almost literally holes in the wall: tiny storefronts or basements, minimally adapted for their new uses. In Boston's South End in 1900, building owners converted house basements into small dining rooms managed, as Wolfe put it, by women "of uncertain experience." The atmosphere was dark, hot, and unfriendly. The beverage included with the meals could be either coffee or tea (one could not always be sure which it was, Wolfe said). However, the table d'hôte meals of four dishes cost as little as 20 cents each. Model boardinghouses run by home economists and settlement volunteers could not set a table at such low prices. At small storefront places in the industrial areas, the lunch fare was likely a cheap stew (potatoes,

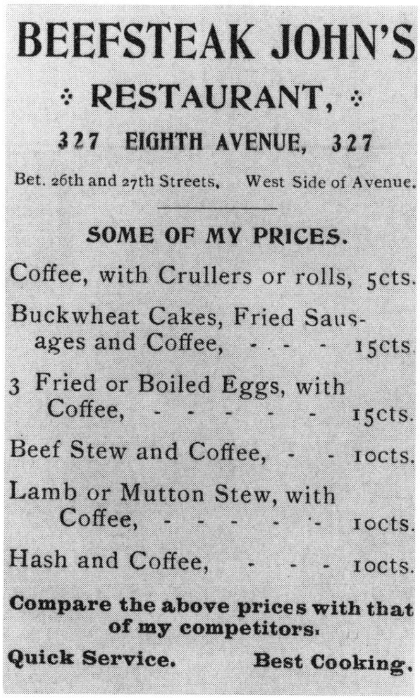

FIGURE 4.19.   Wallet card advertising a beanery-style fast-food emporium in New York City, 1901.

FIGURE 4.20.   Child's Restaurant, a dairy lunchroom in New York City, ca. 1900.

carrots, and as little meat as possible) served with bread, pie, and coffee. Later, cafeterias and small counter-and-booth luncheonettes in
rooming house areas continued the traditions of the small eateries.
Through the 1960s, they remained a frequent haunt of rooming house
residents.[66]

Larger basement restaurants offered similar bargains but better atmosphere. In the 1880s and 1890s, large and profitable places known
as "three for two" restaurants catered to rooming house patrons, offering three 10-cent courses for two bits (25 cents). These eateries were a
variation on the "beef and" restaurants, serving beans with a hefty cut
of beef or pork, that sprang up after the Civil War.[67] Richardson, in the
New York she knew during the late 1890s, occasionally treated herself
with a good meal and a cup of hot coffee at a dairy lunchroom or quick
lunchroom (fig. 4.20). Dairy lunchrooms were in large storefront
spaces, attractively remodeled with white tile walls. They opened early
and closed late. In some, tidy waitresses gave rapid service; in others,
patrons picked up their food and ate at side-arm chairs. From a fairly
large bill of fare, patrons could have a full dinner for 15 cents, order
items à la carte for 5 to 7 cents, and efficiently pay the cashier in her
cagelike desk.[68]

Meals in smaller new cafés were an even bigger treat for roomers
who wanted a special dinner out. The range of Bohemian cafés in
rooming house districts were typically known throughout the city for
their informal dress, casual manners, and reasonable prices. Most cafés
commanded a street view through plate glass windows and also had
electric lights and fans. They were clean and attractive and had linen
tablecloths. A steady café diet could cost $4.50 or $6 a week, as even
spare breakfasts cost 20 cents; lunches, 25 cents; and dinners, 35 cents.
Inexpensive hotel dining rooms essentially offered the same service
(fig. 4.21).[69]

For convivial alternatives to the cafés, rooming house residents could
turn to bars and saloons. Eating in a saloon was clearly working-class
behavior and hence suspect for young people who aspired to the middle
and upper class. Yet in 1912 a Philadelphia housing reformer defended
the saloon with a positive description:

[Patrons at a saloon] could have a good dish of soup by purchasing a glass of
beer for five cents. Often there is an egg, a clam, a fried oyster, or reed-bird

FIGURE 4.21. A small hotel's dining room. For rooming house residents, the Hotel Gianduja in San Francisco's North Beach was a typical place for a special dinner.

HOTEL GIANDUJA DINING ROOM, 1541-1549 Stockton Street, S. F.

given free with every drink. . . . For a very small price a hungry man can get as much as he cares to eat or drink. . . . As a rule the food is good, well-cooked, and palatable.[70]

Furthermore, he said, "That air of poverty which unfailingly pervades the cheap restaurants, and finds its expression in cheap and dirty table linen, is wanting in the saloon."[71] Polished oak or mission tables greeted saloon patrons (fig. 4.22). Richardson, too, was surprised one day when her fellow laundry workers whisked her through the women's entrance to a saloon. "Whatever the soup was made of, it seemed to me the best soup I had ever eaten in New York," she wrote, adding that she would "never again blame a working man or woman for dining in a saloon in preference to the more godly and respectable dairy-lunch room."[72] In the early 1900s, many saloons required that hungry patrons buy two beers to get the free lunch.

Other competitors to cheap cafés were illegal hot plates in one's room. Landladies often supplied these, to the concern of fire marshals. Regular diets of snack foods were available at the many neighborhood bakeries, delicatessens, grocery stores, and fruit stands. Their ready-to-eat bread, cake, cheese, and pickles supplemented the hot-plate fare.[73] Not only rooming house residents but also permanent guests at nearby midpriced hotels availed themselves of the delicatessen supplies.

In both the older, revamped neighborhoods like the Fillmore and the newer areas like the Tenderloin, the local dance halls and bars (or after

Prohibition, the local lunch counters) often had a group of regular neighborhood customers. To the horror of her colleagues, the sociologist Margaret Chandler found a high degree of social cohesiveness in these groups. Social circles focused on one person's room or more frequently around a particular lunch counter, bar, or street corner. Some lunch stand groups behaved much as they might have in small towns. People stopped several times a day or night; on occasion, owners cooked up special meals for their regulars and extended them credit.[74] This social cohesion stood in sharp contrast to the alienation, anonymity, and illegal behavior that also characterized the mixtures of rooming house districts.

Beyond the edge of propriety.   For people who wished to be anonymous and unnoticed, life in cheap hotels could be ideal. In a rooming house district, a small town Simple Simon might be teased less than he had been at home. People who wanted to live a liberated or illegal life

FIGURE 4.22.   A plain saloon. After work hours, construction workers mix with young clerks in this San Francisco saloon. Note the lunch counter at the rear.

could do so in rooming houses and lodging houses more easily than in most other settings. For alcoholics or drug addicts, the fear of being discovered, the desire to be near some people like themselves, and the need to be close to supply sources brought them to hotels. Addicts could have seclusion if they wanted it, and desk clerks fended off investigators and pesky caseworkers.[75] Landladies might not remember or even know a new tenant's name. The frequent change of address possible at hotels, perhaps with a corresponding change in name, helped runaways elude their parents, reformed people escape their past, and criminals evade the police.[76] For anyone who wanted to melt into the physical maze of the city, such anonymity and the large number of rooming houses offered the perfect settings.

Given the large number of people seeking entertainment and anonymity in rooming house districts, red-light or vice zones logically overlapped with rooming house areas. In 1910, three-fourths of the parlor houses in American cities were in the rooming house and tenement fringes of the central business district. The architectural arrangements for small rooming houses in the 1910s could be almost identical to those built for parlor houses: rental store space on the first floor—inevitably a saloon in houses of prostitution—with parlors and the madam's suite on the second floor and many bedrooms on the third floor. For the prostitute residents, the madam's parlor house functioned as a boardinghouse or rooming house. A madam often listed her business in the city directory under the category of lodgings; notorious black sex clubs were sometimes advertised as buffet flats.[77] This overlapping of hotel life and prostitution was heightened in New York by a state vice law of 1896, which inadvertently produced "Raines Law hotels." Under the new statute, saloons could no longer offer free lunches, and hotels alone could sell liquor on Sunday and then only with meals. "In consequence," complained one legitimate New York hotel keeper, "every gin-mill in New York is now a hotel. It is easy to create a hotel. All you need is 10 microscopic bedrooms and some permanent sandwiches." At the turn of the century, Manhattan and the Bronx had 1,407 certified hotels, and 1,160 of them had apparently sprung up in response to the Raines Law.[78]

By the 1920s, decreases in general prostitution ironically led to an increase in prostitution in hotels. Business for women prostitutes had declined with the rise of the flapper—or more correctly, with shifts in social mores for women that allowed women to be more sexually active and independent. Prohibition and Progressive Era attempts to protect young men—particularly the soldiers of World War I—from the Victorian versions of prostitution had decimated the flagrant red-light districts of many cities. Growing use of the automobile for sexual encounters moved prostitution to new locations. For the prostitution that remained downtown, hotels played a larger role as prostitutes' homes and as places of assignation. In San Francisco, a major vice crackdown of 1917 saw police raiding "hotels, lodging houses, and flats on streets which had never before known a house of prostitution." In national surveys in the 1920s, streetwalkers were found to be operating out of hotels twice as often as old-style bordellos.[79] Any of these social problems at times led rooming house residents to look for other housing options.

DOWNTOWN ALTERNATIVES TO ROOMING HOUSES

At least according to social ideals, if roomers left rooming house life, they either joined the protective circle of a private family or began to cook for themselves. In so doing they stepped up in status. While living with a family or cooking for themselves they were less overtly dependent on commercial entertainment and public dining, and less involved with the tainting mixtures of rooming house districts. However, both family and apartment alternatives confronted rooming house residents with serious problems. Living with a family worked directly against the individualism so encouraged by work places and youth culture. The limited and erratic income of rooming house residents militated against proper apartment life. The apartment option that roomers could afford, the light housekeeping room, actually lowered their status.

Problems of living with a downtown family.　Boarding or lodging with a family was *the* major alternative to living in a commercial boardinghouse or rooming house, and it was also the most commonly chosen downtown life-style for young single men and women. For families in the middle and upper class, boarders were extra income, companionship, or people taken in as a favor to relatives. In such households, boarders often filled unused rooms. For wage-labor families with irregular incomes, boarders were essential. The income they

FIGURE 4.23. A Slavic boardinghouse dining room in a factory district near New York City, 1912. Photographed by Lewis Hine.

provided helped to pay medical bills or make monthly payments on a looming seven-year mortgage with a balloon payment at the end. Boarding with families was particularly common in working-class family districts and family slums, often located next to rooming house districts because their residents depended on many of the same kinds of jobs (fig. 4.23).

Boarding with a family offered more traditional home-style conviviality, more social respectability, and generally better food than hotel life. Immigrants tended to board for only a short time and then set up independent households.[80] Unlike immigrants, American-born migrants to the city often chose boarding as a long-term housing choice. The eighteen-year-old lumber clerk, Will Kortum, had started his San Francisco life in a hotel in 1905 but soon wrote home that he planned to move in with a family in a nearby working-class district:

I am getting tired of this hotel and restaurant life and as soon as my pay is raised will look for board in a private family. . . . They say that . . . if you are lucky it is just like being at home.[81]

Kortum moved into a private boardinghouse on Eleventh Street, in the South of Market area, where he lived with the housekeepers—a young Swedish woman and her little girl—and seven other paying guests. He found that boarding with an immigrant family meant a sharp decline in personal comforts:

FIGURE 4.24. Flats and single-family houses at the edge of San Francisco, ca. 1890s. Roomers who stayed with families in such settings were isolated from downtown life.

The meals are good, at least they are a great improvement in the restaurant fare, but otherwise there are but few comforts: no water in the room, poor bed, very small room, and bare of furniture. I shall look around for something better and wish I had never moved here at all.[82]

Kortum's new room supplied fewer personal needs independent of the boarding household. "My moving is an easily accomplished act," he said, "but costs 50 cents every time so I must be more careful."

This dissatisfaction with boarding with a family matched a general trend. Many boarders sought more independence and freer association with friends. Young people who lived in outlying family districts had a half-hour streetcar ride every time they wanted to visit companions, go dancing, or see a movie (fig. 4.24). Returning home, family boarders had to worry about missing the last streetcar for the night.[83] Other concerns were about privacy, as reported in this case:

"Miss G.," a public school music teacher, did not like rooming with a family. When she had phone calls, the family had to listen to one end of the conversation. If she slept late on Saturday morning she felt she was inconveniencing the family—and the children made such a ruckus she could not rest anyway. . . . She repeatedly took guests for a walk rather than use the parlor.[84]

Another woman complained, "The family from whom I rented a room were inquisitive and prying. I'm sure they investigated my room during my absence. The bathroom was occupied for prolonged periods."[85] Once these women had sampled the personal freedom and independence of hotel life, they felt that it would be impossible for them to board in a private home again. Lily Bart, Edith Wharton's heroine in *The House of Mirth*, eventually chose the anonymity of a commercial boardinghouse over living in a friend's house. To Lily, "the promiscuity of small quarters and close intimacy seemed, on the whole, less endurable than the solitude of a hall bedroom in a house where she could come and go unremarked among other workers."[86]

Light housekeeping rooms.   Light housekeeping rooms were the cheap apartment-style alternative to rooming house life. They were typically one- or two-room suites in flimsily adapted former houses or apartments, usually in declining neighborhoods (fig. 4.25). By the 1920s, the hallmark of a housekeeping room was the "ubiquitous gas plate" on an old crate in a corner of the bedroom, with a rubber hose leading from it up to the wall gaslight fixture.[87] To keep cooking grease from splattering the wallpaper, tenants pinned newspaper against the wall. A pail of water might serve as a sink. There was usually an improvised pantry made by a large soap box, with cheap curtains on the front. Elsewhere, housekeeping meant simply that several tenants shared both kitchen and bath. Managers of light housekeeping units typically supplied a table, two chairs, a bureau, a few dishes, and a few cooking utensils.[88] As with rooming houses, daily management was left to resident women who leased the buildings as a business. By all accounts, housekeeping rooms were sanitary and social problems. They were technically not hotel units because of their cooking arrangements, although some surveys included them in the ranks of single-room occupancy. Even when owners borrowed names like "apartment hotel" or "residence club" for their furnished room buildings, the lineage of these operations led directly back to the worst nineteenth-century slum traditions. In 1939, two-fifths of San Francisco's substandard housing units were housekeeping rooms. The advantage for the landlord was

FIGURE 4.25. Kitchenette apartment buildings (light housekeeping rooms) on South Parkway in Chicago, 1941.

income: a building cut into two-room units brought twice the monthly rental income that it produced as five-room flats.[89]

Housekeeping rooms were often crowded by families who had fallen on hard times; social workers called them "dejected families" (fig. 4.26). Unlike poor immigrant families in tenements, tenants in housekeeping rooms were usually born in America and often white. Their trip to housekeeping rooms began when they defaulted on the mortgage on their house, stored their furniture, and moved into some sort of hotel while the breadwinners recovered from illness, continued to drink, or looked for work. If the family's finances continued to decline, they often lost their furniture for nonpayment of storage fees.[90] Thus, they found themselves locked into life in housekeeping rooms. Other families came to choose it over the option of having a full-fledged apartment; when social workers helped them obtain a flat and furniture, the families moved right back into cheap furnished rooms. For such households, the social workers reserved the labels "shiftless" and "tramp families."[91]

More expensive apartments were usually out of the question for people in the rooming house price range. The barriers were entry costs and application barriers more than the monthly rents. Matrons in the YWCA cautioned that "it was a risky thing for two or three girls to take an apartment together" because "if one dropped out the remainder were then forced to bear the financial burden" until a new room-

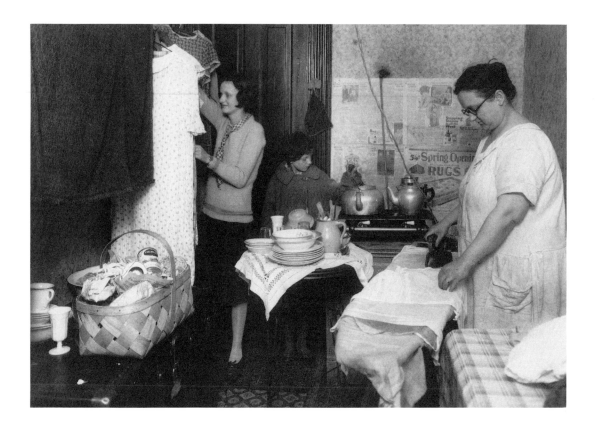

FIGURE 4.26. Housework in light housekeeping rooms in Chicago, ca. 1929. Note the rubber tube connecting the gas wall fixture to the hot plate.

mate could be found.[92] Even when respectable and inexpensive downtown apartments became more available, young single people had neither the nest egg nor the job security to buy the furniture, linens, and kitchen equipment that apartments required. Unmarried or poorly employed people also had a slim chance of getting a lease from apartment managers. Furnished one-room efficiency apartments solved some of these problems, but at $25 to $30 a month they were beyond economic reach. They outpriced an unfurnished four-room garden apartment in the suburbs (table 2, Appendix). So, until their income improved, the low-income renters stayed in housekeeping rooms or in a rooming house.

SCATTERED HOMES VERSUS MATERIAL CORRECTNESS

Whether rooming house tenants lived in a converted single-family house, a generic loft, or a purpose-built rooming house, their home was scattered up and down the street. They slept in one building and ate in another. The surrounding sidewalks and stores functioned as parts of each resident's home: the dining room was in a basement near the corner of the block, and the laundry was three doors over; the parlor and sitting room were at a bar, a luncheonette, a billiard hall, or a favorite corner. Residents of midpriced and palace hotels could use their neighborhood as their homes, too, but for them it was a choice; the more expensive hotels, with their full housekeeping and dining services, were self-contained like private houses.

The scattering of the home reflected the increasing social and cultural autonomy that some young men and women expected. Their work lives also encouraged them to be footloose and independent. Hotel life allowed all tenants—especially single people—to push that personal privacy and autonomy to a new limit. This was a schism between the family districts of the city and the places that embodied nonfamily life. Rooming house life plugged the individual directly into the high-voltage currents of the industrial city—liberation and independence very different from that offered by a room of one's own within a family.[93] The hotel room, even with the acoustical group life that remained in cheaper hotels, was unhinged from the social contracts, tacit supervision, and protection that went with most other types of household life. Absent were the architectural arrangements so important to the maintenance of the nuclear family concept and family proscriptions of behavior.

As Joanne Meyerowitz has observed, the people in the rooming house areas of American cities were leaders in the increasing secularism and decreasing moralism that were reactions to Victorian mores. Of all the social experimentation that rooming house areas supported (and that the urban economy had engendered), most notable were new rules for sexual and social relations between men and women. In rooming houses, men's and women's lives crossed constantly. Gendered realms were scarcely circumscribed in the way that suburban or rural standards prescribed and that the spatial arrangements of polite households reinforced. Single women in rooming houses shared hallways with single men, without any familial or community supervision. Unlike the better hotels, in rooming houses there were not even servants or clerks to observe the activity.[94]

By the 1890s, rooming house areas had earned a reputation for what we would now call a sexually integrated youth subculture. Later, taxi-dance halls, movies, Bohemian restaurants, and cabarets opened the subculture into a wider commercialized landscape of personal desire. An emblem of this different subculture in the years before the depression was the fact that rooming house districts were areas where women could smoke and dance in public.[95] For young people in family districts, such recreations were optional excursions. For rooming house tenants, they were part of the daily walk to work, and part of their home scattered up and down the street.

Not all rooming house life constituted a culture of opposition, however. In their new social and sexual public lives, rooming house residents may have been flappers or dance hall sheikhs; they may have openly flouted a great many values of the middle and upper class. They were *using* rooms in new ways, but they held on to the material propriety of the middle and upper class, especially in relation to individual life in their own rooms. Their concerns about room furnishings suggest that their rooms—not their favorite café or dance hall—stood most clearly for their personal selves and their places in the world. As one social worker put it, turn-of-the-century clerks and secretaries had personal standards higher than commercial wages would justify.[96] They managed their marginal economic and cultural status by keeping one foot in rooming house culture and another in the material culture of private family life.

In 1905, Will Kortum showed his concern with family standards by his choice of building and room furnishings in San Francisco's South of Market area. On finding a place to live, he excitedly wrote home, saying that on his first day in town he had found a fine place to live:

The hotel is a new one, not entirely completed and everything is neat and clean, although not large. My room is very light, has hot and cold water, double bed, bureau, wash stand, chair, and small table. [It also has a] closet for clothes.[97]

In fact, Kortum *had* found a good building—a six-story hotel with an elevator and over half of its street length devoted to its own lobby and saloon.[98] However, his father expressed concern over the choice, and rightfully so: Kortum's hotel was only a hundred yards from the very center of San Francisco's hobo labor market. A few days later, the young man wrote this back to his father:

Rest assured that my present place of lodging is no low class hotel, but a clean, plastered room and that the bed is also clean and comfortable.[99]

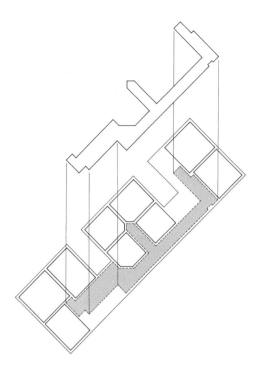

FIGURE 4.27. Diagram of the Delta Hotel second-floor plan, comparing the regularity in the shape of the private rooms and the snake-like public hall space.

Kortum's letters show all the material concerns we would expect of someone brought up in a respectable middle-income family house in a small California town of the 1890s. He noticed that the room was "not large" but "very light." He listed the pieces of furniture carefully; he had plainly seen less attractive rooms at this price range. Other key words were also there: "clean room," "clean bed," "not a low class hotel." He had an individual sense of the line between the propriety of the middle and upper class and the hygienic problems of some working-class life. His room was in every way proper. But he had not yet learned caution about living above a saloon or being associated with a casual laborers' neighborhood. Kortum's decent room, with its minimal pieces of furniture, was clearly his material foothold in the realm of middle and upper class culture. Furniture lists set out by people such as Will Kortum and Dorothy Richardson are practically a mantra in the literature of rooming house life.[100]

In architecture, too, owners and designers gave individual rooms the most attention. Floor plans of purpose-built rooming houses emphasized small, nearly square rooms, all of a similar size and with reasonably equal access to light wells. A diagram of the rooms at the Delta Hotel of 1906, for instance, shows this regularity and the primacy of individual space (fig. 4.27). Owners and landladies knew that rooms like these would rent. In sharp contrast, the hallways and public spaces

of rooming houses were often leftover labyrinths. The twisting hallways mirrored the convoluted social lives of rooming house residents,
fashioned between the interstices of work and personal identity. Plans
like those of the Delta Hotel were very much against the architectural
conventions for hotels of the midpriced or palace rank, where owners
and designers strove to keep hallways far more presentable and regular.

Thus, even single rooms and their furnishings were important anchors for people in a social and cultural limbo. To confirm further that
they still had some claim to social and cultural propriety, rooming
house residents only had to compare themselves to the denizens and
material culture of the least expensive rank of hotel life, the cheap lodging houses.

OUTSIDERS AND CHEAP
LODGING HOUSES

THE GREAT REFORMER JACOB RIIS UNDERSTOOD cheap lodging houses. He had lived in them as a young immigrant in New York. He had smelled and listened to conditions in 25-cent hotels, 10-cent flophouses, and free police station lodgings. In *How the Other Half Lives*, his famous slum exposé of 1890, the only kind of hotels that Riis mentioned were cheap lodging houses. As he put it, "There is a wider gap between the 'hotel'—they are all hotels—that charges a quarter and the one that furnishes a bed for a dime than between the bridal suite and the everyday hall bedroom of the ordinary hostelry."[1] Riis's photographs explain why, when reformers wrote the words "cheap lodging house," readers could almost see the authors curling their upper lip in disgust (fig. 5.1). To say "cheap lodging house" was to say "dirty tramp."

Most lodging house denizens were not dirty tramps but unskilled day laborers whose work included digging ditches and carrying materials to extend and to finish the turn-of-the-century city. In the backgrounds of Riis's photographs were remnants of the old city: wooden shacks, leftover piles of dirt and gravel, stretches of weeds, and vacant lots. Much of the American city in 1890 was not only old and dilapidated; much was also raw and unfinished. Riis and his fellow reformers hoped

FIGURE 5.1. A hammock-style cheap lodging house. A Jacob Riis photograph of Happy Jack's Canvas Palace on Pell Street in New York City, 1890s.

to keep slums of all kinds, including cheap lodging houses, from the permanent and proper parts of the city then under construction.

Both low wages and their own subculture kept casual laborers in cheap lodging houses and out of better hotels or other housing. In better neighborhoods, rooming house residents were merely *down* on the socioeconomic ladder; however, the low-income men and women who lived in cheap lodging houses were both down and *out*. They were unwelcome in most of the city but nonetheless essential for the volatile urban and rural economy. The owners and managers of cheap lodging houses not only responded to the hierarchies of the casual laborer subculture but also negotiated an uneasy three-sided truce among unskilled single workers, the captains of industry and agriculture who employed them, and the urban residents who saw the workers—at best— as a necessary evil.

ESSENTIAL OUTCASTS

To outside observers, the gangs of hired laborers at construction sites or in farm fields seemed to be members of a single category: tramp. However, casual workers themselves pointed out vital differences within their caste, often using a three-line rule of thumb:

A hobo works and wanders.
A tramp dreams and wanders.
A bum drinks and wanders.[2]

All three groups of men appeared unattached to a family; they had few possessions, enjoyed recreational drinking, worked intermittently, and traveled often. People in the categories of tramp and bum did the most to give casual laborers a bad reputation, yet they made up only a small share of the whole group, for instance, only 2,500 out of Chicago's 100,000 casual workers. Tramps and bums were migrant *non*workers, often dirty and slovenly. Hoboes were workers who often shared or aspired to many middle-income values.[3] Together, hoboes, tramps, and bums represented a hotel group that writers—historically as well as today—have erroneously called "homeless men." The casual laborers who lived in cheap lodging houses were no more homeless than the mining kings or opera divas who lived in palace hotels (fig. 5.2). Hotels were also an integral part of the casual labor supply and its culture.

FIGURE 5.2. The Waco Hotel, St. Louis. When photographed in 1939, rooms were 25¢, 35¢, and 50¢ a day. Note the tavern and restaurant on its ground floor.

Nels Anderson, a hobo who later went on to become a University of Chicago sociologist, defined the true hobo as the "in-between worker, willing to go anywhere to take a job and equally willing to move on later." In rural and remote wilderness locations, hoboes dug ditches, carted bricks, and tended animals in the construction of mines, railways, highways, and oil fields. In farm regions, hoboes followed the harvests of grain, corn, fruit, potatoes, beets, cotton, or hops. During the winter, smaller numbers of men did lumbering or cut ice. According to Anderson, most boys or men moved out of the hobo work force within ten years of entering it.[4] In city locations, gangs of casual workers toiled over the menial tasks involved with building industrial plants and street railroads, paving streets, laying pipe and wire for gas and electric systems, and erecting new buildings. Casual laborers were also former carnival workers, part-time sailors, and extra hands for industrial and shipping peaks at docks, warehouses, and factories (fig. 5.3).[5] In the 1920 census, San Francisco registered over 17,000 general laborers and another 7,000 people working as longshoremen and sailors (table 4, Appendix).

In the economy of the nineteenth century and early twentieth century, demand for hobo labor fluctuated wildly, even in comparison with the unstable work conditions for skilled workers. A bumper crop, a new railroad company, sudden demands for lumber, or an oil boom instantly employed thousands of new people and created the need to house them. Just as instantly, business downturns wiped out those positions. A slowdown in 1908 meant that American railroads employed 236,000 *fewer* men than they had employed the year before. When work was plentiful, hoboes came to the city to sign up at employment agencies catering to casual laborers; the agencies then sent them back out to distant labor sites. Some California farm workers migrated to and from the same San Francisco hotel for over fifty years.

Due to the fluctuation of casual laborers' work, summer occupancies in cheap lodging houses could drop to 40 percent of capacity. When rural work for casual laborers declined sharply in the winter months, large numbers of hobo laborers returned to the city. By late November, urban lodging houses were at full occupancy and beyond. Lodging house keepers doubled up people in rooms and set more cots out into the hallways. The residents lived as long as possible on their summer earnings and picked up odd jobs, but winter urban work was also

scarce. During January, February, and March, industrial employers in San Francisco cut their work forces by an average of one-fourth (a cut of 12,000 jobs in 1921).[6] Cheap lodging houses were also permanent residences for stationary casual laborers or the "home guard," men spending some stationary years before resuming hobo life or formerly migrant men too old or unwilling to go back on the road.

Urban casual laborers were paid by the day and lived by the day. Often resisting the tedium of a steady job, they worked from a day to a week at jobs. Their indoor work included stints as porters, janitors, waiters, dishwashers, or potato peelers. In "King of the Road," Roger Miller summarized the immediate work-hotel relationship: in 1964, "two hours of pushing broom" bought an "eight by twelve four-bit room."[7]

Photographs and reports from the turn of the century show that workers' hotel districts were not full of elderly, hard-drinking men, as the 1950s stereotypes of those districts suggest. Riis declared in 1890 that he found a high proportion of able-bodied men in New York's Bowery—"young men, unsettled in life, . . . fresh from good homes, beyond a doubt with honest hopes of getting a start in the city and making a way for themselves" (fig. 5.4).[8] At the turn of the century, at least one casual laborer out of eight might be under twenty years of

FIGURE 5.3. Sailors' boardinghouses photographed in 1913, Steuart Street, San Francisco. These waterfront structures had survived the fire of 1906 and could thus remind San Franciscans of Victorian hotel slums.

FIGURE 5.4. Police station lodgers, including two young men. In the 1890s, Jacob Riis photographed the bare comforts of this police station lodging room in New York City, where he had slept in 1870.

FIGURE 5.5. Racial segregation in cheap lodging houses. A hotel on Beale Street in Memphis, Tennessee, 1939.

age, and most were in their middle years. After World War II, the elderly proportion increased; in Sacramento in 1953, men over fifty-five comprised about one-third of the lodging house population.[9]

In some regions of the United States, new immigrants and racial minorities made up significant parts of the casual labor markets. In 1880, a fourth of San Francisco's hired laborers were single Chinese men no longer sent out to do far-flung railroad and field work. They comprised almost 90 percent of the 3,000 employees in the cigar and tobacco industry and over half the labor force in the boot and shoe manufactories. A dual labor agency system prevailed in San Francisco through the 1920s; Japanese and Chinese workers were hired from "Oriental" employment agencies.[10] In other cities, blacks were the more significant racial minority in the single laborer population, and blacks had the most trouble finding housing. In 1925, a black carpenter complained to authorities that he was unable to secure a lodging house room in San Francisco; all the cheapest hotels had drawn the "color line" (fig. 5.5).[11]

Before World War II, in spite of the notable presence of minority casual laborers, in large cities most casual laborers were white and American-born. They were usually in-migrants from the countryside, where mechanization had made them superfluous. Almost all had permanently separated from their families. In fact, these were distinctly *non*family, nonhousehold people. The few who had wives or children were rarely in contact with them and had cut off most other typical family ties as well.[12]

When a lifelong single laborer became feeble or too old for hard physical work, he survived with odd jobs and rough domestic work such as raking leaves or shoveling cinders. As such work gave out, as it did during the 1930s when younger men competed for marginal jobs, the older men went on starvation economy programs, moved to the cheapest lodging houses, lived on as little as 25 cents a day, and then pawned what they could of their possessions (including overcoats and eyeglasses) to pay their hotel bills, trusting to odd jobs for their food. As a last resort, single laborers applied for work or aid at a mission, a Salvation Army wood yard, or a soup kitchen. After age sixty-five, all but the strongest were forced to go to an almshouse or hospital for at least part of the year.[13]

Although lodging houses were overwhelmingly a male workers' realm, women lived there as well. In 1890, a San Francisco reporter asked the keeper of a 10-cent lodging house what he did when women applied for a room. "If they've got the money [15 or 20 cents] we try and put them in a room by themselves," answered the desk clerk. When the reporter asked what happened if they did not have the money, the clerk replied, "Well, if they've only got ten cents, or the other rooms are full, they have to take their chances with the rest."[14] Women were as many as one out of ten migrant workers during the depression; national estimates then ranged from 14,000 to 50,000 women on the road. In New York City's Bowery district, perhaps the nation's most famous lodging house zone, out of the sixty-three cheapest hotels, three were for women and four for boys. In most cities, commercial and social services for women were not nearly as well developed as those for men. Bertha Thompson, better known as Box-Car Bertha, wrote about using women's informal information networks to find urban housing, often shared with other women.[15] Nonetheless, cheap lodging house districts had the most skewed gender distribution of all types of residential hotel areas, as shown in a series of age and sex pyramids drawn for Chicago in 1920 (fig. 5.6).[16] Even in the cheap lodging house pyramid, with its dramatic curve for men, women make up a clearly discernible proportion, many of them living in small dilapidated rooming houses that had sunk to lodging house prices and standards.

Urban lodging houses also served as repair stations for work place casualties. In the decades when few employers paid for incapacitating injuries at work and when few workers had a labor union or insurance, handicapping accidents or job-caused diseases sent thousands of single workers each year to permanent hotel life in the city. Casual laborers knew the county hospitals, dispensaries, and medical colleges in large cities. In 1911, according to Alice Solenberger's study of one thousand men in Chicago's cheap lodging houses, one-fourth were either temporarily crippled or permanently maimed.[17]

The most desperate lodging house denizens were those whose incomes made housing hard to find and who in addition had the bad luck, marginal psychiatric state, or personal weaknesses to keep them out of all housing except commercial hotels, police stations, or public institutions. These outcasts often became permanently unemployed and castigated as "industrially inefficient." Solenberger deduced that 9 percent of the dependent tramps and bums—the people who dreamed and drank more than they worked—did so because they were mentally ill.

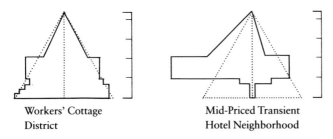

Workers' Cottage
District

Mid-Priced Transient
Hotel Neighborhood

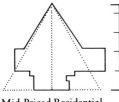

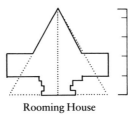

Mid-Priced Residential
Hotel Neighborhood

Rooming House
District

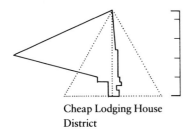

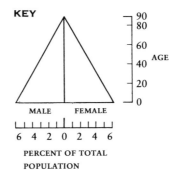

Cheap Lodging House
District

KEY

90
80
60
40 AGE
20
0

MALE   FEMALE

6   4   2   0   2   4   6

PERCENT OF TOTAL
POPULATION

FIGURE 5.6. Age-sex pyramids for Chicago hotel
neighborhoods in 1920. Dotted lines indicate the national average, with young people at the base, elderly at
the top. Males are on the left of each pyramid, females
on the right. Men particularly predominate in cheap
lodging houses; women are prominent in rooming
houses and midpriced areas.

Heavy drinking also led to underemployment of hotel residents, although only a tenth of the drinkers in lodging houses may have been true alcoholics. Reports of cocaine, heroin, or morphine addiction also came from the cheap lodging houses more often than from the more polite hotel ranks.[18]

Low-caste professional crooks found both shelter and a continual supply of hapless victims in cheap hotels. When migrant workers got to town, the tricksters and prostitutes were ready for them. Robbing men while they were drunk or asleep became something of a specialty near lodging houses. Narcotics sellers, bootleggers, and pickpockets could also be found in hotel areas of all sorts.[19] Outside observers assumed everyone was a criminal in San Francisco's Barbary Coast, the zone of rooming houses, boardinghouses, saloons, and manufacturing buildings located between Chinatown and the piers. In cheap San Francisco hotels in the nineteenth century, the verb "to shanghai" replaced "to crimp" for the process of drugging or knocking out sailors and then sending them out to sea as unwilling crews on ships (while the lodging house master pocketed the saved-up pay the sailor had just given him). Reporters said conditions in other ports were similar or worse.[20] On the subject of criminals living in lodging houses, Riis and other reformers loved to quote New York's Police Superintendent Thomas Byrnes, the most famous detective of his era. In the 1880s, Byrnes had traced 27 percent of the city's police book arrests to men who lived in the cheap hotel district. The lodging houses, he said, were "nurseries of crime."[21]

In spite of the dire pronouncements of people like Byrnes and early sociologists, single casual laborers did not lead socially disorganized lives. The historian Robert Slayton has shown how casual laborers thoroughly knew their place within an elaborate social hierarchy. To match the general outline of the workers' social structure and income variations, hotel owners offered a hierarchy of cheap lodging houses.

NO-FAMILY HOUSES

Hoboes, home guard workers, tramps, and bums constituted a tough group of customers. However, hotel owners and managers rose to the challenge, spurred on by the potential for reliable profits. As Slayton has argued, the value and cash price of different types of lodging houses were based on the degree of privacy and autonomy they offered their residents. The higher the price, the greater the privacy.[22] The lower the price, the more one lived in a group. From top to bottom, however, cheap lodging houses were home to people largely living outside the family and without access to the rest of the city; lodging houses were the ultimate "no-family house."[23]

Architecturally, cheap rooming houses shared features with their richer rooming house cousins. Typically, neither rooming houses nor lodging houses had dining or restaurant facilities. Only when they were very large or in old midpriced hotel buildings did they have any lobby or reading room on the ground floor. Their neighborhood locations sometimes overlapped. Nonetheless, prospective tenants quickly learned to distinguish an inexpensive rooming house from a cheap lodging house. The respectable rooming house operator always charged by the week or the month; the cheap lodging house keeper charged by the day and only occasionally offered weekly rates. To reach the stairs of a smaller lodging house of the nineteenth century, tenants often had to walk through a saloon where the bartender doubled as the desk clerk. In other buildings, the doors between street and stairs often gave clear architectural signals—the better rank of dwelling usually having side windows and more of a setback from the sidewalk.[24] Interior features, however, were most important. Once one left the doors and the stairs, lodging houses showed themselves to be very different from rooming houses.

Rooms, cubicles, wards, and flops. Price normally separated lodging house amenities into three very distinct levels: (1) full private rooms for 25 to 40 cents a night; (2) semiprivate cubicles or open wards for 15 to 25 cents a night; and finally, (3) flophouses that charged from 5 to 10 cents a night for a dry space on an open floor (fig. 5.7).[25] All these prices are for the 1920s.

For 40 cents, the tired laborer in a private-room lodging house had a room, 10 feet by 10 feet or smaller in dimension. In 1913, a San Francisco health inspector gave this telegraphic description of a small 40-cents-a-night lodging house used by both men and women:

Folsom Street rooming house. Three-story frame. Saloon on first floor. Thirty-nine rooms [upstairs]. Skylight in hall does not ventilate. Five inside rooms on

FIGURE 5.7.   Cheap lodging house rates. The entrance to a skid row hotel on West Main Street in Norfolk, Virginia, in 1941.

FIGURE 5.8.   Hotels on the Bowery in New York City, photographed in 1986. These tall lodging houses and other structures remain from the years before World War I.

FIGURE 5.9. Cubicles in a high-ceilinged loft space, photographed before 1923. The partitions are about 7 feet tall.

each floor have window in unventilated hall. One fire escape; one stairway; large hall; four toilets; four baths; twelve stationary basins. Hot water in bath rooms. . . . Many rooms have double beds.[26]

As the inspector's figures show, each floor had a men's and women's bathroom, for a ratio of one bath to every ten rooms. In most cheap lodging houses, the one to five rooming house ratio fell to one to ten or one to twenty—a ratio hovering at or below the legal minimums.[27] For the entire building, in Chicago or New York, five or more stories were common (fig. 5.8). In smaller cities, three or four stories were the rule.

Inside the 40-cent lodging house, the minimum list of room furnishings might be only a dilapidated bed (sometimes with a straw mattress), one rickety chair, and a hook for clothes. At the very best, conditions might match those of the largest cheap lodging house in San Francisco, the Central Hotel, where the 440 rooms were tiny, but most had a small dresser and a basin with hot and cold running water.[28]

For only 25 cents (again, in 1920s prices), the tired and nearly broke renter could stay in either a cubicle- or a ward-style lodging house. The patrons called the cubicles "cages" or "cribs": they were stalls made of wood or corrugated iron partitions about seven feet high. These partial walls offered visual privacy inside large loft spaces whose ceilings were ten to fourteen feet high (fig. 5.9). Having several hundred cubicles in one building was not unusual. The cubicles measured as little as five by seven feet for a single bed or seven by seven feet with two cots or a double bed. The remaining area inside a cubicle left room for a chair and space for the occupant to pull off his or her clothes.

In cubicle hotels, the manager's provision of a chair was not always assured but very handy. Veteran lodgers folded their clothes and placed them *under* the chair to prevent their being hooked with fishing tackle from over the partition. Cubicles earned their "cage" nickname from the chicken wire that managers stretched over the open tops of stalls to prevent thefts and to keep people from sleeping in the spaces without paying. After the installation of electricity, each cubicle might have its own 15-watt bulb; before then, gaslights overhead lit the whole space.[29]

The cubicle room's great significance—having a private space to lock and a room for coming and going as one pleased—was the most important boundary in the range of privacy and independence offered by cheap lodging houses.[30] At the next lower level were the open dormitory wards, areas crowded with rough homemade bunk beds or cots. In such a dormitory area, each guest had at the most a locker for clothes. If one did not have a locker, one World War II resident remembered, "one major problem was what to do with your wallet when you took a shower."[31] In some dormitory wards, tenants could gain access to the room only after dark; at 6:00 A.M. the sleepers would all be roused and moved out. Seasonal peaks at urban industrial sites or months of high unemployment packed the dormitory areas with residents. Edith Abbott gives this graphic description of a ward-type lodging house in a good working-class suburb near Chicago in the 1920s:

The beds were not clean, and very often were occupied by relays of men, the day shift and the night shift, the bedding scarcely becoming cold after one occupant had left it.... This is known as the "hot bed."... The beds were usually left unmade, a higher rental being charged if the boarding-housekeeper attended to their making.[32]

Most cheap lodging houses offered a mixture of rooms, cubicles, and wards to compensate for fluctuations in occupancy. A Folsom Street hotel in San Francisco offered 10-cent beds in a dormitory behind the first-floor saloon, 15-cent cubicles in the interior of the loft spaces above, and a few 25-cent cubicles that had windows on the street or alley. Of the 101 licensed cheap lodging houses in New York City in

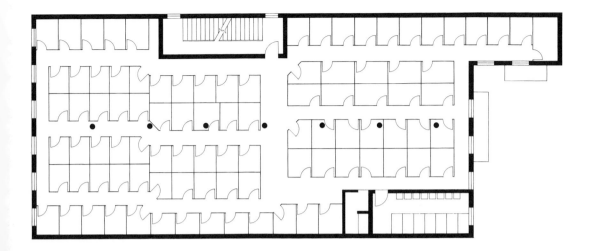

1905, 36 were of the full-room or cubicle type, 34 were of the open ward type, and the remaining 31 had both wards and cubicles. It was typical to put wards on the remote upper floors of tall buildings and cubicles on the second or third floor (fig. 5.10). Thousands of people in most large cities lived whole seasons and from year to year in cubicle and ward hotels.[33] Cubicle lodging houses had a direct building-type equivalent in crib or cage bordellos, some of them with hundreds of tiny cubicles, some fit with window shades that rolled up when patrons put in coins. Other bordellos and cheap lodging houses had canvas walls instead of matched lumber partitions.[34]

FIGURE 5.10. Typical floor plan with cubicles, ca. 1900. Reconstructed from a rough 1980s diagram of the Kenton Hotel on the Bowery in New York City. Varied cubicle sizes and angled passageways were common.

If a cubicle hotel offered heat (not all of them did), it came from over-worked and red-hot stoves often strategically blocking the narrow pas-sages between cubicles. In some lodging houses, the only conditions worse than the heating supply were the vermin, general filth, and hor-rific smells, all resulting from the conditions of the tenants themselves, bad hotel maintenance, and poor ventilation. Lice, other bedbugs, and mice were constant problems. A San Francisco reporter wrote that "the persistent scratching of the sleepers proclaimed that their beds had other tenants that were not asleep."[35] During cold weather, people in the front or rear cubicles closed their windows, thus sealing the venti-lation for the whole floor. In hot weather, the few windows (open or not) were completely inadequate. In short, year-round there was virtu-ally no ventilation at all. In some corners, odors of urine or foul cloth-ing overwhelmed tenants and visiting inspectors alike. Spittoons were everywhere, and one observer wrote that "it is the general custom in

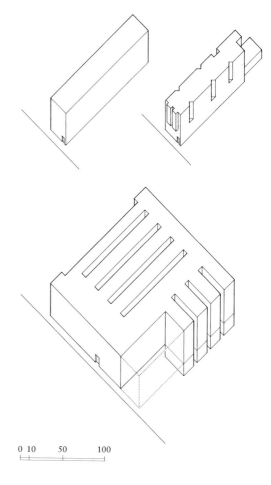

FIGURE 5.11. Three types of cheap lodging houses. All were built in San Francisco from 1906 to 1909. *Top left,* a 39-room hotel annex in a loft structure with no specialized light wells; *top right,* a 35-room hotel on the two upper floors with below-code light wells; *bottom,* the Central Hotel, with 440 tiny rooms and minimal light wells satisfying early codes.

0 10   50   100

lodging houses to require those who spit profusely to spread a newspaper on the floor beside their beds."[36] In some cubicle hotels, as few as two toilets served 180 occupants. Bathtubs or showers may have been absent altogether. Residents might find one common drinking cup per floor and common towels that one critic compared to "those in a fourth-class printing office." Managers kept staff to a minimum; therefore, the beds, walls, and floors stayed unclean.[37]

Not surprisingly, disease conditions, social concerns, and fire dangers brought cheap lodging houses repeatedly to the attention of city officials. In 1917, the state of California outlawed construction of new cubicle hotels. Since that time, code enforcement and downtown development have gradually eliminated all cubicle rooms in San Francisco, although their use continued in the city through the 1950s. In Chicago, a 1963 sample of lodging house residents found that 75 percent of the 10,690 respondents still lived in cubicle hotels. Nine percent lived in missions, and only 16 percent lived in private room hotels. In a 1986 estimate, New York City still had 3,500 people living permanently in cubicles and dormitory beds, some of the buildings dating from the 1890s.[38]

Most cubicle lodging houses were in temporary buildings or general-use lofts erected with light industrial or warehouse uses in mind (fig. 5.11). The Bonanza House was a 55-foot by 100-foot loft building that stood next to several similar buildings on San Francisco's Market Street in 1885. In the basement were a saloon and a bakery oven; an eating establishment occupied the first floor. The second and third floors were lodgings, probably of the cubicle sort, and a shoe factory occupied the top floor.[39] Not all cubicle hotels were such large structures. In 1906, the builders of Thomas Turish's lodging house in San Francisco's South of Market district fit sixteen rooms into what today would look like a long two-car garage—a one-story wood frame structure on a back alley lot with no apparent source of heat.[40]

Not even cubicle conditions matched the lowest lodging house variant, the flophouse. Ten-cent flophouses often occupied two or three floors of a loft building—one similar to those used for cubicle hotels but usually in poorer condition. Flops had no permanent installations whatsoever, rarely even beds. Some had mattresses or piles of rags with a blanket available. Others had long rows of canvas hammocks. Others simply offered customers a dry place on the floor where they could unroll their newspapers or bedrolls. Flophouse owners offered no lockers; there was little need of them since the tenants typically owned very little. Most flops did not open until winter, when migrant workers surged into the cities. They were temporary operations and moved from year to year, yet even flophouses with simple canvas slings could turn a profit. Riis knew one otherwise respectable and wealthy New Yorker who operated three such establishments and made $8,000 a year clear profit.[41]

Still lower on the commercial scale were informal private lodging houses—unlicensed dives where a lodger could sleep in a corner of a tenement room for 5 cents, or for 3 cents curl up in a sheltered hallway and not be moved out until morning. By the 1920s, the owners of all-night movie theaters had added to the urban landscape a variant of the flophouse. Local law in some cities (including San Francisco) closed movie theaters at night. Local law in other cities, such as Los Angeles, allowed people to sleep all night for 5 cents in an uncomfortable wooden seat in a room that was at least dark and dry, if not well ventilated.[42]

While conditions in urban lodging houses could be bad, they were often better than those offered at distant road excavations, mines, or lumber camps. The nineteenth-century U.S. Army set the hoped-for standards for the peacetime industrial army; real conditions could be much worse. At one lumber camp in 1916, inspectors found tents with men crammed into triple makeshift bunks with only straw for mattresses. At Baltimore's suburban Sparrows Point steel plant in the 1890s, two thousand laborers (mostly recent immigrants and blacks) rented space in the plant's barracks—long rows of one-room shanties, 10 feet by 14 feet, built of rough pine boards and roofed with tar paper. Each room housed four men, who provided their own mattresses, stove, and fuel; only after 1904 were a shower house and cookhouse available. Low rent and direct proximity to work were the advantages; at $2 to $3 per month per man, only charity lodging houses could have beaten the price.[43]

Subsidized missions. The urban provisions for day laborers and the elderly poor alarmed politicians, philanthropists, and social activists. They waged sporadic campaigns to offer subsidized alternatives to the cubicle and flophouse hotels, just as institutional alternatives were provided for the other hotel ranks. Some attempts were minimal. In the 1890s in Chicago, for instance, the city opened up the floors of the City Hall; on winter nights as many as two thousand people slept there. More commonly, police rounded up (or took in) street denizens in downtown police stations overnight. There, the tenants found stern, clean, and usually unpadded benches or plank platforms for beds (fig. 5.12). Police lodgings served a relatively small group. In 1889 in New York City, only 400 people—half of them women—slept in the police lodgings each night, while an average of 13,000 New Yorkers slept in commercial lodging houses.[44]

Progressive Era reformers lobbied strongly for better public facilities. New York opened America's first municipal lodging house (other than police lodgings) in 1896. By 1902, seven other large American cities had such buildings, and up to World War I the numbers grew. At these, indigents could sleep a few nights on an iron cot and receive two meals

a day—at least rolls and coffee—if they agreed to put up with interrogation, fumigation, a shower, a promise of docile behavior, and often at least two hours a day chopping wood or cleaning alleys. During periods of high employment, the number of lodgers dropped sharply. During World War I, most cities closed their lodging houses for lack of use; cities reopened their shelters as the rural economy worsened in the 1920s and rapidly augmented them during the depression. By the 1920s in progressive states, counties augmented urban shelters with county relief homes or work farms.[45]

A few philanthropists also subsidized the construction of landmark workers' hotels. The benefactors relinquished the usual 15 percent or more made on urban real estate investments but expected a safe 6 or 7 percent return nonetheless. The most famous East Coast example, the 1897 Mills Hotel built by Darius O. Mills, covered an entire block

FIGURE 5.12. The men's lodging room in a New York City police station typifies overcrowding in a makeshift institutional flophouse. To both sides, note the feet of men sleeping on platforms and chairs.

FIGURE 5.13. Exterior view of the Mills Hotel No. 1, built in 1897 as a subsidized lodging house on Bleeker Street in New York City.

FIGURE 5.14. Schedules and regulations posted in a mission window in Dubuque, Iowa, 1940.

front in Greenwich Village and visually dominated the neighborhood. By the 1960s, its social situation had devolved to such an extent that it became the first hotel in New York to be called a "welfare hotel," but that was hardly Mills's intention (fig. 5.13). Its designer, the well-known reform architect Ernest Flagg, included 1,500 well-ventilated cubicle rooms, each five by seven feet.[46] On the West Coast, the palace of workingmen's lodgings was San Diego's Golden West Hotel, a three-story concrete structure of 450 private rooms designed in 1913. While the Mills Hotel is now remodeled as a chic condominium, the Golden West is still a workingmen's hotel. Urban philanthropy standards were also matched at the better company towns built in the United States after 1900.[47]

In 1891, the Salvation Army opened its first U.S. operations in New York; ten years later, they had forty-four missions in the country; by the 1920s, their numerous buildings and enthusiastic marching bands automatically invoked images of a fundamentalist struggle to save souls and to offer free or nearly free beds and food. The Salvation Army was one part of a wide range of missions and shelters that various benevolent groups began to sponsor after the Civil War. Some were simply basement or upper-floor flophouses, and their sanitary problems rivaled the worst commercial conditions. The field notes about one shelter in St. Paul tersely said, "Charitable Institution. . . . Old Opera House made over; Fire Marshall condemned it."[48]

The supervision in institutional lodging houses was, of course, as notoriously strict as that in municipal lodging houses (fig. 5.14). Institutional lodgings were generally cleaner than cheap commercial lodgings, and they also offered meals, either free (in return for a sermon or prayer meeting) or at very cheap rates. A work shift at San Francisco's Salvation Army wood yard, for instance, entitled men to a bed ticket and a 20-cent meal ticket that could be split into a 5-cent and a 15-cent meal. At the wood yard (a vacant lot) men cut and stacked cords of wood for sale to the public. Some missions also gave out tickets redeemable for meals or lodging at nearby commercial establishments. In a few large northern cities, separate "Negro Corps" were formed; southern Salvation Army services for blacks were segregated until the Supreme Court's decision on segregation in 1954.[49]

For single hoboes, housing options other than cheap lodging houses or missions were slim. Their chance of securing a polite apartment was no more likely than attaining a berth on a luxury ocean liner. Groups of single laborers occasionally ganged together to rent a tenement space and to hire a cook. The places they could get were in the worst tenements or back rooms and cost $1.50 each per week in 1910. In the mid-1920s, a clean-living casual laborer might (with a persistent search) secure a windowless hall bedroom in a low-end rooming house for $2 to $3 a week, probably around the corner from a cheap lodging house. For comparison, a cubicle room or flophouse cost $2 or less a week.[50]

ZONES FOR SINGLE LABORERS: SKID ROW AND CHINATOWN

By the 1950s, most Americans had learned to use the pejorative term *skid row* for large areas of cheap lodging houses and their surroundings. But before the 1950s, these areas—with their high concentration of hotel housing—were very different places, for which the term *single laborers' zone* might be more appropriate. Even if polite citizens had rarely been to a skid row area, the names of those areas evoked vivid images. People often knew the area by the name of its major street: in

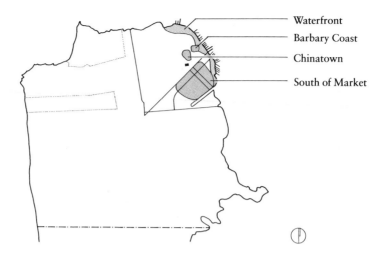

Waterfront
Barbary Coast
Chinatown
South of Market

FIGURE 5.15. Single workers' neighborhoods in San Francisco. The small black rectangle is Union Square. Streets indicated in the South of Market are Third, Fourth, and Howard.

New York, the Bowery; in Minneapolis, Upper Hennepin Avenue; in Baltimore, Pratt Street; in Boston, Scollay Square; in Chicago, the Main Stem on West Madison Street; in Los Angeles, South Main Street.[51] Large cities typically had more than one single laborers' zone, and San Francisco had three: Third and Howard streets in the South of Market, the waterfront and Barbary Coast area, and Chinatown (fig. 5.15). Common characteristics of the people inhabiting these districts were unskilled and low-paid work, living outside of a private household of any sort, and being ostracized from the rest of the city. Differentiating the fates of the various districts were the survival of the jobs, the nature of activities mixed into the district, the degree of social ostracization, and competition for the land itself.

The migrant workers' South of Market.   San Francisco's huge district south of Market Street had several neighborhoods within it, most of them packed with immigrant families living in tiny cottages and three-room flats. Before World War II, the area was overwhelmingly white. In 1960, the population of the district was still over 75 percent white, with 14 percent black and 9 percent Asian. The South of Market flour mills, sawmills, refineries, printing plants, and machine shops generated large numbers of jobs for skilled workers and unskilled casual laborers.

Outsiders knew Third Street and Howard Street as *the* South of Market; these streets were the core of the casual workers' South of Market (fig. 5.16). Migrants often arrived in the railroad freight yards and walked north along Third Street. By the time they reached the corner

FIGURE 5.16. Third Street in San Francisco, 1953. Above the first floor virtually every building is a workers' hotel built before 1920. Today, this is approximately the location of the Moscone Convention Center.

of Third and Howard they would have found all that they needed to be at home for the day, week, or month. A 1914 survey estimated that 40,000 single men lived in the South of Market at the peak of the winter, and half of the city's cheap lodging house rooms were in the district.[52] About a third of these men were permanent city residents.

By the turn of the century, Third and Howard streets were a typical single and migrant laborers' zone, a place that mixed cheap work, cheap rooms, cheap liquor, and cheap clothes. At its heart were multiple employment agencies in rented storefronts. Seven major employment offices competed next to each other on Howard Street between Third and Fourth, a very long block that is the site of the present-day Moscone Convention Center; other, similar agencies were located in the surrounding blocks.[53] Early in the day and in times of high employment, the agency clerks filled their shop windows and the interior walls with chalked placards listing jobs. At the beckoning of "800 HANDS TO COLUSA—SOUTHERN PACIFIC RR" or "40 SHOVELERS—4TH STREET," the men would be off to work for the day or the month. Outside the

FIGURE 5.17. A labor agency on New York City's Lower West Side, 1910.

labor agencies men would stand and wait to register for work or for other listings to appear (fig. 5.17). In 1907, Nels Anderson and a friend stood on Omaha's great hobo employment center, Douglas Street, and estimated that they could see a thousand men on the streets and sidewalks. In slack times, the sidewalks outside the labor agencies were still the prime outdoor loitering and meeting spots of the workers' zone. People often loitered on the sidewalks throughout the year in such districts because there was no place to sit other than in a bar, card room, or other commercial establishment.[54]

Other prominent elements of the South of Market were workingmen's saloons. Along Third, men found the greatest concentrations of workers' saloons, many with back room "bookie joints" that were legal until 1938. By 1910, San Francisco's saloons no longer served a free lunch, but they offered hearty 10- to 15-cent meals with the purchase of a glass of beer. Nearby were a distinctly grubby class of pool rooms and penny arcades. An occasional amusement hall, concert saloon with its cheerful and gladdening bathing beauties, and later, cheap movie theaters all added to the mix along the ground floors. Upstairs through much of the zone would be the cheap rooms, cubicles, and dormitory spaces of the lodging houses.

Single laborers' zones also offered essential retail services for the workingman. San Francisco's South of Market had fifty-one second-hand clothing stores, twenty-one of them on the employment-office block of Howard Street alone. Retailers offering new clothing did not do so for "gents," as in the rooming house districts, but called themselves "outfitters": they sold serviceable boots, Levis, heavy shirts, and gloves for distant work camps. Trunk shops and storage locker businesses catered to men leaving town for a season. Radical bookstores supplied reading material aimed at a workers' revolution. A third of the city's pawn shops were also in the district, not far from charity missions and the Salvation Army "institute" or wood yard, which was on a side street. There were barber colleges offering free haircuts, medical and dental schools offering low-cost clinics. Men could also get dental work done on credit in the single workers' zone. In San Francisco, Greek migration was strong after 1910, and the local colony of Greeks began to run South of Market tea- and coffeehouses and inexpensive restaurants frequented by single men. In the evenings, some of the shops offered exotic dance shows. Houses of prostitution or assignation were never far away, but the single workers' zone in any city had fewer women and children visible on its streets than any other residential or commercial district of the city.

Bargain eating shops filled the interstices of the South of Market. Near cheap lodging houses workers always found the most reasonably priced food. A few large lodging houses had inexpensive eateries in them and offered American plan rates to their residents. Most lodging house tenants at the turn of the century, however, relied on saloon fare and the cheapest 5-cent to 15-cent lunchrooms available. For breakfast, San Francisco's Bolz Coffee Parlor promised "three of the largest doughnuts ever fried and the biggest cup of coffee in the world" for 10 cents. Coffee Dan's advertised "one thousand beans with bread, butter, and coffee" for 15 cents.[55] On a crash economy program, a man or a woman could eat three meager meals a day for as little as 30 cents in the mid-1920s. One elderly man gave this minimum-price daily menu:

Breakfast: "coffee and," 5 cents; sometimes with mush, 5 cents extra
Noon: hash, soup, bread, and coffee, 10 cents
Supper: stew, bread, and coffee, 15 cents[56]

At such rates, neither food nor service enticed the diners' palates. Over-worked waiters got plastered with food; stale bread and sour milk were common.[57] The cheapest meals were mission provisions given out free (fig. 5.18).

Life in the South of Market and other American migrant workers' areas began to change in the 1920s because of shifts in the demand for cheap work. As owners mechanized their factory, farm, mine, road-building, and lumber operations, they dramatically cut the need for casual migrant workers. The remaining migrants began to drive rickety automobiles to their work; in Kansas in 1926, for instance, over half the harvest workers came to the wheat fields by car. Having gradually lost the business of robust migrant workers who arrived by train, districts like the South of Market began to be identified more with the home guard.[58]

San Francisco had two other well-known single workers' areas. The Barbary Coast, although much tamed after its rebuilding from the 1906 fire, was still considered a disorderly district. It housed a great number of San Francisco's single sailors and longshoremen.[59] Inexpensive rooming houses and cheap lodging houses dominated the housing supply, mixed with various wholesalers' lofts, bawdy saloons, and houses of prostitution. San Francisco was the base for thousands of military men, and in their off-duty hours they often gravitated to the Barbary Coast (to the chagrin of their officers). After World War II, with the rapid decline of work for San Francisco's break-bulk water-front, the port workers were no longer needed; the recreational culture of the area was seen as an increasing threat. Not surprisingly, the Barbary Coast and waterfront areas were early targets of official and private redevelopment beginning in the 1950s. In the adjacent Chinatown, however, the neighborhood in 1990 stood much as it was rebuilt after the 1906 fire, and had similar uses.

Racial rooming house districts: The Chinatown example. The racial ghettos of many cities have had a high number of inexpensive hotel homes. San Francisco's Chinatown was somewhat unique, since the Chinese were imported as inexpensive laborers early in the city's history and were allowed, even after the fire, to remain in their downtown location—a three-block by seven-block Chinatown crammed with

boardinghouses and lodging houses. In some ways, Chinatown was much like the Anglo South of Market. Chinatown had many privately owned cheap lodging houses and some better rooming houses; in 1980, half of the area's housing units were still in SROs. Chinatown's streets and basements were filled with affordable retail services and employment offices. There were counterparts to the missions, although Christian missions in Chinatown more vigorously took on acculturation as well as salvation. The population was largely male—but for a different reason. Until the 1960s, federal law forbade importation of wives and created a bachelor society in Chinatown. Wage conditions for the Chinese were even worse than those faced by American-born casual workers. Because of ghetto confinement, the Chinese neighborhood could not expand in spite of population pressures. Hence, the hotel housing conditions were worse. Whites, especially city officials and the police, saw Chinatown as a convenient place to dump (or not see) unsavory characters and illicit activities, even though this meant that gambling

FIGURE 5.18. Compulsory prayer before dinner at a charitable mission, Dubuque, Iowa, 1940.

houses, brothels, and drug dens were mixed with a law-abiding population of workers. As in other racial ghettos, a few local residents profited from the dumping process.[60]

Chinatown hotel buildings built after the 1906 earthquake, on their exterior, looked just like their counterparts in the South of Market or waterfront areas. The rooms and windows were similar sizes, often matching code minimums. Inside, however, the forces of economics, management, and ownership forced densities four times those assumed in the building standards. The Chinatown lodging house rooms were crowded with bunk beds. Men commonly slept in shifts, and tenants often did their own cooking in simple communal kitchens. To help each other ignore this appalling population density, Anglos used cultural stereotypes such as "the Chinese tolerate crowding better than white people." Whites (not aware that Chinese were rarely allowed to own property) also defended the densities by pointing to Chinese-managed family association buildings, which had similar densities on their living floors. The multiuse family association buildings functioned in part as subsidized lodging houses. On the ground floor would be commercial spaces leased to leading association members; on the second and third floors were crowded hotel rooms that housed bachelor members; on the top floor were offices, meeting rooms, or social halls for the entire association.[61]

San Francisco's Chinatown was neither monolithic nor completely Chinese. Almost immediately it became an important tourist zone and (on a square-footage basis) probably did far more profitable retail business than did the Howard Street businesses. White workers and non-Chinese Asians also lived in significant numbers on the edges of Chinatown. In the late 1800s, Mexican workers lived directly to the east. After 1900, Manilatown—a concentration of thirty-seven hotels housing up to 10,000 Filipino workers—straddled the border between the core of Chinatown and the Barbary Coast. The workers used the Lucky M Pool Hall as their informal information center. San Francisco's International Hotel, of 1977 eviction fame, was a workers' hotel of a fairly typical 184-room size built in 1907 (fig. 5.19). Twelve stores filled the ground floor, and billiard halls and a well-known nightclub were housed in its basement.[62] A block to the west, in 1939, the permanent residents of the border-location Clayton Hotel revealed the

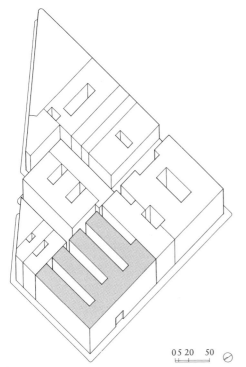

FIGURE 5.19. Axonometric view of the International Hotel and surrounding buildings in Manilatown, San Francisco. The 184-room hotel (shaded) was built in 1907 with more generous light wells and larger rooms than average. In this block, most structures are hotels.

0 5 20   50

area's ethnic and racial mixture: 25 Filipino, 15 Chinese, and 22 white workers.

While most Chinese were segregated into Chinatowns, city authorities on the West Coast allowed Japanese immigrants to operate and live in rooming and lodging houses in several districts of the city, usually outside of Chinatown. Some white workers preferred Japanese-leased hotels because of their management style. In San Francisco's Western Addition, Japanese-managed hotels seem to have been racially mixed; in the South of Market, all-Japanese residents were more the rule.[63]

Until the 1930s, San Francisco had a very small black population. However, in other cities lodging house districts for blacks were similar to San Francisco's Chinatown. Like Chinatowns, black lodging house districts crowded workers (who were paid less than their white counterparts), suffered from double housing standards in city inspection and code enforcement, and endured a high proportion of unsavory uses dumped there by outsiders. The several-block area of cheap lodging houses in the middle of Chicago's Black Belt was a prime example. It served thousands of black workers who were hired by the railroads and meat packers, where blacks could get jobs earlier than they could in most other industries (fig. 5.20). In 1990, it remained as one of the largest remaining SRO concentrations on the city's South Side.[64]

Another lodging house pattern, front-gate lodgings, served workers stranded at an eccentric industrial location. For large factories initially built beyond the edge of the city, speculators often built nearby clusters of rooming and lodging houses as well as family houses and flats. San Francisco's Union Iron Works, for instance, employed up to 5,000 men but was four miles from Third and Howard. The hour walk each way to and from the factory cut too much into the casual laborer's day. By 1900—with the factory owners actively encouraging the development—the workers could choose from over thirty commercial wooden rooming and lodging houses and almost as many saloons within three blocks of the factory gate (fig. 5.21).[65]

Rationales for lodging house life.   For the men and women who lived in cheap lodging houses, the looming advantage was low price. But cheap lodging houses had other advantages. For the indigent elderly, the advantage of ambulatory independence in a central location was particularly prominent. (This was true of other ranks of hotel life as well.) As long as older tenants could walk, they could meet their own needs. California researchers found that elderly residents cherished their independence. Anderson described areas of a few blocks that satisfied all the employment and services needed by former hoboes. A great many of the aged men and women who lived their last years in cheap lodgings lived in grim surroundings. Yet the psychological benefits of maintaining their personal choice and self-reliance seemed to be the most important attractions of staying in hotel housing, just as it is for the elderly in hotel housing today.[66] For workers, cheap hotels and their staff also provided specific stabilizing services. Before 1925, in the heyday of the cheap lodging house districts, men could turn over their summer earnings to the hotel proprietor, who acted as banker and bursar. This ensured that the hobo or sailor would not lose all his money in one first spree.[67]

For the most outcast people—drifters, unemployables, thieves, or prostitutes—rooming houses simply offered a place to be. Technically, state laws required hotel managers to accept any reasonable person for one night, although managers did not have to accept everyone on a weekly or monthly basis. On occasion, however, landlords welcomed

FIGURE 5.20. Hotels for black workers on Chicago's South Side. The Hotel Warner and Memorial Hotel on Cottage Grove Street, photographed in 1950.

long-term tenants who were outcasts elsewhere. Poor casual laborers made up a reliable market for slumlords and honest landlords alike. By renting to hoboes, building owners with a warm heart or a dilapidated and unrentable loft space could invest very little money and yet reap a tidy profit. A madam could pay substantially higher leases than other tenants and pay additional sums under the table to the building owner, to district politicians, or to the police. The flophouse floor, even with its vermin, was still a viable commercial space.

The financial pressures on managers who leased cheap hotels probably did the most to open places for outcast people. Each month the lease had to be paid. Only rented rooms brought income. When rooms were going empty, or where the architectural or sanitary conditions were already at a low ebb, undesirable tenants were better than no tenants at all. Managers of "no-tell hotels" that allowed men to take women to their rooms found that they could charge a higher rent. Harvey Zorbaugh asked one hotel keeper how many married couples there were in her house. Her answer: "I don't know—I don't ask. I want to rent my rooms."[68] As long as couples paid, she did not oversee their moral life as old-fashioned boardinghouse keepers might have done. Such management realities, taken to their extreme, fostered the worst social and physical conditions of all types of inexpensive hotels.

FIGURE 5.21. Line of wooden rooming houses near the Union Iron Works shipyards in San Francisco, photographed just before demolition in 1918. The closest building was probably intended to be temporary.

For so-called homeless men, cheap hotels and the area around them were also more than shelter. They were a significant part of hobo identity, just as suburban houses became important for family identity in the middle and upper class. However, unlike suburban houses or better hotels, cheap lodgings were more important as a *type* of building than as individual structures. The way casual laborers relied on built space contrasted with the manner of the middle and upper class. Wealthy hotel dwellers lived in highly individualistic buildings; their hotel homes were part of an elaborate and individuated material culture system. Midpriced or palace hotel residents could further anchor their identities with their professions, marriage partners, personal pedigrees, and clothes or other possessions. Single laborers, who moved often and easily from one cheap lodging house to another, relied on a more generalized use of the city fabric. They lived largely within a nonmaterialistic and verbal subculture. The social organization and membership in the American day laborer's subculture relied less on unique possessions and more on story telling and social drinking. While less individually anchored to specific buildings, casual laborers were nonetheless identified with hotels as a group. The anthropologist James Spradley has maintained that flops (places to sleep) made up the most significant set of words in hobo language and culture; no other American group had so many words for places to sleep.[69] Other recent research suggests that, among no-family people, setting in large part can *become* lifestyle. The hotels, street corners, parks, and businesses of cheap lodging house districts—even though fluidly used and seen as virtually interchangeable—provided an essential and meaningful backdrop for the single laborers' individual and social worlds. Cheap lodging house districts socially countered the low esteem of hobo employment and provided an island in a hostile dominant society.[70]

Employers and bankers could see advantages to lodging house life, too. The individual freedom of people living completely apart from a family and without material possessions dovetailed precisely with the needs of employers for maximum flexibility and control over a set of workers. The single, more atomized residents of cheap hotels could adjust more easily than family-tied workers to the whimsy of economic demand for a risky new business or a sudden big contract.[71] At a more abstract level of capital circulation, commercial single-room housing had additional benefits for landowners and managers of the middle and upper class. When thousands of workers lived as part of a family or boarded with a family, that rent money went into the family sector; it went back into the control of the private urban community. Hotel life, however, channeled the workers' rent and food money directly into commercial circuits, retail hands, without passing through a private household. More than in family tenement districts, the money of hotel life went into commercial entertainment and commercial socializing. The architecture of the no-family house also displayed these uneasy truces between the renters, the owners, and the employers of the city.

FRONTS FOR EMBARRASSING ECONOMIC REALITIES

The contrast between the core of downtown and any one of the single laborers' districts rarely failed to jar streetcar and automobile travelers. An equally sharp boundary existed between the facades and interiors of the cheapest hotels. Before 1900, the architectural exteriors of lodging houses usually matched interior conditions. The exteriors of the

FIGURE 5.22. San Francisco's International Hotel, photographed in 1977 as demonstrators fought to stop its demolition. The handsome design of the 1907 facade contrasts strongly with its spare lodging house interiors.

run-down, cheaply constructed wooden lodging houses of the nineteenth century stood out like sore thumbs. They *were* sore thumbs: social embarrassments, cultural concerns, and architectural eyesores. However, between 1900 and 1920, with no single great inducement, thousands of landowners in American cities were building more polite facades for their lodging houses, exterior images that matched the new commercial world of downtown. The new structures of course reflected production peaks, especially those of World War I. Yet there seemed to be new cultural rules for these buildings.

Keeping in step with national trends, landowners in San Francisco built remarkably schizophrenic lodging houses. The facades and interiors were disassociated; the exterior design and building materials said little or nothing about the uses of the upper floors or the people who lived inside them (fig. 5.22).[72] The interiors of lodging houses were the most reliable material clues to the social and economic standing of their initial residents. The extreme plumbing ratios, minimum air wells, lack of furniture, and narrow hallways made residents immediately and constantly aware not only of their income but also of their place in society (fig. 5.23). Especially for white and American-born workers, the interiors of cheap lodging houses reinforced their cultural alien-

FIGURE 5.23. Surviving cubicles in a Bowery Hotel. When photographed in 1986, the area was being used for storage. Note articles resting on the wire ceilings of the cubicles.

ation from the rest of urban society.[73] As capital investors saw it, the interiors of cheap lodging houses were embarrassing necessities for agricultural and industrial production and for commercial and transportation service. In contrast to the interior conditions, the architectural exteriors could easily have been mistaken for lofts or small office buildings of the period.

Admittedly, institutional forces nudged the owners along in their decisions to build in this way. New building codes and their efficient enforcement brought grudging interior changes.[74] But beyond specifying brick construction to stop fires and enforcing various height and bulk limitations to guide building density, neither city nor state bureaucracies had stipulated that owners of purpose-built lodging houses commission the construction of nice facades. Indeed, "nice" is the word for the lodging house facades built after 1900: they were dressed up, made more presentable than their forebears (fig. 5.24). The phenomenon was notable in both rooming houses and lodging houses but more remarkable in the cheaper hotels.

The presentable yet schizophrenic facades built after 1900 were one strategy used by landlords to erase embarrassing images of the social and economic marginality in their properties, and to erect reassuring

FIGURE 5.24. A dressed-up lodging house facade in Chicago, contrasting with a more literal side view. Photographed in 1954.

images of greater cultural uniformity. Of course, landowning citizens also built polite exteriors for individual and personal reasons: for future flexibility and better resale values, for personal pride, or for the desire to be more high-minded business people. The new lodging house facades offered the potential for casual workers' neighborhoods to appear to be respectable, minimally threatening, and permanent. Choosing to give cheap hotels facades that were commercial and not residential was an attempt at making them culturally acceptable both to their residents and to outsiders. The public could imagine that the people inside the new buildings were perhaps not so drastically different a subculture as first-floor sidewalk scenes suggested. For outsiders, at least, the respectability of nice facades visually linked the workers' low-priced hotel subcultures to the high-priced environments of the dominant culture. The resident hoboes could appear to share with business people the bridge of commercial culture. For the hoboes themselves, the exterior architectural images might also have helped them to feel more a part of the great commercial core of the metropolis.

For their part, the architects of cheap lodging houses (or, more probably, the skilled drafters working for small contracting firms) also exerted their professional and personal desires for a more elegant city, even though their powers for individually influencing buildings of this class were extremely limited. These structures were economically destined to be generic buildings. In reality, the designers' most essential contributions rested in making the floor plans work while getting the most rentable space out of a cramped downtown site.

The schizophrenic relationship of the lodging house facades and their interiors declared that these sorry material conditions were probably the best that the urban political economy of that era could do—reasonably dress up the front and nominally clean up the interiors. It is significant that the owners dressed up the fronts by their own initiative, while the slower improvement of interior standards required a vigilant network of professional reformers and a succession of political battles.

The quality of life and the eventual life spans of cheap lodging houses were thus linked not only to the employment of their residential customers but also to the work of reformers and a specific generation of owners—the people who, after the turn of the century, built hotel life more permanently than it had ever been before. These improvements notwithstanding, in the eyes of politicians, the public, and professional reformers, neither the interiors nor the facades of *any* lodging houses would ever be adequate. The critics did not want lodging houses and their residents to merge with the city but to vanish entirely. In fact, a coalition of critics intended to prove that no one should live in hotels of any kind—palace, midpriced, rooming house, or lodging house. Given their interests in the hotel business, the hotel property owners naturally stood to disagree. The wide range of the hotel industry itself would prove to work against their common interests.

BUILDING A CIVILIZATION

WITHOUT HOMES

IN 1919, THE SOCIAL HISTORIAN ARTHUR CALHOUN told his readers, "It would seem that our current capitalism is willing to try the experiment of a civilization without homes."[1] Calhoun saw hotel life as an experiment driven primarily by desires for commercial profits and real estate returns. Indeed, the people who built and managed hotels saw their investments and businesses as a natural and necessary part of the city economy. At the scale of individual buildings, hotel managers were key figures. They orchestrated staffs to manage life inside their hotels and did their best to make a personal gain. Building owners could also affect a wider sphere. When they individually improved their properties they often collectively changed an entire neighborhood as well. Hotel owners, like other downtown landowners, welcomed and fostered a more organized, more rational city of increasing architectural specialization and clearer social stratification. The individual actions of hotel owners—with those of other downtown landowners—combined to specialize whole districts and thereby revamped the nature of living downtown.

OWNERS AND MANAGERS

No architect or real estate agent wanted to admit it, but the success of a hotel relied more on management than either ownership or architecture. Well into the twentieth century, hotel advertisements and facades listed the manager prominently (fig. 6.1). In the nineteenth century, people held hotel keepers to be consummate business operators. When Americans doubted someone's cleverness they would say, "He's a fine man, but he can't keep a hotel."[2] Americans were also not surprised when a woman successfully managed a hotel, as women were assumed to possess myriad household management skills.

Most owners had to compete at luring good managers to their hotel. Some owners became their own hotel managers. The San Francisco entrepreneurs Edward Rolkin and George D. Smith epitomize two common types of the combination owner-manager. Both made fortunes from hotel keeping. However, Rolkin was a Polish immigrant, and Smith was a well-born Californian. They did not belong to the same clubs and probably rarely met. Their different social class positions limited them to reasonably specific patterns. However, as leading hotel keepers who were both owners and managers they set the pace for their respective contemporaries.

Stratification of owners. A hotel investor's available capital naturally affected the size of his or her building and the duration of ownership. Small-scale business people and professionals tended to buy small hotels on the fringes of downtown as income property. They held on to their properties for long periods. Well-connected and large-scale capitalists secured the big downtown hotels that often had faster turnover in ownership and were thus more liquid investments. Owner-managers like Smith and Rolkin fit into a pattern between these two groups.

The cheap lodging houses of San Francisco attracted more large-scale investment than did rooming houses, but the investors were rarely people of high social status. Judging from a San Francisco sample of hotel ownership from 1910 to 1980, over half of the lodging house rooms in the city were built or held by people who were of relatively low social standing but who often had amassed enough wealth to own citywide strings of lodging house properties.[3] The strings usually included the largest and most profitable cheap hotels. The owners of

FIGURE 6.1. Prominent proprietor's sign on a nineteenth-century hotel. This waterfront hotel, probably of the rooming house rank, was photographed on West Street in New York City about 1890.

cheap lodging houses typically ran hotels as their primary business; unlike wealthy investors, they were not merely investing surplus income.

At the time of the earthquake in 1906, the fairly young Edward Rolkin already owned twenty small hotels. His hotel buildings were not well insured (they may have been so dilapidated that they were uninsurable), and his total disaster insurance settlement was only $2,500. Rolkin still owned twenty parcels of prime South of Market land, however, and with these as collateral he continued to build and buy hotels throughout the neighborhood. As in the prefire years, he and his wife lived in and actively managed the hotels, moving every few years as he bought a new one (fig. 6.2). From 1906 to the 1920s, Rolkin acquired several new choice properties, including four of the city's largest workers' hotels and some of the most notorious as well. From 1906 to 1911, he worked to assemble the four South of Market lots he needed to build his new 375-room Reno Hotel, named after the first hotel he had managed in the city. As a result of such entrepreneurship, Rolkin was a

FIGURE 6.2. A four-alarm fire at one of Edward Rolkin's hotels, The Denver House, in 1952. Located on Third Street at Tehama in San Francisco, the hotel had 180 lodging house rooms.

millionaire by the 1930s.[4] He and his wife, Arline, seem to have lived in their hotels until about 1935, when (in old age) they removed to a comfortable but merely middle-income district of town (fig. 6.3). A similar string of cheap San Francisco lodging houses was owned in the 1920s by Jules, Louis, and Joseph Marty. They held at least nine workers' hotels in Chinatown and the South of Market. In their private lives, the Marty brothers and their wives and children lived in the relatively ordinary Mission district, an area where immigrants emerged into the lower end of the middle and upper class.[5]

Not all inexpensive hotels had immigrant owners. In San Francisco, especially for a *small* new lodging or rooming house on the edge of downtown, the archetypical builder and owner was a doctor or the proprietor of a small downtown retail business. In over half the sample cases, the doctor or business owner lived in Pacific Heights, a well-known and expensive enclave of the city's middle and upper class. The Portland Hotel, a wretched wooden cubicle hostelry that the city tried

FIGURE 6.3. The modest house of a millionaire skid row landlord. Edward Rolkin's house at 1275 Stanyon, San Francisco, 1992. Rolkin and his wife lived in their various hotels until late in life. This is the only house they ever bought.

to condemn in 1916, belonged to a brass works manager who lived in the suburb of Berkeley. The owner was probably holding the hotel as a possible expansion site for his machine shop. He sold the hotel to an ophthalmologist from Pacific Heights who owned it for a much longer time. On a lot on Sixth Street, an optician built the Delta Hotel, a downtown rooming house, and the family held the property from 1906 to 1959. The Sierra House near Columbus and Broadway belonged to a family of wholesale grocers from 1909 to 1944; the first generation of the family lived in Pacific Heights, and their children watched the property from Piedmont, an exclusive suburb fifteen miles away.[6]

In another common pattern, a real estate developer would assemble a parcel of land, build a hotel, and then sell it to a lawyer, doctor, or other financially secure person. Two to four such investors often joined in a partnership to buy a building. Like individual owners, the original partnerships of the early 1900s seem to have held hotels as fairly long-term investments. This rule held until the turn-of-the-century investing generation died—in San Francisco, typically until the 1940s or early 1950s.

The Pacific Heights style of individual ownership or two- or three-person partnerships held particularly true for rooming houses. Such middle and upper class owners, detached from the direct management of their hotel properties, seem to have made up the bulk of the owners for the large areas considered "zones of transition" during the 1930s.

Yet the original owners rarely saw the so-called transition take place. They typically willed the hotel to sons or daughters, who also held on to it as an investment. Until the mid-1960s, these heirs held the property for its immediate income, tax write-offs, and speculative value. The property value may have been relatively low, but as part of the site for tomorrow's office tower or expanded factory, the rooming house land could quadruple in value.[7] Therefore, in these zones of transition especially, neither the original nor the inheriting ownership generations were primarily building a civilization without homes. Rather, they were holding land in order to build something else. The civilization without homes was a side effect. In contrast, when Rolkin built a hotel, he chose its location, design, and management with the intention that it be a permanent cheap lodging house.

A real estate market below the level of small new hotels was composed of small *used* hotels. As with other downtown property, the price of an older hotel relied more on the value of its land than that of the structure. In the 1920s, one wooden rooming house of thirty-nine rooms southwest of San Francisco's downtown sold for as little as $14,000—approximately the price of a duplex in an outlying streetcar district of the city.[8]

Generally, only the already wealthy—those with substantial inherited capital or a name that invoked the significant trust of lenders—could count on the loans required to build or buy large polite hotels in the heart of downtown. They usually did so as one of several investment vehicles. Midpriced hotels were built by people of substantial means—not the highest elite but often people who already had other good properties in the city. For a midpriced hotel of one hundred rooms in San Francisco, the owners would very often be a partnership of two such families, one of whom had inherited a choice downtown lot. Sarah Pettigrew (whose deceased husband had been an officer in a wholesale grocery firm) and Mary E. Callahan built the substantial Hotel Victoria in 1907–08, creating the plot by assembling two adjacent downtown lots (fig. 6.4). Sarah's brother managed the hotel for a time.[9] Edward Beck built the 106-room Colonial Hotel in 1912, directly next door to the family's Beck Apartments. Joseph Brandenstein, an early resident of the city and a wealthy tobacco importer turned investor, built the Hotel York on one of his larger properties. He himself lived in an appropri-

FIGURE 6.4. The Hotel Victoria on Bush Street, San Francisco, in December 1934.

ately large Victorian mansion in Pacific Heights, near the holders of the Levi-Strauss company fortune.[10]

Hotel properties in the core of downtown tended to turn over more frequently than rooming and lodging houses in the periphery. The Hotel Victoria's original owners, Pettigrew and Callahan, sold to another woman in just two years. Major changes of ownership occurred again in 1917, 1921, and 1934.[11] The palace-rank Hotel Bellevue, when its founding family sold it in 1916, saw two rapid turnovers until a resident owner and manager bought it in 1923.[12]

At the very top of the hotel property market were the builders of palace hotels, usually people competing to lead the city's finances and high society. Moneyed families not in the opera- or museum-endowing circle could erect palatial new hotels to gain or control social leadership. In San Francisco, trustees of the Charles Crocker estate, which was based on the notoriously unpopular profits of the Southern Pacific Railroad, decided to compete with the stodgy Palace Hotel by building the St. Francis Hotel. (The site of the Crocker mansion itself became the site of the Episcopal cathedral). Not long afterward, on the Nob Hill site that Comstock silver king James Fair had bought for his mansion, his daughter built the Fairmont Hotel. Terraces cascaded down the hill from the Fairmont; its opulence, hilltop views, and relatively quiet location made it a residential favorite for wealthy tenants and a monument to the Fair family.[13]

Grand hotels did more than open a route for nouveaux riches to memorialize a fortune. On occasion, grand hotels also allowed bright, enterprising people to wedge themselves into the highest strata of society, as shown by the career of George D. Smith and his family. Smith was an engineer born and educated in Berkeley. He worked professionally at his father's mines and also forged his own Nevada political connections and mining profits. His wife, Eleanor Hart, was from a solid Central Valley business family with impeccable pioneer California credentials. In 1922, when Smith was thirty-three years old, he and his wife moved to San Francisco to join George's sister in leasing and personally operating two hotels. Having undergone this self-paced hotel management training for a year, Smith gave up his other property interests to build the city's elegant Canterbury Hotel. Four years later, with his sister remaining as the manager at the Canterbury, he bought the Nob Hill site of the razed Mark Hopkins mansion. (Hopkins had been another of the Southern Pacific Railroad owners.) Smith then constructed the eighteen-story Mark Hopkins Hotel, instantly one of the palace hotel landmarks on the West Coast (fig. 6.5).[14]

Smith believed in downtown living, and he built and managed for it. In the plans for both the Canterbury and the Mark Hopkins he included larger-than-usual rooms with larger-than-usual closets, which adapted very well to the needs of permanent residents. At the Mark Hopkins, he called for a number of self-contained residential suites with refrigerators and electric kitchens. Permanent residents had claimed half the rooms of the Mark Hopkins before it opened, and its residential clientele remained substantial through the 1950s. In 1929, Smith gained controlling interest in the Fairmont Hotel across the street; for a time he managed both hotels, remodeling aggressively. Smith and his wife continued to live in the Mark Hopkins until 1962, and they raised their family there. Smith's business acumen and buoyant personality explain the success of his profitable hotel career as much as his remarkable access to loans. His reputation remains that of a model hotel keeper.[15]

Smith's personal involvement in his hotels was more typical of the nineteenth- than of the twentieth-century hotel owner; nonetheless, his

FIGURE 6.5. Recent photograph of the Mark Hopkins Hotel, opened in 1927 on the site of the Southern Pacific Railroad magnate's mansion. The corner of the Fairmont Hotel can be seen to the left.

capital management matched the modern owner. Except for the Mark Hopkins, he sold all of his luxury hotels after only a few years. Smith and Rolkin were both leaders in the hotel business, but because they combined ownership and management, they were exceptions. More typical owners relied on hired managerial talent.

Managers. As many as nine out of ten owners of large hotels did not personally manage their property. To the owners, the hotel was often strictly a real estate investment, no more meaningful to them than a speculative office building or warehouse. They typically leased the building to a manager for one to ten years. The contract details varied: a high fixed fee per year gave the owners a guaranteed income and left the remaining profits to the managers; leases at lower annual rates gave the owners a percentage of the gross receipts. Either method repaid construction loans quickly and gave the owner relatively worry-free income as long as hotel business was good at that location. At the turn of the century, owners proudly announced the cost of the lease (along with the cost of the building if it was new) in the local newspapers. In 1909, for instance, the Haas Realty Company began a $95,000 hotel just two blocks from San Francisco's Union Square. While construction was under way, they sealed a lease with the first manager, who over ten years was to pay the company $177,600 to operate the 108-room hotel and its ground-floor German grill.[16]

Hotel furniture often belonged to the manager, not the building owner; change of management included the sale of interior furnishings. In the 1890s, new furniture and fittings of an elegant family hotel might cost $400 a room, while a few blocks away, the manager of a cheap rooming house might pay only $50 a room. In the midpriced hotel range, the fittings, furniture, and dining room equipment could cost as much as 60 percent of the cost of the building.[17]

Published guides existed to help managers decipher the commercial metabolism of the United States, but most hotel owners and managers relied as much on hunches and personal experience.[18] While bargaining on a lease for a hotel with a bar and dining room, the astute hotel manager counted on the bar for positive cash flow. Dining rooms, other food service, and hotel entertainment offered virtually no chance for profit; at best, they broke even. The bar, however, generated a hefty share of the hotel's income and often paid rent, heat, and light for the whole building. Similarly, store rentals on the ground floor often carried the hotel's interest charges and some of the mortgage principal.[19]

Managers needed leadership ability, sound judgment, and good legal counsel for the daily demands of coordinating a complicated staff. At a polite hotel, that meant a 24-hour supply of maids, bellboys, elevator operators, kitchen assistants, janitors, and plumbers, along with a sizable number of clerks and midlevel supervisors. Much of the hotel management literature chronicles labor strife and methods to reduce it. To keep good workers nearby, builders of large hotels often constructed rooms in the attic or at the back of the hotel as living quarters for a share of the employees. Owners of gargantuan hotels like San Francisco's Palace built neighboring rooming houses with one hundred rooms or more, largely rented to their staff. Rooming houses and cheap lodging houses required a smaller but equally essential supply of maids and repair people.

Besides assuring the necessary staff support, the motive of a hotel manager was filling as many rooms as possible every night. In 1930, a hotel management report put it this way:

Hotel business differs from the general run of manufacturing in the perishability of its product. Time . . . is the major item that a hotel man has for sale. Every unsold room in his house every night represents an irretrievable loss, for that night will never return.[20]

To attract and keep permanent residents, managers of all types of hotels had to give appropriate attention to their clients, and the manager-tenant relationship was often very personal. Palace hotel managers personally assured wealthy clients that they would have the same suite each year and welcomed them with flowers and a personal note in their room when they arrived. Other managers chatted with tenants daily, or if they were managing a rooming house with elderly residents they helped them read and write letters, do their shopping, make doctor's appointments, or arrange ambulance service. At cheap lodging houses, good clerks made a point of greeting tenants by name and playing host to the group in the lobby to give them a sense of belonging and being at home (fig. 6.6). During strikes, rooming house keepers won loyalty from tenants by extending credit until the strike was over.[21]

When Prohibition cut off bar receipts, even more of the manager's attentions went to maintaining high room occupancy. By the 1920s, in a larger hotel a room occupancy rate of 70 percent was usually needed to break even. Seasonal changes in occupancy were another cash flow reality. When transient guest numbers were low in most palace and midpriced hotels, managers often took in more permanent guests. Monthly room rates were always substantially lower than the prorated daily or weekly rates—often only a fraction of the daily rate—but nonetheless managers could count on that residential income to cover fixed operating expenses.[22]

On similar sites, hotel buildings were known as potentially higher income properties than apartment buildings. Hotels made less money than apartments during business troughs but much more money in busy seasons. Apartments usually offered relatively steady cash flow year-round.[23] After 1920, real estate investors with a small amount of

FIGURE 6.6. Desk clerk in a cheap lodging house in Dubuque, Iowa, photographed in 1940. Note the casual arrangement of chairs.

capital, or those who wanted to rely on a housing investment as a significant part of their day-to-day income (for retirement income, perhaps), seem to have preferred apartments over hotels.

In the 1890s, the majority of the midpriced family hotels in San Francisco were run by women managers, and women managers were also reasonably common in other types of hotels. A California journalist explained in 1892 that the woman in business may have been questioned in some quarters, but "as a manager of large family hotels and rooming-houses, she is an eminent success" (fig. 6.7).[24] In 1900, up to 95 percent of American rooming house keepers were women. In most cities, about half of these rooming house operators were widows; the married rooming house operators typically had husbands who were wage laborers. Income from small rooming houses was more touch and go than at larger hotels. Unless the woman owned the building, its revenue was not substantial. The small rooming house operators leased their building by the year and bought the furniture on time payments. Typically, both the lease and the furniture purchase were arranged through a real estate broker who specialized in such deals and either owned the buildings outright or managed them for investors.[25] In spite of the meager income available, becoming a rooming house keeper was one of the occupations most available to mature self-supporting women before World War II. Older waitresses, for instance, commonly dreamed of leasing a rooming house instead of slinging hash in a cheap

FIGURE 6.7. Desk clerk in a small rooming house in San Augustine, Texas, 1939. Even in the nineteenth century, women were commonly hotel keepers.

restaurant. Yet many women went broke in their first year, not realizing the seasonal shifts or other expenses. They lost the money they had paid on the furniture and had to forfeit everything to the rooming house brokers. The brokers then easily found another recently widowed woman willing to invest her small nest egg on a rooming house venture. Rooming house real estate brokerages were so shady that some hotel brokers, to appear reputable, overtly advertised "strict conformance to upright business principles."[26]

Cycles of investment and construction. Particular years were noted for surges in all types of hotel investment. San Francisco directories record how quickly the number of hotels changed in response to potential business (fig. 6.8). Peaks of hotel listings coincided with surges in the local and national business climate, particularly in response to increased industrial and office employment, wars or other widespread investment stimuli, and surges in tourist travel. Troughs in the number of hotels corresponded to employment and travel slumps.[27]

Mercantile and industrial expansion—and the ensuing population movement—triggered good business for hotels of all types. The first major peak in San Francisco's hotel listings, from the mid-1890s to 1905, followed production surges for the Spanish-American War, discovery of gold in the Klondike, and increasing Philippine and Pacific

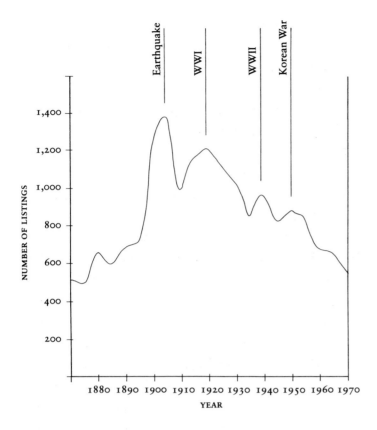

FIGURE 6.8. Graph showing total number of hotel listings in the San Francisco directories from 1870 to 1970.

Basin trade. It also coincided with the stimulation of Pacific Coast business due to the promise of the new Panama Canal trade and the rapid growth of population and markets in the American West.[28] San Francisco's great earthquake and fire of 1906 only briefly interrupted hotel business. In the aftermath, a great many hotels were built for workers and for households displaced by the destruction. No drastic land-use changes occurred in the rebuilding; the fire merely hastened and highlighted gradual developments already under way in real estate investments for the center section of the city.[29] At the scale of individual lots, the average hotel business before the fire had about 30 to 60 rooms; after the fire, each business listed in the directory was more likely to be on a lot twice as large and to have from 40 to 100 rooms.[30] Thus, although the number of individual hotels in San Francisco peaked in 1906 (the year of the fire), the peak in hotel *rooms* came after World War I.

Hotel keeper E. M. Statler called World War I "the best five years American hotels ever had." (He could not have imagined the boom of

World War II.) Wartime meant expanded employment. New hotels of all ranks were built or converted for war demands, and each wartime boom stretched all existing hotels to their maximum potential—and sometimes beyond. War industry workers packed into lodging houses and rooming houses while the better hotels did thriving business with war-materiel brokers, production engineers, government officials, and military officers. The only single-room housing operations that languished in World War I were the free municipal lodging houses and other flophouse adjuncts in some cities, which were made less necessary by high wartime employment. The Chicago Municipal Lodging House closed entirely in 1918–19 because of lack of applicants.[31]

After World War I, generally, only the directors of philanthropic rooming houses (such as new YWCAs) and owners of midpriced and palace hotels added to the stock of hotel rooms. Again, the San Francisco case is typical.[32] From 1918 to 1921, manufacturing employment decreased in San Francisco industries by 4,000 employees, down almost 10 percent; by 1925, it had dropped by another 4,000. Hence, private downtown housing investors in San Francisco built neither lodging houses nor rooming houses after World War I. A share of this downtown decline also resulted from mechanization in the work place and the steady relocation of industries to the edge of the city.[33]

Within these broad swings in hotel business, several market processes operated. Perhaps the least rational were those behind the building of palace hotels and some midpriced hotels. Beginning in the 1820s, each generation of city business leaders felt compelled to adorn their town with a state-of-the-art hotel—usually larger and more lavish than strictly necessary—to assure their city's regional or national stature. In the 1920s, palace hotels began to vie even with office skyscrapers as the largest buildings in major cities. Not all of this was sheer boosterism. For two centuries Americans have responded positively to size in hotels as they have responded to size in other commercial attractions. The biggest hotel in town also commanded monopoly rates and the largest conventions.

In the battle between city boosters in different towns and between different expensive hotels, design and fashion as well as size figured prominently. As the competition between a city's better hotels increased, the owners and managers came to rely more on the tools of high-style design, attention-catching interior decorating, spectacular cooking, and innovative engineering. In every generation, owners and their architects informally settled on a prevailing facade style for hotels; for interiors, managers and their designers changed the reigning style almost twice as often. Thus, to remain in fashion, hotel managers had to search for better chefs constantly, redecorate about every ten years, and significantly remodel or add new wings at least once every twenty to twenty-five years. Watching the constant competition between grand hotels, Sinclair Lewis observed that "next to love, nothing loses its rank so quickly as a leading hotel."[34]

When hotel owners demanded ever-larger hotels to pay for ever-more-expensive downtown land, architects responded with new types of floor plans. On larger sites, designers provided wings of rooms separated by larger and wider light wells. In an "E" or "C" shape, the floor plans yielded more rooms with two- and three-way exposure for better cross-ventilation and light. Engineering also set new hotel fashions. For every passing decade's conspicuous innovative gadget—calling-card elevator, exuberant lighting display, ice water tap, or built-in radio—managers installed many more machines to reduce labor costs. By 1900, the design and outfitting of hotels had become complex enough so that a few architecture and engineering firms specialized in hotel design and did a significant share of the nation's large hotel business.[35]

The use of elevators particularly revolutionized hotel life. With elevator access, the rooms on upper floors (once the cheapest rooms) became the most expensive. By the 1920s, tower views from high palace hotel rooms had become another aspect of hotel living that expensive private houses could not outdo.[36] In San Francisco, it was George Smith who best captured the skyscraper view. In 1939, to compete with new post-Prohibition bars and nightclubs opening throughout the city, he opened the Top of the Mark at the remodeled crown of his hotel, where a penthouse apartment had been. Smith also hired the talented architectural office of Timothy Pfleuger to give the Top of the Mark the Manhattan sheen of Art Deco style.[37]

Managers who chose not to compete in the size, chef, or gadget game typically dropped their hotels to a lower rank of clientele by cutting the amount of service, closing lavish dining rooms, or changing from American plan to European plan rates. With such cuts in service, a palace hotel could be profitably run as a midpriced hotel. In the late 1920s, so many boosters had built so many good hotels that in most cities

FIGURE 6.9. The Gateway District of Minneapolis, photographed in 1939. Through the filtering of clients, this Victorian midpriced hotel district had shifted to cheap lodging house status.

there were price wars and substantially lower transient occupancy rates. Simultaneously, motels and auto courts were beginning to cut into the family travel market. Such overbuilding stimulated more permanent occupancy to fill the rooms. Managers lured tenants with ads proclaiming, "Occupancy from October! Lease from January! Fifteen months for the rent of twelve."[38]

For all types of hotels, shifts of social cachet, demographic changes in surrounding neighborhoods, or losses in nearby employment triggered the process of filtering: first, former permanent guests gradually filtered *out* to newer, more comfortable, or better-located quarters; second, to keep occupancy levels high, managers at the older hotels lowered their prices, allowing less affluent tenants to filter *in*; finally, the remaining earlier tenants left, feeling that their social standing, comfort, or safety was in jeopardy. In any American city, it was not unusual in the 1920s to see handsomely designed and fashionable family hotels of the 1880s that had devolved to inexpensive rooming houses for unskilled or unemployed workers.[39] Cheaper hotels, too, filtered to lower-income tenants (fig. 6.9). In the core of San Francisco's South of Market district, the managers of several hotels built in 1906 had by 1919 discontinued polite hotel services and given up the term "hotel"; they simply ran their establishments as more casual rooming houses or lodging houses. On one block alone, three out of four hotels had seen this conversion.[40]

To maintain high profits in spite of lower rents, owners of rooming or lodging houses could reduce repair budgets and employ only minimally skilled managers or staff. What observers called the "visual decay" of rooming house districts was usually the evidence of inept or uncaring management and the literal erosion of architectural fabric: first cosmetic facade deterioration and then more serious structural dilapidation from decreased maintenance.[41]

Like the question of when to launch a new hotel business, the question of when to leave the hotel business was often prompted by the general urban metabolism and how it affected the neighborhood, hotel clientele, competition for the hotel site, and the cash flow of the property owner(s). If hotel managers could not sell their rooms to either tourists or permanent guests, and if shifting to cheaper clients did not work, owners often looked to office rentals or other nonhotel uses. At appropriate downtown locations hotel owners could rent rooms, whole floors, or the whole hotel as offices. Even in colonial times, hotels had mixed offices and sleeping rooms. In 1906, the Grand Central Hotel in San Francisco was consciously built to be *either* office or hotel space, and it saw both uses. The elegant Hotel Whitcomb served as San Francisco's city hall for a time after the great fire. About 1920, the owners of New York's Manhattan Hotel (even though it was the birthplace of the Manhattan cocktail) converted the twenty-four-year-old building to offices. Other hotel owners converted their properties to private hospitals (or vice versa). After 1945, however, demands for better electrical service, lighting, and air-conditioning made such office and hospital conversions less feasible.[42] When all else failed, a major old hotel's downtown site usually brought the owners a good price as the location for a new office tower. The most notable example of such conversion is the block that held the original Waldorf-Astoria Hotel, where the Empire State Building now stands. At times even perfectly profitable and viable hotels were torn down, revealing tensions that can exist between owners and managers. If the owners were convinced they could profit more by closing the hotel and changing the building's use—and if the managers had lost their lease—no basis remained for the hotel to be in business, other than emotional appeals by the managers or clients.

Especially at the scale of the Empire State Building but also at more modest sites, the actions of individual owners and managers had a great influence on the surrounding blocks. Hotels collected large numbers of people who were a market for other retail services nearby. The hotel's staff also exerted a pressure for their own housing and for their retail needs. These influences, plus their voice in urban governance as landowners, gave hotel builders important roles in rebuilding downtown neighborhoods in a more organized way.

SPECIALIZATION FOR SINGLE USE

At the turn of the century, downtown renters and landowners were actively rejecting mixtures of different people and activities that had been common and widely accepted as late as 1880. In the old city, even plutocrats proudly built their mansions on streets that included middle-income people and plots with inferior improvements and wildly varying qualities. Not even the most wealthy could guarantee a proper setting for their homes (fig. 6.10). Noxious factories could blight next-door flats or tenements. From their own perspective, factory and workshop owners saw nearby dwellings as a blight; as industries expanded their production, they needed larger unencumbered sites and fewer neighbors who complained about smoke and noise. With less mixture and more logical land-use patterns, private downtown builders and clients hoped that business growth might be more predictable, employees healthier, and clients more conveniently available. In such a reformed city, future property and business investments would also be more secure and less threatened by the encroachment of slums. Sites would be assured of maintaining their "highest and best use"—usually interpreted to mean their most valuable use for private return within some rational sense of the public good. The timing for this desired shift in land-use attitudes hinged on the growing size and complexity of cities, new industries, traffic problems, and the social and cultural repercussions of high-density mixtures of different people and competing projects.

FIGURE 6.10. Residential land-use conflicts on San Francisco's Nob Hill during the 1870s. In the foreground, the white mansion of the Southern Pacific Railroad's chief lawyer stands next to a very ordinary 1870s middle-income row house. At the rear is the Victorian pile of the Crocker mansion. Crocker wanted to own his entire block to properly distinguish his home. His last remaining neighbor refused to sell, so Crocker built a 30-foot wooden "spite fence" around the parcel. Photographed in 1878 from the tower of the Mark Hopkins mansion.

Privately, on new land at the edge of the city developers could impose covenants or simply own tracts large enough so that rational control for the owners' best interest was guaranteed. Publicly, cities did not have the legal power to enforce greater separation and organization until the 1920s. Instead, downtown builders privately replaced the old city's heterogeneity on a site-by-site basis, gradually and informally creating more specialized zones. By the 1890s, rudimentary district specializations—industrial apart from commercial, commercial apart from residential, workers apart from middle-income people—were becoming fairly implicit goals of private city building.[43] Hotel owners played their part. As they changed their individual properties they not only helped to specialize hotel life but also whole districts in which those hotels stood and, inevitably, the nature of living downtown.

In the gradual drive for specialized urban space, hotel owners first specialized designs for distinct hotel building types. From the very earliest experiments, palace hotels were purposely built as permanent and unique parts of the city. In 1829, the architect Isaiah Rogers had designed the Tremont House in Boston as a monument, just as George D. Smith demanded that his architect make the Mark Hopkins a singular monument on the San Francisco skyline. However, from 1880 to 1930, San Francisco's other types of hotels varied widely in the specialization of their buildings (fig. 6.11). In 1880, over a tenth of San Francisco's midpriced hotels were still in reused grand houses. By 1910, all operators of midpriced hotels were in structures intended solely for hotel uses, probably reflecting their clients' higher expectations for private bathrooms and the rebuilding from the fire of 1906.[44]

Before 1900, as a rule, developers made cheap hotels a less permanent part of the city: the lower one's social status, the more impermanent was one's hotel. Compared to the investors in expensive hotels, the actions of San Francisco rooming house investors provide an apt case of slower specialization. They chose architectural flexibility so that if the hotel scheme did not work, they could easily use the structure for something else. In 1880, half of the rooms in the city's rooming houses occupied the upper floors of fairly undifferentiated commercial structures. The building envelope provided few or no housing-style amenities such as light wells or other residential adaptations. Rooming house owners changed their minds rapidly at the turn of the century, probably spurred by client expectations raised by improvements in single-family houses. In 1910, only 5 percent of the rooming house rooms were in general-purpose commercial buildings. At that same time, 17 percent of rooming house rooms were in converted houses due to the dislocations of the fire. By 1930, owners had rebuilt many of their properties, so that 90 percent of the people in rooming houses lived in specialized buildings, not ad hoc structures. By that year, landlords had also increased the average size of a rooming house to about sixty rooms—twice the 1910 average.

Predictably, the slowest architectural specializations came in hobo hotels. Up until the turn of the century, only a small share of San Francisco's cheap lodging house rooms were in buildings constructed for that purpose; more often, owners of a downtown house or commercial loft building roughly converted it for lodging house use. The temporary

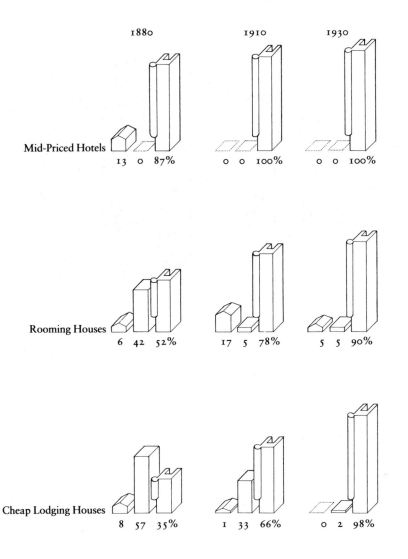

1880   1910   1930

Mid-Priced Hotels

13 0 87%   0 0 100%   0 0 100%

Rooming Houses

6 42 52%   17 5 78%   5 5 90%

Cheap Lodging Houses

8 57 35%   1 33 66%   0 2 98%

FIGURE 6.11. Increasing specialization of San Francisco hotel buildings. Note especially the number of rooming houses and cheap lodging houses in ad hoc structures in 1880 and 1910.

KEY

Converted Flats or Houses

Converted Commercial Buildings

Purposely Built as Hotels

FIGURE 6.12. An example of a specialized cheap lodging house built in 1909. The Central Hotel, built by Edward Rolkin at Third and Brannan in San Francisco, had 440 small rooms and several storefronts across the first floor, including a large saloon and dining room. It was later converted to apartments as shown in this 1992 photograph.

arrangements built for the lodging house residents reflected many things: their marginal rent-paying ability, the lack of housing inspection or adequate health inquiry for these groups in San Francisco (true in most other cities as well), and the condescension of landowners toward their tenants. Also, owners of downtown land acted as if they hoped and expected that the laborers would soon go away. Because of its central location or location adjacent to industrial areas, the land under cheap lodging houses was still considered too valuable to devote permanently to casual laborers. By about 1900, however, perceptions were very different. Many landlords had realized that lodging house residents were a permanent group and that it made good economic sense to design buildings especially for them. San Francisco's Edward Rolkin became a leader in this process as he rebuilt his properties after 1906. He assembled larger sites around his best lots and hired inexpensive architects to make the largest and most particularized hotels San Francisco's laborers had ever seen: brick bearing-wall structures like that of the Central Hotel (fig. 6.12). On other lots, owners were doing the same thing—but not all the owners, since in 1910 a third of the cheapest hotel rooms were still in temporary loft-type quarters, often with completely wooden construction. Nonetheless, by the end of World War I, virtually all lodging houses in San Francisco were purpose built at an average size of about sixty rooms each.[45]

As noted above, for owners, the better facades of cheap hotels were fronts for embarrassing realities. For residents of inexpensive hotels after 1900, being in a purpose-built hotel (rather than an ad hoc adapted house before 1900) usually meant better physical conditions: wider light wells, better ventilation, and private room sinks. Specialized cheap lodging houses had at least the required minimum of a one to twelve ratio of baths to cubicles. San Francisco's city administrations varied notoriously in ability and honesty and started effective building regulation comparatively late. Nonetheless, by the mid-1910s sporadic enforcement of the city's regulations had begun and may account, in particular, for the increase in minimum standards in lodging houses by the time of World War I.[46]

For city residents in general the new, larger, and more specialized rooming houses and cheap lodging houses made a distinctly different visual impact on the streets of the city. Compared to their predecessors, the new hotels were often taller, located on more prominent corner sites, and more visually insistent. The large painted advertisements on the structures' blank sides announced the availability of steam heat, low weekly rates, locational advantages, and often a nearby ice cream parlor or clothing emporium. The new visual impressions of these more architecturally defined structures were also surrounded by more particularized neighborhoods.

The organization and separation built into individual hotel buildings were parts of the larger specialization of whole neighborhoods. Hotel owners hammered out more distinct hotel districts from 1880 through 1930, each with a different range of services. Palace hotel builders learned to keep their buildings and neighborhoods more exclusive and insular by putting most tailor shops, newsstands, and restaurants into interior arcades.[47] Meanwhile, designers of midpriced hotels and cheaper apartments kept equivalent services open to the sidewalk.

San Francisco's Western Addition became an old-house rooming district in an uneven process but one that was typical of rooming house areas in other American cities. From 1900 to 1930, people in the property industry seemed to disagree about whether the Western Addition was becoming a converted-house district, an area of new purpose-built rooming houses, a zone of middle-income apartments, or simply a slum. After the fire of 1906, many neighborhood landowners converted their large Victorian era houses into rooming houses to serve emergency needs; within a few years, a good number of these people had converted their houses back to single-family use—either as rentals or for their own homes. Others, however, built rooming house additions on their lots, creating a diverse mixture of rental conditions and lower prices. These attracted new residents and increased the area's ethnic and racial diversity. Meanwhile, through the 1920s, other developers assumed the area should resemble lower Nob Hill; they speculated in large lots, built tall apartment buildings, and drove up land values. Finally, during the building hiatus of the depression, the slum perception took over. The majority of the house owners had moved away; absentee owners could not rent out large units. They converted their houses to flats, ad hoc apartments, or light housekeeping rooms and stopped investing in repairs or improvements. They held on to their Western Addition properties, hoping for a resurgence of land values. As the perception spread that the area was indeed a slum, more owners individually shifted to rooming house and light housekeeping use. During World War II, Japanese families were removed to internment camps, and the black population in the area increased from 5 to 30 percent. Through 1945, the rents were high enough to make these income properties too expensive for San Francisco's housing authority to acquire, but the area had been officially tagged as a problem zone. Neither property leaders nor planners had a positive view of a good rooming house zone being developed in the Western Addition, although in the 1920s that had been a viable future for the district.[48]

In similar ways, individual landowners specialized skid row areas but usually without the vacillation that marked the Western Addition. The concentration of cheap lodging houses in the Third and Howard area in the South of Market was a steady progression. In 1880, only about a third of the residents in that area had rented rooms in family homes or hotels. By 1900, that proportion had increased to one-half, and it continued to grow. By the late 1920s, the most densely settled blocks of San Francisco were no longer in Chinatown but in the blocks of lodging houses clustered at the core of the laborers' zone.[49]

The individual changes wrought in the South of Market responded to changes in industrial employment from both the invasion of new uses and the retreat of former residents. From 1880 to the mid-1920s, distant railroad and agricultural projects throughout the West became larger, and the number of hobo laborers increased, doubling and then tripling the San Francisco cheap hotel market. In 1900, San Francisco's South of Market area still had many ethnic families and commercial

family services located on side streets or alleys, mixed with small
lodging houses and rooming houses. As owners of industrial facilities
bought up land and as family-tied workers moved to be closer to new
skilled work sites, family services began to be more scarce. Astute lodging house owners like Rolkin were ready to buy up any available lots.
By 1930, lodging house developers had cornered most of the major
sites in a wide area around Howard, Third, and Fourth streets. The
massing of building along the major streets was impressive (fig. 6.13).

As single workers' zones became more separated, organized, and
specialized, there were fewer reasons for other city residents to enter
them. Workers' zones became the most alien and repugnant commercial districts in the city for middle and upper class suburbanites. Sinclair Lewis presents George Babbitt as a real estate man who knows
most of Zenith building by building—especially central and suburban
Zenith. However, for Babbitt the workers' zone (where he goes to buy
bootleg gin) was merely a "morass of lodging houses, tenements, and
brothels."[50] While the effect of specialization of San Francisco's Howard and Third streets made them alien to suburbanites, the process had

FIGURE 6.13. Workers'
hotels vying with downtown
offices in permanence and
prominence. The last two
blocks of Third Street in the
South of Market, looking
toward San Francisco's
financial district, 1929.

FIGURE 6.14. A small corner hotel at Pacific Street and Powell, in San Francisco, 1926.

a different effect on male low-income laborers who lived elsewhere. Areas like Howard and Third remained familiar haunts for their evenings away from their new homes in the cottage districts. The South of Market concert saloons, billiard halls, and other establishments were places where they felt at home—a sense they had in few other districts in town. The neighborhoods were also fertile ground for union activists and liberal and radical political workers.

For the property industry, collectively hammering together fashionable hotel zones, rooming areas, or single laborers' zones helped to ensure steady real estate income. Another effect of specialization was the prominence it gave to outlying experiments in hotel life at the turn of the century; they became more prominent because they became more exceptional. Throughout the nineteenth century, a few rooming houses with public dining rooms could be found in fairly scattered locations in middle-income and working-class neighborhoods. By 1900, these hotels in outlying streetcar districts were more concentrated. Commercial nodes at the intersections of two lines typically had three or four hotels or rooming houses built above corner grocery stores and other neighborhood shops (fig. 6.14). The neighborhood hotel could be a place for Sunday dinner excursions. Proper single-family houses might also have had a hotel as a neighbor. Especially before 1920, a few landowners with property close to a major avenue expanded the residential capacity of their lots by building a residential hotel much larger than

the surrounding houses but not above the two-story height of the neighbors' houses. Elsewhere, the site of former mansions provided space for large new apartment hotels (fig. 6.15).

Not everyone heralded the specialization of hotel buildings and downtown housing districts as a desirable change. The more definite building types of hotels, the more definite neighborhoods, and even the outlying experiments were problems for some urban critics, usually people outside the property industry. The criticisms and concerns also had a definite class bias: examples of hotels built and managed for the middle and upper class were often treated very different from hotels built for the working class, and the concerns were rooted in street perceptions.

FIGURE 6.15. Experimentation with hotel life in formerly prestigious residential areas, photographed in the 1940s. The large H-shaped Belmont and Buckingham apartment hotels, *top left,* replaced former mansions on half of a city block in Denver's Capitol Hill district in 1917. Developers built the other apartment buildings a generation later.

PUBLIC IMPRESSIONS AND RESIDENTIAL OPPOSITION

Within San Francisco's development and specialization, George Smith and Edward Rolkin lived and worked in widely separated spheres. Smith, through his success in elegant downtown hotels, became a leading booster of the city. He was vice president of the Golden Gate International Exposition, a director of the Chamber of Commerce, president of the Downtown Association, and treasurer of the San Francisco Convention and Visitors Bureau. He retired in 1961 at seventy-two years of age and sold his share of the Mark Hopkins for a reputed $10 million.[51] As true urbanites, after retirement he and his wife moved to a fashionable downtown apartment near Union Square. Rolkin, an immigrant, never fully retired and personally managed his string of hobo hotels until he died in 1941 at the age of ninety, a social outsider with a real estate fortune of $2 million. He had served on the California State Board of Equalization, but his most important social or civic organization seems to have been the Independent Order of Oddfellows. Rolkin's obituary dubbed him the "Landlord of Skid Row."[52] Although both Smith and Rolkin trained themselves, built large hotels, and personally managed them, they remained in the two separate worlds of residential hotel life: on the one hand, the culturally acceptable; on the other, the merely necessary.

Most middle and upper class citizens came to perceive the negative, necessary side of hotel life far more clearly than its positive, more culturally acceptable side. The specialization of hotel buildings and districts as well as the lives of their residents helped to exacerbate the negative public perceptions. In the 1880s, downtown housing and the mixtures of the old city comprised a large share of San Francisco's extent. In addition to the downtown core, a third or more of the residential neighborhoods still had occasional commercial single-room housing and retail uses. In those large areas, such mixture was a part of everyday urban experience (fig. 6.16). By 1930, the city's number of hotel rooms had quadrupled; the ratio of hotel rooms per person in the city was substantially higher than in the 1880s. The concentration of hotel life in the downtown core had expanded significantly. However, outlying neighborhoods with an occasional residential hotel represented only a tenth of San Francisco's extent. The new city of more single-purpose areas—areas for only residence or only production—stretched for miles. Thus, by 1930 one of the most salient features of downtown housing had become its dramatic contrast with the outlying residential districts. Together, the expensive and cheap downtown residence zones comprised an island of urban life very different from that in the rest of the city.[53] People outside the suburban family model or

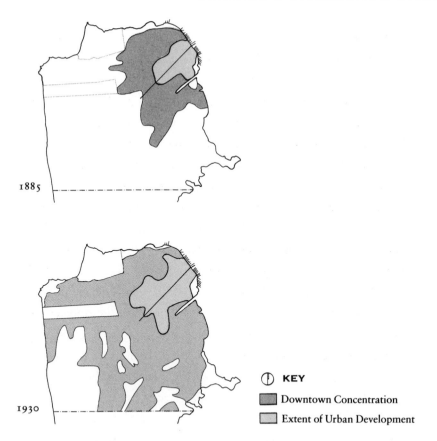

1885

1930

KEY

Downtown Concentration

Extent of Urban Development

who chose family life in an old city mode were increasingly concentrated downtown.

The gradual architectural specialization of the city from 1880 to 1930 helped to make positive hotel life less visible to people of the middle and upper class (as was the case with George Babbitt) while it made negative hotel life more visible. As always, well-dressed middle-income hotel dwellers melted into the downtown crowd.[54] Meanwhile, for well-to-do citizens the people who symbolized social and personal failure became more vividly associated with hotel homes. While a relatively small percentage of successful people were known to live in hotels, a very high proportion of hoboes, poor single clerks, drunks, and prostitutes were known as hotel residents. From the carriage, streetcar, or automobile one was far more likely to remember a bum who had passed out in front of a cheap lodging house than the happy thirty-year-old clerk walking to his rooming house. Among single-family house dwellers, the best-known aspects of the cheap hotel zones became their culturally questionable recreational pursuits. In zones of converted houses, the ROOMS TO RENT signs and the rooming houses

FIGURE 6.16. Comparison of the extent of old city mixture in San Francisco, 1885 and 1930. As the city grew after 1900, dense mixtures of housing and commercial activities became a much smaller proportion of the city's total area.

they represented came to be seen as the *cause* of urban blight rather than the side effects of underlying migration, layoffs, real estate speculation, or expansion of the business district.

The new permanence of the downtown housing districts was even more significant than their specialization. As downtown landowners like Rolkin and the various Pacific Heights professionals built their larger buildings on more prominent street corners, they announced that the alternative hotel life-styles were not a passing phase. The downtown housing areas were not, as one Chicago sociologist had labeled them, a "zone in transition." The owners of the new brick, steel, and concrete residential hotel buildings had clearly built for at least sixty years—the same life expectancy of the adjacent office and loft buildings. The permanent residential interiors of the new hotel buildings signaled the potential for a long-term zone of opposition to the cultural ideals behind the new city. In 1917, the California state senator, Lester Burnett, used dire predictions of persistence to exhort his colleagues to pass a stronger housing act. Where "*only* apartment houses, hotels, and lodging houses are built," he said, referring to San Francisco, "the city blocks are becoming a mass of buildings of steel and brick so solidly constructed *as to last a century or more*." [55] At the time of the San Francisco fire, Senator Burnett might have seen the city's ad hoc wooden hotels as temporary necessities, a passing urban phase. Like the shanty city required for the workers who built the gleaming new capital of Brasilia, San Francisco's minimal hotels had seemed a necessity for the building and rebuilding of the new city. When the city was finished, Burnett and others felt that the cheap lodgings would collapse like packing crates and that their denizens would go away or somehow move to new single-use suburbs. However, when the workers' housing became permanent—"as to last a century or more," as Burnett put it—observers became alarmed (fig. 6.17).

The specialization of downtown buildings also fueled the separation between the culturally acceptable and merely necessary hotel realms, as shown in the careers of George Smith and Edward Rolkin. Smith knew the polite hotel's need for skilled managers. At the end of his life he generously endowed San Francisco's professional hotel and restaurant school, which was named after him. Rolkin left a substantial sum to an agricultural school in Poland but gave nothing to train managers of cheap lodging houses; academically trained managers were not part of

the concept of running low-caste hotels. New clerks got only on-the-job training, as is still the case today. The distinct social relations of Smith's and Rolkin's hotel worlds meant that Smith enjoyed fraternal relationships with his customers, while Rolkin had paternalistic relationships with his. Smith, an avid golfer, advised Mark Hopkins guests on the local courses; Rolkin left a sixth of his estate to purchase candy, tobacco, and other treats for the residents of the county relief home, many of whom would have been his former tenants. The hundreds of absentee hotel landlords in San Francisco had even less direct relationships with their clients than Rolkin. However, they did leave distinct regions of the city that they had collectively built.

Rolkin knew that he was operating marginally reputable businesses—at least in the view of middle and upper class culture, yet he died during World War II with his hotels at absolute peak capacity. To that same polite culture, Smith seemed beyond reproach. Oddly, Smith lived to see the unraveling of the residential life that he had built into the Canterbury, Mark Hopkins, and Fairmont hotels. He also saw one of America's first giant urban renewal projects of the 1950s raze most of Rolkin's properties and guarantee the value of his own. The work of both Rolkin and Smith came to be attacked for threatening the cultural and social life of San Francisco. As both of these men built, leased, and traded hotels they had also unconsciously been generating opposition to their investments. They were "current capitalists" willing to "try the experiment of a civilization without homes." At stake were more than profits or architecture. The grander cultural critique had to do with

FIGURE 6.17. Temporary versus permanent structures in San Francisco's South of Market district. The simple wooden rooming house (*right*) contrasts with the brick housing structure (*left foreground*) at Folsom and Ninth streets, 1927.

how "home" was to be defined in the United States, in how many different ways, and by whom.

By 1970, a generation after Smith and Rolkin's time, many of the downtown real estate assumptions that seemed so permanent in the 1920s had evaporated. People had stopped building outlying hotel experiments by the time of the Great Depression. The confident Nob Hill/Gold Coast/Upper Fifth Avenue projections for elegant residential hotels also were unrealized. By 1970, the current capitalists of America, in Calhoun's terms, seemed suddenly *not* interested in the experiment of a civilization without homes. The broad cultural critiques of hotel life, seemingly ignored by the owners and managers of hotels, were to play a major role in that change.

HOTEL HOMES AS A
PUBLIC NUISANCE

OBVIOUSLY, A GOOD NUMBER OF HOTEL RESIDENTS and owners held positive views about hotel life. However, many opinion makers saw residential hotels as caldrons of social and cultural evil. At a national convention in 1905, the noted American housing reformer Lawrence Veiller condemned both residential hotel and tenement life for their serious social consequences:

The bad effect upon the community of a congregate form of living is by no means limited to the poorer people. Waldorf-Astorias at one end of town and "big flats" at the other end are equally bad in their destruction of civic spirit and the responsibilities of citizenship.[1]

Attacks like Veiller's on any "congregate form of living" had their historical roots in generations of middle and upper class complaints about urban density, mixture, and diversity—key aspects of hotel living. From the mid-nineteenth century to Veiller's time, negative ideas about downtown life had been enunciated and reinforced by literary commentators, housing professionals, and public officials. In the views of hotel critics, all hotels were suspect. Expensive hotels encouraged wasted lives, empty glamour, and rejection of traditional gender roles. These practices endangered the dominant culture of the middle and upper class and set poor examples for the working class. Since large proportions of the city's shiftless laborers, social misfits, thieves, and prostitutes lived in cheap hotels, reformers also assumed that hotel life must be an important part of the cause. By 1900, several generations of hotel criticisms were becoming woven into the housing reform opinions of the complex Progressive Era, which flowered from about 1890 to 1920.

HOTEL CRITICS AND REFORM RANKS

The downtown environmental activists of the Progressive Era, like their colleagues in other parts of the movement, were generally self-appointed and wealthy businessmen—or their wives or minions—who volunteered their time and considerable talents for public good. These people were driven by equal parts of Protestant Christian charity, veiled self-interest, genuine noblesse oblige, and fear that their gigantic cities were out of control. The market-driven locations for industries and transportation had juxtaposed staggering numbers of new immigrant workers and ragged regions of noxious uses that overwhelmed earlier zones of middle and upper class residences, shops, and offices. Small-scale real estate and building practices seemingly had exacerbated slums, pollution, illness, and confusion about future land values (fig. 7.1). To the reformers, American privatism and boss politics were creating an unworkable city, one where not even the buildings of the wealthy could be guaranteed safe futures.

Given their personal class origins, most progressive reformers did not see low wages, uneven work availability, or industrial leadership as being primarily culpable for the urban chaos. In the building of cities, capitalism had merely gone too far. Like other Progressive Era figures, urban activists initially attacked the problems of downtown living as moral and cultural failures. They saw new ethnic, religious, and political subcultures as threatening to hard-won changes in polite family life. Along with the upsurges of American nativism during the nineteenth century came concerns about the serious personal and material culture cleavages between immigrant and native-born, poor and rich, unattached and family-tied, lawless and law-abiding.[2] Using a similar di-

chotomy, critics of hotel life framed their housing attitudes with two extremes: the slums of downtown and the exclusive new zones of single-family houses at the edge of the city.

FIGURE 7.1. A Telegraph Hill slum with street urchins, ca. 1885. Scenes like these spurred San Francisco housing reformers to action.

The reformers were convinced that stronger, centrally ordained, and better-enforced building rules would bring uplift to the lower class and civic betterment to the city as a whole. The new regulations and central planning would shore up the mainstream of the economic system and also maintain the power of the leading elite. Better housing meant not only better environmental health but also better social control. Promotion of material progress became a prime tool of social engineering.[3]

About hotel life, the mainstream reform opinions were usually negative and remarkably uniform, although progressive reformers were not a monolithic movement and often held contradictory views. A few fringe activists genuinely *promoted* hotel life.[4] However, several basic tenets underlay the environmental activists' beliefs and behavior. First, the reformers shared good liberal arts educations; their views were stimulated by literary and social reform figures such as Thoreau, Emerson, Ruskin, and Carlyle; novelists such as Edith Wharton and Theodore Dreiser; and decades of journalistic travel accounts and city exposés, particularly those in the style of the pioneering New York journalist Jacob Riis. Second, in spite of occasional rhetoric to the contrary, the environmental reformers desired a monolithic culture. They admired individuality as exemplified by Thomas Edison or Theodore Roosevelt, but they did not widely value pluralism, heterogeneity, and diversity as related attributes.[5] Third, through most of the nineteenth century and early twentieth century, they were imbued with environmental determinism, the belief that good environments would automatically create good people. Determinism also spurred belief in the obverse—that bad housing caused psychological, social, economic, and medical problems.

The ideas of scientific management and engineering efficiency, along with a great trust in physical solutions for social problems, also figured heavily in the intellectual bulwarks of progressive reformers. The early years of the 1900s were a golden age to focus on a problem, independently gather systematic data on it, proclaim oneself an expert, and thereby create a private or public post to solve it. Frederick Winslow Taylor and his followers were saving their industrial clients millions of dollars by doing systematic research and then finding the One Best Way to shovel coal or run grinding machines. Even social work from 1890 to 1917 aimed for universal attainment of a "normal standard of living"—a phrase that assumed an efficient One Best Way to live. That way, of course, was the way reformers themselves had lived in middle and upper class suburban families.[6] The activists rarely doubted that their own values were the best values. As one housing critic wrote, "Whatever home means for us, it means to others, for human nature is the same, and physical nature is the same, and mental laws are unvarying."[7]

As a solution to urban problems, reformers also promoted a centrally planned shift from the old city to the new city, from multiple use and mixture toward sorting and single use. One official group phrased it like this:

Industry, business, and home life may flourish in the same community if they are distributed according to an intelligent community plan. Without a plan, moral, sanitary, and economic slums are created.[8]

Within such value systems, hotels of all ranks came to be seen as prime elements of "moral, sanitary, and economic slums."

Concern with urban housing attracted the work of several overlapping and usually cooperating professional groups, most notably, housing experts, public health advocates, social workers, architects, and social scientists. Housing experts often took a leadership role, and foremost among them was Veiller, hired as a full-time housing official in New York in 1898. As the author of path-breaking model housing codes and later as an organizer and director of the National Housing Organization, Veiller was for twenty years the most important shaper of housing ideas in the United States. Nationally, a few dozen other experts formed the nucleus of consulting, research, writing, and lobbying about housing in the years before World War I. Their roster included traveling consultants like Carol Aronovici and housing philanthropists such as Alfred T. White and Robert W. Deforest.[9] Through professional meetings and personal contact, this small circle of housing experts knew one another well; most worked for strikingly similar committees of concerned business people. When Veiller preached that he was offended by the bad effects of the Waldorf-Astoria, he knew that his fellow housing activists agreed.

Groups of health reformers were similarly well organized. Their professions had gained great power with the public acceptance of the germ theory of disease and with discoveries in bacteriology; hence health reformers had the best ammunition to promote new housing laws (fig. 7.2). In the architectural realm, public health officers helped define minimums for room size, ventilation, and plumbing. Especially within the climate of environmental determinism, illness could be inextricably linked to places, and thus tuberculosis and pneumonia were "house diseases"; rooming house areas made women "drab, anemic, and disagreeably pathetic."[10] Social scientists and politicians also transferred powerful ideas of biological hygiene to the potentially dangerous concepts of social hygiene and moral contagion. Veiller borrowed from health reformers and stretched determinism even further:

FIGURE 7.2. Health poster from 1910. Hygeia, the ancient Greek goddess of health, is represented as sheltering the single-family house, trees, and the baby while she shuns the old city's density, dirt, disease, and crime.

We know now . . . that poverty, too, is a germ disease, contagious even at times; that it thrives amid the same conditions as those under which the germs of tuberculosis flourish—in darkness, filth, and sordid surroundings.[11]

The historian Roy Lubove has noted that reformers devoted little thought to *proving* these elusive but seemingly self-evident relationships. Nonetheless, belief in public health models fueled influential housing opinions.[12]

By 1900, social workers, settlement house residents, and scientific charity organizers also participated frequently in the critique of hotel housing. These people taught immigrants the one "American" way of life, diffused new ideas of hygiene, and testified for better housing laws and new building projects. People with influential opinions included Edward T. Devine, a social work administrator, educator, and (after 1896) general secretary of the New York Charity Organization Society. Powerful figures such as Grace and Edith Abbott, Sophonisba Breckinridge, Florence Kelly, and Lillian Wald included housing reform in their labor research, settlement house work, and codification of social work. In the 1920s, Edith Abbott was named dean of the University of

Chicago's new School of Social Service Administration. In Boston, Robert A. Woods and his wife, Eleanor Woods, directed South End House, where settlement resident Albert Wolfe did his masterful study of rooming houses.[13]

Leading architects and planners of the Progressive Era often entered housing reform in their roles as designers of model housing and new public space, usually representing the desires of major landowners. A few architects, notably, Ernest Flagg of New York, combined housing activism with major commercial work. Influential citizens hired designers such as Daniel Burnham, Charles Mulford Robinson, and John Nolen to wrap real estate rejuvenation schemes in the classical City Beautiful garb of civic betterment.[14]

After 1900, university professors, often in the social sciences, became a more prominent influence among professional uplifters and the white-collar ranks of all the environmental reform groups. For several decades, Harvard sociologist James Ford summarized housing work. He was the associate director of Hoover's Conference on Home Building and Home Ownership in the 1930s. The University of Chicago was perhaps the most exciting and influential academic center of practical urban ideas and training. In addition to Hull House and the School of Social Service Administration, the university's sociology department engendered an entire school of thought. Robert E. Park, one of the most important American scholars of race, ethnicity, and urban life, in 1916 became the first president of Chicago's Urban League. Park and other faculty members like Ernest W. Burgess attracted graduate students such as Harvey Zorbaugh, Nels Anderson, and Norman Hayner— each of whom did important work on hotel housing. The first department of city planning eventually emerged at the University of Chicago, heavily influenced with the urban ideas of the Chicago school of sociology.[15] By the 1920s, professors often conferred the most powerful expert status on negative opinions about downtown living.

In hotel life, these overlapping sets of reformers saw challenges to the new urban order in at least three distinct realms: the well-being of the family, the development of the individual, and the safety of society as a whole. The following discussion traces each realm of cultural and moral critique from the mid-1800s through the Progressive Era itself and then beyond into the 1920s. The organization of time is in many short, parallel strands rather than one long cable. Each cluster of negative professional opinions about hotel life is presented with its own chronology.

CONCERNS FOR THE FAMILY

Nineteenth-century industries and businesses created work environments and work lives that were increasingly isolating, large-scale, and controlled by people distant from the family. In response, the role of home and family as the most important and nurturing sphere of life took on greater importance, especially to housing reformers. As Veiller put it, "Where there are no homes there will be no nation." In 1911, Dr. Langley Porter (the founding president of the San Francisco Housing Association) wrote that the "health of the individual, physical and moral, and health of the community, physical and moral, both depend in no small degree on the dwelling in which the individual is housed." People who felt (as another activist put it) that home and family were the "crucible of our happiness" saw the notion of people living alone, or family groups living in uncharacteristic ways, as a clear danger to several aspects of the Victorian middle-income family.[16]

Undermined domestic roles and rituals. Women who lived in hotels—particularly those residents of palace and midpriced hotels who could afford the alternative of a single-family house—ran the risk of becoming spoiled by caravansary comforts. They also inevitably violated the Victorian requirements of true womanhood—being a proper mother and an active homemaker.[17] In 1857, the editors of *Harper's Weekly* declared that hotel women were "rapidly becoming unfit not only to be mothers, but to be wives, and members of society at all" (fig. 7.3). They could "neither work, nor talk, nor cook, nor make a bed." Worse yet, they spent "their whole life in gossiping with people of both sexes who are as idle as themselves."[18] Early critics also warned that the inappropriately lavish habits and empty materialism learned in expensive hotels would follow young couples into their mature years.[19] In 1905, Edith Wharton saw the fulfillment of such prophecies. She characterized fashionable New York hotel women as socially objectionable:

FIGURE 7.3. This reposing room in a Turkish bath, about 1904, typified the self-indulgence and empty lives that hotels made too easy for women of wealth.

[They were] . . . wan beings as richly upholstered as the furniture, beings without definite pursuits or permanent relations, who drifted on a languid tide of curiosity from restaurant to concert hall, from palm-garden to music room, from "art exhibit" to dressmaker's opening.[20]

It was all, Wharton said, a "vast, gilded void of existence." Other commentators found midpriced hotels less gilded but still empty. In 1923, hotel maids told Hayner that life at a midpriced hotel "made bums out of women." Their days consisted of sleeping until noon, shopping, playing bridge, taking beauty naps, dressing for dinner, and going out in the evening. One maid called the late-sleeping women "sun-dodgers."[21]

Interior decorating—assembling the middle-income family's material individuality—relied particularly on the mother. Critics wrote that a hotel mother could not "create that atmosphere of manners and things around her own personality, which is the chief source of her effectiveness" and her power over her husband and the development of her children.[22] Data in the 1920 census alarmed Bertha Nienburg, who wrote that Rochester, New York, had 11,500 married women (out of 74,000 total) who were eating at restaurants or living with relatives and thus not keeping house. These women, said Nienburg, may have been "succeeding in their function as guardians of the family," but they were "not contributing to the permanence and stability of civic life through the maintenance of homes."[23] An unhappy woman who had lived in a hotel concluded that "the only endurable kind" of day to have while living in a hotel was a "day busy elsewhere."[24]

Ironically, "being busy elsewhere" was exactly why hotel life appealed to many women of the middle and upper class. Part of the hotel's threat to the true cult of womanhood was that it freed women with nontraditional lives—those who had paid vocations (as doctors, teachers, or secretaries) or active volunteer careers (with charities or other organizations)—from the roles of decorating, entertaining, and doing little favors for their families. Inasmuch as such women threatened the dominant culture, their hotel homes were a threat as well.

Also prominent in the sins of hotel life was its reputation for breaking the ritual and privacy of the family dinner table. William Dean Howells said that for the proper family, private dining was the "moral effect of housekeeping." At the table, or in the parlor after meals, the ideal family was supposed to linger for conversation, companionship, and reading or embark on spontaneous family excursions. Public dining flaunted the model family meal supervised by the mother, presided over by the father, and attended by children at their accustomed chairs receiving instruction (figs. 7.4, 7.5).[25] To the 1903 editors of *Architectural Record,* communal dining was "the consummate flower of domestic irresponsibility, . . . the sacrifice of everything implied by the word 'home.'"[26] In restaurants or in boardinghouses, regular seats could not be assigned, and parents could not discipline their children without feeling public scorn. Families did not even have to eat at the same time. If they *did* eat together, they often scattered after the meal: father to the lobby to talk with men about business or politics, mother to a bridge party, daughter to a dance, and son to the billiard room. Hotels presented almost no friction of distance to retard this family dispersal, while suburban settings imposed a great deal of such friction. Burgess put it in the terms of an urban sociologist: the "small family group in apartment houses and residential hotels" was "the most notorious illustration of effectual detachment from the claims of kinship."[27] The lack of control in the dining room extended to the rest of the hotel home. In common halls or public lobbies, strangers and chance acquaintances had ready access to children. Mothers could not strictly control what their children saw in daily life.[28]

Also threatening the mainstream role of wives was the fact that hotels made possible a cultured, civilized life for men without the aid of a woman. To be sure, cheap lodging houses did little to substitute for women's care. So, too, the stereotypical homeless or single man was a nasty, gruff brute who proved how much men needed the civilizing influence of a home with a woman to take care of him (fig. 7.6). However, hotels in the better price ranges could provide domestic care as well as, or better than, a woman could. In some cases, then, the maxim "what every man needs is a good woman," became "what every man needs is a good *hotel*."[29] Hotel life not only threatened to spoil men and women for predetermined roles but also threatened to erase the roles themselves.

Individualism versus marriage and child rearing.   Observers of hotel life saw resident pipe fitters, maiden aunts, and mobile professional people as abnormal for several reasons. Beginning as early as the 1840s, critics worried that hotel life delayed marriage for single residents; for married couples, hotel life also seemed to delay child bearing.[30] According to Wolfe in 1906, the distractions of living downtown rendered people selfish and self-centered and emphasized "the individual life at the expense of the family and the home." Marriage became "too great a sacrifice"; children meant "expense and trouble and constant attention and 'being tied down at home.'" The American standard of living, he continued, was becoming an individual standard rather than a family standard. Roomers learned very soon the art of

FIGURES 7.4 AND 7.5.   Two of a series of 1871 *Harper's Weekly* cartoons by Thomas Nast comparing hotel and home life. *Left*, the tranquil and protected family dining room; *right*, a rough and noisy dining room in a mid-priced hotel of that period.

"seeking everywhere the greatest *individual* comfort at the least expense.[31]

Hotel living did imply childlessness. On the one hand, hotel and rooming house zones had the lowest birthrates for most cities and stood in sharp contrast to home-ownership areas with their high marriage rates and birthrates. In 1900, 95 percent of those owning houses in San Francisco were married, and 81 percent had children. Looking at these phenomena, social scientists and reformers did not assume market sorting as an explanation, that is, that unmarried childless people simply chose hotel housing. Instead, the reformers concluded that hotel housing *caused* the antifamily phenomena.[32] Based on the long history of problem children in hotels, housing professionals and hotel residents agreed that the environment suited children poorly.

To social arbiters, worse than delayed marriage or child bearing was never marrying at all. About one-tenth of the American population typically has never married, and as much as one-third of New York City's population lived alone in 1930. Yet, through the 1950s, Americans widely considered the condition of being unattached as either temporary or abnormal. The premier housing scholar, James Ford, wrote that having few contacts with married couples, children, and people outside one's own age and sex group tended to make the lives of hotel people seem aberrant. Wolfe spoke of marriage "rescuing" tenants "from the rooming house world and its sophisticating, leveling, and contaminating influences." Chicago social workers visited groups of workingmen who were sharing apartments and were surprised that the men were "extremely friendly," as if hospitality and friendliness were found only in family households.[33]

The relative absence of children was responsible for much of the un-natural character of single-room districts. Zorbaugh, the Chicago sociologist, felt that children were the real neighbors; childless districts therefore lacked a key catalyst of neighborly feeling. Sociologists noted that children forced adults to plan and hope for the future and to consider other-directed action. While child-filled tenements sparked hope (or its frustrated form of outrage), hotel housing rarely evinced either.[34] In order for there to be a proper neighborhood for children, the majority of American middle and upper class families also typically demanded yards or gardens. The reliance on yards as social separation zones related to another cluster of hotel critiques.

Demands for separation and low density. For centuries, wealthy burghers in Europe lived only a floor or two away from their place of work and from their poorest employees, apparently with no significant contagion of poverty. By 1900, in America, such density, mixture, and adjacency were becoming highly suspect in the view of reformers. Critics chided comfortable hotel families who lived in suites of rooms for having a lack of privacy. Residents in cheaper hotel types were criticized for living with too little space per person and for mixing disparate activities in the same room.[35] Reformers blamed some rooming house crowding and mixture on un-American housing standards brought by immigrants from southern Europe, where large families often lived in one or two rooms. Social workers also deplored as "a demoralizing lack of privacy" the European habit of having the same bedroom occupied by grown brothers and sisters. Hull House social workers called a married couple and a child living in one or two rooms an "irregular method of living." What was combined in one room, they said, should have been separated and sorted out in "parlor, bedroom, clothes closet, dining room, kitchen, pantry, and even coal shed." Building inspectors

FIGURE 7.7. Pathological proximity. A rag picker and a middle-class woman, at such close quarters, emphasized the social schisms of urban life in 1875.

ruled that cooking in bedrooms caused vermin problems, dirtied bedding, and problems of inadequate ventilation of cooking odors.[36]

The fear of mixture and the desire for separation also manifested themselves in critiques of the "lodger evil"—the practice of families taking in unrelated men or women as renters. Lodgers often shared family bedrooms. Also seen as unwanted mixture were the "invasions" of housing districts by corner grocery stores, multiple dwellings, small factories, and repair shops. In reformers' eyes, lodgers blighted home interiors just as mixed land uses and traffic congestion blighted residential streets and suggested transitional social character (fig. 7.7).[37]

At the turn of the century, social workers and settlement house leaders also encouraged families to stop mixing social life, family relaxation, and work areas of the home. Most often, this had occurred in the crowded family kitchen—in tenements, then called a living room. Instead, the reformers urged immigrant families to invest in a formal parlor. As Lizabeth Cohen has stressed, separating kitchen and parlor functions met reform goals of creating sharp divisions between public and family interactions and of separating family members from one another within the house.[38]

Between 1870 and 1920, separation *between* family dwelling units and between commercial and residential land uses also became increasingly urgent imperatives. Jacob Riis decried that 80 percent of the

FIGURE 7.8. The possible
horrors of shared plumbing.
A basement toilet room in
a New York City tenement.

crimes in New York City were perpetrated by individuals who had "either lost connection with home life, or never had any, or whose home
had ceased to be sufficiently separate, decent, and desirable."[39] The
word *separate* was notably first in his list of the necessary criteria for
housing. The poor maintenance and overuse of shared toilets in slum
residences led reformers to urge building codes that required private
toilets and baths for each dwelling unit (fig. 7.8). The majority of architecturally oriented reformers saw dense urban housing as "promiscuity in human beehives." Decongesting the city called for smaller
buildings, more open space, and spreading population out along suburban transportation lines. Interwoven with these desires was a growing preference for the open-lot house, set back from the street and from
its neighbors, in place of the more urbane row building that nudged
close to the sidewalk.[40]

Apartments and hotels, the critics said, also possessed the inherent
flaw of shared entrances and halls. The term "apartment house," one
committee said, was "simply a polite term for tenement." In the views
of most reformers, store owners were no longer to live above the store,
nor apprentices to live immediately adjacent to their work. To progressive reformers, any multiple dwelling inherently lacked "domestic quality"; moreover, the poor acoustical privacy of shared dwellings would
intensify marital discord. There was, as one critic put it, "a short cut

from the apartment house to the divorce court."[41] Yet compared to such perceived threats to families, hotel life was held as an even greater hazard for single people.

HAZARDS FOR THE INDIVIDUAL

The lives of single people in hotels invoked repeated reform critiques. The youth culture and recreation zones in rooming house districts were causes of alarm. Yet overarching all was the lack of parental and neighborly supervision of the sort that critics assumed to exist in traditional small towns. Ironically, some hotel residents felt too closely watched in hotels; they complained about feeling "very much in the public eye, . . . living in public, eating in public, and all but sleeping in public." A writer who had lived in a fifty-four-room hotel for thirteen years said she overheard servants having frequent conversations about guests; furthermore, she said, each guest was "carefully watched by certain 'old tabbies'" who lived there.[42] Yet, in the eyes of late Victorian and Progressive Era observers, this hotel surveillance packed too little social pressure to counter the environment's sexual temptations or its professional crime.

Sexual immorality and improper recreation. According to mainstream reform views, the potentials for personal immorality—frequent sexual liaisons outside marriage—loomed much larger for people living in hotels than for people in suburban houses. The reasons seemed clear: in hotels, members of the opposite sex lived on the same hallways, had the right to visit one another's rooms, and could come and go quietly. New people moved in weekly or monthly. Sexual immorality, in fact, was *the* problem that prompted the settlement house resident, Albert Wolfe, to publish his exhaustive 1906 study, *The Lodging House Problem in Boston.* He decried many evils of rooming house life but identified sexual immorality as the "darkest aspect." Reformers in many cities described unmarried couples living together as major evidence of a "general loosening of moral texture."[43] Each time a landlady said, "What my tenants do is their own business as long as they pay their rent on time," she had substituted commerce for traditional social controls. Rooming houses, others said, had lost the "personal element in life."[44]

Along with their focus on sexual offenders, reformers also focused on the mixture of wayward souls with other, impressionable people. Hotels and rooming houses, said Wolfe, exuded an "atmosphere of moral laxity" that was dangerous for virtuous country people who had been thrown into the deep water of city life. "Consciously or unconsciously, the influence of imitation will be at work," he wrote. "If we stay in Rome long enough, we do as the Romans do."[45] Matrons in San Francisco concurred with Wolfe. The housing danger for a single girl in the 1920s was no longer the white slaver but the gradual breaking down of spiritual and moral standards as a result of improper surroundings and companionship. The cheapest residential hotel rooms, the matrons added, caused the most overcrowding, worst sanitation, and greatest "moral strain."[46] The high incidence of venereal disease among roomers and the number of abortion clinics in rooming house neighborhoods underscored concerns about sex, as did the belief that the temporary sexual liaison was "one avenue through which the prostitute class, both of men and women," was recruited.[47]

Prostitutes did live in some hotels, and they could both learn and practice their trade there (fig. 7.9). The shadier rooming houses associated with beer gardens and commercial amusement gardens were almost sure to be places of assignation. In 1915, housing inspectors in Stockton, California, wove their concerns about prostitution into a survey of rooming houses located over saloons:

Women openly solicit in booths in the saloons and take men to the rooms upstairs. In one house the inspector observed that every man accompanied by a woman was asked whether the room was desired for "only a little while or for the night."[48]

In other cities, larger hotels also came in for criticism because prostitutes mixed too easily with tenants. Reformers reiterated that in hotels, both men and women lived next door to "fearful possibilities."[49]

Since people of the same sex routinely shared a hotel room (and sometimes shared a bed) without comment, homosexual couples blended without notice into the upper ranks of hotel life. But in cheap lodging houses and missions, where visual and acoustical privacy was difficult, social investigators made careful note of homosexual solicitation and activity. The sociologist of hobo life, Nels Anderson, reported that homosexual practices among male migrant laborers were fairly

FIGURE 7.9. Prostitute thieves plying their trade with the help of an elegant hotel room. A cautionary view from the *National Police Gazette*, 1879.

common. Although he said they were not *more* frequent than in other all-male situations—prisons, the army, or the navy—these relationships concerned the parents of adolescent boys doing migrant work.[50] Such realities added to the sexual taint of hotel life.

More prevalent than sexual immorality were the perceived dangers of drinking, dancing, café life, and cheap amusements. Together they created another side of the "bright light district" and rooming house youth culture that affronted reformers (fig. 7.10).[51] Similar problems, most vivid in the elite hotels, were associated with all types of hostelries. Elbert Hubbard, author of the popular *A Message to Garcia* and an enthusiastic booster of Craftsman-style bungalows, characterized the residents of expensive hotels as "a gilded, gabby gang of newly gotten rich, or the offspring of such." The flashy hotels were places "where the vampire finds her hunting-ground, and the riot of the senses is complete; where flunkies flunky without ceasing, and the parasite is at

FIGURE 7.10. Signs of dangerous commercial and residential mixture, 1936. This Kansas City drovers' hotel advertises housing and beer at the same location.

home."[52] The *Saturday Evening Post* tersely called hotel life "the time killer industry." Chicago social workers acknowledged surprise at encountering families that seemed to *like* living in furnished rooms and rooming houses because they desired "the excitement that can be found in the rooming-house neighborhoods."[53]

Temperance crusaders aimed their hostility at hotel operators as well as at saloon keepers. The housing expert Carol Aronovici, in a study of cheap lodging houses in St. Paul in 1917, took pains to photograph empty liquor bottles in the rooms. During Prohibition, some hotels engaged directly in bootlegging; at better hostelries, the bellmen often sold or gave telephone numbers for obtaining bootleg liquor. In 1921, the highly publicized death of a drunken woman during a party given by Roscoe (Fatty) Arbuckle in San Francisco's St. Francis Hotel gave the term "Arbuckle party" to any wild hotel room celebration.[54]

The volatile combination of fast and close dancing, alcohol, and the absence of chaperones spelled trouble to reform-minded people wherever it occurred—in a grand hotel or in a cheap dive. In 1883, a Methodist church in San Francisco listed dancing *twice* among its list of sinful city amusements. Indeed, many of the cafés frequented by hotel residents also featured daily dancing and introductions of men and women by café employees (fig. 7.11).[55] Some palace hotels scheduled weekly and then daily tea dances. In 1917, a concerned citizen published a newspaper article entitled "Afternoon Teas First Step Toward

FIGURE 7.11. Postcard view of the Cave Cafe and Grill, near San Francisco's rebuilt Barbary Coast, ca. 1920. The back of the postcard promised "something doing all the time"—exactly what worried reformers about unchaperoned social life.

Depths; Evolution of Good Girls to 'Flappers' of the Bright Lights Is Subtle Transition."[56]

Pathological proximities and isolation.   Another, less visible hazard of hotel life, according to critics, was its potential for leading to a life of crime. Reformers saw this risk particularly in cheap lodging houses, where young people might mix with the most hardened criminals. The chief of New York's secret police branded the laborers' hotels of the Bowery as "nurseries of crime." He claimed that the peril peaked when a young man was nearly broke and he checked into a 15-cent lodging house:

[The young man is then] ready for the tempter whom he finds waiting for him there, reinforced by the contingent of ex-convicts returning from the prisons after having served out their sentences for robbery or theft. . . . In nine cases out of ten, he turns out a thief, or a burglar, if indeed, he does not sooner or later become a murderer.[57]

To his credit, the police chief saw lack of work as the root cause of this progression, but this was lost in related discussions. In a conversation with Riis, a New York police court justice vowed that the 10-cent lodging houses more than counterbalanced "the good done by the free reading room, lectures, and all other agencies of reform." He continued that "such lodging houses have caused more destitution, more beggary and crime than any other agency" he knew.[58] In the twentieth century, Los Angeles police routinely searched for law offenders in the cheap hotels

FIGURE 7.12. Suspicious isolation and improper material life. The caption for this photograph in the 1919 report of California's Commission on Immigration and Housing read, "Is the housing problem merely a problem of *houses*? Can we expect this man to be 100 percent American?"

and rooming houses near the railroad station. Raymond Chandler's detective character, Philip Marlowe, repeatedly visited hotels "whose clerks were 'half watchdog and half pander' and where nobody except Smith or Jones signed the register."[59]

A different but also negative side to the illicit adjacency of hotel life was the friendless life also possible there: the painful isolation for those who did not *want* to be alone, or those who were pathologically withdrawing from human company (fig. 7.12). According to one hotel resident, a hotel filled with people having fun could be "the most lonely place in the world." Rooming house residents with no friends in the area could write poignantly about the "cramped and awful loneliness of a hall bedroom." Young people who did not frequent dance halls or lively cafés but passed them frequently were constantly reminded of their own solitude.[60]

Zorbaugh—whose personal loneliness during his Chicago fieldwork added to his sharp distaste for hotel life—said that hotels carried individualization "to the extreme of personal and social disorganization." Rooming houses "were a world of atomized individuals, or spiritual nomads."[61] As proof, Zorbaugh presented the following statement of a young rooming house woman who had moved to Chicago from Emporia, Kansas, for fervent but futile study as a violinist:

One gets to know few people in a rooming-house, for there are constant comings and goings, and there is little chance to get acquainted if one wished. . . . There were occasional little dramas—as when a baby was found in the alley, and when the woman in the "third floor back" took poison after a quarrel with her husband . . . when the halls and the bathrooms were the scenes of a few minutes' hurried and curious gossip. But the next day these same people would hurry past each other on the stairs without speaking.[62]

Whether or not single-room housing caused such isolation, lonesomeness was part of the territory.

Frequently published reports of suicides kept vivid the public image of pathological isolation in hotels and rooming houses. One hotel manager explained that after gaslights and gas heaters became standard equipment, suicide in hotel rooms was more common; suicide with gas was easier than using a gun or a razor blade.[63] Dozens of novelists set suicides in single-room housing. Hurstwood, the erstwhile husband in Dreiser's *Sister Carrie*, lives his last months in cheap rooming houses where he "toils up" the inevitable "creaky stairs." In a tiny room with gas jets "almost prearranged" for what he intends, he eventually kills himself with a final antisocial phrase, "What's the use?"[64]

THREATS TO URBAN CITIZENSHIP

Suicide and individual isolation worried Progressive Era housing reformers, but more troublesome was the isolation of hotel residents as a group. Even when they were not acting en masse in some political agitation, hotel people seemed to be forming subcultures that deepened the social schisms of the time and weakened the cultural hegemony of the middle and upper class. Reformers saw these dangers as an assault on the urban polity as a whole.

Insufficient materialism.   By 1900, most Americans had settled into the belief that form of tenure—owning versus renting—could be used reliably to discern someone's social position in much the same way that race, income, occupation, and education were used. In interviews, poor house owners in Chicago said that owning a home made them "real

Americans" and gave them a means of achieving personal control over their world.[65] Since so many Americans anchored their personal and civic identities to their homes, reformers saw those who did not (or could not) as insufficient, deviant, or unhealthy. In short, renters were second-class, or perhaps third-class, citizens. Early observers warned that the rental aspect of hotel life's "dissipation" would engender "a distaste for steady and persevering application to anything."[66] Housing policymakers (property owners themselves) firmly agreed that both apartments and hotels would breed bad citizenship. In 1910, Veiller said this about apartment renters:

It is useless to expect a conservative point of view in the workingman, if his home is but three or four rooms in some huge building in which dwell from 20 to 30 other families, and this home is his only from month to month. . . . Democracy was not predicated upon a country made up of tenement dwellers, nor can it so survive.[67]

California housing activists concurred that the home, not rental property of any kind, was "the bulwark of good citizenship." Other California critics complained that if migrant workers saved money, it was only to send the money back home rather than invest it in the local economy. The migrants therefore had little desire to improve their living quarters.[68]

In an otherwise path-breaking book on urban housing, the influential planner Henry Wright flatly explained multiple-family homes as a result of irresponsibility:

[The inception of the apartment house] was brought about by the vaguely defined need of families whose habits were of a semi-transient nature, or those who did not care to assume the responsibilities of the independent house, and yet neither desired nor could afford the luxury of hotel life.[69]

Wright was one of many housing activists to carry Veiller's ideas into decades of later practice.[70]

For the business elites who directed Progressive Era housing reform, the bonds of rootedness and civic responsibility were woven out of mortgage payment receipts: personal financial interest in city real estate. Home ownership guaranteed accumulation of goods through thrift and self-denial. For some analysts, renters also undermined the

FIGURE 7.13. A building considered dangerous to civic virtue. A typical small apartment hotel in New York City, 1903.

stability of centralized bank and mortgage control because they paid scattered individual landlords.[71]

Within the realm of renters, a distinction between hotel dwellers and apartment dwellers arose over the *amount* of personal possessions needed for a proper American home. Unlike apartment dwellers, hotel residents rented both their space *and* their furniture (fig. 7.13). To social observers and public policymakers, this unrootedness crossed the last boundaries of civic propriety. Official rhetoric required citizens to own furniture and dishes as the minimum evidence of stability and civic worth. For Wolfe, household goods and furniture were "those last anchors of men and women to a sense of ownership and permanent interest in a fixed abode."[72] Furniture was an important minimum for Edith Abbott, too. The great evil of the rooming house, she asserted, was neither landlord profit (as some reformers said of tenements) nor sanitary danger. Instead, it was "the degradation that comes from a family living in one room with broken, dilapidated furniture, without responsibility or a sense of ownership, . . . [with] nothing of their own."[73]

For hotel and rooming house residents, the American dream of owning one's own house, yard, and furnishings often did not match the necessity of mobile careers and occupations. That mobility itself constituted another realm in the cultural threats of downtown living.

FIGURE 7.14. Citizenship not encouraged here. Part of a winter bread line at the Bowery Mission in New York City, photographed by Lewis Hine in 1906.

Mobility and vagrancy.   Virtually no one wanted hoboes and other overtly mobile people to be citizens of the city. Officials and the public automatically assumed the worst about hoboes (fig. 7.14). "The doctrine that the American tramp is a pariah and that he ought to be kept such is not often formulated so bluntly, but it embodies the underlying doctrine of the American method in dealing with the tramp," wrote William Stead in 1894 in *If Christ Should Come to Chicago.* Stead accurately reported that the bum was generally and unfairly seen as "outside the pale of human sympathy, . . . an incorrigibly idle loafer, a drunkard, a liar, and a reprobate."[74] Johanna Von Wagner, a Progressive Era tuberculosis inspector in California, candidly expressed the pariah view as she described the residents of San Francisco's cubicle hotels in 1913:

The inmates of these places are human wrecks, old and young, diseased or habitual drunkards; others have failed in the struggle for existence, and [there are] those who from the beginning were never able mentally or physically to compete with their fellow men, their condition making it all the more urgent that they be compelled to live in a more sanitary environment.[75]

To Von Wagner and the general public, the casual laborer's style of life was not only alien but abhorrent, vagrancy and travelers having been mistrusted by Europeans for centuries. Single hoboes and casual laborers were not only poor and unmarried but also violated even more basic American values: cleanliness, sobriety, self-control, steady employment, material possessions, and commitment to home and family. Where "pariah" was too honest a term for such people, writers substituted the term "homeless man." By 1900, vagrancy as a legal term also meant begging, loitering, street walking, and indigence. Chicago School sociologists did occasionally associate creative social change with mobility. More often, however, they linked mobility to vice districts, bright light areas of the city, divergent types of people and activities, and general social disorganization.[76]

Hoboes were not the only mobile people to be mistrusted, however. Robert Park conflated "the hoboes, for example, and the hotel dwellers" as "unsettled and mobile . . . [and] stabilized only on the basis of movement, tribal organizations, and customs."[77] In 1915, in his famous article, "The City," Park used hotel life as a metaphor of metropolitan social disintegration:

A very large part of the population of great cities . . . live much as the people do in some great hotel, meeting but not knowing one another. The effect of this is to substitute fortuitous and casual relationships for the more intimate and permanent associations of the smaller community.[78]

Two generations of Chicago students applied Park's concepts. Ernest Mowrer wrote that the "emancipated" families in hotels had "casual or touch-and-go" relations with their neighborhood. Zorbaugh decried the social breakdowns in Chicago's cheap rooming houses as well as in expensive Gold Coast apartment hotels. The Gold Coast, he claimed, was merely a "location," not a neighborhood. The existing solidarity was one of "caste rather than of contiguity." In rooming houses, he said, "there is not even gossip, no interest, sentiment, and attitude which can serve as a basis of collective action. Local groups do not act. Local life breaks down. . . . The last vestige of community has disappeared."[79]

Park's student Norman Hayner put the worst possible construction on mobility in his 1920s study of hotel life. For instance, he interviewed a well-paid man and his wife, married four years, who moved often because the man established new sales franchises for electrical appliances. Hayner denigrated them as a "childless tramp family moving about from apartment to hotel and never staying in one place more than four or five months."[80] Edith Abbott, in her book summarizing twenty-five years of social work in Chicago, sympathetically presented immigrants and blacks as hapless victims. However, for the families living in furnished rooms—overwhelmingly American-born white people—she displayed obvious disgust and exercised her most invective prose. Such families were "an objectionable class [that is] unstable, irresponsible, and shiftless," for which little could be done.[81] To professors of the Chicago School, moving frequently undermined the power of neighborhoods, and the areal neighborhood was an essential element, if not *the* essential element, in the definition of community. This definition took long-term root at the core of the city planning profession and of suburban design policies.

Mobility meant not only a poorly formed community but also apathetic and corrupt voters. Community fund solicitors and census workers complained that clerks at polite hotels automatically intercepted their attempts to canvass hotel residents. One census director said that hotel people were "so bent on having a good time that duty to the city means nothing whatever to them."[82] Although one study found that a third of Chicago's permanent rooming house residents voted, a precinct captain from nearby complained that it was "useless to try to get the people from the rooming houses to go to the polls."[83] Proprietors of some large boardinghouses became notorious for organizing their tenants in political-machine voting scandals. In New York City, both major parties regarded residents of cheap lodging houses as potential paid voters.

When hotel residents *were* independently organized and active, they became a community that menaced middle and upper class order. San Francisco's South of Market area saw violent workers' outbursts in the

FIGURE 7.15. The howling wolves of urban disease assailing the suburbs. This health poster of 1910 promoted the protective wall of health reform. The original caption read, "How high is the wall in your town?"

1870s and in 1885, 1891, 1893, and 1902.[84] The national march of Coxey's Army in 1894, reinforced by the later organizing attempts of the Industrial Workers of the World (IWW) from 1912 through the 1930s, proved to the public that rooming house and lodging house people could act as a community. Even when laborers were not marching, the presence of Socialist bookstores and Marxist lecturers and devotees in the single laborers' zone reminded observers of nascent unrest.[85] No matter what outside observers made of hotel patrons' political leanings, hotel districts also represented reservoirs of yet other hazards.

Risks to urban real estate and biological health. At a very practical level, the fire and health menaces of cheap downtown hotels worried downtown landholders. Inspection reports and newspaper exposés repeatedly spotlighted old, poorly built, and badly managed hotels as perilous firetraps. Some rooming and lodging houses had no fire escapes; some had hallways and stairways too blocked or too narrow for egress. In other buildings, managers had padlocked the fire doors. A typical fire report in 1924 concerned a three-story wooden hotel in Los Angeles where thirty-five people died because of inadequate and defective fire escapes. Officials routinely reminded builders that cheap wooden hotels threatened the adjacent buildings, the entire neighborhood, and the hotel inhabitants.[86]

Fire dangers paled next to the health risks that cheap hotel areas represented to reformers (fig. 7.15). A California state housing report on San Francisco lodging houses complained that since the buildings housed thousands of "irresponsible" men "careless as to their general personal habits and cleanliness," they presented "an ever constant danger to the health of the entire city." The report stated that shared toilets and baths, especially when poorly maintained, spread diseases among all the tenants; the constant moving from lodging to lodging carried infection to other buildings. Inspectors declared that lodging house rooms posed an additional health risk: they cited vermin-covered beds and blankets reeking with filth and soaked with wine. In most San Francisco lodging houses, sheets were changed (at the most) twice a week—not necessarily for each new occupant of a room; only one-fourth of the establishments ever fumigated their blankets.[87] Von Wagner, the tuberculosis inspector, vividly summarized the dangers:

The cheap class [of hotels] with ten to twenty-five cent beds, are not only breeding places for various diseases, but also centers of infection, especially tuberculosis. We know from past history that plague, cholera and smallpox originated in cheap lodging houses. Therefore, they should be eliminated. They are all unfit for human habitation.[88]

Von Wagner also shuddered at the use of common towels and common drinking cups, holdovers of nineteenth-century hotel practices. Notably, because of the earthquake and fire of 1906, the San Francisco buildings in question were less than ten years old at the time of these descriptions. Conditions in other cities were often worse.

More than any other critique, enforcement of fire and health codes brought reformers into early face-to-face conflicts with building owners. These confrontations revealed deep schisms in progressive reform. In their family *tenement* literature, activists like Veiller, Park, and Abbott attacked the greed of individual landlords who often held relatively small and scattered properties. However, when the reformers wrote about *hotel* problems, they mentioned landlord greed much less and argued more against hotels on cultural and social grounds. In the search for the root of the hotel housing problem, the tenants and their culture were seen as guilty.[89] It was easier for reformers to nominate themselves as caretakers of culture than to question the property industry.

Challenging culture instead of profit or class was not necessarily dissembling behavior on the part of the housing activists. The attempts to establish new ideas about centralized control of land use and building types were openly fought to preserve property values that matched those of downtown or suburban landowners. One of the ironies of the Progressive Era was that reformers fought monopolies but often helped big business as well. Small-scale downtown owners or slumlords rarely had the ear of the reformers, while big landholders with prominent downtown blocks of land were often reform allies and charity organization directors. Concerns about moral problems thus merged easily with concerns about real estate values without seriously challenging the American city's established power structure.[90]

HOTEL HOMES AS A PUBLIC NUISANCE

Like the reformers' ironic positions on real estate values, the negative hotel housing opinions voiced by literary critics, housing activists, health officials, and social workers were not without their internal contradictions and exceptions: hotel housing did not provide proper individuality and personal expression, yet it fostered selfish individualism; hotel housing was pathologically isolating, yet it was not sufficiently private; no one supposedly met anyone in hotels, yet lodging houses were meeting places of great danger. Outright hypocrisy characterized other critiques: amusements enjoyed by wealthy people (billiards for men after dinner; cotillions for all) were wrong in commercial settings or when enjoyed by wage laborers and families struggling to enter the middle and upper class. Some critiques were simply myopic: the people who saw the pathologies of rooming houses rarely mentioned the parallels in other housing types, such as the breaches of sexual mores at weekend house parties of the wealthy or elderly widows pathologically isolated in middle-income suburban houses.

A few social commentators did understand and accept the hotel population's nontraditional ways of living. The Chicago sociologist Day Monroe was one of these exceptions. In a study of Chicago families she noted that "certainly fewer than 20 percent" of the people living in hotels exemplified the supposed "social waste, unproductive leisure,

or even family disorganization" that others automatically associated with hotel life. The majority of women living in hotels had good reasons for being there and represented social well-being, Monroe said.[91] Charles Swanson wrote his doctoral dissertation on the social backgrounds in Lower West Side districts of Manhattan, areas analogous to the Chicago rooming house area analyzed in Zorbaugh's *Gold Coast and Slum.* Swanson failed to find the social pathologies described by Zorbaugh. He saw "no area of anonymity, of desolation, loneliness, and lost personalities." He said that quite the contrary seemed to have been true, since Bohemianism strictly tabooed such qualities.[92]

Nonetheless, with such occasional exceptions, after 1890 the case *for* hotel life was rarely stated forcefully or officially. By the 1920s, the case *against* hotel housing options had successfully been assembled. Stated most simply, to its critics the continued existence of hotel life worked against the progress of the grand new city. In the biological analogies of the day, the residential hotel buildings themselves served as incubators of old-city pathologies. For the reformers working on the new city, single-room dwellings were not a housing resource but a public nuisance (fig. 7.16).

In 1910, Veiller published a major model housing law to help promote such legislation throughout the United States. For each section of the proposed law, he provided capsule explanations. In his explanation

FIGURE 7.16. Rooming house in Lancaster, Ohio, 1938. As a photographer, Ben Shahn caught the irony of a single worker's life-style labeled "first class."

for the definition of "tenement," Veiller was careful to emphasize the following point:

[The definition of tenement] does not include hotels nor lodging houses. It should not do so. [***] The problems of the common lodging house occupied by homeless men or homeless women are totally different from the problems of the tenement house occupied by families. The two should not be confused.[93]

The asterisks inserted in the quotation indicate an automatic leap in Veiller's mind, a leap made by virtually all reformers of his day. Any single-room life automatically meant the worst possible case, which Veiller castigated as the "common lodging house" filled with "homeless men and women." Writing to his audience of legislators, lawyers, and lobbyists, Veiller was careful to note in another section that activists could not *legally* label hotels and lodging houses as nuisances, since common law and the jurisprudence of the time recognized only sanitary or health problems as worthy of legal exclusion. Even the cheapest lodging house, when new, did not present the health problems that tuberculosis officers found in older ones. But Veiller clearly implied that hotel buildings *were* public nuisances. The wholesale adoption of Veiller's building codes in many states, including California, proved that reformers elsewhere agreed.

To someone watching the building of the city up to 1920, all the antihotel work of the Victorian and Progressive Era reformers might have seemed for naught. They had enunciated antihotel opinions but typically had not stopped new residential hotel construction or operation. Reformers had accomplished changes of rhetoric more than changes of action. In fact, the early 1920s were a boom period for hotel building and hotel living of most sorts. However, while the laws were not yet adequate to eradicate single-room homes, American law had begun to recognize residential hotels as a nuisance. The foundation of professional and public opinion encouraged by the Progressive Era reformers would serve to exclude the option of hotel homes in urban culture as developers rebuilt the old city of pre-World War I and expanded the new automobile suburbs. Housing action of the future would ensure new homes that were uniformly separate, sanitary, and (most of all) centrally approved.

FROM SCATTERED OPINION

TO CENTRALIZED POLICY

CRITICIZING HOTEL LIFE WAS ONE THING; effectively controlling it was another. By 1910, reformers had established the idea that hotel housing was a public nuisance. From 1900 through the 1940s, interlocking groups of reformers and landowners transformed objections about hotel life into practices to control living in hotels. For the goals of the culturally and socially reorganized new city to succeed, aberrant forms of housing had to be prevented and removed—slum and hotel alike. Yet gaining control was neither automatic nor preordained. Hotel housing was entrenched in some areas and in others, still expanding (fig. 8.1). A few handfuls of reformers had to do more than galvanize public opinion against the notion of living in hotels; they also had to establish whole new governmental organizations and procedures to give cities and states the necessary legal and bureaucratic power.

At first, California's housing officials developed innovative views of hotel living as a viable (if problematic) part of the state's housing stock. Yet after experimentation with policies different from those of the Midwest and East, California reformers adopted more negative hotel attitudes; as expert actions shifted from the state to the federal level, the power and the uniformity of antihotel policies increased as well. In the 1890s, Californians believed that incremental improvements—

FIGURE 8.1. Rooming house sign near the Iowa State Capitol, 1940. Legislators in Des Moines did not have to walk far to see single room occupancy as part of the slum problem.

moral conversion of one person at a time, remodeling of one building at a time with codes and inspection—were enough to eventually achieve the desired uniformity. By the 1920s, land-use planning and zoning provided stronger responses to hotel life. In spite of these efforts, complete central control remained beyond official grasp. Finally, in the late 1930s, the planners' projects gathered momentum from the dangerously paired strategies of narrow ideals and deliberate ignorance, the policies that would prove nearly powerful enough to eliminate hotel life altogether.

FORGING FRAMEWORKS FOR HOUSING CHANGE

Early housing reform organizations in California had elements similar to their models and counterparts on the East Coast. Dedicated volunteer activists privately defined a problem, became the leading experts as they gathered the best (or only) information, galvanized the support of people with influence, and having talent and good timing, shifted quickly from doing small local projects to influencing major legislation. When a friendly administration established an official agency, the lead

FIGURE 8.2. Portrait of Simon Lubin in 1913. Lubin had just begun his work as president of the Commission of Immigration and Housing.

private reformer became the public agency head.[1] Thus, in California as elsewhere, the circuits of information and the conduits of antihotel opinion were directed by a relatively small number of people.

In California, the housing reform process was exemplified by the work of a wealthy volunteer named Simon J. Lubin and his creation, the state Commission on Immigration and Housing (fig. 8.2). Lubin's commission, a classic Progressive Era enterprise, had an enormous influence on the state's housing, planning, and zoning. Lubin was born to a wealthy Sacramento and San Francisco family. He went to Harvard University, and in his last two years there (from 1900 to 1902) he devoted himself to immigration problems. This work provided Lubin's tie to Lawrence Veiller and the national network of reform centered in New York. In 1903–04, Lubin lived at Boston's South End House, a social settlement, where he met such important housing experts as Albert Wolfe, Robert Woods, and Eleanor Woods. After living for an additional two years in a settlement in the slums of New York's Lower East Side, Lubin returned to Sacramento and went to work as an officer of the family business, a large international retail and wholesale dry goods company. His chance for more social activism came in 1912 with the election of a reform governor, Hiram Johnson. Lubin talked Johnson into forming a temporary commission on immigration which Lubin chaired. The following year, the state legislature created the permanent Commission on Immigration and Housing (CIH) with Lubin as chair and with a full-time staff of twenty headquartered in San Francisco.[2]

More than Lubin's lobbying motivated Johnson and the legislature to create the CIH. In 1912, California had no slums of the style found in New York, but Californians were convinced that employment stimulated by the new Panama Canal would bring tidal waves of southern European immigrants to the state's cities. Demonstrations by the IWW, marches by migrant workers, and riots and killings on one of the Central Valley's giant ranches had also focused attention on the problems of migrant workers and their dwellings.[3]

Lubin enthusiastically picked up where a small local reform group, the San Francisco Housing Association, had left off after three years of work (1911–1913).[4] He also actively strengthened California's ties to national reform. He carried on an active correspondence with his Boston contacts, with experts at Hull House in Chicago, and with New Yorkers whom he hoped to attract for the executive staff of the agency. As a matter of course, Lubin joined the National Housing Association, and Veiller personally provided books, reports, and advice.[5] Lubin chaired the CIH for ten years, gave thousands of dollars to cover staff travel and research expenses, and spent weeks personally training the eventual succession of executive staff. By personally serving as a connecting link, Lubin helped to make an efficient transfer of ideas from the East Coast to the West Coast; the CIH staff routinely cited Veiller, Woods, Breckinridge, and Abbott in their publications.[6]

Lubin and the CIH generally shared and reinforced the values of California's major downtown property owners. As an officer of a large company, Lubin was well connected to the business and real estate communities (fig. 8.3). He also knew labor issues firsthand, as the family business employed a small army of skilled clerks and unskilled warehouse workers. To Lubin, better housing meant a more reliable working force with fewer turnovers in staff.

In retrospect, large-scale land developers and investors clearly needed expertise like that of the CIH to organize city services and to guarantee investments, just as the reformers needed the influence of the large developers to build the new city. Regulating undesirable development was one method of improving the value of urban real estate generally. However, the regulation of downtown and edge-of-the-city development helped the biggest developers most and hurt the "curbs-

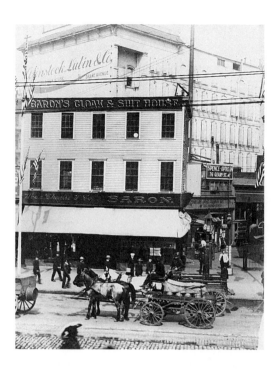

FIGURE 8.3. Side view of Weinstock Lubin's store in San Francisco, ca. 1900. Simon Lubin's father was a founding partner of a dry goods enterprise whose retail store loomed over Market Street a block from Union Square.

toners," people dealing only in a few lots at a time. This congruence of CIH reform and big business was an irony typical of the Progressive Era. On the one hand, housing reformers fought to regulate land-owners and unscrupulous builders and educated the public about the fraud of the landlord class. On the other hand, the reformers had to join with the largest developers and downtown interests to operate and to get legislation passed.[7]

As if to demonstrate the bureau's alliance with downtown business interests, between 1912 and the late 1920s, the CIH jumped whole-heartedly into the California campaign for city planning and zoning, although those issues did not directly impinge on housing and immi-gration. Glowing reports about city planning—reported as "really more important than the housing problem, or the sanitary problem, or the transportation problem" (since it dealt "with the interrela-tion of them all")—appeared frequently in CIH publications.[8] As an example of overlapping interests, in 1914, Lubin and the CIH sup-ported Charles Cheney, a young San Francisco architect and planner, to travel throughout the Northeast and prepare an ambitious exhibit to convert state legislators to proplanning and prozoning opinions. Cheney's father was Berkeley's preeminent commercial realtor, head of the Chamber of Commerce, and a prominent member of the California

Real Estate Association (CREA). In 1915, the CIH, CREA, and other supporters of central planning won the political debate. The legislature gave California municipalities the right to appoint city planning commissions, develop long-term plans, and regulate the subdivision of land. The assumption—correct or not—was that compared to politicians, experts would be more objective and scientifically more value-free in shaping the city.[9] After 1940, city planners were to become prime actors in the fight against culturally aberrant hotel housing.

The most focused housing projects of the CIH were two habitation laws, one passed in 1917 and one passed in 1923.[10] With these uniform laws applied to all communities in the state and with the active assistance of the CIH, most large cities in California had at least nascent city planning and zoning by the early 1920s. Furthermore, the people involved had the service of a set of central bureaus for comparing work and disseminating information and influence. Also by the 1920s, adding to their old health departments, most large California cities had appointed the first trained housing inspectors for their building departments.

These reform actions boded ill for the commercial experiment of hotel living. Thirty years earlier, the New York police inspector, Thomas Byrnes, had said that cheap hotels were "not a case for a palliative; as Emerson would say, it is a 'case for a gun'—for the knife, the blister, the amputating instruments."[11] The work of people like Lubin, Cheney, and the CIH and the aid of their laws, competent staffs, and zealous building inspectors meant that California's antihotel reformers not only had the knife and the blister for slum clearance but also the amputating instruments to begin removing the institution of hotel residence.

EARLY ARENAS OF HOTEL CONTROL

As reformers organized to fight urban architectural problems, they did not move from one strategy to another in a simple chronological line or scale of intervention. Nor were all of the measures Progressive Era developments. Some of the strategies, particularly moral codes, had been tried in California well before 1912 and the founding of the CIH. The targets also shifted. The reformers aimed their building codes particularly at cheap lodging houses and the worst rooming houses—the bottom two-thirds of the hotel market. Zoning promised to control the entire market but only in the new sections of the city.

Enforcement of moral codes.　　At the simplest level, reformers sought to control what they perceived as aberrant social lives by controlling the behavior itself. Beginning in the nineteenth century, various San Francisco reform committees fought for city controls against the sins of downtown life; they did this as a part of their mission hall programs, temperance promotion, and dance hall crusades. In 1903, the city's Board of Supervisors passed a set of mild restrictions against dancing, gambling, sexual solicitation, and cross-dressing. The city's gambling and whorehouse activities continued unabated.[12] In 1913, the state passed the Red Light Abatement Act, allowing authorities to close prostitution houses for up to a year. The Northern California Hotel Association joined the coalition that lobbied against the law, fearing that enforcement could too easily be brought against hotel owners. American entry into World War I stimulated a high wave of concern about vice districts. The ever-active Simon Lubin—with an eye to hotel connections with prostitution and as a member of a Sacramento welfare commission—railed against police corruption that kept "unregulated hotels and lodging houses spreading venereal diseases among the soldiers" at the local army camp.[13] Not all sexual alarms about hotels focused on prostitution or troop safety. Some social agencies recommended that hotel managers bar boys under the age of seventeen from cheap lodging houses, or at least prevent boys and men from rooming together, because of the dangers of homosexuality. For similar reasons, reformers elsewhere urged police to keep city boys from loitering or playing in streets and parks near the cheap lodging house districts.[14]

In 1919, federal Prohibition eliminated drinking in hotel bars and dining rooms and thereby slashed the most lucrative profits of hotel operation. The California Anti-Saloon League and the local WCTU, however, could do little to enforce Prohibition in San Francisco. As in the hotels of other cities, Prohibition merely moved drinking from the management-supervised areas of San Francisco hotels to private rooms, with dire consequences for furniture maintenance and cleaning bills.[15]

Parlor reform—the campaign to require sitting rooms in tenements and rooming houses and thereby to encourage quiet home life—was a milder moral reform that also affected hotels. In 1927, the Girls Hous-

FIGURE 8.4. Creating social reform by changing individual behavior. Men taking a compulsory shower in a New York City public lodging house, ca. 1900.

ing Council of San Francisco decried the long absence of rooming house parlors. Blocked from their goal of laws requiring sitting rooms, the matrons of San Francisco (like women's groups elsewhere) compiled a private registry of rooms. Volunteers inspected each address in the San Francisco registry and judged its respectability, cleanliness, and comfort. The resulting list was designed to prevent single girls from getting into morally dangerous situations when they followed up newspaper ads for a room. Some YMCAs offered similar services for men.[16] This regulation of behavior by private inspection was another means of changing or enforcing individual action.

For hoboes and other poorly dressed people, control of behavior was more direct and often rougher. When police caught drunks or panhandlers out of bounds in San Francisco, they were summarily sent back to the parts of the city "where they belonged" and roughed up if they did not go kindly. The showers required at least once a week in some municipal lodging houses were yet another means of inducing new behavior as well as hygiene (fig. 8.4).[17]

Control over hotel life simply by control of behavior proved ineffective. Prohibition's financial effects on hotels were unintended side effects and hurt the better hotels more than the cheap rooming houses. Laws regulating drinking, dancing, and other social life required constant enforcement that was impossible to provide. In contrast, regulating the environmental conditions of cheap hotels offered an approach that was literally more concrete and, to most observers, far more effective.

Building and health codes.   Initially, housing activists were often convinced that building code enforcement was *the* answer to better housing for the poor. "The solution of the housing problem," Veiller wrote, "is to be found chiefly in legislation preventing the erection of objectionable buildings and securing the adequate maintenance of all buildings."[18] As part of the general implementation of codes, regulation writers attacked fundamental problems of hotel safety and sanitation: firetraps, dark rooms, inadequate plumbing, and insufficient ventilation (fig. 8.5). An entire system of codes had to be implemented. After initial passage of the ordinance came the training of staff to review plans, inspectors to check construction of new buildings, and often another set of inspectors to find later management violations.

San Francisco's earliest attempts to regulate hotels and lodging houses began in 1870 with an ordinance requiring sleeping rooms with at least 500 cubic feet of air space for each lodger; the state passed a similar ordinance in 1876. These laws were primarily aimed at the dwellings of single Chinese laborers. A Sacramento newspaper editor protested the discrimination, asking, "What better right has a Chinaman than a white man to be ventilated?"[19] However, enforcement was used not for environmental improvements but mostly for racial harassment. By the turn of the century, an occasional health inspector did invoke the 1876 law for the worst white lodging houses. San Francisco's other early hotel ordinances were concerned less with health and safety and more with licenses and fees, that is, until the 1906 earthquake and fire.[20] In the first year following the fire, the corrupt administration of boss Abe Ruef and Mayor Eugene Schmitz allowed almost any rebuilding scheme, which outraged reformers. In a political backlash of 1908 and 1909, activists rewrote the city plumbing and building

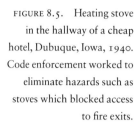

FIGURE 8.5. Heating stove in the hallway of a cheap hotel, Dubuque, Iowa, 1940. Code enforcement worked to eliminate hazards such as stoves which blocked access to fire exits.

laws. For the first time, health inspectors had the power to close non-conforming buildings. Also for the first time, San Francisco building owners experienced serious code enforcement; in 1909, the permit office rejected 75 percent of all the applications submitted. The single section of the new city building codes aimed specifically at hotels allowed cubicle-type rooms only in the most permanent and fireproof buildings; new, large, hastily constructed wooden lodging houses were outlawed.[21]

All subsequent hotel code restrictions came from the state. In 1909, California's legislature approved the first state housing law, a virtual carbon copy of the tenement code Veiller had written for New York City. California housing activists were not happy; they said legislators had been duped by the state's builders into allowing the densities of six-story Manhattan-style tenements when such buildings had not yet appeared in California cities.[22] The only mention of hotels in the 1909 state law was a significant "stables/lodging houses/rag storage" clause copied from Veiller:

No horse, cow, calf, swine, goat, rabbit, or sheep, chickens, or poultry shall be kept in a tenement house, or within 20 feet thereof on the same lot, *and no tenement houses or lot or premises thereof, shall be used for a lodging house,* or stable, or for the storage or handling of rags.[23]

Like Veiller, the California legislature had classified cheap hotels along with cattle and volatile rags as a prohibited nuisance use.

In 1913, prompted now by Lubin and his CIH experts in Governor Johnson's reform administration, state officials passed a short seven-page act specifically regulating hotels and lodging houses. The provisions of this act and other early actions show that the CIH, compared to its eastern counterparts, more actively included hotels in the public vision of housing. The CIH included officials from hotel organizations in their deliberations; they warned the city officials of Stockton, California, that they should supervise the construction of hotels as well as tenements or else slums would spring up. The first CIH housing survey included twenty-nine cheap lodging houses along with an area of immigrant cottage tenements.[24]

In 1917, the CIH pushed the legislature further. The state passed a trio of housing acts: a single dwellings act, a new tenement house act, and a comprehensive hotel and lodging house act that was very innovative. The new hotel act was thirty-nine pages—matching in detail the forty-one-page tenement act. The CIH properly crowed that its hotel law was "the most comprehensive in the U.S."[25] The Californians were breaking with standards automatically imported from elsewhere and were responding to local conditions with local ideas. This experiment in regional diversity would prove to be relatively short-lived.

Laws of other states had stronger details, but in its general conception, California's 1917 hotel act showed the framers' close familiarity with cheap hotel life. They allowed existing cubicle rooms to remain, and they included guidelines for open dormitory rooms; however, they outlawed new cubicle hotels.[26] Most important, the act set lasting bath-to-room ratios for the cheapest lodging houses: a separate water closet and shower on each floor for each sex, at the minimum ratio of 1 per 10 rooms or guests. Owners of existing hotels had to bring their toilet room ratios up to 1 to 12. These were strict requirements for the times. San Francisco's old requirements had been a ratio of 1 toilet room to 25 guests; New York required 1 water closet per 15 beds. The California hotel code matched the minimum window areas, room sizes,

FIGURE 8.6. Window well in a San Francisco hotel built to the city's 1909 codes. Later state housing acts forbade narrow air wells like this one at the National Hotel, a large rooming house on Market Street.

FIGURE 8.7. An imposing inexpensive hotel on two lots next to smaller downtown rooming houses. The scale of San Francisco's 82-room Hillsdale Hotel, built in 1912 on Sixth Street in the South of Market, was the wave of the future for this building type.

and floor area per occupant in concurrent tenement house standards (fig. 8.6). In the new tenement act, the CIH had also rewritten Veiller's "stables/lodging houses/rag storage" clause so that it no longer included lodging houses as a nuisance use.[27]

The new California housing codes also worked for greater separation of people within more specialized rooms. Hotels and apartments were to have separate toilets for employees and guests. The 1917 code also contained this language about the separation of cooking and sleeping:

Food shall not be cooked or prepared in any room except in a kitchen designed for that purpose. Floors of kitchens and rooms in which food is stored shall be made impervious to rats by a layer of concrete . . . or a layer of sheet tin or iron or similar material.[28]

Local housing inspectors later had inspection forms listing "cooking and sleeping in the same room" as a violation category along with infractions such as "undersize rooms," "overcrowding," and "insufficient toilets." Kitchen measures like these were aimed at illegally subdivided houses and other light housekeeping rooms whose owners avoided inspection by not declaring cooking uses. Unbending rules on separate kitchens would become a major hurdle for the maintenance of hotel life after World War II.[29]

State housing inspectors kept up the code pressure on cheap hotels. Of the total inspections made in California cities in 1918, miscellaneous dwellings (largely shacks) required 26,000 inspections. More hotels were inspected (6,900) than tenements and apartments (5,900). By the 1920s, local San Francisco authorities had established a separate department of hotel and apartment inspection.[30]

Building codes had more specific effects than moral codes. For existing California hotels, code enforcement often raised rents but also spurred significant improvements for residents. As full-scale building inspection in San Francisco began in the 1920s, inspectors could— and did—push landlords to provide more livable amounts of ventilation and plumbing. Surviving records suggest that by 1930 even landlords like Edward Rolkin had brought their cheapest lodging houses close to the toilet and sink codes, even if the hotels did not benefit from regular cleaning.[31] For the rooming house rank, codes tacitly encouraged San Francisco speculators to provide larger, more prominent buildings (fig. 8.7). In 1910, small rooming houses with 15 to 40 rooms in a three-story walk-up building outnumbered larger rooming house buildings three to one. By 1930, three-fourths of the rooming house rooms in San Francisco were in large five- and six-story buildings with 70 to 160 rooms and elevator service. Along with efforts to reduce management costs and use more efficient mechanical systems, codes played an important part in this jump in scale (fig. 8.8). The larger light wells and more complicated plumbing also made the new, more specialized rooming houses less likely to be converted to commercial uses without substantial waste and unrentable space.

The more expensive hotels in San Francisco already had standards far above the code minimums. Thus, owners of the better hotels had little to fear from city housing inspectors, except for permanent guests who kept trying to cook in their rooms. One change seemingly a result of the 1917 codes was the end of California experiments with buildings that mixed rooming house units in apartment buildings. One such structure had thirty-six rooms with baths down the hall (all in the back of the building) and forty-five full-fledged apartments.[32]

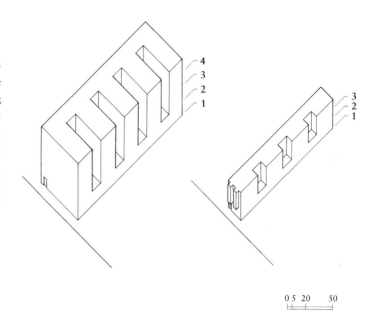

FIGURE 8.8. Typical sizes of rooming houses before and after effective building code enforcement in San Francisco. *Right*, a 26-room structure built in 1910 with small air shafts; *left*, a 157-room structure built in 1915 with the required larger air shafts.

0 5 20   50

Except in rare condemnation cases, building and sanitation codes *controlled* hotels but did not *eliminate* them from the housing stock. Research on Chicago has shown that codes enforced there in the 1920s made new cheap lodging houses unprofitable—thus retarding new construction of such hotels.[33] In San Francisco, the hotel supply was already plentiful and probably overbuilt after World War I. These uneven results of code regulation discouraged even Veiller. He wanted more of the city to be rebuilt, not just brought up to code minimums. More than once he expressed a wistful desire that New York "might be purified by fire, and that whole sections might be thus destroyed."[34]

Veiller's influence, along with his National Housing Association's focus on codes, waned in the 1920s. Codes were seen less as primary tools of social and cultural control and more as assurance for mortgage lenders and insurance agents. In other city departments, however, planners had been hammering out a way not simply to control the present but to control the future of the whole city.

Zoning to control future growth.   Citizens who shared the vision of the new city were uniformly concerned about mixed land use and high residential density. These were problems beyond the scope of building codes and good intentions (figs. 8.9, 8.10). Over the heads of all urban land investors hung the vultures of uncertainty and unpredictability, or as one developer put it, the problem of "premature and avoidable de-

FIGURE 8.9. Street view of middle-income two-family and four-family houses on Avon Street in Oakland, California, constructed between 1910 and 1925. The light-colored Avon Hotel, *at rear,* appears to be another house.

FIGURE 8.10. The Avon Hotel as it appears in the middle of the residential block. Most zoning codes outlawed reproducing experiments like these.

preciation."[35] Moreover, one owner's adherence to codes had no automatic effect on buildings next door. If neighboring properties were sharply incompatible, spewing out noxious fumes, or crowded with the urban poor, then the value and potential use of even the best new building was sharply diminished.

The real estate industry in San Francisco, like its counterparts in other cities, first encouraged the use of restrictive covenants at the edge of the city to exclude nuisance uses, to prohibit subdivision of houses, and to disallow selling or renting to blacks, Asians, or Jews. The largest use of restrictive covenants in San Francisco came in the new elite sub-divisions opened on the city's western side. But developers still worried that construction on the adjacent tracts could spoil their property values.

Closer to downtown, in the Western Addition, real estate promoters had the opposite problem. They wanted to ensure that the district would reach a higher density and do so with uniform heights and uses. Some Western Addition owners were building ten-story apartment towers on prime lots, but their structures stood next to old two-story Victorian houses or light housekeeping rooms (fig. 8.11).[36] Expert reformers taught that widespread land-use zoning, not covenants, would be the logical solution to keep such "old conditions in the larger cities" from "reproducing themselves" in outlying districts. Paul Scharrenberg, one of the five CIH commissioners, promoted zoning in San Francisco as a means to guide "right city growth." Veiller, too, called for zoning specifically "to keep apartment houses and hotels out of the private-residence districts."[37]

Whether one was using restrictive covenants or zoning, controlling land-use mixture and density carried negative implications for hotels. Banning retail activity from a housing neighborhood attacked one of the vital notions of hotel life—the home that was scattered up and down the street, with one's bedroom in one structure, the dining room at the local café, and so forth. Banning multiunit buildings next to lower-density structures struck at the notion of ad hoc rooming houses. As local and national zoning precedents were set, these implications for California hotels came more sharply into view.

San Francisco's zoning act, passed in 1921 and slightly modified in 1927, had typical antihotel provisions. For most unbuilt areas within the city limits, the act established "first residential districts" featuring the new city ideals of separate, single-family houses. Only religious, professional, and bucolic uses could be mixed with the residences; commercial mixtures were banned (fig. 8.12). Musicians, doctors, and dentists could work out of their home but not plumbers or auto mechanics. Nurseries, farms, truck gardens, and greenhouses were allowed but not corner grocery stores or bars. Zoning thus made uniform land use and desired densities as enforceable as the requirements for interior plumbing.

FIGURE 8.11. Nonuniform development in the northern reaches of San Francisco's Western Addition, 1927. Investors saw a surviving Victorian-era house like this, probably a rooming house, as a threat to the property value of the tall buildings.

FIGURE 8.12. The "intrusion" of an auto dealership into a residence district. Illustration of negative land-use mixture from a 1920 article promoting zoning.

Hotels were allowed in three of the other zoning categories. Mapped as "second residential areas" were the city additions built from 1880 to 1921. In such areas, the zoning ordinance allowed apartments, hotels, and six specified neighborhood institutions (libraries, for instance); however, new stores would not be allowed. Existing streetcar corridors with their lines of shops were in the commercial category, and hotels were allowed there. After a series of political appeals, hotels were also allowed in heavy industrial districts.[38]

With so many areas of San Francisco open to hotels in 1921, the effects of zoning may not seem significant. Indeed, the antihotel ideas within zoning ordinances did not initially affect hotel life significantly; yet they reshaped a debate that had dramatic effects several decades later. On the one hand, zoning gave city officials centralized power over the form of future locations for hotel life. On the other hand, zoning drew a very effective *cordon sanitaire* around the old city as it had been built by about World War I, to keep old city ideas from contaminating the new city. In these respects, zoning came to be powerful in several ways.

First, the inflexible administration of zoning cut off suburban hotel experiments such as the hotels built over corner groceries or corner bars in new additions to the city. Zoning laws and opinions could have been written to keep only the *worst* aspects of mixed use and mixed building types out of urban expansion. Bulk, occupancy, or lot-coverage guidelines written as performance criteria rather than as absolute proscriptions might have allowed hotel managers to continue experimenting with expensive one- or two-story hotels whose form, image, and clientele would have blended even with new automobile suburbs. Ample precedents for such congenial mixtures could be found in country clubs that coexisted with the most exclusive suburbs.[39] Had suburban developers actively fought for such variety in early applications of zoning, they probably would have won over the experts' objections.

Second, zoning retarded the establishment of new rooming houses even in those extensive older areas of San Francisco designated as second residential districts. New hotels were entirely legal in these areas, but zoning forbade other new commercial uses. Hence, the critically important tenant services and cash flow from first-floor business were unhinged from the rooming house business above, sharply reducing profits.[40]

Third, the long strips of commercially zoned blocks on either side of streetcar and new automobile through-routes proved to be inhospitable to new hotel life. The older streetcar strips and nodes already had a mixture of hotels and rooming houses. At the newer edges of the city, hotel residents found incomplete commercial services, a narrow range of prices, or too little variety: eating at the same inexpensive restaurant every day did not support convivial hotel life. Farther out, in nascent automobile strips, pedestrian life was unpleasant.

A fourth effect was a consequence of eliminating rooming houses in suburbs. Rooming houses had allowed women to make a living within one of their traditional roles, keeping house.[41] Zoning in effect eliminated expansion of these women's businesses.

Fifth, a succession of court decisions supported the elite and professional opinion that hotels should be excluded not only from the growing edges of the city but also from the *entire* city. It did not matter that hotels were popular or necessary or chosen as homes by a fraction of the downtown public.

The early court cases testing zoning show the degree to which hotels and rooming houses were on the minds of urban land-use experts. Initial state supreme court reviews disagreed about such basics as any land-use exclusions and zoning's uses of the police power; thus, excluding hotels, flats, and apartments from areas of single-family houses was logically more difficult for the courts. *Miller v. Los Angeles,* an influential case heard in 1925 before the California Supreme Court, summarized several earlier antihotel court opinions. The judges upheld the exclusion of a four-flat building from an area of single-family houses, and their opinion ranged widely to discuss apartments and hotels as well as flats.[42] They admitted that "undoubtedly, many families do maintain ideal home life in apartments, flats, and hotels" and that "in many single family dwellings there is much of dissention and discord." Nonetheless, the court also assumed that life in apartments and hotels was never chosen:

Few persons, if given their choice, would, we think, deliberately prefer to establish their homes and rear their children in an apartment house neighborhood rather than in a single home neighborhood. . . . It is needless to further analyze and enumerate all of the factors which make a single family home more desirable for the promotion and perpetuation of family life than an apartment, hotel, or flat.[43]

This ruling influenced other courts. The Minnesota Supreme Court in 1925 rationalized exclusion of multiple-family structures as a reasonable reaction to urban population pressures.[44] A judge in Cleveland, Ohio, bluntly repeated the opinion that apartment buildings not only spread infectious diseases but also promoted immorality.[45] Many of the court opinions invoked expert academic scholarship—like that of the Chicago school of sociology—to reject apartments and hotels as valid housing. A law review article said "sound sociological arguments" led to the belief that open-lot houses were better than flats.[46] In fairly subtle ways, the decades of objections to hotel life by national figures such as Veiller, Woods, Abbott, and Park and California figures like Lubin and Porter had an important effect.

The gathering of antihotel opinion was particularly clear in 1926, when the Supreme Court of the United States handed down its decision on *Euclid v. Ambler,* the landmark zoning case concerning a Cleveland, Ohio, suburb and a small local realty company.[47] Writing for the court, the archconservative justice, George Sutherland, not only upheld the private house ideal but also helped to relegate all hotels and apartments into the category of hazards for the new city. Sutherland found no problem supporting the exclusion of *industrial* activity (as a nuisance) from residential areas; more difficult, he said, would be the "creation and maintenance of residential districts, from which business and trade of every sort, including hotels and apartment houses, are excluded." For this exclusion, the court could not rely solely on the concept of nuisance. Instead, said Sutherland, the court was convinced by "much attention at the hands of commissions and experts" that apartments and hotels, like steel mills, were a hazard to public health and safety when they were placed next to single-family houses (fig. 8.13). Within one year after *Euclid v. Ambler,* forty-five states had enacted enabling legislation for local zoning. Municipal and state courts were henceforth freed from the narrow confines of the common law of nuisance and police power that had constrained the limits of earlier building and health codes.

FIGURE 8.13. An apartment and tourist hotel in a residence district of the San Francisco Bay Area suburb of Alameda. Opinions on the mixture of houses and hotels varied widely: the city's Chamber of Commerce began this hotel in 1926, the same year as the *Euclid v. Ambler* ruling. In the 1990s, small bungalows and Victorian houses still abutted the hotel on two sides.

In 1932, President Herbert Hoover summed up the argument: "Zoning and city planning save waste, reduce ultimate costs, and add attractiveness and other social values to stable investment values for home owners."[48] For Hoover, investment stability was the ultimate social aim, just as it was for the majority of those who gained from the notion of an immutable new city. When reformers elevated the ideal of the privately owned American home as the single goal of national policy, the idea grew dramatically in power. This single-minded focus on the single-house concept would become in itself another strategy for eliminating hotels and apartments.

DOCTRINAIRE IDEALISM AND DELIBERATE IGNORANCE

Codes and zoning prompted immediate, specific actions. Their effects could be measured and plotted. Two later and more veiled strategies—setting narrow housing ideals and consciously creating holes in official intelligence—were seemingly less direct. Nonetheless, they became much more powerful and pervasive actions in the long run, in part because they were prescribed from a national level.

Working for a single ideal. When urban reformers set their architectural agenda for the new city, they realized they had to do more than control bad housing. They also had to promote correct housing, their favorite being the uniform and protected single-use residential district of private houses with open lots. An underside of the process of defining housing ideals was the necessity of drawing the line where housing stopped and mere shelter began—or as later urban renewal officers put it, the line between standard housing and substandard housing. The definition of "standard" would come to insist on private kitchens and private baths, precisely the two items that most hotels did not provide.

At Hoover's presidential conference on housing in 1932, the Committee on Housing and the Community enunciated again the housing specialists' long-standing model:

The ideal conditions for *any* family would be a single detached house surrounded by a plot of ground, with adequate lawns and facilities for a small flower and vegetable garden and play space.[49]

The 1932 committee closely matched the phrase "any family" with the single detached house: like the California Supreme Court, they could not conceive of a minority opinion among people who preferred apartment or hotel life. Moreover, electric trolleys, automobiles, and longer-term mortgages had made the open-lot house more possible.

For several generations, preeminent concern for the welfare of children had figured heavily in the evolution of the reformers' choice. When Veiller spoke of "labor" and "workingmen" he meant laboring men with families, and inevitably he followed with a reference to "making family life possible" or concern for "wives and families." Veiller insisted that the "*normal* method of housing in America" should be small houses on their own "small bit of land," offering "a secure sense of individuality and opportunity for real domestic life" and the suburban advantages of healthful play for children.[50] The CIH proudly published its model rural work camps for single workers but never considered model dwellings for single workers in the city. In 1915, the commission proclaimed that the comprehensive city plan "should provide for detached one-family houses, with lawn and room for rear garden. This is the ideal arrangement."[51] Soon the ideal form of housing became the only acceptable form.

Whether or not they housed children, apartments and hotels both fared poorly in expressions of housing ideals. E. R. L. Gould, the founder of New York's City and Suburban Homes Company, reminded his colleagues that for the better-paid worker, model apartments would be (at best) an intermediate stage between the "promiscuous and common life" of existing city forms and "the dignified, well-ordered life of the detached house." Edith Elmer Wood wrote that "the only excuse for apartments is for celibates, childless couples, and elderly people."[52] In practical application, however, the apartment had to be accepted in local and national construction programs. Physical separation of each family unit remained of paramount importance—the minimum elements of division being the private kitchen and private bath for each unit.[53]

For some time a minority of reformers doubted the necessity of private kitchens for every family. Social workers at a national conference in 1912 called for an indoor bathroom for each low-income family but not private cooking. New York City's housing reformers, however, had insisted on private kitchens in definitions of tenements and apartments written in 1887 and 1910. In these influential codes, an apartment was a unit in a building for three or more families "living independently of one another and doing their own cooking."[54] By the 1920s, the kitchen gained universal consideration as an essential element in the definition of a dwelling unit. By 1950, the U.S. Census defined an apartment's "separateness and self-containment" on the presence of separate cooking equipment for each household.[55]

Limiting the housing ideal required that hotels and lodging houses be legally defined as inferior to apartment buildings. That process had begun with the writing of state building codes but was most effectively accomplished with the establishment of the Federal Housing Administration (FHA). Under Title I of the National Housing Act of 1936, Congress stated that property improvement loans could be secured for *any* residence or commercial building, specifically *including* hotels and clubs. Yet the act also required that the FHA eliminate risks as much as possible for the investors of the funds.[56] That was the sticking point. The 1936 FHA *Property Standards* set the most influential definition of proper housing to that date, with strong exclusionary language about hotels. Although the guidelines defined a dwelling as "any structure used principally for residential purposes," they carefully stated that "commercial rooming houses and tourist homes, sanitariums, tourist cabins, clubs, or fraternities would *not* be considered dwellings within the meaning of the National Housing Act" that had created the FHA. A proper living unit required a private kitchen and a private bath.[57] Although this proscription was largely meant to exclude ad hoc rooming houses from federal aid, it was to prove handy in discriminating against single-room housing with or without federal aid.

Simultaneously, the minimum *Property Standards* stated that "the [insured] property should be located in a neighborhood homogeneous in character," a neighborhood sure to avoid "inharmonious land uses." In the FHA's codification of the real estate industry's values, residential hotels and their mixed-use neighborhoods were categorically "undesirable community conditions"; they "decreased mortgage security."[58] National underwriting manuals of the FHA appraisers gave low ratings to any residential property in a crowded neighborhood, one with racial mixtures, or one with a mixture of "adverse influences" defined as stores, offices, or rental units. These redlining policies extended the biases of zoning to the realms of investment and repair funding. Simultaneously, controls over rental properties were more complicated than for owner-occupied housing; most loans for repair of existing structures were small and short term. With the FHA it was easier to purchase a new building. Hence, FHA insurance helped new houses and apartments at the urban edge far more than any housing or infill in the center city.[59] In the 1950s, many cities further narrowed the definition of a standard dwelling by rewriting their older zoning ordinances to exclude rooming houses from the definition of multiple-family dwellings.[60]

With the national FHA property standards, underwriting manuals, and the increased importance of the income tax preference for single-family house ownership, real estate lobbyists and housing activists had successfully established suburban single-family houses and occasional apartments as the sole ideals for new American house types (fig. 8.14).[61] Meanwhile, during the depression and World War II, other government offices began a hotel control process far less observable but much more insidious.

Deliberate ignorance as a professional strategy. The early activities of the San Francisco Housing Association and the CIH demonstrated that learning about a problem often brought administrative power to

new urban professionals. Later experts proved that ignorance could also have power: if urban experts deliberately created ignorance about a problem, that issue was assured relative oblivion—assuming there was no political activism on the part of the public. Perhaps it was his observance of similar effects of nineteenth-century government administration that led Goethe to write, "There is nothing more frightening than active ignorance."[62]

One sociologist's research in 1948 uncovered the process of deliberate ignorance to be notably at work in regard to single people and hotel life. Arnold Rose exhaustively surveyed the literature about the living arrangements of single people, especially in the settings of rooming houses and cheap lodging houses. From a low point before 1890, interest gathered until 1915 and relapsed into disinterest after 1920.[63] San Francisco's Progressive Era interest closely matched Rose's model. The State Tuberculosis Commission had inspected the city's hotels carefully; the earliest CIH surveys in the city included problem hotels and led to the state's hotel acts of 1913 and 1917. The drop in California interest after 1920 matched the national trend.[64]

FIGURE 8.14. The New Deal housing reformer's minimum. The model town of Greendale, Wisconsin, photographed in 1939, just after its construction.

Idealistic studies of families and children and the simultaneous omission of single adults also helped to allow the growing professional disinterest in nonfamily households. As usual, Veiller serves as both exemplar and partial cause. At no time was he notably interested in single people or their housing. On a visit to San Francisco in 1902, he reported that the poorest living quarters were the "homes of the longshoremen, situated near the docks, . . . containing two families each." To be near the docks and those duplexes, Veiller had to walk past blocks full of rooming houses and hotels for single longshoremen, but he apparently did not notice them. He concluded, in fact, that San Francisco had no tenement problem at all.[65] In 1903, Veiller and Deforest's massive two-volume collection of articles about America's housing problems contained only a few passing mentions of hotels. In his 1910 book, *Housing Reform,* Veiller mentions hotels only once, in the context of high-class hotels. His chapters on housing investigations were written only for apartments and single houses.[66] In short, as Veiller and others framed the urban housing concerns of the United States, they purposely left hotels out of view.

Activists elsewhere reproduced the blind spots in the New York models. When San Francisco finally appointed two housing inspectors for the Board of Health, the commissioners dubbed them "tenement house inspectors," thereby setting a narrow focus for them. Similarly, reports by the San Francisco Housing Association dodged the subject of hotels. When they investigated housing problems in Telegraph Hill and North Beach, San Francisco's reformers incredibly made no mention whatsoever of workers' rooming houses or hotels, which dominated the Broadway border of both districts. The later work of the CIH was similarly silent in this regard.

Even during the positive wave of interest that crested in 1915, for every large book on family housing, usually only a slim article appeared about nonfamily people. By the 1920s, that token measure dwindled as well.[67] Consider how Edith Abbott discussed 60,000 men of downtown Chicago in her exhaustive summary of Chicago housing surveys undertaken between 1910 and 1936:

There are, of course, the large numbers of those who live in cheap hotels, boarding houses, and "flops"—the casuals who come and go in the "flophouses" near the loop. . . . No attempt will be made at this point to discuss the

hotels or shelters for single men since our interest here lies largely in the housing of families and in the tenements where families live.[68]

Abbott had a purely negative impression of hotel life derived from
skewed samples. For her chapter on Chicago rooming houses, she relied on a 1929 thesis about a sixty-unit residential hotel; the thesis was
based *only* on the five to ten families from the building (over five years'
time) who had come to the United Charities offices for assistance. The
thesis was based on the worst possible cases.[69]

Even that bastion of social statistics, the U.S. Census, largely ignored
hotels—both as an industry and as homes. Although hotels ranked
fourth or fifth in income and number of workers among American businesses in 1905, the editor of a hotel journal expressed his general
frustration:

We have no figures, no statistics, no official rating . . . which we might compare
with other industries. Our government which counts every mule, every bushel
of wheat, which has figures on every possible production, has nothing to relate
regarding legitimate hotel keeping.[70]

The editor was complaining that the census office reported only the
number of hotel keepers, not distinguishing size or type of hotel. Census takers, of course, did enumerate individual hotel residents as part
of the U.S. population. But the census staff has never aggregated those
statistics to show accurately how many people have lived in hotels. The
figures typically mix residents of hotels and rooming houses into those
in other "dwelling units," or with military personnel, indigent residents
of institutions, or residents of convents, monasteries, dormitories, or
sorority houses.[71] These figures, at best, can supply only rough estimates. In 1930, the U.S. Census Bureau did publish a special report on
the hotel industry, but it did not discuss permanent residents.[72]

Hotels continued to be out of focus for housing activists and city
planners in the 1930s. In the seven report volumes of Hoover's national
conference on housing, neither single-room housing nor the housing
of single people was mentioned. The hundreds of excellent New Deal
studies, reports, outlines, discussions, and conferences about housing
problems included only very negative information about single-room
housing, mostly on so-called homeless men, their urban flophouses and

shantytowns, and rural CCC and FSA labor camps.[73] Academic coverage of hotel housing continued to be virtually nil in the 1930s.[74]

As the depression wore on and instructions came more efficiently from Washington, D.C., instead of from local officials, New Deal reports—especially real estate reports—became increasingly conservative about including hotel information. The remarkable series of real property surveys is the most salient example. The first comprehensive real estate survey supported by federal funds was made in 1933–34 in Cleveland; most major cities followed suit in succeeding years. A revived San Francisco Housing Association had surveyed the Western Addition in 1933; other partial surveys were done of San Francisco in 1934 and 1936 to identify sites for clearance and renewal. These reports were done under municipal rather than federal guidelines, and all of the reports prominently featured hotels as part of the city's housing stock.[75] These early works were overshadowed by the much more ambitious citywide *1939 Real Property Survey* of San Francisco.

San Francisco's *1939 Real Property Survey* and its subsequent influence provide a stunning case of how deliberate ignorance can be created and perpetuated. For the survey, a small army of field enumerators collected room-by-room data about hotels as well as door-by-door counts of apartments, flats, and houses. However, following federal guidelines, the office staff then systematically excised hotels from the survey's compilations. In their summary volume, the staff devoted only 7 out of 253 pages of discussion and tables to San Francisco's residential hotels.[76] The meticulously detailed survey had found that one-third of both substandard dwelling units and ill-housed people of San Francisco were in hotels, but the staff hid this fact in procedural tables buried in the Appendix of the report volumes. The survey directors ignored the state's long-standing legal definition of hotels, split hotel housing into several different and conflicting categories, admitted that their survey of the 34,000 "primarily one-room dwelling units" in hotels was "an incomplete coverage for this type of permanent residence," and mildly suggested further study.[77] The 1940 U.S. Census of Housing (the first national census of housing) repeated the problems and biases of the real property surveys. The census collected information about hotels but annihilated that information in its reporting techniques.[78]

In 1941, the San Francisco Housing Authority reviewed the *Real Property Survey* and did ferret out comments about the city's nearly

five hundred hotels. The housing staff assumed the hotels had only recently been "converted from commercial to residential uses," erroneously supposing that all had been transient accommodations before the depression. Sounding a great deal like Edith Abbott, the San Francisco planners wrote that "due to the fundamental differences between these two types of dwelling units [hotels versus houses and apartments], the primary analysis and report on housing in San Francisco will exclude the dwelling units in converted hotel structures" (fig. 8.15).[79]

FIGURE 8.15. Statistically invisible hotel. Using 1930s guidelines for real property surveys, the long and narrow Hotel Frederick in Kansas City contained no housing units. Note "weekly rates" promoted on the sign.

The basic data of the 1945 Master Plan for San Francisco—including its recommendations on land clearance—came directly from the *1939 Real Property Survey*. The San Francisco Planning Commission incorrectly described the building types in the city's worst redevelopment areas as "generally three or four story flats or, as in Chinatown, tenement-type apartments."[80] The units in Chinatown were largely SRO hotels. In the South of Market, hotels were also a major share of the building fabric. Similar gaps of logic and description continued to appear in subsequent reports. The vacuum of information was such that in 1966, when William Wheaton and other housing experts compiled an authoritative 470-page series of readings on urban housing, the only words on residential hotels or housing for single, transient, or unattached people were in a five-page reprint of a twenty-year-old article by Arnold Rose.[81] Until the 1970s, the well-meaning planners of San Francisco, like their contemporaries in other cities, continued their policy of carefully not studying hotels.

The omission in San Francisco's urban surveys of single-room housing units and the people who lived in them (rich or poor) seems incredible in the light of their downtown prevalence. Planners and officials in hundreds of other cities repeated the omission. This was neither oversight nor negligence but active repudiation. As Rose had warned in 1948, it was as if the people in hotel settings "were thought to be nonexistent, or at least entirely impoverished so that they could not expect anything by way of adequate housing."[82] He warned that this housing and its population presented an important problem, but his call to action fell on deaf ears. Rose became the Cassandra of today's single room occupancy crisis.

Because of the definitions of a proper American home, apartment units and their renters fared better. From the turn of the century, apartments were carefully watched and carefully counted as important resources. Writers and citizens heralded the building of apartment units as important housing additions to the city. The same was not true for most single-room options. Cheap apartments became a public concern and a public necessity; cheap hotels, if they were noticed at all, remained a public nuisance.

BUILDINGS AS TARGETS AND SURROGATES

To a downtown observer in 1945, the collective effects of all the attempts at hotel housing control—moral reforms, building codes, promotion of housing ideals, zoning, and deliberate ignorance—might have seemed ineffectual. Virtually all of the old rooming houses and cheap hotels were still standing. Where they had been torn down, it seemed that independent builders (such as the South of Market's Edward Rolkin) had simply replaced the old structures with larger and more threatening structures for the same resident groups.

Although the reformers seemed unsuccessful at first, their battles highlighted the active roles these ordinary buildings played in skirmishes over the cultural engineering of the city. Buildings were more than passive strongholds of an old urban order and more than sullen threats to a new order. New buildings were also active tools for creating the kind of urban culture that officials desired. Buildings, old and new, were also surrogate targets, substitutes for more radical or thorough solutions to human problems that were beyond the activists' power. Albert Wolfe, for instance, wrote in 1906 that the only real cure for the Boston rooming house problem would be job security and fair wages for the "mercantile employee as well as the skilled mechanic, the female stenographer as well as the man beside her." In private correspondence among themselves, the members of California's Commission on Immigration and Housing admitted that the most efficacious approach to slum conditions would be a land tax; simultaneously, they admitted that this solution was far too radical to overcome the opposition of private real estate interests.[83] Because reformers could not feasibly put such far-ranging issues on the agenda, they settled on buildings and land uses as surrogate targets.

At each higher level of government, the cultural control of housing became increasingly abstract and isolated. This abstraction was an inherent weakness built into the urban housing agenda after 1900. As reformers, lobbyists, and their bureaucratic machinery catapulted ideas from city to state and finally to the federal level, antihotel policies not only gained power but lost knowledge of local cultural diversities. As the San Francisco and California cases show, the ever more consolidated building codes and zoning definitions (ending with the FHA guidelines) had thwarted creative variations in local housing survey practice and sensitivity to local needs. In the decades after World War II, more centralized, more professionalized, and increasingly isolated housing staffs gained greater power for using buildings as tools of reform and as surrogates for greater action. The consequences of two generations of biased regulatory reforms, doctrinaire idealism, and deliberate ignorance would become massively apparent to the people managing and living in hotels after 1945.

PROHIBITION

VERSUS PLURALISM

RESIDENTIAL HOTEL LIFE CAME CLOSE TO BEING COMPLETELY eliminated in many American cities between the depression and the 1980s.
During those decades, American investors reconfigured the urban
economy and the meaning of downtown. By stretching the city in some
places, they forced changes in others, simultaneously rearranging the
way people used all four ranks of hotels (figs. 9.1, 9.2). These changes
did not eliminate the hotel market, as some hoped; however, they al-
tered it substantially and created the base for the SRO crisis.

A central aspect of hotel life after 1930 is that it depended on an
aging supply of buildings; virtually no one built a new residential hotel
between 1930 and 1980.[1] During those years, changes in residential
hotel supply occurred roughly in three phases. From the depression to
1960, most observers saw an oversupply of hotel rooms. From 1960
to 1970, the SRO crisis became apparent, and Americans began to
forge new policies concerning hotels. Since 1970, continuing losses and
problems have been balanced with increasingly widespread attempts to
stabilize existing hotels and to construct new ones. The hard-won continuation of hotel life reveals the importance of minority choices—both
public and professional—in making public policy.

LOSING GROUND: CHANGING CONTEXTS, 1930–1970

Although urban renewal alone is often blamed for the SRO crisis, earlier and more diffuse forces also sharply affected the residential hotel market. These included work place shifts caused by the depression, World War II, and office expansion, as well as shifts in highway and parking construction, American traditions of retirement, and the treatment of mental illness.

New migrations. The depression was a boon to anyone who had inexpensive housing to rent; especially for inexpensive hotels, hard times meant steady and often overflow business. In skid rows, older and more desperate casual workers piled up. Among the many new urban residents were married men from farms and small towns who left their families to look for work in the city and young girls who shared rooms while they worked as secretaries, putting off college or starting a family. While managers of San Francisco's expensive hotels worried about staying in business—occupancy rates at the better hotels often fell below 60 percent—owners of Western Addition rooming houses found that by cutting repairs they could maintain an after-tax income ranging from 8 to 17 percent.[2]

After 1939, employment surges for World War II production overwhelmed every price level of hotel housing in America and led to the all-time peak in hotel residents. At the better hotels, managers gave priority for rooms to foreign diplomats, production contractors, and military officers in special training. Occupancy rates averaged more than 82 percent, higher than the best rates of the 1920s. However, at many good hotels social elegance and lavish meals faded.[3] Elsewhere in the city, landlords—with the blessing of local and federal emergency housing offices—hastily converted buildings into rooming houses or cheap lodgings. In the districts close to San Francisco's downtown, conversions created hundreds of new rooming houses.[4] Rosie the Riveter and her male colleagues found themselves in emergency dormitory and barracks-style housing, often modeled on traditional lodging and rooming houses. In addition, one nondefense worker moved to the cities for every war-related worker; more than half lived in single-person households, and most were under thirty years old. These wartime conditions caused social workers to worry that one-fourth of the young

FIGURE 9.1. Geary Street in the early 1950s, before urban renewal. A commercial node in a hotel district in the Western Addition, San Francisco.

FIGURE 9.2. Geary Street at the same location, 1992, after urban renewal. A few older buildings, *middle right,* survive, but the new rules of land use, building type, and transportation have eliminated the former rules of the street.

male migrants were "living in flophouses and cheap hotels in the worst sections of the city." In racial ghettos where restrictive covenants constrained expansion, the influx of new minority war workers often meant severe overcrowding.[5]

Ten years after the wartime boom, residential hotel life was beginning to wane in the older expensive hotels, which were catering more to conventioneers than to smaller numbers of local elites. Rent controls imposed on hotel keepers during the war had also made them wary of permanent residents. At the new palace and midpriced hotels of the 1950s and 1960s, owners looked strictly for transient and convention business. To keep prices down for the new clientele, managers ordered chefs to find additional ways to trim the elegance of their menus and service; culinary talent scattered, and private restaurants took up more of the deluxe dining business.[6] The conversion of most top hotels to strictly tourist business helped to stop a 150-year pattern—the generational shift of elite permanent guests from a fading hostelry to the next largest and more socially prominent hotel. The dwindling population of middle and upper class hotel residents entrenched themselves where they were. The middle-aged and elderly high-income residents tended to collect at fewer and older hotels that maintained more traditional dining service and avoided conventioneers. The new social elites, if they lived downtown at all, usually did so in exclusive apartments perched on top of parking garages. The entrenchment in palace hotels cut into the former glamour of hotel life as the number of glittering and notable permanent guests declined. It also interrupted the process of filtering. Fewer good residential rooms were being vacated; hence, fewer residential rooms filtered to a lower price range.

Even after World War II, the rooming house market flourished as a result of the continuing influx of single and mobile young adults, most without cars. Organizations of boarding homes for women remained active into the mid-1950s. In 1951, the creators of the science fiction film *The Day the Earth Stood Still* could present rooming house life lived by a single mother. The suburbs held few housing opportunities for these young people; suburban jobs and the new, boxy blocks of inexpensive suburban apartments would not be created in sufficient numbers until about 1960. Meanwhile, in neighborhoods near colleges and technical schools, the boom in enrollments during the 1940s and 1950s kept whole blocks of rooming house establishments busy. Yet

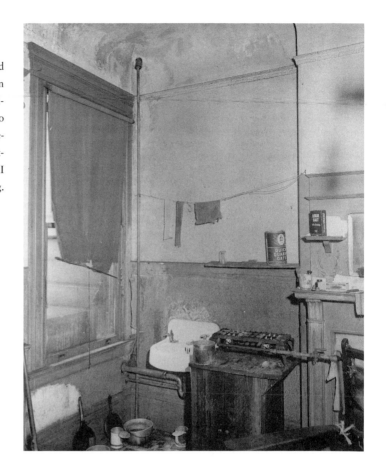

FIGURE 9.3. Jerry-rigged sink and hot plate, Western Addition, 1949. Slum conditions in this San Francisco neighborhood's light housekeeping rooms had been exacerbated by World War II overcrowding.

some supplies of rooms at this price range were literally losing ground. Middle-income families in houses and apartments less often needed to take in roomers. The roomers still in the market were less likely to be of the same race or ethnicity as the landlady, further discouraging rooming house life. In the better neighborhoods, many owners of small midpriced hotels converted their buildings to apartments by adding kitchens and private baths, often with public assistance. Particularly in tenement districts or racially transitional neighborhoods, overcrowding, poor management, and the accumulation of needed repairs turned hastily converted wartime rooming houses into slum housing (fig. 9.3).[7]

Making room for offices and cars. The most overt pressure on residential hotels came from the expansion of downtown office and retailing districts, which began again in earnest with the urban renewal of the 1960s. The case of San Francisco is typical. A downtown growth coalition of retailers and real estate developers was expanding the downtown to accommodate the huge increase in office work created by the immense investment wealth of California and the city's expanded role in Pacific Rim trade. In the 1930s, total office space in San Francisco had stayed nearly static. During the 1940s, developers doubled the city's office capacity, often using lofts and temporary space. During the 1950s, owners made the wartime increases permanent, and capacity grew another 30 percent, making San Francisco fourth in the nation in terms of total office space. By the mid-1970s, San Francisco was second only to New York City as a center of international commerce and banking, second only to Boston in its ratio of office space to population. For the millions of square feet of additional office buildings needed, developers began to bid for sites in the South of Market.[8]

Simultaneously, other government policies and private speculative investment patterns also eroded the basis for hotel living. The sheer primacy and publicly secured profits of suburban single-family houses overshadowed most notions of investing in downtown apartments or residential hotels. Continuing policies of redlining meant that lending institutions often refused loans to rooming or lodging house areas. Meanwhile, at least in San Francisco between World War II and 1960, a generation of hotel owners literally died out. Unlike the patterns of the past, the inheritors (who no longer lived in the city but in elite suburbs) sold the hotels their forebears had built. They invested the money in suburban real estate they understood or in other sectors of the economy. Those prosperous optometrists who still lived in San Francisco's Pacific Heights were more likely to band together to build a medical office complex in suburban Dallas than to buy anything in the South of Market.[9]

Transportation investments acted on yet another series of fronts. To connect the new suburban city with the rebuilt downtown, traffic engineers and automobile-owning consumers called for new freeways and plentiful parking. Downtown highway and garage building hit directly at rooming and lodging house areas, beginning as early as the 1930s. California's transportation engineers planted highway approaches and viaduct routes—first for the Bay Bridge and later for freeways—directly through San Francisco's South of Market and the Western Addition, demolishing thousands of hotel rooms.[10]

Although highway construction leveled lower-cost hotel blocks, the automobile was *not* inherently an enemy for people living in midpriced and palace hotels, at least not in the short run. If anything, for the middle and upper class, automobiles could be a boon to living downtown. In the early 1920s, a study at a south side lakeshore hotel in Chicago found one-fourth of the permanent residents had cars. Where motels cut into downtown tourist business, hotel managers could cater to additional permanent guests. To compete with motels, hotel owners also obtained garages and prominently advertised their parking. Permanent guests with automobiles enjoyed garage access as well; some small hotels offered backyard or side yard parking (fig. 9.4).[11] Thus the automobile per se did not seriously affect hotel housing choice.

In the long run, however, and for the majority of hotel residents, automobiles and hotel life did not mix. The residents of downtown rooming and lodging house neighborhoods found themselves looking out at freeway ramps or giant ditches built for six lanes of traffic, or contending with traffic noise and exhaust generated by automobiles on new through-roads and one-way pairs of downtown streets. In the areas of former single-family houses that owners had converted to rooming houses by the 1950s, parking became a major issue. Planning authorities wrote that parked cars without proper off-street spaces automatically caused blight. Neighbors harangued rooming house owners to provide off-street parking so their tenants' cars would no longer clog the streets or fill unsightly vacant lots (fig. 9.5).[12]

Other changes for hotel tenants.   As suburban employment surged for people with cars, the situation for non–car-owning residents of cheap rooming and lodging houses became grimmer. White-collar work continued to boom downtown, but blue-collar work did not. As part of the shift of use from streetcar and railroad to automobile and truck, workshop employers and shipping firms moved to outlying highway locations. San Francisco's port lost cargo traffic to more modern ports; buildings in San Francisco's South of Market became underused. Elsewhere in the downtown, employers were eliminating jobs through mechanization. Supervisors called for steadier family-tied workers instead of politically volatile, floating groups hired for short periods. Adoption of shorter workdays meant that more employees had time for commuting to more distant homes. These factors drastically changed the needs for downtown housing and the social roles of workers' districts. Younger laborers and family men did not pass through the skid

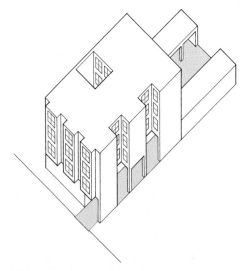

FIGURE 9.4. Small residential hotel with automobile parking in the back. The Hotel Eddy, with about 16 units, was a concrete frame structure built in the early 1920s in San Francisco's Western Addition. The two carports at the back sheltered 10 cars.

FIGURE 9.5. Informal parking lot adjoining a rooming house in Omaha, Nebraska, 1938.

row as often as they had in the 1940s. Older, hard-to-employ men and the home guard were no longer a substrata but a primary proportion of the population (fig. 9.6). By 1960, welfare departments were referring more unemployed downtown people—especially the elderly—to hotels for temporary housing that tended to become permanent. As Joan Shapiro has written, this was often the beginning of an unplanned and unwilling interdependence between social services and hotel owners.[13] In 1961, officials from Minneapolis, Kansas City, and Norfolk seemed confident that demolition of several blocks of their respective

FIGURE 9.6. Older postwar population left on Howard Street in San Francisco's South of Market, 1953.

skid rows had permanently scattered their residents.[14] Enough vacancies still existed so that, indeed, most people displaced from the cheapest lodging houses *could* find some other place to live, probably at a higher proportion of their income or savings.

At middle-income levels, the national redefinition of old age brought other changes in the residential hotel market. Social security began to supplement retirement incomes in 1935. Fewer elderly men and women lived with their children, and people over sixty-five years of age began to create a new consumer market. Commercial care for the elderly and the supply of units in bona fide retirement communities improved markedly between 1940 and 1970, competing with yet another role played by midpriced hotels and rooming houses.[15]

A sudden influx of former mental hospital patients constituted a massive change for SRO tenancy. In the mid-1960s, the well-intentioned (and budget-cutting) decision of many states to mainstream mental hospital populations had been coupled with promises of halfway houses and group homes. Modern psychiatric medicines made this release possible. In California, the population of the state mental hospitals declined from 37,000 to 7,000 between 1960 and 1973. However, the halfway houses were never established. Patients were essentially dumped into downtown hotels where neither hotel staff nor residents were prepared for the care required by these new neighbors. In conversation, tenants and managers alike often mention the arrival of publicly supported but inadequately served mental patients as the last blow to pleasant SRO life downtown. As one hotel owner put it, "Suddenly you weren't managing a building; you were running a nut house."[16]

In spite of all these shifts, not all residential hotels were dying. Through the 1960s, hotel rooms at every price range were a smaller but still surviving and viable housing market. A sizable population of healthy, usually single, and often elderly people still lived downtown in hotels and chose that style of housing. By the late 1960s, the formerly ample supplies of lodging house rooms were filling up. In the cheapest hotels that remained open in 1970, the arrival of new desperate tenants and the departure of the better tenants (for better hotels, apartments, or suburban life) left thousands of hotels packed with what one social worker in the mid-1970s described as "a human residue of the elderly and poor."[17] Ironically, the market-driven declines in hotel life were largely intended and carefully planned as part of the official rebuilding of downtown.

OFFICIAL PROHIBITIONS OF HOTEL LIFE, 1930–1970

While some urban changes informally influenced hotel residents, other changes—most of them officially devised within various phases of urban renewal—aimed directly at the eradication of hotel life. Urban renewal accomplished many important things, but it also deservedly earned many critics. In most cities, renewal was racially biased; renewal often lined certain landholders' or contractors' pockets more than it should have; building the new downtown frequently became an exercise in personal empire building at the service of the downtown business elite. Urban renewal was also a period of hotel resident removal. Hotel housing was absolutely foreign to the aims and legal limitations of public housing. During the decades of urban renewal, officials moved from making antihotel policy to attempting to eliminate hotels; this prohibition was part of their scheme to end all urban blight and poor housing.

The assumptions behind the planned elimination of residential hotels seem to have been very much like the notions behind the national Volstead Act and its attempt to eliminate all alcoholic beverages. Prohibitionists assumed that if they took away the supply of a mistrusted part of the material culture, then the use and need would end as well. Just as the stubborn public refusal to give up drinking hindered the intended social benefits of the Volstead Act, so too the continued existence of hotels seemed to block the promise of the new city. These policies provided major fuel for the later SRO crisis.

Definitions of blight as condemnation.   The rebuilding programs that preceded full-scale urban renewal were of modest scale. During the New Deal, demolition was typically done lot by lot in keeping with the federal policy of equivalent elimination. The idea was to remove slum housing at exactly the same rate that public replacement housing was built. For each new public housing unit completed, a dilapidated housing unit elsewhere had to be condemned, repaired, or demolished.[18] Ironically, hotels escaped early public demolition because only accepted housing units (those with private kitchens and baths) could be considered for equivalent elimination.

The idea of blight, however, helped post-World War II planners do wholesale bulldozing of U.S. hotel stock. The concept of blight (as opposed to the concept of a slum) summed up the officially perceived problems of the old city. Hoover's 1932 Conference on Home Building and Home Ownership defined a slum as an area of *social* liability; that same area, the panel concluded, might continue to be profitable for its owners. A blighted area, however, was an *economic* liability—a district whose property values were so depreciated that they returned less in taxes than they cost in public services. By the late 1930s, downtown landowners were particularly concerned about depressed property values in hotel areas. Politicians worried about such zones because of their reduced tax revenues and high costs of services. The Hoover conference's committee on city planning and zoning used cheap hotels and mixed uses as their prime examples of neighborhood blight.[19]

The 1945 law that enabled urban renewal in California required that blight be demonstrated before clearance, and it gave a multipage definition that planners summarized as follows:

[Blighted areas are] areas compactly built . . . with indiscriminate mixtures of industry, business, and housing, having large percentages of substandard dwellings and absentee ownership, lacking adequate open spaces, play grounds, and gardens, and presenting ugly, depressing vistas on the public streets.[20]

Greenery and designerly vistas were to be preferred over any old city social values.

During the New Deal, the areal extent of blight had been detailed by real estate experts working on real property surveys. In San Francisco's survey, completed in 1939, the majority of substandard dwellings were so classified because they contained shared toilets or baths. Forty percent of the Western Addition's population (50,000 out of 86,000) shared baths or kitchens with other households. In a 1935 survey, 80 percent of the Western Addition's units had been found in good repair. Thus, dilapidation was not generally a problem. However, by 1946, the cost of police service to the area was reported to be ninety times that of newer middle-income areas.[21] In the official maps of blighted areas, different sorts of hotels fared differently. In 1939 and 1945, the mid-priced hotels and better rooming houses of the Tenderloin area were not marked; these postfire structures were of masonry construction, had good plumbing, and were still profitable. For the same reasons, the two blocks directly south of Market Street also fared well. The blocks of the waterfront, Chinatown, the Mission district, and South of Market—with many wooden buildings and far more mixed uses— fared worse (fig. 9.7). Predictably, blight and proposed condemnations were thickest in the Western Addition.

In 1945, the federal bulldozer was not yet at the door in San Francisco, but it was on its way for the vast majority of SRO rooms. "No amount of enforcement can change blighted neighborhoods," wrote one planner about San Francisco after World War II. He continued, "Nothing short of a clean sweep and a new start can make the district a genuinely good place in which to live."[22]

Nonbuilding as eradication.   The clean sweep of hotels came not only with the tearing down of former single-room districts but also with the decisions about what types of buildings should fill the empty

FIGURE 9.7. Reformer's-eye view of rooming houses in San Francisco, 1947. One local newspaper published this picture, which shows the back of the structure, with the caption, "Exterior of typical Western Addition Rooming House." The house was four blocks from City Hall.

blocks. That is, the official prohibition of hotels entailed both clearance and *nonbuilding,* active refusal to build, repair, or subsidize residential hotels with public funds. Publicly funded housing of World War I and World War II had included hotels and dormitories, although for the most part these were temporary structures. Nonbuilding had become officially ordained with the establishment of the Federal Housing Administration during the New Deal. Through the 1970s, the federal government funded or assisted virtually no hotel-style public housing other than college dormitories and too few studio apartments that might have replaced midpriced hotel housing.[23]

In concert with federal policy (which in turn was tied to federal funding), local bureaucracies in charge of rebuilding downtown usually had to avoid the construction of hotel housing. San Francisco established its city housing authority in 1938, and its foremost priority was to build suburban-style apartments for urban families—putting the idealist strategy into concrete. The authority's first three projects were three-story walk-up garden apartment buildings set in ample open space.[24] After the war, in 1945, came the time for larger-scale work. As experts were doing in other states, California city officials convinced the legislature to give special city authorities the power for complete urban renewal: designating blighted areas, replanning and replatting the blocks, and (unlike the New Deal scheme of public construction and management) then selling the land to private developers.[25]

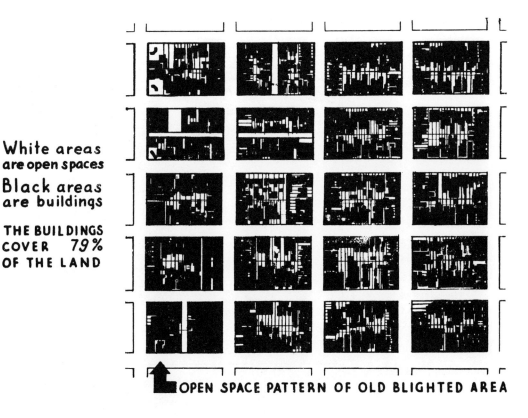

White areas
are open spaces

Black areas
are buildings

THE BUILDINGS
COVER 79%
OF THE LAND

OPEN SPACE PATTERN OF OLD BLIGHTED AREA

San Francisco's first clearance under the new rules was to be in the Western Addition; it was to be a total redevelopment initially slated for 280 city blocks. In a widely circulated 1947 report commissioned by the city Board of Supervisors, planners and architects developed a detailed plan for a study section nearest the civic center and downtown (figs. 9.8, 9.9). At the time, the Western Addition clearance was correctly criticized as "Negro removal," but the project was also hotel housing removal. In 1947, the planners still assumed a single developer would rebuild the study area. The staff, the planning commission, the supervisors, and the mayor agreed that the neighborhood demographics were to remain the same. Out of 445 hotel units existing in the area, the experts liberally proposed to keep 200. Yet out of the 3,799 new housing units they proposed to build, *none* were hotel units. Of the households throughout the Western Addition, 36 percent were to continue to consist of one person, with a much higher proportion of single households in the blocks close to downtown, like the study district. Thus, the sample area plan called for 56 percent of the new units (2,139 out of 3,799) to be two-room efficiency apartments consisting of a sleeping-studio room, an adjoining kitchen-dining room, and a bath-

FIGURE 9.8. Map of an urban renewal study area, drawn to emphasize the density of San Francisco's inner Western Addition, 1945. From a report of the City Planning Commission.

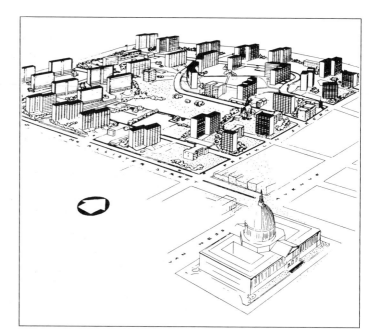

FIGURE 9.9. Proposal for the inner Western Addition, suggesting removal of the old housing and replacement with single-use public housing towers. San Francisco City Hall is in the foreground.

FIGURE 9.10. An idealistic SRO upgrade proposal, 1947. As rooming houses were torn down, efficiency apartments like these were originally envisioned for the rebuilt Western Addition.

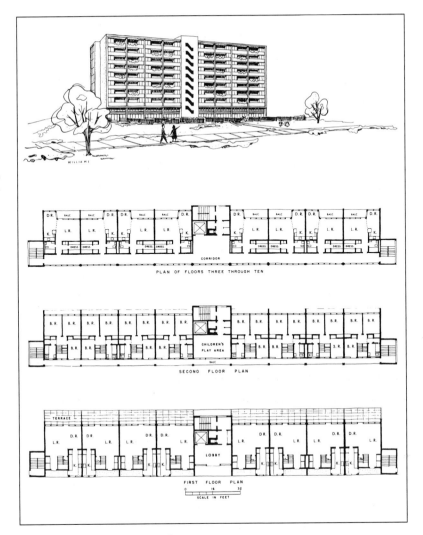

FIGURE 9.11. Apartment towers proposed for the Western Addition, 1947. The eight upper floors were to be efficiency apartments that would replace rooming house units. At the lowest level were two-story town house units for larger households.

room (figs. 9.10, 9.11).[26] This very liberal proposal was in effect an idealistic SRO upgrade.

The 1947 proposal was part of a strategy to establish the city's redevelopment agency, which was founded in 1948. Mayors hostile to renewal prevented the San Francisco Redevelopment Agency (SFRA) from acting in any significant way from 1952 until 1959.[27] During the seven-year hiatus, changes at both the local and federal levels meant that the idealistic scheme for rehousing of the Western Addition's residents was largely lost. By the 1960s, the urban renewal plan for the district was very different. For market rate housing, the mix of unit types was left to the discretion of individual developers. For housing with public subsidies, the programs themselves usually dictated larger units for larger families; heavy-handed administrative pressure from Washington also pushed the mix toward one- and two-bedroom units and away from studio units. For the first phase of redevelopment, data from 1971 show that only 16 percent of the units were studios or efficiencies—in a city where over half of the people waiting for public housing were single elderly people who needed small units. In the second phase, the SFRA's own study found that more than 4,000 of the displaced households (61% of all households) were single-person and more than half, nonwhite. Data on apartment-size mixtures are strangely not available for this phase of the redevelopment, but the proportion of studio units was probably less than 16 percent. Meanwhile, deliberate ignorance continued unabated. A thorough 1967 interagency report on San Francisco's housing did not mention SRO or other hotel units in the city.[28]

Other proposals were more radical than the 1947 San Francisco proposal and even less successful in gaining either local or federal approval. An earlier proposal, one which probably inspired the San Francisco planners, was made during the New Deal by Harvard professor James Ford. For New York City he suggested huge new SRO replacement hotels within larger housing projects. Ford was concerned not only for single people in existing hotels but also for the estimated 200,000 lodgers who lived with New York families. Ford argued that if proper quarters were available for the lodgers, then they would not crowd into the new family housing. For potential housing sites both on the Lower East Side and in Harlem, he recommended interspersing ten-story elevator buildings for family housing with similarly scaled SRO buildings. According to his scheme, some of the SRO structures would have been segregated by gender; others were to accommodate men and women on separate floors; still others would have contained small efficiency apartments in addition to single rooms. He also advocated rehabilitating New York's existing rooming houses. Even in the heady days of New Deal experimentation, however, Ford's ideas had been flatly rejected.[29]

In 1952–53, Catherine Bauer and Davis McEntire proposed that the Redevelopment Authority of Sacramento build an entirely *new* SRO workers' district at a new location to clear the city's West End skid row for more upscale uses. To house the state's largest agricultural labor pool, Bauer and McEntire suggested 3,000 cubicle rooms of relatively permanent occupancy and 1,500 dormitory beds for migrants, all built above commercial spaces, all to be owned by the city and leased to private managers. At the going rates of 75 cents per night and $7 per week, the project would have been largely self-supporting. Bauer and McEntire admitted they were up against extant federal policies, especially Section 207 of the National Housing Act (which recognized only rental units "of design and size suitable for family living"). Sacramento's redevelopment agency actually concurred with the plans, and several private developers were interested in Bauer and McEntire's proposal. However, the difficulties of finding cheap land and the lack of appropriate federal programs killed the brave project.[30]

The proposals for San Francisco's Western Addition, Ford's SROs in New York, and Sacramento's West End were exceptions in the general tide of urban renewal ideas but not rarities. Their existence proves that at least some local leaders and housing designers saw the continued need for and viability of hotel housing, or something very close to it. Yet, the official nonbuilding policy for hotel projects, especially after the mid-1950s, reveals how monolithic housing policies were. The vast majority of public housing proposals gave only lip service to one-person households, in large part because needs for larger households were equally or more pressing, politically more visible, and keyed into the doctrinaire single focus on the family. While public programs avoided building *new* hotel units, parallel actions by many of the same agencies were destroying existing residential hotels.

Making tenants invisible.   As with the SFRA's applications of blight and nonbuilding, the actions of other hotel-closing agencies were not (in their own minds) aiming the wrecking ball at the homes of the poor but "eliminating dead tissue," "applying the scalpel," "clearing away the mistakes of the past," and building "an attractive new city." About a Norfolk, Virginia, hotel district, one planning journal editor reported in 1961 that "progress had reached the demolition stage." Local agents crowed that they had "reduced to rubble . . . scores of flophouses not renowned for adding luster to their city's good name."[31]

Because officials did not consider hotels to be permanent housing, during the official massive downtown clearances from 1950 to 1970, people living in hotels were not tallied as residents. Hence, when a

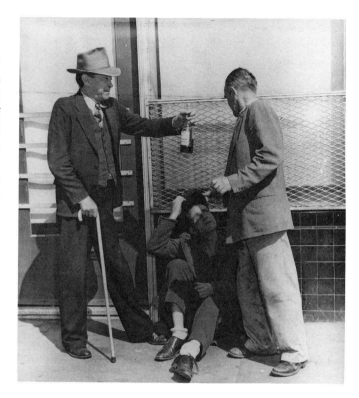

FIGURE 9.12. Helping to make skid row residents look bad, 1956. This picture of a bottle club in the South of Market was carefully posed by a San Francisco newspaper photographer. Fostering such stereotypes lessened concern about SRO demolition.

city demolished an SRO building, "no one" had been moved, and no dwelling units were lost in the official counts and newspaper reports (fig. 9.12). In reality, of course, hundreds of thousands of SRO people and homes were being removed. Deliberate ignorance had become a cultural blind spot that made hotel residents invisible both to officials and to the public. A 1970 planning study in San Diego found only 100 people living in the city's large single workers' district, which was being considered for demolition. Local hotel housing advocates protested. A second count in 1975 found 499 people in the same district; after another protest, a third count found 1,000 hotel people still living in the district—and this after several hotels had closed because of the official pressure. In some cities, the people removed were difficult residents: bums, psychotics, or other marginal people. But the vast majority were not marginal. By making them invisible, experts made the rough handling of such people easier.[32]

Relocation costs gave city officials another reason to make hotel residents invisible. The 1961 Housing Act provided up to $200 for a *family* displaced by renewal but gave no guidelines and granted no federal funding for single individuals. To fill that gap in the law, the Urban

Renewal Administration in Washington authorized local authorities to pay each single SRO person a relocation fee of $5, approximately cab fare out of the neighborhood. "Transients," those who had lived fewer than ninety days at a hotel, did not even qualify for the $5, although many local agencies paid the token relocation fee to any SRO tenant who applied.[33]

In San Francisco's redevelopment of the South of Market, politicians and downtown leaders deemed a large clearance was necessary for what eventually has become the huge Moscone Convention Center and its adjacent Yerba Buena Gardens. In the blocks to be cleared during the 1960s, 91 percent of the households were single, and most were white; 97 percent lived in hotels. A surprising 41 percent of the 240 families in the renewal area also lived in hotels. Later studies estimated that about 40,000 hotel rooms were destroyed, although city officials kept no tally.

Initially in areas like the Western Addition and South of Market, the opposition of hotel residents was neither strong nor organized. Instead of fighting a seemingly impossible battle, tenants took their $5 relocation fee and moved. To their credit, the staff in many urban renewal agencies attempted to give SRO tenants help in finding a new home; in some cases, the appointed social workers made repeated visits and multiple notices. The SRO residents, tending to be fiercely independent and suspicious of authorities, usually had ample reason to mistrust overtures from urban renewal agents. In any case, up until the early 1960s the vast majority of the tenants moved on their own, without help. Long after the supply of inexpensive SRO housing had reached a critical stage, these tenants still thought they could find a new place.[34]

In the late 1960s, hotel tenants met increasing frustration in finding rooms. The losses in rooms had far outpaced the losses in clients. No national figures exist for the number of SRO hotel rooms destroyed before 1970; estimates usually refer to "millions" of rooms closed, converted, or torn down in major U.S. cities. Including the hotels closed in small towns and medium-sized cities would double the number of units lost.[35] Alarmed by the simmering political and health implications of relocation and the declining quality of life in inexpensive hotels, a few pioneering planners, social workers, public health officials, and journalists recognized the beginning of an SRO crisis.[36] During the 1960s, this new corps of SRO advocates began to chip away at the unfair stereotypes about hotel life. Their work coincided with a growing pro-fessional and public disillusionment with downtown renewal. The pub-lication of books such as *The Death and Life of Great American Cities* in 1961, *The Urban Villagers* in 1962, and *The Federal Bulldozer* in 1964 had galvanized critiques of urban renewal processes and goals.[37] Among housing officials and planners, the time was ready for a more widespread change of heart about hotel life. Unfortunately, for many hotel residents, this revised view would be too late.

SINCE 1970: CONFLICTS SURROUNDING HOTEL LIFE

Before 1970, the elimination of SRO units was encouraged by govern-ment policy, often against the objections of private hotel owners. Since 1970, hotel housing advocates have hammered together a pro-SRO movement and won converts in official life. Pro-SRO activists continue to be haunted by critics and by the underside of hotel life. Nevertheless, since 1970, officials and owners have changed sides. Growing numbers of public officials have moved to conserve hotels, while more owners want to close or raze their buildings. The following summaries can in-troduce only salient moments and principal themes in the gradual building of a national pro-SRO movement after 1970. Not presented here—but available in the cited literature—are the complex historical processes which supported and delayed each case: urban and regional economies, local power structures, and myriad participants. For each failed SRO campaign noted here, a great many more occurred. Other positive examples also exist, but in more modest numbers.

The coalescing of a pro-SRO movement. Between 1967 and 1973, the political situation of hotel life changed dramatically. The climate of American political activism and awareness of minority needs had reached critical mass. As part of reforms aimed at urban renewal, ar-guments began to be heard locally and in Congress for the inclusion of hotel residents in public housing programs.[38] Responding to these ar-guments, Congress passed the Uniform Relocation Act in 1970. This policy change marked 1970 as a major pivot year in the political his-tory of SROs. For the first time, redevelopment agencies and other fed-erally funded groups were legally required to recognize people living in hotels as bona fide city residents; if a residential hotel was to be demol-

FIGURE 9.13. A hotel tenants' meeting in San Francisco's South of Market, 1973. Members of Tenants and Owners in Opposition to Redevelopment (TOOR) confer with their lawyers in a hotel lobby.

ished as part of a public project, the agency had to help the hotel tenants find new housing, just as if they were apartment dwellers. Twenty years of official removal had made SRO units hard to find, and the process of assisting tenants was difficult. Most critically, the budget outlays were substantial: each hotel dweller was to receive the $200 household dislocation allowance, compensation for moving costs, and up to $83 a month for four years if the new housing cost more than 25 percent of the individual's income; the total was not to exceed $4,000.[39] Suddenly hotel residents were both visible and very expensive for the urban renewal process.

Simultaneously, SRO tenants had learned their rights and with community activists had organized themselves more effectively. Because urban renewal was early and done on a large scale in San Francisco, the local movement against it was an important national example. In 1968, South of Market hotel tenants began organized protests of the relocation for what became Moscone Convention Center and Yerba Buena Gardens (fig. 9.13). In December 1969, courts issued the first restraining order against the San Francisco Renewal Agency, and the court battles continued for four years. The residents proved to the court that adequate replacement housing did not exist in the city, and the court forced the SFRA to develop over 1,500 units of new housing in the area. Developed by a nonprofit community group, Tenants and Owners Development Corporation (TODCO), the first new replacement housing opened in 1979.[40]

San Francisco was only one early center among several engaged in full-fledged fights to revise plans for urban renewal and to save SROs. In Boston SRO tenants stopped progress on a renewal program. So did tenants in New York's Greenwich Village and on the Upper West Side. The New York Mayor's Office of SRO Housing was opened in 1973 to work on social programs and tenant protection laws. Other groups were working to rehabilitate hotels and improve their management. In 1975, a pro-SRO group in New York City, Project FIND, leased and moved into the 308-room Woodstock Hotel, located near Times Square.[41] These projects saved only a few hotels from demolition but did create a new and embarrassing climate of public relations. Suddenly hotel owners, city housing authorities, redevelopment agencies, and other people with anti-SRO views had to work hard to prove that residential hotels were an urban blight of culturally aberrant buildings where only marginal people lived.

Unfortunately, the Uniform Relocation Act could not decree an instant change in the SRO attitudes of all housing officials in Washington, D.C., or in local agencies; at first, the act exacerbated harassment of residents and hastened hotel demolition. From 1970 to 1980, an estimated one million residential hotel rooms were converted or destroyed, including most of the Yerba Buena area (fig. 9.14).[42] Hotel owners generally did not want help to stay in business, in large part because of the potential profits from the expansion of downtown offices. In the 1970s, downtown office construction suddenly started a new boom and developers began to offer hotel owners handsome prices for their properties. Then, as now, the land underneath most residential hotels had more market value than the buildings. In New York, an empty hotel was worth two to three times that of an occupied building because the new speculator owner could more quickly rehabilitate it for a new use or tear it down.[43] Then, as now, to encourage the perception of hotels as blight, public and private owners understated the positive side of hotel living and overemphasized the problems in bad hotels. In day-to-day management and long-term goals, the lines between public and private ownership often blurred. Redevelopment agencies (through eminent domain) and city governments (through tax foreclosure) frequently became unwilling landlords for remaining residential hotels. To manage their hotel programs, they often hired anti-SRO people from the property industry, not pro-SRO people from social welfare offices.

FIGURE 9.14. Ken Roth, a South of Market hotel resident in the 1970s, watching the demolition of his San Francisco neighborhood for the Yerba Buena project.

For the stubbornly positive SRO buildings with sound structures and tenants neither marginal nor easy to dislodge, both public and private landlords developed an arsenal of tools to create problems where none have existed before. Although the techniques were perfected in the early 1970s, many remain in use. To generate vacancies, one of the most effective means was to reverse normal management principles and to harass the tenants: replacing friendly, long-term staff with churlish employees; suddenly lowering the standards for admissible tenants; and loosening security, stopping maid service, or permanently removing clean linen from stock. Other owners deliberately aggravated tenants by shutting off heat and hot water for long periods, locking toilet rooms, not repairing (or entirely closing down) elevators in six-story and eight-story buildings, plugging room locks, seeing that mail and messages were "lost" (particularly for tenants who were demanding their rights), not letting Meals on Wheels attendants deliver food, spraying for roaches while tenants were still in the room, taking the furniture out of the lobby, falsely advertising no vacancy so the hotel emptied, and sending gangs of thugs along with eviction notices to intimidate tenants. The agents of one hapless San Francisco hotel owner had the poor judgment to use the roach-spray-in-an-occupied-room technique while one of Mayor Dianne Feinstein's aides was visiting the tenant. One New York landlord went at the steel stair landings of his building with a hammer and chisel; after five flights of stairs had thus "collapsed," the building had to be vacated because of failure to comply with fire safety laws.[44]

In San Francisco, struggles like these eventually led to the International Hotel dispute and eviction of 1977, which was another turning point in national opinion about SRO homes and SRO people. After eight years of nationally publicized eviction struggles, at 3:00 A.M., 330 police officers and sheriff's deputies converged on the hotel, which stood at the edge of Chinatown. After vociferously protesting the court orders to do so, the sheriff had finally come to evict about forty elderly Chinese and Filipino residents who remained in the 184-room hotel. On nearby sidewalks more than 2,000 demonstrators protested. Many of the public knew the hotel's location not only because of its residents but also because of its large basement nightclub, the hungry i, which in earlier years had headlined Barbra Streisand, the Kingston Trio, Dick Cavett, Bill Cosby, Dick Gregory, and Woody Allen.[45] After the eviction battle, the owner of the property, the Four Winds Corporation of Singapore, immediately razed the building. Fifteen years later, the site was still empty, except for the archways of the remaining basement walls, where the hungry i had once been. There, on cold nights, homeless people huddled to get out of the wind.

The tenants in the International Hotel lost their single-room homes, but like tenants in earlier cases, their fight helped to raise new questions about the intersections of hotel life, property rights, and social services. For instance, the year following the eviction, the staff of the U.S. Senate used the case for the introductory example in an information paper about the SRO crisis.[46] Owing to the fights of the 1970s, the formerly invisible realms of hotel life finally began to appear regularly in public spotlights, with front-page newspaper articles headlined "Rooms of Death," "Heatless Hotels," and "Struggle over Downtown Continues." Through the 1980s, the *New York Times* prominently featured SRO stories nearly once a week. The Gray Panthers and other senior groups also came to be instrumental in several fights.[47]

Another important example of the turnaround process since the 1970s is the experience of Portland, Oregon. About the same time as the last fights at the International Hotel, a private group remodeled Portland's Estate Hotel with a city loan; in 1978, neighborhood leaders formed the nonprofit Burnside Consortium (now called Central City Concern) to coordinate services and to preserve other housing. In 1979,

Andy Raubeson was appointed director of the consortium and saw immediately that SRO hotels were a prime priority for his skid row clientele. "It just seemed too obvious," he says, "that we had to champion the housing stock." His organization began leasing and then buying hotels, eventually renovating more than five hundred units.[48] The Burnside experience emphasizes the growing realization that proper management—often subsidized by a nonprofit organization—is a key to maintaining low-cost hotel life. As part of the Portland action, in 1980, U.S. Rep. Les AuCoin, a Democrat from Oregon, persuaded Congress to make SROs eligible for federal low-interest rehabilitation loans and then for Section 8 housing funds. These and other successful programs have put Portland in the forefront of municipal efforts to preserve SROs.[49]

With the federal Omnibus Reconciliation Act of 1981 and the Stewart B. McKinney Bill in 1987, hotel housing moved further toward better housing status and became eligible for a few other subsidies. With cruel irony, these official changes of heart began just before the Reagan and Bush administrations slashed public housing funds by 80 percent.[50] The widespread implementation of the new policies was thus deferred.

The legacy of problem hotels. In spite of a generation of pro-SRO work and the gradual but growing official acceptance of hotel life, the problems of the past continue to haunt the progress of the present. At the worst hotels, not only the buildings are residues. So are the owners and managers. For many owners, a net loss helps their tax accounting. Such owners are unwilling to put money into their buildings; they hire the cheapest possible managers, who rarely have any training and never stay very long in the demanding and often dangerous business. Many managers lack the simple bookkeeping acumen to maintain profitable cash flows. Observers in Portland saw hotels where repair investments as small as $15 per room (for fixing a broken sink, window, or toilet) could have restored one-fifth of the vacant rooms to full weekly and monthly rents. For other managers, costs of labor and of maintaining desk, telephone, linen, and housekeeping services have risen at a rate greater than reasonable rents.[51]

The most deteriorated rooms and disturbing social conditions in hotel life do not necessarily occur in the cheapest hotels but in those where managers and owners are completely callous, inept, underpaid, or overwhelmed. Most simply, these locations can be called "problem hotels." A subset of problem hotels are those where the owners and managers have given up any attempt at lobby surveillance and where no one screens or controls troublesome residents, guests, or behavior. Social workers call such places "street hotels" or "open hotels."[52] The daily conditions around problem and street hotels disturb even SRO advocates. In a street hotel, the negative stereotypes of hotel tenants ring true: a majority are unemployed, addicted to alcohol or narcotics, mentally ill, or otherwise chronically disabled. The tenants exhibit little capacity for normal social life or collective political action. Single parents may leave children unattended for long periods. The residents might include someone who likes to throw knives at walls or a heavy drinker who routinely vomits on the hall carpets or urinates in the elevators. In street hotels, lobbies and halls are unsafe because speed freaks attract or bring "bad trade" into the building. The desk clerks do nothing to screen out these people. Other tenants collect stolen weapons or other contraband items in their rooms. The more vulnerable tenants are often brutally beaten and robbed by the tougher ones. Tenants in problem hotels expect to see psychotic behavior or erratic anger.

Safety and health hazards also darken life in problem hotels. Children fall to their deaths from unprotected windows or open elevator shafts. Uncollected garbage piles up in the halls; rats jump from can to can. Some residents hoard toilet paper; then because no toilet paper is available, other residents substitute newspaper, which clogs the toilets. Because the maintenance staff is minimal at best, the toilets can remain out of commission for a long time. Eventually, when angry tenants break toilets with baseball bats and angry landlords refuse to replace the shattered plumbing, even those not incapacitated by alcohol use the halls for toilet rooms.

The fire hazards of problem hotels match their social and health risks. Fire escapes may be wooden; panic hardware is absent on the doors; no alarm system has ever been installed, or the aging system is out of order. Smoking in bed causes frequent mattress fires. Tenants (or landlords) intentionally set other fires. Because the electrical wiring in the rooms is old and intended to run only one 60-watt bulb, overloaded extension cords to refrigerators and hot plates routinely blow fuses or start fires. Managers and tenants put out the fires by themselves if they can; if they call the fire department, fire marshals may inspect and then close the building.

The people and activities from these problem SRO buildings spill out into the surrounding neighborhoods. Socially marginal residents and their friends congregate outside the door. They panhandle passing pedestrians, or rant to them about imaginary fears. Garbage (called "air-mail" by hotel residents), epithets, and urine can be hurled from open windows onto surrounding sidewalks.[53] New York's Hotel Martinique, made infamous by Jonathan Kozal's study *Rachel and Her Children*, exemplified many problem hotel dimensions of the mid–1980s. Kozol detailed a case in which crowding, lack of services, and corruption had created a nightmare for family groups. The supply of the city's public housing apartment units and affordable apartments had lagged so far behind need that social workers were forced to dump clients on a temporary basis that was essentially permanent and very expensive for the public. Dangers and privations endured by single people and by the elderly in problem hotels can be equally serious, and are often similarly intertwined with public assistance.

Problem *motels* for permanent residents have begun to reflect the degree to which the American city has become a suburban city. Where highway traffic has shifted away from a motel and the units are over a generation old, managers have hung out signs advertising WEEKLY AND MONTHLY RATES. At the more expensive examples are salesmen on temporary assignment and construction workers in town for a season. There, the system works. Elsewhere, residential motels often shelter very low income residents. Families unable to afford other housing and recent immigrants sometimes fill whole motels that have the worst management. Many of the families, like those in light housekeeping rooms in the 1920s, have their furniture in storage. In 1985, officials estimated that Orange County, California, had 15,000 people living in motels, along boulevards such as Katella Avenue near Disneyland. South of San Francisco, hundreds of families and single-person households live in residential motels that line access roads to the Bayshore Freeway not far from the airport. The Memphis, Tennessee, motel where the Reverend Martin Luther King, Jr., was killed in 1969 had become a residential motel and a haunt of prostitutes by 1988, when residents were evicted to convert the structure into a museum of the

FIGURE 9.15. A three-story rooming house, the Hotel Harris, virtually quivering before the onslaught of new office tower development in Denver, 1983.

civil rights movement. Even the wealthiest counties can have serious residential motel problems. The citizens of Westchester County, north of New York City, refuse to build adequate low-income housing but pay $3,000 per month for each of hundreds of residents in miserable motels where the maids steal medications and a reputed 80 percent of the residents use crack cocaine. Often without cars, parents cannot reach jobs or take their children to school.[54]

Many of the eradication processes that destroyed good hotel homes in the 1960s and 1970s have remained in force (fig. 9.15). Through the 1980s, professional "housers" or housing activists were typically not converted to pro-SRO views. Cushing Dolbeare, long-term director of the National Low Income Housing Coalition in Washington, D.C., admits that people like herself were the hardest to convince. She notes that housers "assumed that the requirement for a kitchen and a bath for each unit was always supposed to be in a housing proposal." She was not personally involved in the pro-SRO movement until 1981.[55] Some housing advocates still expect that preserving hotel housing will undermine family housing minimums and that the cities will not have the ability to enforce occupancy standards of one or two people per room even for elderly people. All hotel rooms, the doubters say, will soon be overcrowded with single mothers with three children each. In 1985, when many people could only choose between living on the street or in an armory shelter, a HUD program director still stated that in rehabbed structures "asking people to give up a private bathroom is an awful lot."[56]

Official actions continue to reverse earlier progress. In 1989, the U.S. Supreme Court eviscerated New York City's 1985 moratorium on SRO conversion or demolition, although rent stabilization laws continued to protect most of the city's long-term tenants. In California, for more than twelve months after the Santa Cruz and San Francisco Loma Prieta earthquake in October 1989, planners and hotel residents of several cities had long struggles with officials of the Federal Emergency Management Agency (FEMA) over whether or not residential hotels qualified as dwellings for more than $50 million in repair or replacement funds.[57] The debate sounded a great deal like the debates of the 1960s. "The wave of the future may be an undertow," warns SRO activist Richard Livingston. "For each hundred hotel units that we fight to save, a thousand are torn down or converted. We are moving rapidly backwards."[58]

The problems of living at the lowest-priced hotels are serious, but many of them are inherited from generations of misunderstanding. Prohibition, the national ban on alcoholic beverages lasted only thirteen years. The national prohibition of single-room housing lasted more than sixty years and is not yet completely rescinded. Many public officials have come to realize the importance of SROs at precisely the same time that their redevelopment agency has just torn down the city's last publicly owned—and usually largest—SRO buildings.

Nonetheless, shifting policies and programs in several cities show a viability for hotel life and suggest that public vision *is* widening. Hotels remain the cheapest private housing available downtown. Hotels are less ideal than apartments, especially for families with young children. However, as numerous activists put it, for the most difficult to house people in the city, hotels work "better than shelters and better than the streets."[59] In bad hotels, a change of owners and better management can create a very different home environment, even for hotel and motel tenants with very low housing budgets. Where managers strictly control lobby entrances, carefully screen residents, and keep up building maintenance, the type of tenants and their living situations change dramatically. Managers at positive SROs still serve their tenants not only as tough-minded rent collectors and rule enforcers but also as social workers, part-time grandparents, or political advocates. Significantly, rents in successful SROs are *not* necessarily higher than in street hotels, although as the price rises, conditions generally improve. The profitability of a good residential hotel lies in higher occupancy rates with less turnover.[60]

For public housing provision, hotels make economic sense, too. As Bradford Paul has put it, for the cost of one new HUD Section 8 studio apartment, 4 or 5 hotel rooms can be rehabilitated in San Francisco (with its stringent seismic safety requirements); 12 to 15 rooms can be rehabilitated in Portland; or 35 to 40 rooms can be rehabilitated in city-owned hotels in New York.[61] Seeing figures like these, more and more elected officials and representatives have begun to join pro-SRO forces, spurred by the worsening homeless situation. More cities have passed and enforced ordinances to slow the conversion or demolition of residential hotels. Several mayors have created special offices for hotel housing and encouragements for rehabilitation. In the early 1980s, the New York mayor's office began offering six-month training courses (two nights a week) and internships for SRO managers.[62] These experiments in a new attitude about downtown hotel life, in addition to each one hundred hotel units that are saved, may have an importance far greater than their initial numbers. The wave of the future may be a wave of change.

THE PROSPECT OF PLURALISM IN HOUSING

The argument of this book is fairly straightforward. Public and professional housing attitudes—in particular, doctrinaire idealism and deliberate ignorance—have devastated an important supply of American urban housing. Between 1800 and 1960, hotel entrepreneurs and their clients and staffs developed both good and bad traditions of hotel life, responding especially to the needs of urban employment. By the time of the Civil War, hotel life comprised four distinct downtown subcultures; hotel owners and their architects had unofficially but effectively begun to stratify environments to match those cultures. Simultaneously, housing officials began a one hundred-year campaign to write hotels out of public policy because hotel life undermined middle and upper class cultural ideals and hotel land-use mixtures threatened professional hopes for a new, specialized city. This cultural imperialism fueled the near-annihilation of hotel life. For over fifty years, until the beginning of the pro-SRO movement in the 1970s, public policymakers unnecessarily shelved the high-density housing option of hotel living as a tool of urban life and culture. The history of hotel living affirms that the built environment is not merely a result or a background for human action but a participant, a player in collective human life. The problems of doctrinaire idealism and deliberate ignorance continue to haunt present hotel life and United States housing plans.

Expanding the notion of home. The history of hotel life shows that the crisis in the residential hotel supply was a planned event. So too, solutions to the SRO crisis can be planned events choreographed by residents, activists, officials, owners, and experts. Pioneering groups have begun to build new residential hotels, thereby stretching the boundaries of both the official and public definitions of home in America.

The new residential hotel building types are as varied as their different sites and cities. For lower-income residents, hotel makers are reinventing the rooming house; higher-income residents are seeing variations on the midpriced hotel or motel. For new rooming houses, the trend is to plan fairly large buildings with at least one hundred rooms. Most typically, they are structures remodeled or built with some type of public/private partnership and managed by a nonprofit organization. However, with initial subsidies a few private developers have also successfully developed SRO projects. Because neighborhoods at the edges of town continue to block efforts to build for a diverse population, these hotels continue to be on expensive downtown land. Like the downtown rooming houses of 1910, the new rooming houses rely on commercial rentals on their ground floor to subsidize rents on the upper floors and to provide retail services for a neighborhood where home activities are scattered up and down the street. The new rooming

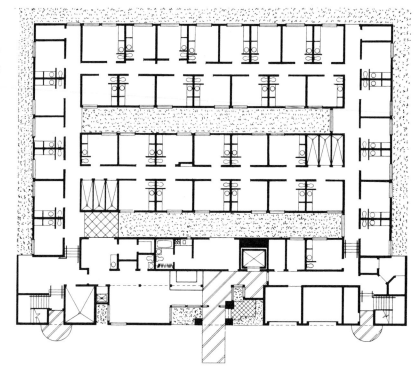

FIGURE 9.16. First floor plan for San Diego's Baltic Inn, opened in 1987. Rooms at the lower part of the plan include the lobby, manager's apartment, and service spaces.

houses require larger lots to accommodate a comparatively large number of parking spaces—more than the 1910 rooming house, which had no parking spaces, and fewer than the typical present apartment requirement of one parking space per unit.

In the early 1990s, about a dozen of these projects in the United States are either newly built or in working drawings. Two West Coast examples are typical. In San Diego, California, the 207-room Baltic Inn opened in 1987. It was the first new SRO building in the city in seventy years and one of the first in the nation (figs. 9.16, 9.17). It marks a new least-expensive version of the rooming house. As one commentator characterized the legal permit battles for the hotel, "San Diego has said, in effect, that it is willing to permit some citizens to live in places most others would not prefer."[63] In Berkeley, California, the Studio Durant project has been planned for a large lot between the city's downtown retail district and the University of California campus. The 198 rooms occupy the upper three floors. At the back of the site (with an E-shaped plan of rooms above) is a large parking area; retail spaces and a generous lobby fill the site next to the sidewalk. The project features timely commercial facade design, as any good hotel owner would have re-

FIGURE 9.17. Street view of the new Baltic Inn, San Diego.

quired in the past (fig. 9.18). The projected construction cost in 1991, $20,000 a room, compares favorably with the $27,000 a room being spent to renovate a residential hotel across town.[64]

The most striking physical changes in these new rooming house buildings include their provision of more social spaces—lobbies, lounges, and shared kitchens—and their improved ratio of baths to rooms. The one to six ratio from 1910 is no longer viable. The Baltic Inn provides the new minimum: a private toilet for each room, simply in a stall behind a curtain, and a room sink on a small all-purpose countertop area. Showers are down the hall. The plan for the Studio Durant, geared to a slightly higher rent, provides each very small room with a private shower and toilet room and a room sink on a longer all-purpose counter built as a cooking area (with a small refrigerator and a microwave oven as standard equipment). The bathroom sink doubling as the kitchen sink harks back to light housekeeping rooms of the 1940s. The tiny built-in kitchen area, which has yet to gain a name, does not make these new dwellings into full studio apartments; in most cases these structures are not designed to meet apartment building codes. Instead, the better plumbing and wiring, the rudimentary baths and cooking

common areas
▾

manager's apartment
▾

handicapped
adapted unit ▶

◂ lobby entrance

▴ retail storefront

FIGURE 9.18. Perspective view of the Studio Durant, a new rooming house planned for downtown Berkeley, California. The architect, David Baker, expresses each of the functional elements on the facade of the project.

units, are responses to age-old demands from both hotel residents and managers. In the past, because the wiring was not adequate, the smells disturbed neighbors, or the food attracted vermin, managers even in palace and midpriced hotels fought tenants who illegally cooked in their rooms. However, the small inexpensive refrigerator has revolutionized food storage. Milk bottles set to keep cool overnight on rooming house window ledges are no longer a telltale sign of residents making breakfasts in their rooms, and vermin can be made less prevalent as well. Making the wiring, plumbing, and cabinetwork more adequate from the beginning is better for both tenants and managers. The increase in bath ratio is completely in keeping with the history of increasing plumbing expectations in dwellings of all sorts in the United States.

Sustaining *existing* residential hotel buildings continues to be essential and even more challenging than constructing new buildings. Because very few purpose-built rooming houses were constructed after the early 1920s, 99 percent of the inexpensive hotel rooms in the United States are in structures that are seventy years old or more. Their heating systems and elevators wore out long ago, and most have been inexpertly patched and repaired rather than replaced. If the buildings have any cooling system at all, it probably consists of those few windows that still operate. The plumbing is as old as the heating; the plumbing ratio usually needs to be improved, at least to one bath for each four rooms. All this refitting has to be done inexpensively and if possible without closing the building entirely. In 1990, using Community Redevelopment Agency funds, advocates in Los Angeles opened 520 newly rehabilitated SRO rooms on skid row and planned to build a new 72-room hotel. The sponsors argue that these SRO services will cost the city $11 a night versus the $28 per night for ward-style shelters. San Francisco has bought and renovated six hotels (with a total of 460 rooms) and turned them over to nonprofit agencies for management. In 1991, the city's Redevelopment Agency—the former archenemy of residential hotels—remodeled a downtown building as mixed apartments and SRO units. The unsung heroes of the hotel housing movement include the architects, managers, and financial backers who devise ways to upgrade structures like these.

Rehabilitated structures provide the widest variation in size and social program. Sheltered dwellings, small board-and-care homes, and halfway houses have made use of modest structures in a variety of settings, even in outlying single-family neighborhoods. In the 1990s, market rents marginally sustain thousands of 30-room downtown rooming houses, anonymous three-story buildings on 25-foot-wide lots often managed by families of recent immigrants. With appropriate subsidies for maintenance, these structures can continue to provide housing, probably at the upper end of the SRO price range. Midsized buildings, from 30 to 80 rooms, are more expensive to buy and manage; most hotel activists say that roughly 100 rooms are needed to make efficient use of a full-time manager and to staff a desk 24 hours a day. The scale of a 100- to 150-room older structure is also well matched to the financial abilities of many nonprofit organizations. The largest inexpensive hotels—those with 400 rooms—often require different sorts of organizations or partnerships for purchase, rehabilitation, and management.

Hotels that fewer people want to talk about are new or rebuilt temporary shelters for people living on the streets or in their cars. These structures may have to be the future equivalents of the lodging house rank—the dormitories, cubicles, and missions from the Progressive Era. They could replace the hastily converted armories, church basements, barely renovated flophouses, and other temporary shelters that have become quasi-permanent while the SRO crisis has intensified. As temporary shelters or as permanent single-room housing, hotels cannot solve the entire housing crisis. But they can help to solve parts of it, especially for single men and women (even some with children) who need to get off the streets, for single working people with low incomes, and for low-income elderly people.

A possible revival is apparent for hotels at more expensive levels, too. Private developers in Quincy, Massachusetts, opened a new sixteen-unit rooming house in 1986, the first purpose-built rooming house constructed in the Boston area in several decades. All over the United States, both public and private developers have reinvented the role of the midpriced hotel in the form of elderly housing developments with household services and common meals. In 1990, one typical Bay Area "retirement hotel" offered a private room, full hotel services, and meals for $1,500 a month and shared rooms for $650 a month. Chains of Hometels and Embassy Suites have begun to combine motel, hotel, and residential hotel features. For rents of $2,000 a month (without meals), expensive new apartment hotels—including a 44-story example in Chicago—essentially re-create the apartment hotel of the early 1900s.[65] The popular television series "Beverly Hills 90210" featured a teenage hotel child for much of the first season. According to the show's writers, the character of Dylan McKay "was supposed to live in the Beverly Wilshire, like Warren Beatty." Dylan is the Eloise of the Plaza for the 1990s.[66]

New and rehabilitated hotel buildings are only one of the new experimental residential structures that promoters are proposing to the American public. Not since the 1890s have so many new types of units, mixtures of uses, and shared facilities been tried simultaneously in the United States. Live-work (loft) structures, "mingles" (apartments designed to be shared or co-owned by two separate heads of household), co-housing (a cluster of separate houses that share cooking, recreation, child care, and open space), and "doubling up" (two households sharing one house to counteract high rents) are examples of a sudden burst of chosen or forced experimentation.[67] These projects, along with hotels, can reasonably be expected to push into more suburban settings as well.

These experiments continue to spark heated debates and are usually slow to gain official permission. Housing activists repeatedly must climb against a hundred-year-old glacial accumulation of skewed textbooks, laws, bureaucracies, and attendant attitudes. Two years or more can easily go by while the sponsors of a new rooming house debate with their financiers, the local planning office, the zoning commission, and finally the city council over procedural questions and definitions, including: Should each room in the rooming house be required to have a separate off-street parking space? Are these units legally apartments? If they are not apartments, what are they? If the minimum permitted room size is relaxed, what happens in the future? How will the management guarantee that future densities will not soon overwhelm provisions geared to one- or two-person households?

Obviously, funding subsidies are a prerequisite for most hotel housing projects at the lodging house or rooming house level. Public funds for construction and rebuilding of hotel housing are urgent, and they are needed in far larger amounts than ever before spent for alternative housing projects in the United States. Taxpayers who balk at these expenditures must be consistently reminded that, according to one analysis, the 1990s home owner deduction from federal income taxes has amounted each year to a $47 billion subsidy for private suburban households, half with incomes over $80,000 a year. This private home owner deduction equals four times the entire annual budget of the Department of Housing and Urban Development.[68] If the economically comfortable can be so handsomely subsidized, in good times as well as bad, then the economically essential—the poorly paid people or elderly people who have played fundamental roles in our economy but at low-paying jobs—equally deserve subsidy.

Along with funds for construction, new programs must be funded for management training, building on the New York City model. Running a hotel was one of the most demanding jobs of the nineteenth century, and it is still a task that requires more than can be learned on the job. The horrors of past and present street hotels and indifferently managed flophouses have repeatedly proved that management is as important as the building itself for successful hotel housing. The current cadre of nonprofit hotel staff cannot stretch to cover the number of improved hotels that are needed in the near future.

The necessity of hotel housing is not decreasing. All indications from those who know the homeless situation point in one direction: the need for inexpensive, nonapartment housing is only going to increase. Alice Callaghan, from the Skid Row Housing Trust of Los Angeles, noted in 1992 that hotels were still the last place available for urban people. Like so many other SRO activists, she stressed that hotels provide the last viable safety net for housing; if people miss this net, they will either become homeless—literally forced to live on the street—or institutionalized.[69] It is significant and a sign of wider public concern that Callaghan was being interviewed for an airline flight magazine. In 1970, her only audience might have been the readers of a social welfare journal. Even a relatively conservative housing expert can now publicly point to the unattached as being the least well-served people in American housing. Peter Salons, of Hunter College in New York, emphasizes that "homeless people are merely the most visible portion of the unattached who need housing; there are many more." He continues that these people "do not all need apartments; they need *rooms.*"[70]

Twenty years of the SRO crisis and of determined study and activism have not produced the massive housing program that is needed, but they have set the stage for such a change. Perhaps the most necessary shift is a broader point of view about urban space, a move away from the monolithic one-best-way approach that gained currency in the late nineteenth century.

HISTORY, URBAN EXPERTS, AND PLURALISM

No single profession is responsible for all of the past misunderstandings and omissions of hotels within the range of American housing types. Nor does any single group have the power to instantly expand the notion of home, one of the most complicated and deeply rooted ideas in culture. Yet designers and planners, past and present, have operated at an important nexus in preserving the status quo as well as in fostering change. In part, this role falls to designers because they are trained to think of the future. Unfortunately, they are rarely educated to understand the present or past, particularly not the ordinary environments of the present and past. This has caused problems in the history of hotel housing. During the Progressive Era, social workers and social hygiene experts most successfully focused on what *existed;* the designers focused resolutely on what *ought to be* and often relished the utopian role they wanted to have, rather than the social servant role they told themselves they were performing. Grounded in the dominant class and its culture—whose values and hopes they usually shared—they wrote the official rules and fashioned leading examples of what was and what was not acceptable housing culture. Mary Burki, Peter Marcuse, Robert Goodman, and others have written about this cultural imperialism that has haunted the public housing movement from its inception. Until the 1970s (and in many cases, continuing into the present), planners and architects defined ideal residential environments of both the suburbs and downtown based largely on their own rarefied personal experience and professional design perspectives.[71] They ignored any conflicting evidence. In 1968, Robert Venturi and Denise Scott Brown wrote that "learning from the existing landscape is a way of being revolutionary for an architect."[72] This is still true.

Other housing professionals exhibit problems with understanding the ordinary past and present. In 1976, an official at HUD explained that his department refused to extend federal housing assistance to SROs because the agency's obligation was "not to subsidize or encourage the establishment of a housing environment which is in any way inferior to those standards of quality which our society has come to expect from the public as well as the private sector."[73] Surely the official was unaware that his agency and its forebears had consciously worked to create those expectations and to foster an overly narrow view of the subcultures that have made up America's housing markets. Policymakers have not only omitted hotel housing and singled out apartments and houses as proper homes, they have also created for themselves an official illusion that all Americans, including all public housing clients, have always wanted houses with private kitchens and private baths. The United States now knows the cost of defining as "homeless" even those people who have lived happily and productively in a hotel for fifteen or twenty years.

The new positive SRO view has thrust housing professionals into a new role, that of cultural pluralist. More architects and planners are learning how diverse social groups live, especially those at the margins of society. Housing officials, who now know more about single-person households, are less likely to be disgusted by a thirty-five-year-old clerk who rents a room without a kitchen or private bath. These same officials now see their role, in part, as defending new and old subcultures and fragile people from unnecessary loss of a place to live. They cannot protect these people from any and all change, but they can direct change for the better interests of a greater variety of people. These new variants of professionals and officials seem to be arriving at a clearer grasp of three central realities in building or managing human environments: that people are diverse; that diversity requires flexible approaches and multiple solutions to problems; and that diverse environments are essential for maintaining important social and cultural options. No one solution can work for all Americans. These ideas mark a major shift from professional attitudes of the past one hundred years.

The misguided but well-meaning attempt to eradicate hotel housing from American cities reveals particularly well the importance of remembering the long-term and double-edged nature of expert ideals and ideology. The nineteenth-century ideal of housing urban Americans in single-family suburbs need not have caused a corresponding problem for downtown housing. These were not inherently incompatible environments. The new city of separate and single-purpose spaces might yet be built to coexist very nicely with the old city of social and commercial mixture, pedestrian convenience, and shared kitchens and baths. Had more housing studies been based on the full urban landscape—what existed and why it was there—the SRO crisis might have been averted or at least lessened, and millions of housing units would still be in service.

Hindsight always makes such lessons easier to see than the historical situations allowed. Yet constant danger springs from what Goethe called "active ignorance." The narrower our attitudes, the more rarefied and abstract our experts' education and values, and the less grounded they are in the total historic and geographic reality of how people use rooms, buildings, streets, and neighborhoods, then the more harmful will be the unintended results of well-meaning public policies. If professional knowledge and public vision are wider, more inclusive, and more pluralistic, the United States is less likely to repeat policy and procedural mistakes like those that caused the SRO crisis, the oversight of hotel life, and the temporary twentieth-century decline in living downtown.

TABLE 1

Estimated Hotel Room Supply in San Francisco, 1880–1930

		1880	1910	1930
Palace hotels	Total rooms in rank	3,360	2,848	7,464
	Residential rooms	672	570	1,492
	Share of all SF residential rooms	8%	2%	4%
Midpriced hotels	Total rooms in rank	1,840	7,768	13,864
	Residential rooms	1,049	3,573	4,575
	Share of all SF residential rooms	12%	13%	12%
Rooming houses	Total rooms	4,240	9,352	17,368
	Residential rooms	3,265	7,014	13,026
	Share of all SF residential rooms	38%	26%	34%
Cheap lodging houses	Total rooms	4,800	21,264	25,428
	Residential rooms	3,600	15,948	19,446
	Share of all SF residential rooms	42%	58%	50%
All ranks	Total rooms	15,440	41,234	64,624
	Total residential rooms	9,606	27,105	38,539
	Residential proportion	62%	66%	60%

SOURCE: Groth, "Forbidden Housing," 325–328, Tables IV-1 to IV-21.

TABLE 2

Costs of Urban Housing Alternatives in the Mid-1920s

		Weekly cost ($)
Palace and midpriced hotels		
1.	Palace hotel, five-room suite with bath(s)	97–210
2.	Palace hotel, two-room suite with bath	60–90
3.	Midpriced hotel, two-room suite with bath	30–42
4.	Midpriced hotel, one room with bath down the hall	6–10
5.	Commercial residence club (one room)	10–20
Rooming house and lodging house hotels		
6.	Rooming house, downtown type, bath down the hall	4–10
7.	Institutional residence club ($8 typical)	3–12
8.	Rooming house in converted single-family house	2½–6
9.	Cheap lodging house, private room	3–5
10.	Cheap lodging house, cubicle or ward style	1–3
11.	Flophouse or Salvation Army home	1–1½
Boarding and lodging with a family		
12.	One room (heated) in a family house	6–12
13.	Elderly person boarding with a family	2–6
Apartment hotels and efficiency apartments (furnished)		
14.	Apartment hotel, very elegant, two-room unit	50–100
15.	Apartment hotel, four rooms with sun parlor, high priced	90
16.	Efficiency apartment, one room with kitchenette and dinette	25–30
17.	Light housekeeping room, bath down the hall	5–6
Apartments, flats, and tenements (not furnished)		
18.	Luxury apartment, five to seven rooms	80–250
19.	Luxury apartment, three rooms	40
20.	Skilled workers' apartment, four rooms in older suburb	12–25
21.	Tenement apartments, lowest price	2–6

Single-family houses (including operating costs)	Weekly cost ($)
22. Mansion with seven servants	385
23. Very fashionable house but a changing neighborhood	160
24. Professional's six-room house, close to center city	50
25. Small house in a cottage district for skilled worker	10–14
26. Miserable four-room cottage or rear house, slum	4–6

NOTE: Most prices are from studies done in Chicago and San Francisco during the years 1923 to 1925. For comparison's sake, monthly and daily prices have been adjusted to reflect weekly costs.

SOURCE: Groth, "Forbidden Housing," 466–471, 494–498; and *San Francisco Chronicle* (Sunday, September 2, 1923).

TABLE 3

Typical Weekly Incomes for San Francisco Occupations, 1920

Employment	Women	Men
Manufacturing		
Foundry and machine shops	$12–14[a]	$35–39
Shipbuilding	13–16[a]	33–38
Bakeries	11–14	28–34
Boots and shoes	10–14	25–30
Clothing, women's	12–15	29–35
Clothing, men's	10–14	29–35
Printing and publishing	12–15	27–32
Food preparations	10–13	22–25
Furniture, band and store fixtures	14–16[a]	20–24
Steam laundries	11–14	20–23
Canning	10–13	20–23
Boxes, bags, cartons, etc.	9–12	19–24
Confectionery	9–13	19–23
Tobacco	10–13	18–21
Trades (only union wages reported)		
Carpenters[b]	—	40–45
Stone masons and setters[b]	—	40
Laborers[b]	—	30
Sewer cleaners[b]	—	38
Teamsters, ice deliverers	—	34
Longshoremen, general cargo	—	43
Longshoremen, clerks	—	36
Laundry mangle hands	—	15
Laundry first-class hand ironers	16	—
Waiters and waitresses	18	21
Salesclerks	18	—
Cashiers	18	—

[a] A very small number of women were reported for these occupations.

[b] These trades had won a 44-hour week; all the other trades listed had a 48-hour week.

SOURCE: California Bureau of Labor Statistics, *Nineteenth Biennial Report, 1919–1920* (Sacramento: California State Printing Office, 1920).

TABLE 4

Selected Employment Groups in San Francisco, 1920

Occupation	Women	Men	Total
Potential residents in palace and midpriced hotels			
Retail dealers and managers	837	10,296	11,133
Owners and officers in manufacturing	177	2,038	2,215
Technical engineers (civil and mech., esp.)	0	2,304	2,304
Bankers, brokers, and moneylenders	50	1,683	1,733
Potential rooming house residents			
Office clerks (nonretail, nonstore)	4,813	12,374	17,187
Sales staff in stores and department stores	4,074	9,606	13,680
Stenographers and typists	8,101	592	8,693
Bookkeepers and cashiers	3,872	3,006	6,878
Machinists	0	6,306	6,306
Carpenters	3	5,793	5,796
Clerks in retail stores	1,403	3,351	4,754
Waiters and waitresses	1,339	3,323	4,662
Schoolteachers	2,492	320	2,812
Food, candy, canneries (semiskilled)	1,085	1,356	2,441
Telephone operators	1,960	92	2,052
Bakeries	53	1,359	1,412
Milliners and millinery dealers	1,147	47	1,194
Printing (skilled and semiskilled)	315	669	984
Potential residents in rooming or lodging houses			
General laborers[a]	684	17,176	17,860
Ship- and boat building (semiskilled)	7	2,815	2,822
Clothing manufacturing	2,001	545	2,546
Longshoremen and stevedores	2	2,404	2,406
Sailors and deckhands (not in U.S. Navy)	2	5,002	5,004

[a] This is the total figure for general laborers listed in all categories.

SOURCE: U.S. Bureau of the Census, *Fourteenth Census of the U.S., Vol. 4, Population 1920* (Washington, D.C.: U.S. Government Printing Office, 1923): 222–238. Figures are for the day of the census; employment may vary substantially in other months of the year.

If the first reference to a work is condensed, the full citation is given in the bibliography. The following abbreviations are used in the notes:

ASPO   American Society of Planning Officials

CIH   California Commission on Immigration and Housing

CSRA   California State Relief Administration

CSS   Community Service Society of New York

CGOPR   California Governor's Office of Planning and Research and the California Department of Housing and Community Development, "Residential Hotels: A Vanishing Housing Resource," a two-day conference, June 1981, in San Francisco

SFHA   San Francisco Housing Association (1910–1912)

SFHACC   San Francisco Housing Authority of the City and County of San Francisco (1930s–present)

SL   St. Louis University Institute of Applied Gerontology

UC-HC   University of California Heller Committee for Research in Social Economics

CHAPTER ONE: CONFLICTING IDEAS ABOUT HOTEL LIFE

1. These figures can be accepted only as rough approximations (and probably undercounts), since the U.S. Census does not compile hotel housing data in a separate category. On underreporting, see Hoch and Slayton, *New Homeless and Old,* 107–123.

2. Dowdee, "Incidence of Change in the Residential Hotel Stock," 28, found 31,000 residential hotel housing units remaining in San Francisco, making up 9.8 percent of the city's total housing units. The city of San Francisco never annexed land outside San Francisco County; hence its urban percentage of hotels as dwelling units is much higher than the reported national 1980 average of 3.2 percent, which (again) is based on poor data. If downtown districts could be compared, hotel percentages might be much closer in various cities. On New York, see Blackburn, "Single Room Occupancy in New York City," 1.1, 3.1–3.12. On smaller California cities, see Deni Greene (director of the California Governor's Office of Planning and Research), I. Donald Turner (director of the California Department of Housing and Community Development), and Jonathan P. Brooks (housing specialist, Redevelopment Agency of Eureka, California), in reports given at the CGOPR conference.

3. Kevin Leary, "San Francisco's Cyril Magnin Dies at 88," *San Francisco Chronicle* (June 9, 1988): A-1, 20–21. Magnin's parents founded the J. Magnin clothing store in 1907. Magnin was its president and driving force from 1936 to 1969; after that, he was the president of an investment firm.

4. Beacon, "Home Is Where the Hotel Is," 16–19.

5. Goldberger, "Seeking the Ideal," 52, 55, 59–60.

6. Beacon, "Home Is Where the Hotel Is"; Carroll, "Home, Home on the Hill," 17.

7. This is a composite character based on interviews by the author and on Erickson and Eckert, "The Elderly Poor in Downtown San Diego Hotels," 441ff. See also Eckert, *Unseen Elderly,* 86–93.

8. Wagner quoted in David Halberstam, "The Brightest Lights on Broadway," *Parade Magazine* (May 18, 1986): 4–5, 6–8. On the YMCA, an interview with Barry Kroll, director of the Embarcadero YMCA, San Francisco, June 2, 1984.

9. This advertisement, unchanged except to delete the name and address (Thor Residential Hotel, 2084 Mission Street) and to substitute "subway" for "BART," was posted at the San Francisco Veterans' Center in fall 1982.

10. Observations by the author while living in the National Hotel in San Francisco during fall 1986. Rents were about $300 a month.

11. Felix Ayson, interviewed in Curtis Choy's documentary film, *The Fall of the I-Hotel* (1983), quoted in Grannan, "International Hotel," 10. Quotation edited for grammar.

12. California Statutes of 1917, chap. 736, sect. 10. The full text, as slightly amended in 1923, continues, "and shall include hotels, lodging and rooming

houses, dormitories, Turkish baths, bachelor hotels, studio hotels, public and private clubs."

13. The legal derivation and history of the word "hotel" is reviewed in an elaborate opinion given in *Cromwell v. Stephens*, 2 Daly 15, 3 Abb. Pr. N.S. 26; see also 19 ALR 517 (1922), 53 ALR 988 (1928), and 28 ALR 3rd 1240 and 1245. On the definition of "hotel" in the federal courts, see *Creedon v. Lunde*, D.C. Wash., 90 F Supp 119. For historical census definitions, see U.S. Bureau of the Census, *Census of Hotels, 1930*. For a historical account with the one-month definition, see Trollope, *North America*, 480–492.

In addition to the number of rooms, some jurisdictions require a hotel to satisfy one or many of the following criteria: a telephone operator, a clerk, a mail or key rack, a lobby, some transient accommodations, and a place for safekeeping of guests' valuables. The WPA-period Real Property Survey in San Francisco considered as hotels only those with a telephone operator, a clerk, a mail rack, or a key rack.

14. In a few rooming houses or lodging houses, tenants have kitchen access to cook meals individually.

15. Historical newspaper articles and duplicate listings under different categories in city directories show that compilers and readers as late as the 1920s had overlapping and rather hazy definitions for commercial lodgings. See Groth, "Forbidden Housing," 34–36, 50–52.

16. The kitchen definition dates at least to 1887. See Lubove, *The Progressives and the Slums*, 18, 26, 169. The full sentence defining a tenement continues, ". . . but having a common right in the halls, stairways, water closets, or privies, or some of them." In 1912, the New York Court of Appeals ruled that an apartment house was not a tenement "if each family had its own toilet, kitchen, and set bathtub."

17. I will leave to anthropologists the battles of defining True Culture. Interpolating from Clifford Geertz, I hold culture to be the mental and physical webs of meaning that people themselves spin—not simply an ideational system but an adaptive and material system. See Clifford Geertz, "Thick Description," in Geertz, *The Interpretation of Cultures: Selected Essays* (New York: Basic Books, 1973): 3–30, and Roger M. Keesing, "Theories of Culture," in B. Siegel et al., *Annual Review of Anthropology* 3 (1974): 73–97.

18. Laffan, "Caravansaries," 176; Hayner, *Hotel Life*, 3; the phrasing of sleeping when tired, etc., is from Siegal, *Outposts of the Forgotten*, 174.

19. Hayner, *Hotel Life*, 104–109, 126, 165.

20. For a classic description of lobby mixtures, see Hayner, *Hotel Life*, 93.

21. Ibid., 147.

22. See Burki, "Housing the Low-Income Urban Elderly," 282; Eckert, *Unseen Elderly*, 84; Werner and Bryson, "Guide to Preservation and Maintenance," pt. 1, 1001–1002. Blackburn, "Single Room Occupancy in New York City," 3.10–3.12, finds a lower preference for SRO life than he expected, al-

though this may simply reflect the grim conditions of SRO life in New York City.

23. For instance, see Phyllis Ehrlich, "A Study of the Invisible Elderly: Characteristics and Needs of the St. Louis Downtown SRO Elderly," in SL, *The Invisible Elderly.*

24. On San Francisco, Dowdee, "Incidence of Change in the Residential Hotel Stock," 38; on New York, Judith Spektor (director of the Mayor's Office of SRO Housing, New York City), at the CGOPR conference, and Susan Baldwin, "Salvaging SRO Housing," *City Limits: The News Magazine of New York City Housing and Neighborhoods* (April 1981): 12–15. Frank, "Overview of Single Room Occupancy Housing," 6–7.

25. Kasinitz, "Gentrification and Homelessness," 9–14; Dan Salerno, Kim Hopper, and Ellen Baxter, *Hardship in the Heartland: Homelessness in Eight U.S. Cities* (New York: Community Service Society of New York, Institute for Social Welfare Research, 1984); James A. Cogwell, *No Place Left Called Home* (New York: Friendship Press, 1983). On options, see Baldwin, "Salvaging SRO Housing," 12; Werner and Bryson, "Guide to Preservation and Maintenance," pt. 1, 1005.

26. For these phrases, I have relied particularly on Ira Ehrlich, in SL, *The Invisible Elderly,* 1–6; see also another early and still useful collection of reports, U.S. Senate Special Committee on Aging, *Single Room Occupancy.*

27. See Deirdre Carmody, "A Report Recounts Problems in a New York Welfare Hotel," *New York Times* (September 30, 1984), which summarizes CSS, "Struggling to Survive in a Welfare Hotel," on the Martinique at Broadway and 32d. This hotel is the corruption-ridden feature of Kozol, *Rachel and Her Children,* which also appeared in serial form in *The New Yorker* in January 1988.

28. On San Diego, Erickson and Eckert, "The Elderly Poor in Downtown San Diego Hotels," 441. The study compared people in hotels priced for middle-income, wage-laborer, and skid-row budgets. On Chicago, Hoch and Spicer, "SROs: An Endangered Species," 11.

29. On New York, Blackburn, "Single Room Occupancy in New York City." The California figures are from Paul Silvern, economic development specialist for the Skid Row Development Corporation, Los Angeles, and Fei Tsen, Chinese Community Housing Corporation of San Francisco, at the CGOPR conference.

30. On single people, Blackburn, "Single Room Occupancy in New York City," 3.1–3.2. On mobility assumptions, Werner and Bryson, "Guide to Preservation and Maintenance," pt. 1. In the full price range of San Diego hotels, Erickson and Eckert, "The Elderly Poor in Downtown San Diego Hotels," reports that the average tenant stayed over three years, matching the average three-year and four-year rates found in residential hotels in other cities.

31. Interview with Ramona Davies, former public health nurse, San Francisco, July 1981.

32. Blackburn, "Single Room Occupancy in New York City," 3.1–3.2. In 1981, speakers from several other U.S. cities gave similar figures at the CGOPR conference. See also Eckert, *The Unseen Elderly,* 2, 26; U.S. Senate, *Single Room Occupancy;* and Ehrlich, "St. Louis Downtown SRO Elderly," 8.

33. Walter Krumwilde in *The American Lutheran Survey* (Columbia, South Carolina), quoted in "Religion and Social Service," *Literary Digest* (October 28, 1916).

34. Eckert, *The Unseen Elderly,* and SL, *The Invisible Elderly.*

35. Ira Ehrlich in SL, *The Invisible Elderly,* 4.

36. Liu, "San Francisco Chinatown Residential Hotels," 2.

37. Cushing Dolbeare, "The Political Obstacles to Decent Housing," Catherine Bauer Lecture, College of Environmental Design, University of California, Berkeley, March 10, 1987.

38. Caroll Kowal in SL, *The Invisible Elderly,* 40.

39. Blackburn, "Single Room Occupancy in New York City," 3–12. Philip Hager, "Singles Make Up Growing Share of Urban Households," *Minneapolis Star and Tribune* (October 30, 1982): 1-S, 5-S; *New York Times* (September 9, 1984).

40. Brad Paul interview, February 26, 1981.

41. Melvin Carriere (vice president, Community Development Division, Wells Fargo Bank, San Francisco) at the CGOPR conference.

42. Dolores Hayden, "What Would a Non-Sexist City Be Like? Speculations on Housing Urban Design and Human Work," *Signs* 5:3 Supplement (1980): S170–S187; quotation on S171–S172.

43. Gunther Barth, *Instant Cities: Urbanization and the Rise of San Francisco and Denver* (New York: Oxford University Press, 1975): 108–127, 182–228; James E. Vance, *Geography and Urban Evolution in the San Francisco Bay Area* (UC, Berkeley: Institute of Governmental Studies, 1964); John R. Borchert, "American Metropolitan Evolution," *Geographical Review* 57 (1967): 301–332; Brian Godfrey, *Neighborhoods in Transition.*

44. On vast numbers, the writer is Samuel Bowles, editor of the Springfield, Mass., *Republican,* quoted in Williamson, *The American Hotel,* 84. On very early San Francisco hotels (1850s–1860s), see Francis J. Mazzi, "City from Frontier: Symbols of Urban Development in Nineteenth-Century San Francisco," (Ph.D. dissertation, Department of History, University of Southern California, 1974): 110–116, 153–174, 189. On boardinghouse keepers, see Wolfe, *Lodging House Problem.*

45. For instance, a pre-World War I surge of hotel building in San Francisco was closely matched in Los Angeles from 1914 to 1915; CIH, *Second Annual Report* (1916): 277. In San Francisco in 1980, the 600-plus residential hotels

in the city had all been built before 1930; most before 1921. The unpublished data were compiled by Scott Dowdee, Department of City and Regional Planning, 1980. After 1900, rapidly growing economies in cities such as Boston, New York, and Chicago challenged San Francisco's nineteenth-century lead in hotel rooms per capita.

46. Groth, "Forbidden Housing," 325–327. Note that these numbers—based on interpolation between directories, insurance maps, plumbing records, and tax files—do not agree with the first national set of hotel statistics, published in U.S. Bureau of the Census, *Census of Hotels, 1930*. See n. 47.

47. As reported in U.S. Bureau of the Census, *Census of Hotels, 1930*, 104, San Francisco's proportions leaned more to the residential side than the national averages. San Francisco had 5 percent mainly transient, over one-third mainly permanent, and 57 percent mixed. This census report was badly skewed, however. It surveyed only members of a national hotel association and included only hotels reporting over 25 rooms. In San Francisco, that meant only 333 hotels when the city directory listed 940 distinct hotel addresses. The sociologist who specialized on hotel life in the 1920s and 1930s, Norman Hayner (*Hotel Life*), concluded that the official census count had largely missed rooming houses and cheap lodging houses as well as many midpriced hotels.

In that same year, a private survey of the total rooms in palace and midpriced hotels in New York found 9 percent of the rooms were only residential, 40 percent only tourist, and 51 percent shifted between residential and tourist use (typescript notes by W. Johnson Quinn, "Hotels in New York and Brooklyn as of February 1st, 1930," New York Historical Society).

48. Palace hotels all advertised nationally for tourists. Only a few midpriced hotels advertised so widely in 1880, but by 1930, 80 percent of them advertised for tourists, still emphasizing homey features and rates for permanent guests. Most reputable rooming house operators avoided transient guests altogether if they could. For cheap lodging houses, Nels Anderson (*The Hobo*, 30) observed that a third to a half of the guests stayed in one hotel for several months or more; most others moved from hotel to hotel but as permanent residents in flux, not as travelers.

49. San Francisco probably had higher proportions in palace and midpriced hotels than these estimates because its warm winters and cool summers brought both winter and summer long-term guests for its expensive hotels. The 1980 figures are based on computerized tax data gathered monthly. The data are still complicated as many rooms shift between tourist and residential use. See Dowdee, "Incidence of Change in the Residential Hotel Stock," viii, 34. Dowdee's report was republished in 1982 by the San Francisco Department of City Planning.

50. Ford, *A Few Remarks*, 222.

51. I am adapting the scheme for class locations set out in Erik Olin Wright, *Classes* (London: Verso, 1985): 64–104, and Michael B. Katz, "Social Class

in North American Urban History," *Journal of Interdisciplinary History* 11 (1981): 579–605. On class as a cultural and economic formation, I obviously rely on E. P. Thompson. I have also used the more recent popular definitions of class in Mary R. Jackman and Robert W. Jackman, *Class Awareness in the United States* (Berkeley, Los Angeles, and London: University of California Press, 1983): 13–41; and for the upper class, G. William Domhoff, *Who Rules America Now?* (New York: Simon and Schuster, 1983): esp. 17–55.

52. David Rocah, "Homelessness and Civil Liberties," *Civil Liberties* (Fall/Winter 1989): 5, 7.

53. For the 1910 and 1930 surveys of San Francisco hotels, lists of existing postfire Chinatown hotels were added to the directory categories, since Chinese hotels were underrepresented in the directory. Mariners' hotels were also likely underrepresented, but these buildings and building records did not survive urban renewal.

CHAPTER TWO: PALACE HOTELS AND SOCIAL OPULENCE

1. Wharton, *The Custom of the Country,* 4–5, 12, 27.

2. Greeley is quoted in Williamson, *The American Hotel,* 116. On travelers' complaints that permanent residents filled the best rooms, see King, "The First-Class Hotel," 177; for an example, see Sala, "The Philosophy of Grand Hotels," 141.

3. On servants in hotels, see Laffan, "Caravansaries," 176; on cost of servants in the West, see John S. Hittell, *The Commerce and Industries of the Pacific Coast* (San Francisco, 1882): 99. The Westward Ho! advertisement is in Lewis, *Work of Art,* 321.

4. Phrases on hotels being built for crowds and notoriously public are from travel accounts written in 1837 and 1875, quoted in McGlone, "Suffer the Children," 420.

5. On the Lick House, see Mazzi, "City from Frontier," 166, 168; most expensive hotels kept the American plan until at least 1900. In 1910, the three best hotels in San Francisco—the Fairmont, St. Francis, and Palace—were all still American plan.

6. On hotels and the American spirit, see Trollope, *North America,* 43, and Sala quoted in Williamson, *The American Hotel,* 116. The local editor was Nat P. Willis in the New York City *Weekly Mirror* (December 7, 1844). On eating alone, see also Trollope, *North America,* 62.

7. Trollope, *North America,* 42, 490–491; see also Williamson, *The American Hotel,* 202–207, and Sala, "American Hotels and American Food," 140.

8. Williamson, *The American Hotel,* 208, 295. For San Francisco, see also Frances de Talavera Berger and John Parke Custis, *Sumptuous Dining in Gaslit San Francisco* (Garden City: Doubleday and Co., 1985).

9. Mark Twain [Samuel Clemens], "'The Lick House Ball' and Other Fash-

ion Reviews," 32–44, in Franklin Walker, ed., *The Washoe Giant in San Francisco* (San Francisco: George Fields, 1938; original essays written in 1863–64): 37.

10. The advertisement is from the 1910 *Hotel Red Book,* for San Francisco's St. Francis Hotel; for a sample of the social room photograph, see the "baronial bridge room" at the midpriced Olympic Hotel featured in the 1935 city directory for San Francisco.

11. The guest is quoted in Boomer, *Hotel Management,* 13. On other privacy, see Hayner, *Hotel Life,* 72.

12. Hayner, *Hotel Life,* 66, 71, 100.

13. Laffan, "Caravansaries," 176.

14. Hayner, "The Hotel," 30, 91, gives these prices for Chicago and notes the minimum at one fine hotel was $25 a week.

15. Compare cases 1, 22, and 23 in table 2, Appendix. See also, "Hotel Life as It Is and Was," 449, and Hayner, *Hotel Life,* 72–73.

16. On Palmer and Leiter, see Lloyd Wendt and Herman Kogan, *Give the Lady What She Wants: The Story of Marshall Field and Company* (Chicago: Rand McNally, 1952): 16–17, 70; on Higginson, see Douglass Shand Tucci, *Built in Boston: City and Suburb, 1800–1950* (Boston: Little, Brown and Co., 1978): 103.

17. Williamson, *The American Hotel,* 210; Van Orman, *A Room for the Night,* 55; Laffan, "Caravansaries," 178; and Mazzi, "City from Frontier," 166, 168.

18. For families at the Palace, see Lewis and Hall, *Bonanza Inn,* 52, 64, 71, 118–123, 140, 216, 247–248; the editor was Fremont Older, editor of the *Bulletin;* see Walton Bean, *Boss Ruef's San Francisco: The Story of the Union Labor Party, Big Business, and the Graft Prosecution* (Berkeley and Los Angeles: University of California Press, 1967): 67. On the St. Francis, see Siefkin, *The City at the End of the Rainbow.*

19. Williamson, *The American Hotel,* 274; the *New York Times* article appeared sometime before October 1, 1907, and the page is reprinted in Dorsey and Devine, *Fare Thee Well,* 139.

20. On the Fairmont and the Mark Hopkins, interview with Gray Brechin, January 12, 1982.

21. The figures on the Lick House come from the 1880 U.S. manuscript census.

22. Mark Twain [Samuel Clemens], "Those Blasted Children" (1864), 18–19, in Franklin Walker, ed., *The Washoe Giant in San Francisco* (San Francisco: George Fields, 1938): 18–23.

23. Sala, *America Revisited,* 344–345.

24. For more on children's facilities, see "The Kindergarten in Hotels," *Hotel Monthly* 3, 22 (January 1895): 12; "When the Apartment Hotel Builds

Playground Parkways in the Air," *Fashions of the Hour,* School Number (1922); J. O. Dahl, "When Does a Play Room Become a Profitable Investment?" *Hotel Management* (November 1925); Hayner, "The Hotel," 92, 100, 145; Hayner, *Hotel Life,* 129–130. The special classes (a French school) were a feature of the Fairmont in San Francisco; see Siefkin, *The City at the End of the Rainbow.* The McAlpin's women's and children's floor had a playroom, an outdoor playground, and a library, in addition to a large lounge and a hairdressing parlor.

25. *The Blue Book* (San Francisco: Theodore J. Hoag, 1929): 550–551.

26. Thompson, *Eloise.*

27. Edmund White, *A Boy's Own Story* (New York: Plume Books of the New American Library, 1982): 70–72, 77–78.

28. Hayner, *Hotel Life,* has an entire chapter on hotel children, 119–131. See also a section in Hayner, "The Hotel," 129–133. The history of hallways as play spaces is reinforced by William Robertson and W. F. Robertson, *Our American Tour . . . 1869* (Edinburgh: Privately printed, 1871): 8–9.

29. On early hotels in Europe, see W. C. Firebaugh, *The Inns of Greece and Rome and a History of Hospitality from the Dawn of Time to the Middle Ages* (Chicago, 1923); Henry P. Maskell and Edward W. Gregory, *Old Country Inns of England* (London, 1912); and Walter Ison, "Pleasure Gardens and Hotels," in Ison, *The Georgian Buildings of Bath from 1700 to 1830* (London: Faber and Faber, 1948): 92–98.

30. King, "First-Class Hotel," 173–175, 178–179; Williamson, *The American Hotel,* 8–9; Boorstin, "Palaces of the Public," 134–147.

31. King, "First-Class Hotel," 177. A later example of such a complaint is in Sala, "The Philosophy of Grand Hotels," 141.

32. Williamson, *The American Hotel,* 13, 16, 23–24, 28; Boorstin, "Palaces of the Public," 136–137; interview with Richard Penner, July 1982. On sharing rooms and beds with strangers, see King, "First-Class Hotel," 186, and Van Orman, *A Room for the Night,* 19, 22, 38.

33. King, "First-Class Hotel," 173–188; Boorstin, "Palaces of the Public," 140.

34. See also Boorstin, "Palaces of the Public," and Williamson, *The American Hotel.* One of the many general histories of palace hotels is Bryan McGinty, *The Palace Inns* (Harrisburg: Stackpole Books, 1978).

35. The principal developer of the Palace Hotel was William C. Ralston, an industrialist, mine owner, and bank president; at his death, the Palace was completed by Senator William Sharon; Lewis and Hall, *Bonanza Inn.* See also the *San Francisco City Directory* (1880): 18; "The Palace Hotel," *Overland Monthly* 15 (September 1875): 299; Mary Goodrich, *The Palace Hotel* (San Francisco, 1930); Williamson, *The American Hotel,* 32, 91.

36. Sala, *America Revisited,* 372.

37. Williamson is careful to note the presence of two-room suites: *The American Hotel,* 17, 53, 56, 92, 115–116; see also King, "First-Class Hotel," 177, 182.

38. Stone, "Hospitality, Hotels, and Lodging Houses," 472–477; Hayner, "The Hotel," 192.

39. Lewis, *Work of Art,* 194–195. TelAutograph is a trademark for a telegraph device that reproduces hand motions at either end of the wire, so one can "write" a personal note to someone anywhere in the world.

40. The life of each palace hotel has spawned several books. For instance, see Eve Brown, *The Plaza: Its Life and Times* (New York: Meredith Press, 1967), and Frank Crowninshield, ed., *The Unofficial Palace of New York: A Tribute to the Waldorf-Astoria* (New York: N.p., 1939).

41. Williamson, *The American Hotel,* 294, and Lewis, *Work of Art,* 331. On the Drake, the *Hotel Red Book,* 1930, 70.

42. For this phase in San Francisco, see Siefkin, *The City at the End of the Rainbow,* 110–111; the Mark Hopkins (at 19 stories) and the Sir Francis Drake (25 stories) are apt tower examples. LeRoy Linnard installed the first hotel radio station in San Francisco in the Fairmont in March 1922.

43. Williamson, *The American Hotel,* 295; interview with Harold Weingarten, March 17, 1986.

44. Hayner, "The Hotel," 28–29, 37; Dorsey and Devine, *Fare Thee Well,* 108–110, 137; Williamson, *The American Hotel,* 273.

45. Carroll, "Home, Home on the Hill," 14, 16–17.

46. Hayner, "The Hotel," 228–229. For correlative sentiments about staff but in a midpriced hotel, see Edith Rosenshine, "The Typical Small Hotel," ca. 1947, MS Collection, Bancroft Library of the University of California, Berkeley.

47. Hayner, "The Hotel," 91.

48. Maria Therese Longworth Yelverton, Viscountess Avonmore, *Teresina in America,* 2 vols. (London: Richard Bentley & Son, 1875): 278.

49. Quoted in Hayner, *Hotel Life,* 114.

50. "Hotel Detective Constantly Battling Smart Criminals," *Hotel World* (March 3, 1923): 35; "Hotel Life as It Is and Was," *Chambers Journal* 21, 7th ser. (June 20, 1931): 441–451, 450; Hayner, *Hotel Life,* 93, 165.

51. "Hotel Life as It Is and Was," 451; Hayner, *Hotel Life,* 167.

52. Williamson, *The American Hotel,* 92.

53. Philo Tower, *Slavery Unmasked* (Rochester, N.Y., 1856): 319, 321, 335–342; also quoted in Calhoun, *A Social History of the American Family,* 2:205.

54. Hayner, "The Hotel," 7, quoting an engineer for the Illinois Bell Telephone Company.

55. For examples of seasonal moves, see Hayner, *Hotel Life,* 65; Tucci, *Built in Boston,* 103; Siefkin, *The City at the End of the Rainbow,* 62.

56. On the Del Monte, see Limerick, Ferguson, and Oliver, *America's Grand Resort Hotels,* 49, 100–107. On resort hotel architecture, see also Evers, Cromley, Blackmar, and Harris, *Resorts of the Catskills.* During any single decade, the truly elite frequented a relatively small number of resort hotels. Other classic examples of the upper-class resort around the turn of the century would include the Broadmoor in Colorado Springs, the Grove Park Inn in Asheville, North Carolina, and the Greenbrier at White Sulphur Springs, West Virginia.

57. Henry James is quoted in Limerick, Ferguson, and Oliver, *America's Grand Resort Hotels,* 97, where the daily round is also listed. On activities, see also Betsy Blackmar, "Going to the Mountains: A Social History," in Evers, Cromley, Blackmar, and Harris, *Resorts of the Catskills,* 71–98.

58. Blackmar, "Going to the Mountains," 79.

59. Ibid., 72, 82–83; Limerick, Ferguson, and Oliver, *Grand Resort Hotels,* 51.

60. Sexton, *American Apartment Houses,* 8.

61. Three early leaders in Boston were all labeled as hotels: the Hotel Pelham; its neighbor, the Hotel Boylston; and the Hotel Hamilton, dating from 1857, 1870, and 1869, respectively. After 1900, apartments would reverse the direction of innovation and come to influence hotel design. On early experimental apartment houses and social hierarchy, see Gunther Barth, *City People: The Rise of Modern City Culture in Nineteenth-Century America* (New York: Oxford University Press, 1980): 46–50; James E. Vance, Jr., *This Scene of Man* (New York: Harper and Row, 1977): 391–406; and John Hancock, "The Apartment House in Urban America," in Anthony D. King, ed., *Buildings and Society* (London: Routledge and Kegan Paul, 1980): 151–189. On fashionable apartments, see James M. Goode, *Best Addresses: A Century of Washington's Distinguished Apartment Houses* (Washington, D.C.: Smithsonian Institution Press, 1988); Cromley, *Alone Together;* Stern, "With Rhetoric: The New York Apartment House," 78–111. On the blurring of apartment and hotel, see also Williamson, *The American Hotel,* 270–271; Sexton, *American Apartment Houses.*

62. The radiator line comes from a sprightly and largely accurate summary of apartment evolution in Beard, "New York Squeezes into the 'Domestic Unit,'" 4; Alpern, *Apartments for the Affluent;* Sexton, *American Apartment Houses;* Westfall, "The Golden Age of Chicago Apartments."

63. For example, see "Apartment House for Jones and Ellis Streets," *San Francisco Chronicle* (July 12, 1907), which mixes many of these terms. From 1903 to 1915, the San Francisco directory had only a single heading: "Apartments—Hotels."

64. Environmental determinism is not invoked here but rather a structurationist explanation for the connections between the social and the physical, the individual and the social. See Allan Pred, *Making Histories and Constructing*

Human Geographies (Boulder: Westview Press, 1990); and Anthony Giddens, "Structuralism, Post-Structuralism and the Production of Culture," with Ira J. Cohen, "Structuration Theory and Social *Praxis*," in Anthony Giddens and Jonathan Turner, eds., *Social Theory Today* (Stanford: Stanford University Press, 1987): 195–223, 273–308.

65. On the palace hotel's role in innovation diffusion, see especially Boorstin, "Palaces of the Public," and Grier, "Hotels as Model Interiors."

66. See Dell Upton, "Another City: The Changing Urban Landscape in Early Republican America," in Catherine Hutchins, ed., *Everyday Life in the Early Republic, 1789–1828* (New York: W. W. Norton for Winterthur Publications, 1991).

67. Henry James, *The American Scene* (Bloomington: Indiana University Press, 1968; first published in 1907): 102.

CHAPTER THREE: MIDPRICED MANSIONS FOR MIDDLE INCOMES

1. Groth, "Forbidden Housing," Table IV-20, 331.

2. See esp. Martin, "Boarding and Lodging," 148–180, and Williamson, *The American Hotel*, 17, 115. On Chicago in 1844, see Boorstin, "Palaces of the Public"; the boardinghouse figure in Chicago included people of lower incomes.

3. Walt Whitman, "Wicked Architecture," *Life Illustrated* (July 19, 1856), reprinted in Emory Holloway and Ralph Adimari, comps., *New York Dissected: A Sheaf of Recently Discovered Newspaper Articles by the Author of Leaves of Grass* (New York: Rufus Rockwell Wilson, 1936): 92–98, 96, emphasis in the original. Whitman could include boarders and hotel guests together in his estimate partly because purpose-built boardinghouses and small hotels of the time so closely resembled each other. See also Barth, *City People*, 41–54.

4. On comparisons with England, see Calhoun, *A Social History of the Family*, 3: 180, drawing on nineteenth-century travelers' accounts. On the prevalence of living in hotels from the 1840s to the 1860s, see McGlone, "Suffer the Children," 414–426. On temptation, see Flagg, "The Planning of Apartment Houses and Tenements," 89. See also J. Lebovitz, "The Home and the Machine," *Journal of Home Economics* 3, 2 (April 1911): 141–148. On almost any family, see Calhoun, *A Social History of the Family*, 3: 239.

5. The residence was the Tubbs Hotel. Beth Bagwell, *Oakland: The Story of the City* (Novato, Calif.: Presidio Press, 1982): 118–123.

6. For examples of this flux, particularly in reference to hotel residents, see Hamilton, *Promoting New Hotels*.

7. Hayner, *Hotel Life*, 78, 105.

8. In San Francisco, according to the U.S. decennial census, the number of

architects doubled between 1900 and 1910 owing to the reconstruction after the great fire of 1906. The number doubled again in the 1940s owing to the impacts of World War II. Comments on western architects following fires rely on research in progress by the architectural historian, Ronald L. M. Ramsay, Fargo, North Dakota. On Louis Sullivan, see Robert Twombly, *Louis Sullivan: His Life and Work* (New York: Viking, 1980).

9. Interview with James E. Vance, Berkeley, California, November 2, 1982, discussing his neighbors and family in the greater Boston area before World War II.

10. The observer is Trollope, *North America,* 484; on ease for renters versus lease and mortgage holders, see Abbott, *The Tenements of Chicago, 1908–1935,* 327.

11. The girl is quoted in Hayner, *Hotel Life,* 113; see also Williamson, *The American Hotel,* 12, 98.

12. Harding's letter is quoted in Hayner, "The Hotel," 248. On Long, "Hotel that Inspired Novel Celebrates 95th Year," *Topeka Capital-Journal* (March 20, 1988): 8-C.

13. "New First Lady is 'Human,' Has Sense of Humor," *Chicago Tribune* (August 4, 1923); Williamson, *The American Hotel,* 288.

14. On Frankfurter, Judith Spektor interview, June 11, 1981; on Earl Warren, see Beacon, "Home Is Where the Hotel Is," 16.

15. On Johnson, see Hank Burchard, "Presidents in Residence: Round Town Digs of Our Chief Executives," *Washington Post* Weekend Section (March 7, 1986): 4–7; for the others see Beacon, "Home Is Where the Hotel Is," 18.

16. Sala, *America Revisited,* 345. Van Orman, *A Room for the Night,* 127, claims hotel life was as respectable as private house life, which McGlone and other historians dispute.

17. On age of marriage in 1890, Andrew Truxal, *Marriage and the Family in American Culture* (New York: Prentice Hall, 1953): 183; Howard Chudacoff, "Newlyweds and Family Extension: The First Stage of the Family Cycle in Providence, Rhode Island, 1864–1865 and 1879–1880," in Tamara Hareven and Maris Vinovskis, eds., *Family and Population in Nineteenth-Century America* (Princeton: Princeton University Press, 1978): 185. On hotel wives, McGlone, "Suffer the Children," 415–426, 456.

18. On 1855, see Edward H. Dixon, *Scenes in the Practice of a New York Surgeon* (New York: De Witt & Davenport, 1855): 209, quoted in McGlone, "Suffer the Children," 417. On furnishings equal to half the building cost, "Our Family Hotels." On 1928 costs, see UC-HC, *Cost of Living Studies. 1. Quantity and Cost Estimate of the Standard of Living of the Professional Class;* the data were collected in 1925–26.

19. Hayner, "The Hotel," 87, 123; Williamson, *The American Hotel,* 28. In San Francisco in 1929 and 1930, city directory advertisements for the Hotel

Harcourt listed prices of $6 to $10 a week. Weekly rates as low as 4.7 times the daily rate were reported for palace and midpriced hotels and 2.5 at rooming houses or cheap lodging houses. The key variables were number of staff and range of services. Groth, "Forbidden Housing," 464–466, 493 n. 104, gives several historical examples of weekly rates versus daily rates.

20. The social worker is quoted in Barth, *City People*, 42; on the school-teachers, see Hayner, "The Hotel," 123.

21. *Harper's Weekly*, "Decline and Fall of Hotel Life" (1857): 274.

22. Gilman, "A Possible Solution of the Domestic Service Problem"; on an Adamless Eden, see Herrick, "Cooperative Housekeeping." On a hundred fires, "Cooperative Housekeeping at Last," *Good Housekeeping* 32 (1901): 490–492; see also Hayden, *The Grand Domestic Revolution*.

23. On mental rovers, see Hayner, "The Hotel," 81, 84–87, 234; and Hayner, *Hotel Life*, 7. On Seattle, see Hayner, *Hotel Life*, 3, 35, 67, 86–89, 99–100, 103. The journalist is Williamson, *The American Hotel*, 127.

24. Louis Wirth, *The Ghetto* (Chicago: University of Chicago Press, 1928): 257–258; the Chicago Beach Hotel percentage is from Hayner, "The Hotel," 234. See also Hayner, *Hotel Life*, 33, 125, 147–148.

25. On O'Neill, see Arthur Gelb and Barbara Gelb, *O'Neill* (New York: Harper and Row, 1974); O'Neill and his wife, Carlotta, did live at San Francisco's Fairmont Hotel for a year in 1944. On guests at San Francisco's Palace Hotel, see Lewis and Hall, *Bonanza Inn*, 267–318. On New York, Harold Weingarten interview, March 17, 1986.

26. Williamson, *The American Hotel*, 4, 275; Hayner, *Hotel Life*, 97–98; Zorbaugh, *Gold Coast and Slum*, 37, 70; Lewis, *Work of Art*, 132–134; the-atrical hotels are given a special symbol in American Travel and Hotel Directory Company, *American Travel Book and Hotel Directory* [The Blue Book, a short-lived competitor to the Red Book], 9th ed. (Baltimore: ATHD Co., 1923).

27. Williamson, *The American Hotel*, 269, 273, 292; see F. Marion Crawford's *Dr. Claudius* on the Brevoort Hotel, which was still standing in 1930.

28. On Willa Cather, see E. K. Brown, *Willa Cather: A Critical Biography* (New York: Avon Books, 1953): 228. Like Cather herself, her character of Thea in *Song of the Lark* lived in a seedy hotel in Union Square when she first moved to New York. On Arendt and Mann, interview with Reeda Yacker, publicity consultant for the Windermere Hotel, May 29, 1987, who based her information on research by Rena Appel. Mann reputedly wrote *Budden-brooks* while at the Windermere; his daughter and her husband lived a few blocks up the street; on Ferber, see Hayner, "The Hotel," 120; on Chaplin and Winchell, "Landmark L.A. Hotel Closes," *San Francisco Examiner* (January 4, 1989): A-7.

29. Promotional brochure for Eighteen Gramercy Park South, an 18-story hotel (Corsa Collection, New York Historical Society).

30. Accounts (see Williamson, *The American Hotel*, 115, 283) mention el-

derly bachelors, spinsters, widows, and widowers as "hotel hermits" but without reporting their relative numbers. Hayner's *Hotel Life* (87) reports that people in Seattle hotel districts were, on the average, consistently older than apartment dwellers, but by no means were the elderly in the majority: 52 percent of the people in Seattle's hotel districts were between 25 and 44 years of age.

31. Sinclair Lewis, *Babbitt* (New York: New American Library, 1961; originally published in 1922): 188.

32. Hayner, *Hotel Life*, 70–71.

33. Ford, *A Few Remarks*, 309. See also Hayner, *Hotel Life*, 62, 71.

34. "Kate Smith, All-American Singer, Dies at 79," *New York Times* (June 18, 1986): A-1, B-10.

35. For security precautions routinely taken in large hotels, see Boomer, *Hotel Management*, 280–283; for interviews, see Hayner, *Hotel Life*, 72.

36. Condit, "Hotels and Apartments," 101–102, 108–109, 150–153, 219. On family hotels, "Our Family Hotels," 12. Hayner mentions the rows, many of which are still standing, in Hayner, "The Hotel," 71.

37. Hayner, "The Hotel," 92, 224–225.

38. Perelman, "Nathanael West," 161; note that Perelman is describing a 16-story residence club; see section on residence clubs, below.

39. Ibid., 161–162. Benslyn, "Recent Developments in Apartment Housing in America," pt. 2, 543–547.

40. The 12-room example is the Lamont, in San Francisco, built in 1911; its managers listed it as a rooming house in the 1930 city directory.

41. Hayner, "The Hotel," 228–229.

42. On service levels, Stone, "Hospitality, Hotels, and Lodging Houses," 475, and "Our Family Hotels," 12; on discriminating chambermaids, Hayner, "The Hotel," 192. In 1892, a leading 220-room family hotel in San Francisco had a staff of only 75 people.

43. Williamson, *The American Hotel*, 56–57, 61–62. The first midprice claim for every room with a bath was the original Hotel Statler in Buffalo.

44. Groth, "Forbidden Housing," 247–250.

45. Hamilton, *Promoting New Hotels*, 48.

46. Williamson, *The American Hotel*, 69, claims that America's first push-buttons were hotel annunciators.

47. Hayner, *Hotel Life*, 3–4, 71.

48. Sexton, *American Apartment Houses*, 5.

49. *Architectural Forum: Apartment Hotel Reference Number,* November 1924, 265.

50. Hayner, "The Hotel," 225–226; Hayner, *Hotel Life*, 106–107.

51. Hayner, "The Hotel," 74.

52. Compare cases 19 and 24 with 1 and 3 in table 2, Appendix. On Chicago family, see Hayner, *Hotel Life*, 72–73.

53. The 1930 ads quoted here are for the Cecil Hotel, at 545 Post, and the

Hotel Regent, at 562 Sutter. These ideal midpriced streets included the palace-ranked Canterbury.

54. On the PPIE, see Burton Benedict, *The Anthropology of World's Fairs: San Francisco's Panama Pacific International Exposition of 1915* (Berkeley: Lowie Museum of Anthropology, 1983). For accounts of the hotel connections for New York City's Crystal Palace exhibition (1850–1855), Chicago's Columbian Exposition (1893), and earlier conventions in San Francisco, see Williamson, *The American Hotel*, 45, 103, 124, and John P. Young, *San Francisco: A History of the Pacific Coast Metropolis* (San Francisco: S. J. Clarke, 1912), 2: 728–729.

55. Williamson, *The American Hotel*, 28.

56. Hayner, "The Hotel," 234.

57. See Groth, "Forbidden Housing," 244–250.

58. Ibid., 246–247; see also Zorbaugh, *Gold Coast and Slum*, 15, 40, 46, 57; on equivalent issues in 1850, see McGlone, "Suffer the Children," 41; for a late example of a successfully converted house, which with an addition had 54 rooms that accommodated 90 to 95 permanent guests (some of whom had been there 13 years in 1923), see Hayner, *Hotel Life*, 115, 147, 178. On the Berkshire, "Our Family Hotels," gives 1883 as its approximate construction date.

59. C. W. Dickey, "The New Claremont Hotel," *The Architect and Engineer of California* 5, 2 (June 1906): 30–32. Dickey was the architect of the hotel.

60. Ford, *Slums and Housing*, 341.

61. Benslyn, "Recent Developments," pt. 2, 543–547; Ford, *Slums and Housing*, 764.

62. Perelman, "Nathanael West," 161.

63. "The Breaching of the Barbizon: A Bastion of Virtue and Beauty Goes Coed," *Time* (February 23, 1981): 122; the literary hotel is Perelman's Sutton Hotel.

64. In 1907, for instance, Mrs. Laura Gashweiler built the Gashweiler Apartment House, four stories tall with 19 two-room units, stores on the first floor, an elevator, and steam heat. Mrs. Gashweiler and her daughter lived in the building and advertised it as a fine "family hotel." Next door, other developers built the 72-room Hotel Artmar (1911) and the Windeler Apartments (1915) with 62 efficiency units. These examples stand on the 400 block of Ellis, near Jones. See "Apartment House for Jones and Ellis Streets," *San Francisco Chronicle* (July 12, 1907), the city directory of 1911, and the building files of the Foundation for San Francisco's Architectural Heritage.

65. Chicago advertisement quoted in Hayner, "The Hotel," 22.

66. Warren, "What the Typical Apartment Hotel 'Looks Like,'" 406–409; *Architectural Forum*, Apartment Hotel Reference Number, 206, 221; Benslyn, "Recent Developments," pt. 2, 540; Hayner, *Hotel Life*, 66. See also, "To Cook or Not to Cook," *Housing Betterment*.

67. Warren, "What the Typical Apartment Hotel 'Looks Like,'" 407, 409; Benslyn, "Recent Developments," pt. 2, 540, 542–543; Hayden, *The Grand Domestic Revolution,* 317.

68. On early examples, Tucci, "Built in Boston," 101; Hayden, *The Grand Domestic Revolution,* 72–74; Carl W. Condit, *The Chicago School of Architecture,* 152. On design standards and guides, Alpern, *Apartments for the Affluent,* 18; Sexton, *American Apartment Houses,* 7; *Architectural Forum,* Apartment Hotel Reference Number 41, 5 (November 1924): 208; for less expensive types, Cash, *Modern Type of Apartment Hotels Throughout the United States;* the original survey cards for the SFHACC Real Property Survey (Bancroft Library) also show the full range of apartment hotel types.

69. One source states that the revolving bed did not make its way to the East Coast until 1914; Beard, "Domestic Unit," 4. On early folding bed competitors and their use in hotels, see "The Holmes Wall Bed," *Pacific Coast Architect* (Portland, Oregon) 3, 4 (July 1912): 454; "The Murphy Bed," *Pacific Coast Architect* 3, 2 (July 1912): 455–456. See also, advertisement in *Pacific Coast Architect* 4 (November 1912): 90. Anne Bloomfield shared these sources with me before her own research was published.

70. SFHA, *First Report* (1911): 48; Taylor, "Efficiency Planning and Equipment," 253–258.

71. Rose, "Interest in the Living Arrangements of the Urban Unattached," 491.

72. The listed figures are an excerpt from "Domicile Status of Families Classified by Occupation of Husband (Unbroken Families in One- and Multiple-Family Households)," Table XIII, Monroe, *Chicago Families,* 66.

73. Monroe, *Chicago Families,* 64, 70–74, 226.

74. Ibid., 78–79.

75. Nathaniel Hawthorne, *The Blithedale Romance* (Boston: Ticknor, Reed and Fields, 1852): 525–528.

CHAPTER FOUR: ROOMING HOUSES AND THE MARGINS OF RESPECTABILITY

1. Richardson, *The Long Day,* 3–5. Richardson used a pen name; her identity is not known. Sarah Eisenstein and others have criticized Richardson's book as mere "middle-class voyeurism," but Richardson displays working-class architectural and social discernment, even if she did not retain a full working-class consciousness.

2. Van Antwerp, "Study of Boarding Homes for Employed Women and Girls."

3. Woods, "The Myriad Tenantry of Furnished Rooms," 955–956. Cohen, "Los Angeles Rooming-House Kaleidoscope," 319.

4. Modell and Hareven, "Urbanization and the Malleable Household," 470–472, 475. See also Peel, "On the Margins," 813–834.

5. A classic source on old-fashioned boardinghouses is Butler, "The Physiology of New York Boarding Houses."

6. Ford, *Slums and Housing,* 341; Wolfe, *Lodging House Problem,* 1–2. Wolfe reports that in 1900, 95 percent of Boston's rooming house operators were women.

7. On San Francisco and Boston, see Groth, "Forbidden Housing," 34–36; on Chicago, see Meyerowitz, "Holding Their Own," 106.

8. Wolfe, *Lodging House Problem,* 6, 38, 42–44.

9. SFHA, *Second Report* (1913): 26; Wolfe, *Lodging House Problem,* 42–59; Zorbaugh, *Gold Coast and Slum,* 69–71. On stoves, see Richardson, *The Long Day,* 5, 27–28, and "The Irvington, S. Hancock's Handsome New Building," *San Francisco Chronicle* (Sunday, March 30, 1890).

10. Wolfe, *Lodging House Problem,* 84, 93; Zorbaugh, *Gold Coast and Slum,* 78; Hoch and Slayton, *New Homeless and Old,* 15–19.

11. Richardson, *The Long Day,* 28–29. Technically, Richardson was in a light housekeeping room, hence the tiny cooking stove and kitchen-style table.

12. Meyerowitz, "Holding Their Own," 43; Hoch and Slayton, *New Homeless and Old,* 17; Richardson, *The Long Day,* 171; Wolfe, *Lodging House Problem,* 36–37; Bessie Van Vorst and Marie Van Vorst, *The Woman Who Toils: Being the Experiences of Two Ladies as Factory Girls* (New York: Doubleday, Page & Co., 1903): 177. On public baths, see Glassberg, "The Design of Reform." On cracked bowls and pitchers, "Remember the Old Hotel of a Decade Ago? Some Place, No?" *San Francisco Chronicle* (January 15, 1919).

13. Fretz, "The Furnished Room Problem in Philadelphia," 2 (n. 1), 57–58; Wolfe, *Lodging House Problem,* 1–2. City directories suggest that "lodging house" was the local term in San Francisco.

14. CSS, "Life in One Room," 1–5; Mostoller, "A Single Room," 191–216. Both articles focus only on New York City.

15. Olmstead and Olmstead et al., *The Yerba Buena Center,* 193–195. The Central Pacific was listed in the city directory under boarding, lodging, and hotel categories.

16. O. Henry [William Sydney Porter], "Between Rounds," in *The Four Million and Other Stories* (New York: Airmont, 1963; first published in 1906): 35. Hoch and Slayton, *New Homeless and Old,* 20.

17. On plumbing, see Hoch and Slayton, *New Homeless and Old,* 48–49.

18. For a literary example, see the comments of Lily Barth in Wharton, *The House of Mirth,* 267, 287–288.

19. Groth, "'Marketplace' Vernacular Design," 179–191. In most cities, the construction of new downtown rooming houses probably continued through the 1920s, so that the years 1880 to 1930 could bracket the building of most examples. However, in the San Francisco sample, no examples were built after 1921, probably as a result of overbuilding larger hotel structures for the 1915 Pan American exposition.

20. The construction date for the Delta is listed as 1906, but in San Francisco records, early dates are unreliable. The Delta, at 41 Sixth Street between Market and Mission streets, had a directory listing in 1910; in 1990, it was still operating as the Whitaker Hotel.

21. John Leighly refers to living in an "upstairs hostelry" in Champaign, Illinois, in 1913; Leighly, "Memory as Mirror," in Anne Buttimer, ed., *The Practice of Geography* (New York: Longman, 1983): 80–89. On bare, creaky, and depressing stairs, see Richardson, *The Long Day,* 45; Dreiser, *Sister Carrie,* 525; Van Vorst and Van Vorst, *The Woman Who Toils,* 195.

22. Will Kortum letter of March 4, 1906, quoted in Olmstead and Olmstead et al., *The Yerba Buena Center,* 232.

23. The Delta has only one bath for every nine rooms, low for the rooming house rank. See Groth, "'Marketplace' Vernacular Design."

24. Girls Housing Council, "Where Is Home?" 22; "Rooming House Problems," *Housing Betterment* 10, 3 (1921): 269.

25. Lewis, *Work of Art,* 6–7. The hotel in the novel is clearly based on the Palmer House in Sauk Centre, Minnesota, built in 1901. Lewis worked there in 1902.

26. Most comments based on the author's observations while living in the National Hotel, San Francisco, in 1986. On not conducting personal affairs behind closed doors, see Chandler, "The Social Organization of Workers in a Rooming House Area," 116.

27. See Mary S. Sims, *The Natural History of a Social Institution: The Young Women's Christian Association* (New York: Woman's Press, 1936); and Sherwood Eddy, *A Century with Youth: A History of the YMCA from 1844–1944* (New York: Association Press, 1944).

28. On independence sought by women, see Meyerowitz, "Holding Their Own," 77, 84–90, 120. In the 1920s in New York, the cheapest women's residence clubs charged $3 to $8 a week, without board; other institutional residence clubs typically charged from $7 to $12 for combined board and room. In contrast, the YWCAs charged 50 cents a day for meals with a dormitory bed or cubicle, up to $1.50 a day for rooms (with meals); Ford, *Slums and Housing,* 755. Girls Housing Council, "Where Is Home?" 14, 18–20, reports similar prices in San Francisco. See also Davidson, "Organized Boarding Homes for Self-Supporting Women in Chicago."

29. U.S. Bureau of Labor, "Boarding Homes, Aids for Working Women," 31–57; Fergusson, "Boarding Homes and Clubs for Working Women," 141–195; Rose, "Interest in the Living Arrangements of the Urban Unattached," 488–489; Girls Housing Council, "Where Is Home?" 14; Meyerowitz, "Holding Their Own," 78–82, 121–122.

30. Clifford Drury, *San Francisco's YMCA: 100 Years by the Golden Gate, 1853–1953* (Glendale, Calif.: Arthur Clark Co., 1963): 233; on integration of blacks, J. Howell Atwood, *The Racial Factor in YMCAs* (New York: Associa-

tion Press, 1946): 48–51, and National Council of YMCAs, *Negro Youth in City YMCAs* (New York: Association Press, 1944): 5–9, 59.

31. Fayès, "The Housing of Single Women," 101; Meyerowitz, "Holding Their Own," 68–76, 122–125. Early large temperance hotels in San Francisco included the Branch House, which accommodated up to 500 people in 160 rooms; "Lodging Houses of San Francisco," *San Francisco Chronicle* (November 6, 1870). In the 1920s, San Francisco had six private organizational rooming houses with 644 beds total.

32. Rose, "Interest in the Living Arrangements of the Urban Unattached," 489; Ford, *Slums and Housing*, 755–759; "Hotels for Women: The Grace Dodge Hotel," *Housing Betterment* 11, 2 (1922): 198–201.

33. In the 1920s, ethnic homes for the elderly charged a monthly fee of about $40 or a lifetime entrance fee of about $2,000; UC-HC, *Dependent Aged*, 26–29, 83–86. Hospitals, institutional residences for the handicapped, tuberculosis sanatoriums, prisons, and army bases add other urban dwellings that the census counts as "institutional group quarters"; few of these met rooming house standards and typically substituted for lodging house quarters.

34. Wolfe, *Lodging House Problem*, 1, 5–6; Wolfe reported that roomers made up 14 percent of the population of Boston's inner wards. See also Peel, "On the Margins," 817; and Zorbaugh, "The Dweller in Furnished Rooms," 84–85.

35. Boston in 1906 had a 1:1 ratio of men to women; Wolfe, *Lodging House Problem*, 82. Data from Chicago in 1929 reported 52 percent men, 10 percent single women, and 38 percent couples; Zorbaugh, *Gold Coast and Slum*, 71. Philadelphia in 1912 had similar ratios; Fretz, "The Furnished Room Problem in Philadelphia," 50. A Los Angeles study in 1949 reported about one-third of the 600 interviewees were women; Cohen, "Los Angeles Rooming-House Kaleidoscope."

36. Wolfe, *Lodging House Problem*, 94. Wives with no outside employment made up 16.5 percent of the sample of 200 women. Stenographers and waitresses made up 8 percent each; dressmakers, 7.5; saleswomen and nurses, 6.0 each; and clerks, 5.0.

37. Employment figures from U.S. Census, *Fourteenth Census of the U.S., Vol. 4, Population 1920*, 222–238; wages from California State Bureau of Labor Statistics, *20th Biennial Report, 1919–1920* (Sacramento: State Printing Office, 1920): 228; on vying with Chinese, see Tygiel, "Workingmen in San Francisco," 23; on few living in commercial housing, Girls Housing Council, "Where Is Home?" 5–6, 37. In the Housing Council's sample, a third of the single women lived away from their families, but only one out of twelve girls lived in a commercial rooming house or hotel. The rest were boarders or lodgers.

38. The San Francisco figures are from the population and occupation volumes of the U.S. Census, 1900–1930. On working-class women in the city, see

particularly Meyerowitz, "Holding Their Own," 21–35; and Cohen, "Los Angeles Rooming-House Kaleidoscope," 317–320. On new white-collar work, see Margery W. Davies, *A Woman's Place Is at the Typewriter: Office Work and Office Workers, 1870–1930* (Philadelphia: Temple University Press, 1982); Elyce Rotella, *From Home to Office: U.S. Women at Work, 1870–1930* (Ann Arbor: UMI Press, 1981); U.S. Department of Labor, Women's Bureau, *Women's Occupations through Seven Decades,* Bulletin no. 218 (Washington, D.C.: Government Printing Office, 1947).

39. On new jobs, U.S. Bureau of the Census, *Census of Manufactures, 1914,* 95, and table 18.

40. Wolfe, *Lodging House Problem,* 92. Clerks made up 13.2 percent of a sample of 7,600 men. Other occupations with 2 or more percent: salesmen, 8.0; merchants and dealers, 5.4; waiters, 4.8; foremen and managers, 2.7; engineers, 2.3; real estate and insurance, 2.1; cooks and stewards, 2.0.

41. Wolfe, *Lodging House Problem,* 1, 5–6, 86–97. Wolfe's account matches closely with that in Fretz, "The Furnished Room Problem in Philadelphia," 67–68. A less statistical and more negative account of male residents is in Zorbaugh, *Gold Coast and Slum,* 69–86. On carpenters, see Tygiel, "Workingmen in San Francisco," 182, and Averbach, "San Francisco's South of Market District." Woodrow Wilson's rooming houses were at 146 North Charles Street and 8 McCulloh Street; Burchard, "Presidents in Residence."

42. On mobility, see Hoch and Slayton, *New Homeless and Old,* 19–20, 23; Wolfe, *Lodging House Problem,* 5, 9, 82–83; Girls Housing Council, "Where Is Home?" 6. On the San Francisco skilled labor experience, see Tygiel, "Workingmen in San Francisco," and Olmstead and Olmstead et al., *The Yerba Buena Center,* 193, 247. The two women are quoted in Hoch and Slayton, *New Homeless and Old,* 20.

43. On age and sex profiles, Zorbaugh, *Gold Coast and Slum,* 8, 71–75, which compares closely with Wolfe's Boston study. A New York study in 1940 and another in Los Angeles in 1949 showed similar proportions: CSS, "Life in One Room," 37–51, and Cohen, "Los Angeles Rooming-House Kaleidoscope," 319–326. On the elderly, UC-HC, *Dependent Aged,* xii, 1, 14.

44. Hayner, *Hotel Life,* 86; Wolfe, *Lodging House Problem,* 66.

45. On ethnic and religious distinctions, see Peel, "On the Margins," 816; Harney, "Boarding and Belonging," 8–37. On blacks, see Hoch and Slayton, *New Homeless and Old,* 24–25; Hayner, *Hotel Life,* 86; and R. D. McKenzie, *The Metropolitan Community* (New York: McGraw-Hill, 1933): 243–247.

46. On roommates and the sexual service sector, Meyerowitz, "Holding Their Own," 146, 47–57. Tygiel, "Workingmen in San Francisco," 204, found 7 percent of the married workers in his sample were in boarding or hotel situations of some sort. The derogatory "charity girl" term and the 38 percent figure are from Zorbaugh, *Gold Coast,* 86ff. On post–World War II, see Chandler, "Social Organization," 12–14, 100–138. On blacks, see Hoch and

Slayton, *New Homeless and Old,* 29; on a different interpretation of Chandler, see Hoch and Slayton, 156.

47. Although Wolfe makes no mention of homosexuality, he does mention several same-sex pairs moving together; Wolfe, *Lodging House Problem,* 84, 93. See Meyerowitz, "Holding Their Own," 10–11; and Meyerowitz, "Sexuality in the Furnished Room Districts: Working Class Women, 1890–1930," paper presented at the Organization of American Historians meeting (April 1986); Hoch and Slayton, *New Homeless and Old,* 22–23; Box-Car Bertha as told to Reitman, *Sister of the Road.*

48. Ford, *A Few Remarks,* 308.

49. Ford, *Slums and Housing,* 343, 759–760.

50. Kortum in Olmstead and Olmstead et al., *The Yerba Buena Center,* 226–227; Wolfe, *Lodging House Problem,* 1–2, 61, 99–103, and Chart VI; Girls Housing Council, "Where Is Home?" 14, 18–20, 24. See also Ford, *Slums and Housing,* 755; Hayner, "The Hotel," 88, 123, 116–117.

51. On the elderly, UC-HC, *Dependent Aged,* 94, on data collected in 1925; on downtown rooming houses, Girls Housing Council, "Where Is Home?" 24; Hayner, "The Hotel," 88.

52. These figures are from the California Bureau of Labor Statistics. For parallel income and household expenditure figures for women in Chicago, see Meyerowitz, "Holding Their Own," 47–51, 221.

53. On the half-mile figure for San Francisco, see Shumsky, "Tar Flat and Nob Hill," 138. On journey to work issues for women, see Meyerowitz, "Holding Their Own," 111–113. For descriptions of pedestrian job searches, see Richardson, *The Long Day,* and Van Vorst and Van Vorst, *The Woman Who Toils.*

54. The Western Addition is centrally located in the city but so named because it was the first plat added at the western edge of the original street grid.

55. San Francisco City Planning Commission, *The Master Plan of San Francisco,* 14–19.

56. *Vertigo,* Alfred Hitchcock, producer (Paramount, 1958).

57. Scott, "Western Addition District," 5–6, 11–12; and E. J. Schallert, *San Francisco Report: A Compendium of Information on Population, Housing, Races, Land Use, and Zoning* (San Francisco: J. B. Little & Co., 1965). Scott does not use the term "Jewish," although both old and new synagogues were prominent features of the area at the turn of the century. On early blacks, see Douglas H. Daniels, *Pioneer Urbanites: A Social and Cultural History of Black San Francisco* (Philadelphia: Temple University Press, 1980); on Japanese, see Godfrey, *Neighborhoods in Transition,* 70–71.

58. On block-by-block mixture, SFHACC, manuscript survey cards and summary schedules for Census Tract J-1 to J-14, in the 1939 Real Property Survey archive, Manuscripts Division, Bancroft Library, University of California, Berkeley. Population figures from U.S. Census.

59. The 1970 census reported 88 percent white in the Tenderloin. Hotel figures include the Civic Center area and a line of South of Market blocks between Mission and Market streets. See Groth, "Forbidden Housing," 301–306, 331bb.

60. Other new areas included with the Tenderloin are the Van Ness/Polk corridor and the Church and Market area. On nearby apartments, see Eric Sandweiss, "Building for Downtown Living: The Residential Architecture of San Francisco's Tenderloin," *Perspectives in Vernacular Architecture* 3 (Columbia: University of Missouri Press, 1989): 160–173.

61. See "Dance Madness," in Kathy Peiss, *Cheap Amusements: Working Women and Leisure in Turn-of-the-Century New York* (Philadelphia: Temple University Press, 1986): 88–114; and David Nye, *Electrifying America: Social Meanings of a New Technology* (Cambridge: MIT Press, 1990).

62. About "gents," see Wolfe, *Lodging House Problem,* 20–33, with quotation from 33, talking about Boston; on the café, E. Idell Zeisloft, *The New Metropolis: Memorable Events of Three Centuries, 1600–1900* (New York: D. Appleton and Co., 1899): 266.

63. The generic elements are drawn largely from Boston; Wolfe, *Lodging House Problem,* 27–33. For overlaps with San Francisco, see Frank Norris, *Vandover and the Brute* (New York: Doubleday & Co., 1914): esp. 5–9, 43–59, 168–181; for New York, see Richardson, *The Long Day.*

64. Glassberg, "The Design of Reform," 5–21.

65. Wolfe, *Lodging House Problem,* 38, 46–48. Noncommercial meal arrangements could vary: in the 1920s, some San Francisco boarders had kitchen privileges, some ate breakfast and dinner with the family, and others ate their meals at a neighbor's house; Girls Housing Council, "Where Is Home?" 6, 24.

66. Wolfe, *Lodging House Problem,* 28, 48–50, 101–103. On the stew, see Meyerowitz, "Holding Their Own," 100. On counter and booth luncheonettes, see Chandler, "Social Organization," and SL, *The Invisible Elderly,* 20.

67. A well-known basement restaurant was in the What Cheer House; see Lucius Beebe and Charles Clegg, *San Francisco's Golden Era: A Picture Story of San Francisco before the Fire* (Berkeley: Howell-North, 1960): 204, and Williamson, *The American Hotel,* 90. On three for twos, see John P. Young, *San Francisco: History of the Pacific Coast Metropolis,* vol. 2 (San Francisco: S. J. Clarke, 1912): 559–560; on beef n' beans, see Zeisloft, *The New Metropolis,* 268.

68. On dairy lunchrooms, see Zeisloft, *The New Metropolis,* 266–268; Richardson, *The Long Day,* 148, 155; Jane Stern and Michael Stern, "Cafeteria," *New Yorker* (August 1, 1988): 37–54, on 40–41.

69. Wolfe, *Lodging House Problem,* 28, 46, 101.

70. Fretz, "The Furnished Room Problem in Philadelphia," 114.

71. Ibid.

72. Richardson, *The Long Day,* 258–259.

73. Wolfe, *Lodging House Problem,* 28.

74. Chandler, "Social Organization," 12–26; she devotes a chapter each to a corner crowd, a tavern crowd, and a rooming house group.

75. Anderson, *The Hobo,* 68, 76; see the recent equivalent of Anderson's cases reported in Siegal, *Outposts of the Forgotten,* 37.

76. For an exaggerated account of this sort of anonymity, see Zorbaugh, *Gold Coast and Slum,* 75. See also Wolfe, *Lodging House Problem,* 138.

77. On building types, see Gentry, *The Madams of San Francisco,* 204, 215–218, 225, describing 130 Eddy Street and 337 O'Farrell in the Tenderloin district; Zorbaugh, *Gold Coast and Slum,* 119–120. On buffet flats, see Chris Albertson, *Bessie* (New York: Stein and Day, 1972): 14, 122–123. On vice zones, see Wolfe, *Lodging House Problem,* 30, 32, 139–141, 171; Abbott, *The Tenements of Chicago,* 306, 313, 322–325; on contemporary views of such locations, see Howard B. Woolston, *Prostitution in the United States,* Publications of the Bureau of Social Hygiene, vol. 1 (New York: The Century Co., 1921): 132–133.

78. The hotel keeper is Ford, *A Few Remarks,* 293–297, with direct quotation on 294. Lubove, *The Progressives and the Slums,* 138; Hayner, *Hotel Life,* 168; Havelock Ellis, *The Task of Social Hygiene* (Boston: Houghton Mifflin, 1912): chap. 9.

79. Zorbaugh, *Gold Coast and Slum,* 120; Gentry, *Madams of San Francisco,* 255, 266–268; Hayner, *Hotel Life,* 172–173; Woolston, *Prostitution,* 147.

80. Modell and Hareven, "Urbanization and the Malleable Household," 471.

81. Kortum is quoted in Olmstead and Olmstead et al., *The Yerba Buena Center,* 234.

82. Ibid., 234; technically, this private boardinghouse needed a hotel license.

83. In 1880, a full two-thirds of the common laborers, teamsters, and carpenters who boarded or lodged had done so with private families. Twenty years later, over half of that group lived in commercial hotels; Tygiel, "Workingmen in San Francisco," 182, 207. On social concerns of family boarders, see Hayner, "The Hotel," 123; Hayner, *Hotel Life,* 70–71; Girls Housing Council, "Where Is Home?" 4, 21.

84. Hayner, "The Hotel," 123.

85. Hayner, *Hotel Life,* 69.

86. Wharton, *The House of Mirth,* 287.

87. Wilson, "Chicago Families in Furnished Rooms," 5; Abbott, *The Tenements of Chicago,* 318; Girls Housing Council, "Where Is Home?" 22.

88. Abbott, *The Tenements of Chicago,* 335; Wilson, "Chicago Families in Furnished Rooms," 3. Compare with the excellent 1940 descriptions in CSS, "Life in One Room," 8–26.

89. Wilson, "Chicago Families in Furnished Rooms," 30, 41; the building

cut into two-room units was in Chicago on the Southwest Side, on West 65th Street. On San Francisco, SFHACC, *Real Property Survey, 1939*, 1:13, 29.

90. Abbott, *The Tenements of Chicago*, 337.

91. Abbott, *The Tenements of Chicago*, 305–338; Mrs. Johanna von Wagner in SFHA, *Second Report* (1913): 26; Wolfe, *Lodging House Problem*, 173. Chandler reported that within two years, two of her friends, both in their 40s, had bought furniture and then abandoned it when they moved; Chandler, "Workers in a Rooming House," 131.

92. "Rooming House Problems," *Housing Betterment* 11, 1 (1922): 73–74.

93. Barth, *City People*, 7–18; Richard Sennett, *Families Against the City: Middle Class Homes of Industrial Chicago, 1872–1890* (Cambridge: Harvard University Press, 1970): 194; see also 62–69, 192–200.

94. Meyerowitz, "Holding Their Own," 3, 8, 196–199; Henry May, *The End of American Innocence: A Study of the First Years of Our Own Time, 1912–1917* (New York: Alfred A. Knopf, 1959); Daniel Scott Smith, "The Dating of the American Sexual Revolution: Evidence and Interpretation," in Michael Gorden, ed., *The American Family in Social-Historical Perspective* (New York: St. Martin's Press, 1973).

95. Meyerowitz, "Holding Their Own," 4, 8–9. See also Peiss, *Cheap Amusements*; and Lewis A. Erenberg, *Steppin' Out: New York Nightlife and the Transformation of American Culture, 1890–1930* (Westport, Conn.: Greenwood Press, 1981).

96. Wood, "Myriad Tenantry of Furnished Rooms," 956.

97. Quoted in Olmstead and Olmstead et al., *The Yerba Buena Center*, 227.

98. Kortum's hotel was the Rio Vista, on Third Street between Howard and Folsom in San Francisco's South of Market district, at the site of the present Moscone Convention Center.

99. Quoted in Olmstead and Olmstead et al., *The Yerba Buena Center*, 227.

100. Novelists such as Sinclair Lewis, Theodore Dreiser, and Edith Wharton often use rooming house furniture to mark their characters' changing socioeconomic status. Wharton gives this list for Lily Barth as the character nears the limit of what makes a socially proper room: a "shabby" chest of drawers with a lace cover, a washstand, two chairs, a small writing desk, and a little table near the bed. Wharton, *The House of Mirth*, 327. See also Dreiser, *An American Tragedy* (Cleveland: World Publishing, 1946; first published in 1925); and John Steinbeck, *In Dubious Battle* (New York: Penguin Books, 1979; first published in 1936): 1–3.

CHAPTER FIVE: OUTSIDERS AND CHEAP LODGING HOUSES

1. Riis, *How the Other Half Lives*, 69.

2. Anderson, *The Hobo*, 87–89, 172–173, quoting Ben Reitman, the self-styled "King of the Hoboes."

3. Hoch and Slayton, *New Homeless and Old*, 41; Anderson, *The Hobo*, 3, 14, 106; Wallace, *Skid Row as a Way of Life*, 18–19.

4. Anderson, *The Hobo*, xviii, xiv.

5. For this labor group in San Francisco, see Nylander, "The Casual Laborer of California"; Wood, "The California State Commission of Immigration and Housing," 3–22.

6. On 1907, Anderson, *The Hobo*, 63–64. On occupancy, see Nylander, "The Casual Laborer of California," 3–22, and Olmstead and Olmstead et al., *The Yerba Buena Center*, 247. On winter layoffs, see California Bureau of Labor Statistics, *19th Biennial Report, 1919–1920*, 231, and Averbach, "San Francisco's South of Market District," 199, 202, 205. California's canning industries employed a work force that was nine-tenths seasonal; two-thirds of the brick and tile makers were seasonal workers.

7. On the home guard see esp., Anderson, *The Hobo*, 41–45, 74, 117–119; and UC-HC, *Dependent Aged*, 63–64. Roger Miller, lyrics from "King of the Road" (Nashville: Tree Publishing Company, 1964).

8. Riis, *How the Other Half Lives*, 69. Specifically, Riis spoke here of young men mingled in the 25-cents-a-night cubicle hotels in the Bowery; not all of these men were migrant laborers.

9. Hoch and Slayton, *New Homeless and Old*, 37–40; McEntire, "Population and Employment Survey of Sacramento's West End."

10. On Chinese, see Shumsky, "Tar Flat and Nob Hill," 49–51. On labor agencies, see Tygiel, "Workingmen in San Francisco," 23. In 1880, the vast majority of San Francisco's tobacco and shoemaking workshops were within three blocks of Chinatown, showing their owners' dependence on the Chinese. In 1900, the 14,000 Chinese were 4.1 percent of the city's total population.

11. California, UC-HC, *Dependent Aged*, 75; Hoch and Slayton, *New Homeless and Old*, 29–32, 38; on blacks in the migrant work force, see John C. Schneider, "Tramping Workers, 1890–1920: A Subcultural View," in Monkkenon, ed., *Walking to Work*, 212–234.

12. One survey found that 60 percent of the older, male day laborer group had never been married and 30 percent had long been widowed. By comparison, in 1920, the national average among all adult males over 55 was only 27 percent single, widowed, or divorced; UC-HC, *Dependent Aged*, 64.

13. UC-HC, *Dependent Aged*, 58, 68–75; and Averbach, "San Francisco's South of Market District," 209. On modern parallels, see Wallace, *Skid Row as a Way of Life*, 199–120, and Spradley, *You Owe Yourself a Drunk*, 76–77.

14. "Ten Cent Lodgings," 9.

15. Weiner, "Sisters of the Road," 171–188; Martin, "Homeless Women," 32–41; Box-Car Bertha, *Sister of the Road*, 9, 13–15, 60–68, 132–134. The low national figure is Box-Car Bertha's; the high figure is from the U.S. Women's Bureau, 1933. On the Bowery, see Kennaday, "New York's Hundred Lodging Houses," 489.

16. R. D. McKenzie, *The Metropolitan Community* (New York: McGraw-Hill, 1933): 245–247. The data were taken from sample tracts of the 1920 U.S. Census.

17. Wallace, *Skid Row as a Way of Life,* 192–194; Anderson, *The Hobo,* 13, 129; Solenberger, *One Thousand Homeless Men.* On unemployables, see Ford, *Slums and Housing,* 346–347; UC-HC, *Dependent Aged,* 68.

18. One expert defined the mentally ill as including the "insane, feeble-minded, or epileptic"; she found only 197 alcoholics out of 1,000 men; Solenberger, *One Thousand Homeless Men.* Another observer cites a 1950s study that found only 8 percent of the excessive drinkers on skid row to be alcoholics; Wallace, *Skid Row as a Way of Life,* 187–188. On cocaine, see Anderson, *The Hobo,* 67, 97.

19. Anderson, *The Hobo,* 5, 15.

20. Richard H. Dillon, *Shanghaiing Days* (New York: Coward-McCann, 1961): 38–45, 212–215; Felix Riesenberg, Jr., *Golden Gate: The Story of San Francisco Harbor* (New York: Alfred Knopf, 1940): 128–132, 153–161, 206, 234–299.

21. Byrnes, "Nurseries of Crime," 355–362; Devine, "The Shiftless and Floating City Population," 160–161; Wolfe, *Lodging House Problem,* 137–138, 181–182.

22. Hoch and Slayton, *New Homeless and Old,* 44, 60–61.

23. I have borrowed "no-family house" from Lars Lerup, who uses the term for a conceptual house design.

24. See saloon stairway photo in Aronovici, *Housing Conditions in the City of Saint Paul,* 59. Liu, "Chinatown Residential Hotels," shows doorway distinctions on 8, 109.

25. On prices, see Anderson, *The Hobo,* 29ff.; Riis, *How the Other Half Lives,* 69–72. Riis gives the prices in 1890 as 25, 15, 10, and 7 cents. The reformer's full phrase for a city's cheapest hotels was often "cheap hotels, lodging houses, and flops." The more generic term for the entire rank was "cheap lodging house." Common variants of "lodging house" added the price, as in "Ten Cent Lodging House."

26. The California State Tuberculosis Commission inspector, Johanna von Wagner, in SFHA, *Second Report* (1913): 26.

27. Groth, "Forbidden Housing," 522–535. In 1910, most cheap lodging house ratios were worse than 1:20; by 1930, most owners had added plumbing, and the ratios were better than 1:20.

28. The Central Hotel, probably built in about 1909, is described in CSRA, *Transients in California,* 181. Its owner was Edward Rolkin, profiled in chap. 6. The building, at 564–586 Third Street, across from South Park, had a bath-to-room ratio of 1:18.

29. Anderson, "Lodging Houses," 595, and Chicago Department of Public Welfare, "Fifty Cheap Lodging Houses," 66–73. Other useful glimpses of cu-

bicle rooms, in chronological order: Riis, *How the Other Half Lives,* 72; Josiah Flynt [Josiah Flynt Willard], *Tramping with Tramps* (New York: Century Company, 1901): 123; Anderson, *The Hobo,* 30, 132; Hayner, "The Hotel," 48–49; Hayner, *Hotel Life,* 29; Ford, *A Few Remarks,* 15; CIH, *First Annual Report* (1915): 80; CIH, *Second Annual Report* (1916): 226–228; Hoch and Slayton, *New Homeless and Old,* 46–47, 101–102. Gentry, *Madams of San Francisco,* 186–187, gives measurements of San Francisco cribs in a cheap prostitution house he saw: height, 6′6″; length, 6′9″; width, 4′6″.

30. Hoch and Slayton, *New Homeless and Old,* 44–45, 60–61.

31. The wallet detail is courtesy of Prof. Warren Roberts, Folklore Institute, Indiana University, describing his stay in a military ward-style domicile in World War II; interview in Newark, Delaware, May 5, 1984. See also Irvine, "A Bunk-House and Some Bunk-House Men."

32. Abbott, *The Tenements of Chicago,* 164.

33. Folsom Street, in SFHA, *Second Report* (1913): 25–26. New York, in Ford, *Slums and Housing,* 346, quoting Kennaday study of 1905; CIH, *First Annual Report* (1915): 80. New York's Kenton Hotel, 333 Bowery, had the top two floors in wards, the next two in cubicles, and the ground floor in commercial uses.

34. Gentry, *Madams of San Francisco,* 186–188, 204, 215–218; Woolston, *Prostitution in the United States,* 104, 139; Abbott, *The Tenements of Chicago,* 112. On canvas partitions in some crib brothels, see Norman Maclean, *A River Runs Through It and Other Stories* (Chicago: University of Chicago Press, 1976): 174–207. On the "municipal crib," a 100-cubicle hotel owned and operated in part by city officials, see Walton Bean, *Boss Reuf's San Francisco,* 45–46.

35. "Ten Cent Lodgings," 9.

36. Anderson, *The Hobo,* 132; see also Kennaday, "New York's One Hundred Rooming Houses," 487, 489; Hoch and Slayton, *New Homeless and Old,* 48.

37. In 1910, the four-story Milton House, near Third and Howard in San Francisco, had 120 rooms (cubicles, surely) yet only 11 basins, 5 toilets, and no baths in the entire structure. On towels, Aronovici, *Housing Conditions in the City of Saint Paul,* 59. On other conditions, see especially Anderson, *The Hobo,* 29, 132; SFHA, *Second Report* (1913): 25; Riis, *How the Other Half Lives,* 69; Hoch and Slayton, *New Homeless and Old,* 48–49.

38. On California, see Groth, "Forbidden Housing," 523–529; on Chicago, see Bogue, *Skid Row in American Cities,* 84; on New York, see Blackburn, "Single Room Occupancy in New York City," 2–8. On codes and enforcement, see chap. 8 below.

39. The Bonanza was at 867–869 Market, near Fifth Street, in the 1880s. It did not survive the fire of 1906. The top-floor shoe factory suggests the building was a commercial loft structure; hence the likelihood that the lodgings were of a minimal sort (Sanborn Insurance Maps, 1885, 1905).

40. Turish's structure, built about 1906, filled its 20- by 70-foot lot at 211 Minna Street, between Third and Fourth streets (a block later occupied by the Yerba Buena Gardens project).

41. Riis, *How the Other Half Lives,* 72. Other sources on flophouses are Anderson, *The Hobo,* 30–32 (see esp. his account of a night in a flophouse); Chicago Department of Public Welfare, "Fifty Cheap Lodging Houses," 68–70; UC-HC, *Dependent Aged,* 74–75; CIH, *Second Annual Report* (1916): 226.

42. CSRA, *Transients in California,* 81–82.

43. CIH, *Second Annual Report* (1916): 50–51; Sherry H. Olson, *Baltimore: The Building of an American City* (Baltimore: Johns Hopkins Press, 1980): 215; U.S. Bureau of Labor, *Housing of the Working People in the United States by Employers,* 1191–1243.

44. On Chicago City Hall, see Hoch and Slayton, *New Homeless and Old,* 53–57. On police stations, see Riis, *How the Other Half Lives,* 72.

45. Mostoller, "A Single Room," 191–216. Hoch and Slayton, *New Homeless and Old,* 55–57; Robbins, "What Constitutes a Model Municipal Lodging House"; "Model Lodging Houses for New York," 59–61; Philpott, *The Slum and the Ghetto,* 98–99. On county measures in San Francisco: UC-HC, *Dependent Aged,* 75. In 1909, a new Municipal Lodging House in New York had showers, a fumigation room, a dining room, a laundry, and six large ward rooms with a total of 912 beds; Charles Zueblin, *American Municipal Progress* (New York: Macmillan, 1902): 102.

46. Reconstructed as condominiums and called "The Atrium," the Mills Hotel No. 1 in 1990 still stood between Bleeker, Sullivan, and Thompson streets. Flagg is known for model tenement house designs as well as for the Singer office building. On the Mills No. 1 as "welfare hotel," see Francis X. Clines, "Hotel in 'Village' Step to Nowhere," *New York Times* (July 16, 1970): 36; "Down-at-Heels Hotel Gets a Natty New Identity," *New York Times* (September 28, 1975): R-1, R-12; Siegal, *Outposts of the Forgotten,* 7–8, 11.

47. "Unique Workingmen's Hotel for San Diego," 80–82. The J. D. and A. B. Spreckels Securities Company sponsored the hotel; its architect, Harrison Albright of Los Angeles, worked from designs by Lloyd Wright. Each room measures 8 by 11 feet, with no cubicles or open wards, and the lobby spaces are cavernous. It is, in fact, more a rooming house rank building than a lodging house. See also Eckert, *The Unseen Elderly,* 42–45.

For a wonderfully detailed account of a company town that had dormitory and rooming house buildings in addition to houses, see Candee, *Atlantic Heights,* 63–109. For a period architect on how to design a proper workers' hotel for a company town, see Kilham, "Housing the Single Worker." Hotels like these dot the company towns of the West and the Southeast.

48. Johnson, "The Lodging House Problem in Minneapolis"; field notes are Aronovici, *Housing Conditions of the City of Saint Paul,* 61. On missions of the 1870s, a good description is Sala, *America Revisited,* 70–71.

49. On San Francisco, see UC-HC, *Dependent Aged,* 73; on Chicago, Hoch and Slayton, *New Homeless and Old,* 57–60. Dorothy Richardson bitterly recalled a charitable home for working girls in Richardson, *The Long Day.* On blacks, see Sally Chesham, *Born to Battle: The Salvation Army in America* (Chicago: Rand McNally, 1965): 252–253.

50. Hunt, "The Housing of Non-Family Groups of Men in Chicago," 145–170.

51. The term "skid row" was derived from the old Skid *Road* section of Seattle, where loggers lived next to the street where logs had been skidded down to the waterfront; Wallace, *Skid Row as a Way of Life,* vii, 13–45. On the distinction between the hobo district of the 1920s and skid row, see Schneider, "Skid Row as an Urban Neighborhood," 167–189; Jackson, "The Bowery," 68–79; Hoch and Slayton, *New Homeless and Old,* 87–93. I have also relied on the early historical study of Leonard Blumberg et al., *Liquor and Poverty: Skid Row as a Human Condition* (New Brunswick: Rutgers Center of Alcohol Studies, 1978), which uses San Francisco as one of three case studies.

52. Averbach, "San Francisco's South of Market District," CIH, *First Annual Report* (1915): 11; Groth, "Forbidden Housing," 331ff. Population figures are from the U.S. decennial census. In Chicago, the winter population of the analogous Main Stem area could be 75,000.

53. Much of the following description relies on Averbach, "San Francisco's South of Market District," 197–218, with material added from city directories, insurance maps, photographs, and skid row descriptions found in Anderson, *The Hobo;* CSRA, *Transients in California;* Hoch and Slayton, *New Homeless and Old;* and Hartman, *The Transformation of San Francisco,* 53–59.

54. Nels Anderson, *The American Hobo: An Autobiography* (Leiden: E. J. Brill, 1975): 85. On no place to sit, see Bauer and McEntire, "Relocation Study, Single Male Population," 4–5.

55. Riesenberg, *Golden Gate,* 250. The year when these prices were in effect is unclear. Coffee Dan's later became popular with middle-income patrons.

56. UC-HC, *Dependent Aged,* 73. This man lived in the South of Market in San Francisco; the original breakfast spelling was "coffee an'."

57. Anderson, *The Hobo,* 33–35.

58. Schneider, "Skid Row as an Urban Neighborhood," 173–180; Anderson, *The Hobo,* xix, 107–108; Averbach, "San Francisco's South of Market District," 210.

59. Bowden, "The Dynamics of City Growth." The neighborhood was centered on Pacific Avenue, just east from the modern North Beach area.

60. Nee and Nee, *Longtime Californ',* 30–57; Connie Young Yu, "A History of San Francisco Chinatown Housing," *Amerasia Journal* 8, 1 (Spring/Summer 1981); Yip, "San Francisco's Chinatown." On Chinatown as a tourist attraction in the 1880s, see Sala, *America Revisited,* 460, 493–494. The Chi-

natown area was bounded roughly by California Street on the south, Powell Street on the west, Pacific Street on the north, and Kearny Street on the east.

61. Yip, "San Francisco's Chinatown," 168–234. In the 1880s, the double building standard for Chinatown was very obvious; in the 1887 edition of the San Francisco Sanborn Maps, see sheets 9 and 13 for shifts in building types at the edges of Chinatown. For an official example of culturally explaining away the situation, see CIH, *Second Annual Report* (1916): 262; on recent crowding in the family association buildings, Chinatown Neighborhood Improvement Center, *Update: Special Issues* (1980): 9.

62. Description from Sanborn Insurance Maps; see Trillin, "Some Thoughts on the International Hotel Controversy," 116–120.

63. On the Mexican population, see Godfrey, *Neighborhoods in Transition,* and CIH, *First Annual Report* (1915): 66. In the late 1800s, Columbus Street was known for its Mexican food. Curtis Choy's film, *The Fall of the International Hotel,* is the most vivid source on Manilatown. According to Hayner, who worked in Seattle, white residents in Los Angeles and Seattle preferred Japanese hotels for their better management; *Hotel Life.* On racial mixtures, see manuscript survey cards in the Bancroft Library for SFHACC, *Real Property Survey, 1939.* The Bo-Chow Hotel, at 102 South Park, was all-Japanese in the 1930s. The Clayton is at 657 Clay Street.

64. On separate black lodging house areas, see Hoch and Slayton, *New Homeless and Old,* 24–26, 29–32. Later steel mills to the south also hired large numbers of black workers.

65. At least 600 cheap SRO rooms were in this outlying cluster; Groth, "Forbidden Housing," 296–301, 331ee.

66. UC-HC, *Dependent Aged,* 72–74; Anderson, *The Hobo,* 69; Hayner, "The Hotel," 87. A recent study is Burki, "Housing the Low-Income Urban Elderly," 279–280.

67. CSRA, *Transients in California,* 120, 186. The authors reported that in San Francisco, only the Scandinavian Seamen's Mission still provided the banking service but that in all hotels, the wiser laborers still paid their room rent in advance when winter or recessions ended their employment.

68. Zorbaugh, *Gold Coast and Slum,* 74; on charging higher rents, see Wolfe, *Lodging House Problem,* 140.

69. Spradley, *You Owe Yourself a Drunk,* 71, 97–107, 252–262.

70. On setting becoming life-style, I have relied on interviews with Jim Baumohl, February 12 and March 5, 1981. See also Anderson, *The Hobo,* 40–57, 87–106; Wallace, *Skid Row as a Way of Life,* 125–134, 166, 179–202; Spradley, *You Owe Yourself a Drunk,* 252–262; and Siegal, *Outposts of the Forgotten,* 42–44, 51, 68. Siegal reports that transient guests used "house" for their room, while longer-term residents used "house" for the whole hotel.

71. Tamara Hareven, *Family Time and Industrial Time: The Relationship Between the Family and Work in a New England Industrial Community* (New

York: Cambridge University Press, 1982), shows how family workers, too, wove flexibility into their housing tenure but with generally much larger swings of time.

72. On the dichotomies of rural facades and interiors, see Henry Glassie, "Folk Eighteenth-Century Cultural Process in Delaware Valley Folk Building," *Winterthur Portfolio* 7 (1972): 29–57; and Thomas C. Hubka, *Big House, Little House, Back House, Barn: The Connected Farm Buildings of New England* (Hanover: University Press of New England, 1984). Commercial buildings of the last 100 years often share this lodging house facade-interior split. See William H. Jordy, "Functionalism as Fact and Symbol: Louis Sullivan's Commercial Buildings, Tombs, and Banks," in Jordy, *Progressive and Academic Ideals at the Turn of the Twentieth Century,* American Buildings and their Architects, vol. 4 (New York: Oxford University Press, 1972): 83–179. On smaller false-front store buildings, see Kingston Heath, "False-Front Architecture on Montana's Urban Frontier," *Perspectives in Vernacular Architecture* 3 (Columbia: University of Missouri Press, 1989): 199–213. Owners and designers used the same calculated, carefully designed dichotomies between facade and interior in the tall brick tenement buildings of New York.

73. The case for the immigrant Chinese laborers living in Chinatowns is more complex, since their household formation and rights to property were limited until the 1960s and since they often cooked for themselves. For black and Latino laborers, racial segregation and ethnic prejudice surely overshadowed the role of residence in this process.

74. Codes and other reforms are explored in chap. 8.

CHAPTER SIX: BUILDING A CIVILIZATION WITHOUT HOMES

1. Calhoun, *A Social History of the Family,* 3:75.

2. "English Photographs by an American," *Harper's New Monthly Magazine* 37 (July 1868): 253–257, quotation on 256.

3. The comments on San Francisco hotel ownership draw from a sample of 40 properties taken at random from the much larger samples of the 1910 and 1930 city directories. Jim Buckley traced the ownership from the present back to 1896 and where possible, correlated all owners with listings in the city directories.

4. "Landlord of Skid Row: Cheap Beds Net $2,000,000 Estate," *San Francisco Chronicle,* February 27, 1941, and city directories. From 1889 to 1904, Rolkin lived and managed the prefire Reno House at 631 Sacramento; by the end of his life, Rolkin was partial or full owner of several apartment buildings, a steam laundry, the Winchester, Irwin, Argonaut, Seneca, Denver, and Colton hotels, together with the new Reno Hotel (375 rooms) and the Central Hotel (440 rooms). Not all of Rolkin's holdings were of the lodging house sort; for instance, the Argonaut, of 250 rooms, was a midpriced hotel that advertised

for travelers and families. The eventual nonhotel home for the Rolkins was at 1275 Stanyon, southeast of Golden Gate Park. After Rolkin's death, his wife, still the holder of an immense amount of real estate, lived in the South Peninsula suburb of Milbrae until her death in 1953.

5. In the 1917 city directory, the Marty brothers advertised a list of their holdings; in 1920, they also bought 662 Clay (128 rooms) and held it in the family until 1953; it is likely that they owned additional properties. In 1917, Jules and Louis Marty lived a few blocks from each other near the intersection of Army and Mission streets.

6. The Portland was at 611 Howard Street, between Second and Third, under the site of the present-day Moscone Convention Center. The Delta, at 41 Sixth Street near Market Street, is shown in chap. 4. The Sierra House, 558 Broadway, is shown in chap. 1.

7. See also Hoch and Slayton, *New Homeless and Old,* 17–18.

8. From real estate prices advertised in the *San Francisco Chronicle* (April 2, 1923); the rooming house was near the Civic Center, the Edwardian flats near Dolores and Army streets in the Noe Valley district.

9. The Victoria, 598 Bush at Stockton, more recently named the Hotel Juliana, has 142 rooms. Pettigrew and Callahan also shared a house in Pacific Heights.

10. The Beck family held the Colonial Hotel until 1958. The Hotel York was at 1499 California at Larkin. On Brandenstein, see Ruth Bransten [Brandenstein] McDougall, *Under Mannie's Hat* (San Francisco: Hesperian Press, 1964): 13–25. Among Brandenstein's earlier holdings had been Sarah Pettigrew's portion of the lot for the Hotel Victoria.

11. In 1909, the second owner, a Mrs. Morris, also managed the Somerton Hotel at 440 Geary.

12. C. H. and Made D. Barber owned and managed the Hotel Bellevue, Taylor at Geary, from 1923 until 1946.

13. Siefkin, *The City at the End of the Rainbow,* 44–45.

14. Smith's sister, Mrs. C. C. Rawak, talked Smith into beginning his remarkable hotel career. He first leased the Biltmore and Cornell hotels and opened the Mark Hopkins on December 4, 1926. "He Built the Mark: San Francisco Hotelman George Smith Dies," *San Francisco Chronicle* (September 25, 1965). In addition to print sources on Smith, I am indebted to an interview with Mr. Smith's son, Hart Smith, in San Francisco on January 27, 1988.

15. Smith (1889–1965), California Historical Society, biography collection; see also Basil Woon, *San Francisco and the Golden Empire* (New York: Harrison Smith and Robert Haas, 1935): 88.

16. On recruiting good managers, see Williamson, *The American Hotel,* 50, 94–95, 245. The San Francisco case is Herbert's Bachelor Hotel and German Grill, at 151–161 Powell Street, near O'Farrell; the 108 rooms had 66 private bathrooms and 11 shared toilet rooms; for the prices quoted, see the *San Fran-*

cisco Examiner (January 10, 1909) and the *San Francisco Chronicle* (January 9, 1909).

17. "Our Family Hotels," 12.

18. A popular reference they might have consulted is Richard M. Hurd, *The Principles of City Land Values,* 3d ed. (New York: The Record and Guide, 1924; first published in 1903). Popular period hotel management guides included Boomer, *Hotel Management,* and Hamilton, *Promoting New Hotels.* Investment and management magazines ranged from national journals such as *Hotel Management* and *Hotel Review* to *The Pacific Coast Hotel Weekly* and *Western Hotel Reporter.*

19. On bar receipts, see Williamson, *The American Hotel,* 143; on store rentals, see Hamilton, *Promoting New Hotels,* 147.

20. Hamilton, *Promoting New Hotels,* 2 (see also 32, 38). See also Hayner, *Hotel Life,* 62–63; and Monroe Adams, "The SRO Elderly from the Perspective of a Hotel Owner," in SL, *The Invisible Elderly,* 15.

21. On sociability of managers, see Williamson, *The American Hotel,* 50, 94–95, 245; and Sala, *America Revisited,* 142, 405. On managers and strikes, see Tygiel, "Workingmen in San Francisco," 324. On the continuing importance of post-World War II managers for low-income residents, see CSS, "Life in One Room"; Shapiro, "Reciprocal Dependence"; and Adams, "The SRO Elderly from the Perspective of a Hotel Owner," 15.

22. Hayner, *Hotel Life,* 32, 35, 38, 62–63; Williamson, *The American Hotel,* 115.

23. Charles Hoch, planner, interview in Chicago, May 28, 1987.

24. "Our Family Hotels," 12.

25. Wolfe, *Lodging House Problem,* 52–80; Hayner, *Hotel Life,* 36.

26. Wolfe, *Lodging House Problem,* 20–21, 58–66. The "honest" broker's quotation is from the 1915 directory listing for the Irwin Keeler Hotel Brokerage Company in San Francisco. Keeler was the city's primary hotel broker and also the publisher of the *Pacific Coast Hotel Weekly;* before the 1915 exposition, four other hotel brokers briefly opened offices. For glimpses of middle-income women running boardinghouses, see "The Experiences of a Boarding House Keeper," and Krag, "How I Made a Boarding House Successful." On the similar ownership and leasing of rooming houses and light housekeeping rooms in San Francisco's Western Addition during the 1940s, see SFHACC, *Third Report* (1941): 12.

27. I borrow language and approach here from Sherry H. Olson, "Baltimore Imitates the Spider," *Annals of the Association of American Geographers* 69 (1979): 557–574. On the graph of San Francisco hotel listings, hotels from two city neighborhoods are partly missing. Comparing the 1910 and 1930 directory listings with recent inventories of Chinatown hotel addresses reveals that only one in seven Chinatown hotels were listed in 1910; by 1930, only half of the hotels in Chinatown were listed in the directory. Seamen's hotels on the

waterfront also seem underrepresented in the directory before 1910. Judging from Sanborn Map records, the building booms in these districts did coincide strongly with the general city economy.

28. William Issel and Robert W. Cherny, *San Francisco 1865–1932: Politics, Power, and Urban Development* (Berkeley, Los Angeles, and London: University of California Press, 1986); Tygiel, "Workingmen in San Francisco," 297. On the 1870s migration to San Francisco and the proportion of manufacturing employees, see Shumsky, "Tar Flat and Nob Hill," 53.

29. Groth, "Forbidden Housing," 236–327; Olmstead and Olmstead et al., *The Yerba Buena Center*. Nancy Stoltz, "Disaster and Displacement: The Effects of the 1906 Earthquake and Fire on the Land Use Patterns in San Francisco's South of Market" (Master's thesis, UC Berkeley, 1983). On general political and physical processes of rebuilding after great fires, see Christine Meisner Rosen, *The Limits to Power: Great Fires and the Process of City Growth in America* (Cambridge: Cambridge University Press, 1986).

30. Groth, "Forbidden Housing," 244–283.

31. Statler is quoted in Boomer, *Hotel Management*, 49. War surges are also discussed in Hamilton, *Promoting New Hotels*, 32, 133–136; and Anderson, *The Hobo*, 260–261.

32. The last major construction of commercial rooming houses and cheap lodging houses seems to have occurred in 1915, based on Groth, "Forbidden Housing," 331-a to 331-x.

33. For 1919, U.S. Bureau of the Census, *Fourteenth Census of the U.S.,* vol. 9 (Washington, D.C.: Government Printing Office, 1923): 132–137; for 1921, California Bureau of Labor Statistics, *Nineteenth Biennial Report, 1919–1920*, 231; for 1925, the *U.S. Census of California Manufactures,* quoted in California Bureau of Labor Statistics, *Twenty-Third Biennial Report, 1927–1928*. On the relocation of jobs, see David Nelson, *Managers and Workers: Origins of the New Factory System in the United States, 1880–1920* (Madison: University of Wisconsin Press, 1975).

34. Stylistic innovation and engineering marvels dominate the design literature about hotels; see Condit, "Hotels and Apartments." On the long American tradition of emphasizing size of hotels above all else, see Trollope, *North America*, 485; and Lewis, *Work of Art*, 148.

35. San Francisco's Baldwin Hotel (completed in 1877, burned in 1898) had two electric passenger elevators and another one for calling cards. The George A. Fuller Company in Chicago and F. W. Nicolls were prominent hotel design firms cognizant of the latest technology. See Condit, "Hotels and Apartments," 101, 150–151, 159; and Hamilton, *Promoting New Hotels*, 13.

36. In the 1920s, one of Baltimore's first new prestige skyscrapers was the 14-story Southern Hotel; Sherry Olson, *Baltimore: The Building of an American City* (Baltimore: Johns Hopkins Press, 1980): 173, 244, 314. On civic pride and hotel skyscraper competition, Boorstin, "Palaces of the Public," 134–147.

37. Pfleuger was *the* 1930s society architect in San Francisco. He designed several landmark structures and often used the famous New York delineator Hugh Ferris to advertise his buildings as thoroughly stylish. Daniel Gregory, "Why Don't You Make It Undulate? The Story of Designing the City Club— An Interview with Michael Goodman," oral history interview for the San Francisco Museum of Folk and Craft, San Francisco, June 6, 1988; also, an interview with Daniel Gregory in San Francisco, September 20, 1988.

38. Hamilton, *Promoting New Hotels,* 1–3, 41, 112, 131–136; E. M. Statler, "The Race for the Guest," *Nation's Business* (June 1928).

39. On the filtering of grand New York City hotels, see Sala, "American Hotels and American Food," 345–356; Williamson, *The American Hotel,* 36–37. For more detailed examples in Chicago, see Zorbaugh, *Gold Coast and Slum,* 26–27, 35–37; Hayner, "The Hotel," 44–45, 87.

40. The block was bounded by Folsom, Harrison, Third, and Fourth streets; the three hotels giving up hotel services were the Clay, the Southern, and the Delmar. Olmstead and Olmstead et al., *The Yerba Buena Center,* 251.

41. For a description of the process as seen by building owners, see Wolfe, *Lodging House Problem,* 72–80.

42. In 1870, one floor of San Francisco's elite Lick House was temporarily converted to offices. Judging from tax records, San Francisco's Grand Central opened as a hotel, served as offices in World War I, and then after the war became a hotel again. Two other notable New York hotels closed due to Prohibition at about the same time as the Manhattan: the Knickerbocker (built in 1906), and the Holland House (built in 1892); farther south along Broadway, below Times Square, several hotels were converted to needle trades in the 1890s. In Louisville, owners converted the rebuilt Galt House (built in 1868) to a warehouse in 1919; Toledo's large Oliver Hotel (built in 1859) met the same fate. See Williamson, *The American Hotel,* 94, 260–262, 270–271, 286–287; Hurd, *Principles of City Land Values,* 107; and Groth, "Forbidden Housing," 116–117, 461–462.

43. For succinct summaries of this process, see Michael P. Conzen, "The Morphology of Nineteenth-Century Cities in the United States," in Woodrow Borah, J. Hardoy, and G. Stelter, *Urbanization in the Americas: The Background in Comparative Perspective* (Ottawa: National Museum of Man, 1980): 119–141; James E. Vance, Jr., "Land Assignment in the Precapitalist, Capitalist, and Postcapitalist City," *Economic Geography* 47 (1971): 101–120; and Weiss, *The Rise of the Community Builders.* On individuals and collective results, see also Borchert, *Alley Life in Washington,* 23, and Sam Bass Warner, Jr., *The Private City* (Philadelphia: University of Pennsylvania Press, 1968): 4.

44. For cheaper hotels, the proportion in former houses appears to be lower because informal boarding and lodging arrangements were not listed in the street directory. For excruciating detail on these rates of specialization and the

various building types they represent, see Groth, "Forbidden Housing," 236–287, 331ff–331hh.

45. This figure includes both complete rooms and cubicles; the capacity of wards or flophouses cannot be computed from San Francisco records; Groth, "Forbidden Housing," 331–332.

46. The details of San Francisco's building codes are outlined in chap. 8, below. Without the coercion of city officials, palace and midpriced hotels usually offered above-code building standards.

47. Compare the Lexington or New Michigan Hotel, 1892, and the Plaza Hotel, 1892, in Condit, "Hotels and Apartments," 153.

48. The physical development of the Alamo Square area of the Western Addition is exquisitely described in Moudon, *Built for Change,* 127, 135–138, 169–170. On land values, see SFHACC, *Third Report* (1941): 12; San Francisco Planning Commission, "Redevelopment of Blighted Areas," 28. Racial changes from U.S. decennial census, 1940 and 1950.

49. Tygiel, "Workingmen in San Francisco," 249, 254–255, 398. On the late 1920s, see Margaret Goddard King, "The Growth of San Francisco, Illustrated by Shifts in the Density of Population" (M.A. thesis, University of California, Berkeley, 1928): 49.

50. Lewis, *Babbitt,* 89.

51. "S.F. Hotelman George Smith Dies: He Built the Mark," *San Francisco Chronicle* (September 25, 1965): 10; Woon, *San Francisco and the Golden Empire,* 87–88; and city directory listings. Smith had sold his interest in the Fairmont in 1941.

52. "Landlord of Skid Row," and city directory listings. Rolkin gave the candy money in trust to the city health department and also left money to Protestant, Jewish, and Catholic orphanages. He and his wife did not have any children.

53. On the contrast of suburb and downtown, salient titles are David Ward, *Cities and Immigrants: A Geography of Change in Nineteenth-Century America* (New York: Oxford University Press, 1971): 127; and Tygiel, "Workingmen in San Francisco," 265–269, 397–398.

54. Zorbaugh, *Gold Coast and Slum,* 46–68.

55. Lester Burnett, in commentary printed with the *State Tenement House Act and State Hotel and Lodging House Act of California* (Sacramento: State Printing Office, 1917). Emphasis added.

CHAPTER SEVEN: HOTEL HOMES AS A PUBLIC NUISANCE

1. Veiller, "The Housing Problem in American Cities," 255–256.

2. This review of the progressives draws primarily on Lubove, *The Progressives and the Slums;* Robert H. Wiebe, *Businessmen and Reform: A Study of the Progressive Movement* (Cambridge: Harvard University Press, 1962): esp.

16–41, 206–224; James Weinstein, *The Corporate Ideal in the Liberal State: 1900–1918* (Boston: Beacon Press, 1968); and Davis, *Spearheads for Reform.*

3. On order in a complex world, see esp. Richard Hofstadter, *The Age of Reform: From Bryan to F.D.R.* (New York: Vintage Books, 1955). On housing as social order, see Lubove, *The Progressives and the Slums,* 82, 131, 214; and Ernest S. Griffith, *The Progressive Years and Their Aftermath, 1900–1920* (New York: Praeger, 1974).

4. Marie Stevens Howland and Albert Kinney Owen, in their scheme for Topolobambo, like several earlier utopian communities, included hotel life; Hayden, *The Grand Domestic Revolution,* 103–108. The conclusion section of this chapter also gives exceptions to the rule.

5. On pluralism, see Lubove, *The Progressives and the Slums,* 187.

6. Samuel Haber, *Efficiency and Uplift: Scientific Management in the Progressive Era, 1890–1920* (Chicago: University of Chicago Press, 1964): 18–74; Harry Braverman, *Labor and Monopoly Capital: The Degradation of Work in the Twentieth Century* (New York: Monthly Review Press, 1974): 85–138; and Donald A. Krueckeberg, "Introduction to the American Planner," in Krueckeberg, ed., *The American Planner: Biographies and Recollections* (New York: Methuen, 1983): 1–36.

7. Albion Fellows Bacon, *Housing—Its Relation to Social Work,* publication no. 48 (New York: National Housing Association, ca. 1919): 8.

8. CIH, *Second Annual Report* (1916).

9. On Veiller, see Lubove, *The Progressives and the Slums,* 117–118, 117–184. For an excellent profile of Chicago reformers, see Steven J. Diner, *A City and Its Universities: Public Policy in Chicago, 1892–1919* (Chapel Hill: University of North Carolina Press, 1980): 52–64.

10. On house diseases, see Bacon, *Housing—Its Relation to Social Work,* 3–4; on anemic women, see Ruth Reed, *The Single Woman* (New York: Macmillan, 1942); Lubove, *The Progressives and the Slums,* 83–84.

11. Veiller, *Housing Reform,* 5.

12. Lubove, *The Progressives and the Slums,* 252.

13. On Woods, see Davis, *Spearheads for Reform,* 8, 24, 33–34; on Hull House and Abbott, see Diner, *A City and Its Universities,* 43–47, 119–153; on settlements, see Mary K. Simkhovitch, *Neighborhood: My Story of Greenwich House* (New York: W. W. Norton, 1938).

14. Mardges Bacon, *Ernest Flagg: Beaux-Arts Architect and Urban Reformer* (New York: Architecture History Foundation, 1986). On Burnham and this theme, see Hines, "The Paradox of 'Progressive' Architecture," 426–448, and Hines, *Burnham of Chicago: Architect and Planner* (New York: Oxford University Press, 1974).

15. Diner, *A City and Its Universities,* 32, 131–132; and Fred H. Matthews, *Quest for an American Sociology: Robert E. Park and the Chicago School* (Montreal: McGill-Queen's University Press, 1977); see also Martin

Bulmer, *The Chicago School of Sociology: Institutionalization, Diversity, and the Rise of Sociological Research* (Chicago: University of Chicago Press, 1984).

16. Veiller, *Housing Reform*, 5–6; Porter writes in SFHA, *First Report* (1911): 6, 8. On the crucible, see J. Lebovitz, "The Home and the Machine," *Journal of Home Economics* 3, 2 (April 1911): 141–148, on 145.

17. See Barbara Welter's classic article, "The Cult of True Womanhood: 1820–1860," *American Quarterly* 18 (Summer 1966): 151–174, and Mary P. Ryan, *Cradle of the Middle Class: The Family in Oneida County, New York, 1790–1865* (New York: Cambridge University Press, 1981): 191–210.

18. "Decline and Fall of Hotel Life," 274. For a finely crafted summary of criticisms from the 1850s and 1860s, see McGlone, "Suffer the Children," 414–426.

19. Robertson and Robertson, *Our American Tour*, 7–10.

20. Wharton, *The House of Mirth*, 274, 276.

21. Hayner, "The Hotel," devotes an entire chapter to women of leisure, 99–127; the quotation is on 102. Other negative comments are from Hayner, *Hotel Life*, 7, 55, 109–110. See also, "The True Story of a Hotel Child," quoted (without citation) in Hayner, *Hotel Life*, 113–114, 129. For earlier views of these critiques, see Fayès, "The Housing of Single Women," 102; and Calhoun, *A Social History of the Family*, 2:238–241, 3:179–182.

22. The comments on decorating are from "Over the Draughting Board," 89–91. See also Trollope, *North America*, 484.

23. Nienburg, *The Woman Home-Maker in the City*, 9.

24. The hotel woman is quoted in Hayner, *Hotel Life*, 74–75.

25. Howells, *The Hazard of New Fortunes*, 80; Ryan, *Cradle of the Middle Class*, 146–165.

26. "Over the Draughting Board."

27. Ernest W. Burgess, "The Family as a Unity of Interacting Personalities," *The Family* (March 1926). On the scattering of family life, see also Hayner, "The Hotel," 55, 66, 93, 125.

28. McGlone, "Suffer the Children," 421; Lubove, *The Progressives and the Slums*, 163.

29. For this insight and this phrase, I am indebted to Frederick Hertz.

30. McGlone, "Suffer the Children."

31. Wolfe, *Lodging House Problem*, 154–155, 161, 162.

32. Hayner, *Hotel Life*, 84, 100; Wolfe, *Lodging House Problem*, 126–129, 165. See the sharp contrast with Monroe, *Chicago Families*, 64, 75–77.

33. On population proportions, see Rose, "Living Arrangements of Unattached Persons," 429–430; Ford, *Slums and Housing*, 768; and Wolfe, *Lodging House Problem*, 165. On Chicago visitors, see Hunt, "The Housing of Non-Family Groups of Men," 146, 165; and Abbott, *The Tenements of Chicago*, 358.

34. Zorbaugh, *Gold Coast and Slum*, 82; see also Hayner, *Hotel Life*, 84, and Siegal, *Outposts of the Forgotten*, xviii.

35. Veiller wrote that the "most terrible of all features" of slums was "the indiscriminate herding of all kinds of people in close contact," in Deforest and Veiller, *The Tenement House Problem*, 1:10. Robert A. Woods and A. J. Kennedy wrote that privacy was necessary for "self-respect, modesty, order, and neatness," in *Young Working Girls* (Boston: Houghton Mifflin Co., 1913): 41–42. For the continuation of this idea in the 1930s, see Gries and Ford, eds., *Housing and the Community*, 5–6.

36. On European habits, see Breckinridge and Abbott, "Housing Conditions in Chicago, III: Back of the Yards," 450; on irregular living, see Abbott, *The Tenements of Chicago*, 316–318, 331, 335–337; on inspectors, see SFHACC, *Real Property Survey, 1939*, 1:13.

37. On the lodger evil, see Veiller, *Housing Reform*, 33; Modell and Hareven, "Urbanization and the Malleable Household," 467–479; Abbott, *The Tenements of Chicago*, 343, 345–346. On planners' historical views about invasion of mixed uses, see Mel Scott, *American City Planning since 1890* (Berkeley and Los Angeles: University of California Press, 1969): 74–75, 128.

38. Cohen, "Embellishing a Life of Labor," 762–763. On the family room as the general purpose room in tenement units, see Cromley, "The Development of the New York Apartment."

39. Riis, *How the Other Half Lives*, 1; on the need for internal and external separation, see also Veiller, *Housing Reform*, 109, 110–112.

40. On beehives, E. R. L. Gould (founder of the City and Suburban Homes Company in New York), 1897, quoted in Lubove, *The Progressives and the Slums*, 110; on the open-lot house vs. row house traditions, Vance, *This Scene of Man*, 59–62, 121–128, 152–153; and Paul Groth, "Lot, Yard, and Garden: American Gardens as Adorned Yards," *Landscape* 30, 3 (1990): 29–35.

41. On shared entries and the short cut, Bernard J. Newman, "Shall We Encourage or Discourage the Apartment House" (ca. 1917), quoted in Douglass Shand Tucci, *Built in Boston*, 125–126; on apartment as the polite term for tenement, Minneapolis Civic and Commerce Association, Committee on Housing, *The Housing Problem in Minneapolis* (Minneapolis: The MCCA, ca. 1915): 89; on domestic quality, "An Apartment House Designed in the Colonial Type," *The Architect and Engineer of California* 48 (February 1917): 1.

42. Hayner, *Hotel Life*, 3, 7, 62.

43. Wolfe, *Lodging House Problem*, 85, 145, 169, esp. 171. On unmarried couples, Wolfe, 64–65, 142, and 171 (quotation on 142). On other cities, Zorbaugh, *Gold Coast and Slum*, 73–86; Abbott, *The Tenements of Chicago*, 327; Girls Housing Council, "Where Is Home?" 23.

44. The personal element phrase comes from Wolfe, *Lodging House Problem*, 173; see also, Hayner, *Hotel Life*, 181.

45. Wolfe, *Lodging House Problem*, 180, 182.

46. Girls Housing Council, "Where Is Home?" 3, 25, 35.

47. Wolfe, *Lodging House Problem,* 142, 180–182; see also Abbott, *The Tenements of Chicago,* 327.

48. CIH, *Second Annual Report* (1916): 226.

49. Wolfe, *Lodging House Problem,* 30, 32, 139, 140, 171. About larger hotels see, for instance, Howard B. Woolston, *Prostitution in the United States,* 139–141; Hayner, *Hotel Life,* 37; Havelock Ellis, *The Task of Social Hygiene* (New York: Houghton Mifflin, 1912): chap. 9.

50. Anderson, *The Hobo,* 144–149; see also CSRA, *Transients in California,* 189.

51. These were the greatest concerns of social reformers as published in the San Francisco newspapers of 1917; Central City Hospitality House, "Tenderloin Ethnographic Project," 17–18.

52. Elbert Hubbard, "A Little Journey to Hotel Sherman," quoted without citation in Hayner, "The Hotel," 159.

53. The *Post* is quoted without citation in Hayner, "The Hotel," 34–35. On furnished rooms, see Abbott, *The Tenements of Chicago,* 323, 337; and Hunt, "Housing of Non-Family Groups of Men," 146.

54. Aronovici, *Housing Conditions in the City of Saint Paul,* 58; Abbott, *The Tenements of Chicago,* 337; Wolfe, *Lodging House Problem,* 137; Hayner, *Hotel Life,* 6, 20–21, 168–170. On Arbuckle parties, Siefkin, *The City at the End of the Rainbow,* 118–126, and Williamson, *The American Hotel,* 143.

55. The sinful amusement list compiled by the Howard Street Methodist Church in the South of Market included "dancing, playing at games of chance, attending theaters, horse races, and dancing parties"; Averbach, "San Francisco's South of Market District," 201. On dance halls, Elisabeth I. Perry, "'The General Motherhood of the Commonwealth': Dance Hall Reform in the Progressive Era," *American Quarterly* 37 (1985): 719–733, on 720–721; see also John Dillon, *From Dance Hall to White Slavery: Ten Dance Hall Tragedies* (New York: Wiley Book Co., 1912). A 1940 study reported that 60 percent of all men present in the dance halls were recent migrants to the city, most of whom lived in rooming houses; CSS, *Life in One Room,* 41–42. On cafés, Central City Hospitality House, "Tenderloin Ethnographic Project," 17–18.

56. Caroline Singer, *San Francisco Examiner* (January 25, 1917).

57. Byrnes, "Nurseries of Crime," 355, 360, quoted in Riis, *How the Other Half Lives,* 69–70. See also Devine, "The Shiftless and Floating City Population."

58. Riis, *How the Other Half Lives,* 69; see also Wolfe, *Lodging House Problem,* 137–138.

59. Cynthia Taylor Roberts, "Stopping the Kaleidoscope: Los Angeles as Seen by Reynar Banham and Raymond Chandler" (Berkeley: unpublished manuscript, November 1981); on Los Angeles police, CSRA, *Transients in California,* 82.

60. On hall bedroom loneliness, a resident quoted in Hayden, *The Grand*

Domestic Revolution, 168; on tenements and dance hall walk-bys, Fretz, "The Furnished Room Problem in Philadelphia," 95–108; and Wolfe, *Lodging House Problem,* 31, 106.

61. Zorbaugh, *Gold Coast and Slum,* 67–68; see also 82, 86, 251. On Zorbaugh's fieldwork, interview with Robert A. Slayton, then a historian with the Urban League of Chicago, in Chicago, on May 29, 1977.

62. Zorbaugh, *Gold Coast and Slum,* 78–79; for the girl's entire life story, see 76–81.

63. On suicide rates, see Hayner, *Hotel Life,* 4; Zorbaugh devotes a whole paragraph to rooming house suicide in Zorbaugh, "Dweller in Furnished Rooms," 87; on gas suicide, Ford, *A Few Remarks,* 25–26.

64. Dreiser, *Sister Carrie,* 554. For other examples see Wharton, *The House of Mirth,* and Norris, *Vandover and the Brute,* 312–338.

65. Constance Perin, *Everything in Its Place: Social Order and Land Use in America* (Princeton: Princeton University Press, 1977): 32–34; on real Americans, see Abbott, *The Tenements of Chicago,* 381. See also John Modell, "Patterns of Consumption, Acculturation, and Family Income Strategies in Late Nineteenth Century America," in Tamara Hareven and Maris Vinovskis, eds., *Family and Population in Nineteenth-Century America* (Princeton: Princeton University Press, 1978): 206–240.

Residential stability did, of course, correlate strongly with house ownership, although those who could buy houses were also those who were most skilled and more likely to be self-employed. See Clyde Griffen, "Workers Divided: The Effect of Class and Ethnic Differences in Poughkeepsie, New York, 1850–1880," in Stephen Thernstrom and Richard Sennett, eds., *Nineteenth-Century Cities: Essays in the New Urban History* (New Haven: Yale University Press, 1969): 59; and Stephen Thernstrom, *Poverty and Progress* (New York: Atheneum, 1971): 118.

66. James S. Buckingham, *The Homes of the New World: Impressions of America* (New York: Harper, 1841), 1:453, quoted in McGlone, "Suffer the Children," 417, 421; and Walter Adams, "A Foreigner's Impression of San Francisco," *The Golden Era* 34 (November 1885): 445.

67. Veiller, *Housing Reform,* 6.

68. On California, see Cohn, *California Housing Handbook,* 6; for an example of the migrant argument used against the Chinese in San Francisco, see SFHACC, *Real Property Survey, 1939,* 1:8–9.

69. Henry Wright, *Rehousing Urban America* (New York: Columbia University Press, 1935): 63.

70. See, for instance, S. J. Herman, "Why Do You Live in an Apartment?" (Lansing: Michigan Housing Association Report, January 1931).

71. On responsibility, see H. L. Cargill, "Small Houses for Workingmen," in Deforest and Veiller, *The Tenement House Problem,* 352; on citizenship, see Veiller, *Housing Reform,* 6; on mortgage control, see Hancock, "Apartment House," 152, 157–158, 182–183.

72. Wolfe, *Lodging House Problem*, 106, 173.

73. Abbott, *The Tenements of Chicago*, 335–336; see also 326–328.

74. William T. Stead, *If Christ Should Come to Chicago* (Chicago: Laird & Lee, 1894): 30.

75. SFHA, *Second Report* (1913): 24.

76. On interpretations of medieval and colonial period mistrust of vagrancy, see Anderson, *Men on the Move*, 32–33; and Robert E. Park, "Human Migration and the Marginal Man," *American Journal of Sociology* 18, 6 (May 1928): 881–893. Beginning in the Middle Ages, European inns were considered the favorite rendezvous of radicals, propagators of heresy, and free thinkers; Williamson, *The American Hotel*, 181. On interpretation of hobo subcultures, see Spradley, *You Owe Yourself a Drunk*, 6–7, 67; Wallace, *Skid Row as a Way of Life*, 129–144; Abbott, *The Tenements of Chicago*, 100–101, 322–324.

77. Park, "Marginal Man," 887.

78. Park, "The City," 607–608.

79. Ernest R. Mowrer, *Family Disorganization* (Chicago: University of Chicago Press, 1927): 111, quoted in Monroe, *Chicago Families*, 67–68. On the Gold Coast, see Zorbaugh, *Gold Coast and Slum*, 65–68, 82, 86, 240, 249–251; on rooming houses, ibid., 248–249, 251. On Park's direct influence on his graduate students, see also Hayner, "The Hotel," 54, 176. Wolfe exhibits parallel ideas in *Lodging House Problem*, 100.

80. Hayner, "The Hotel," 54. Hayner's own dissertation committee apparently filtered some of the author's distaste for hotel life. When Hayner published his dissertation as a book, he deleted most of its positive anecdotes as well as most of its logical organization. In both dissertation and book, he gave extended descriptions of unhappy hotel tenants but lightly reported busy, productive, and satisfied people—perhaps because they would not take the time to talk to sociology graduate students.

81. Abbott, *The Tenements of Chicago*, 305, 307, 314, 317, 338.

82. On New York, see Anderson, *The Hobo*, 151; on polite hotels, see Hayner, *Hotel Life*, 3–5, 72, 181.

83. The study of one-third voting is from Anderson, *The Hobo*, 151, 154, based on a 1923 survey of rooming houses and the better (private room type) lodging houses. On the precinct captain, see Zorbaugh, *Gold Coast and Slum*, 82. See also, CIH *Fifth Annual Report* (1919): 34; and UC-HC, *Dependent Aged*, 68.

84. Anderson, *Men on the Move*, 52–57; Averbach, "San Francisco's South of Market District," 201–205. In the 1870s, the outbursts were by the anti-Chinese Workingmen's Party; in 1885, 1891, and 1902, seamen fought both legally and illegally against their working conditions.

85. Anderson, *The Hobo*, 150–153.

86. On the fire (in Venice, Calif.), see CIH, *Eleventh Annual Report* (1925): 19. Other CIH reports: *First Annual Report* (1915): 80; *Second Annual Report*

(1916): 226. Also, SFHA, *Second Report* (1913): 24; and "Most Lodging Houses Are Perilous Firetraps," 1–8.

87. CIH, *First Annual Report* (1915): 11, 78–80.

88. SFHA, *Second Report* (1913): 24. In Sacramento, which served a large number of agricultural laborers, another report revealed the 33 cheapest lodging houses to be even worse, since no earthquake and fire cleared the pre-1900 buildings. Seventeen of them had no bathing facilities whatsoever; in five, cellars were illegally inhabited; CIH, *First Annual Report* (1915): 86.

89. For instance, typical reports about crowded Chinese lodging houses of San Francisco blamed neither poverty nor landlords but cultural habits. See Elmer Clarence Sandmeyer, *The Anti-Chinese Movement in California* (Urbana: University of Illinois Press, 1939): 51; CIH, *Second Annual Report* (1916): 263.

90. In San Francisco, Mayor Phelan's central landholdings are an apt example. Lubove, *The Progressives and the Slums,* 154–155; Weiss, *The Rise of the Community Builders.*

91. Monroe, *Chicago Families,* 84; see also 61–84.

92. Charles G. Swanson, "Social Background of the Lower West Side of New York City" (Ph.D. dissertation at New York University, n.d. [before 1936]).

93. Veiller, *A Model Tenement House Law,* sect. 2 (14–15).

CHAPTER EIGHT: FROM SCATTERED OPINION TO CENTRALIZED POLICY

1. Samuel Hays in the foreword to Lubove, *The Progressives and the Slums,* x–xi. See also, Davis, *Spearheads for Reform,* 3–39.

2. During the years Lubin was at South End House, Wolfe was there finishing his study for *The Lodging House Problem in Boston.* On Lubin and Veiller, letter from Lubin to Veiller, October 21, 1913; Lubin Papers, Bancroft Library, University of California. Wood, "The California State Commission of Immigration and Housing," 1–42; and SFHA, *Second Report* (1913): 7.

3. CIH, *Second Annual Report* (1916): 8; CIH, *Ninth Annual Report* (1923); Wood, "The California State Commission of Immigration and Housing," 86, 97.

4. The major accomplishments of the group were their role in forming the CIH and a vigorous letter campaign demanding code enforcement; see Wood, *The Housing of the Unskilled Wage Earner,* 284; SFHA, *First Report* (1911): 7, 9, 11, 30–40, 45–46; SFHA, *Second Report* (1913): 7–8, 20–21.

5. Lubin-Veiller correspondence dating from May 14, 1913, to July 7, 1915; Lubin papers, Bancroft Library.

6. For instance, CIH Commissioner J. H. McBride, a Pasadena physician who drafted the major CIH publications on housing, cited Veiller extensively.

See esp., CIH, "An A-B-C of Housing" (Sacramento: State Printing Office, 1915).

7. On California real estate, see Weiss, *The Rise of the Community Builders,* and Weiss, "Urban Land Developers and the Origins of Zoning Laws." In the 1920s, the City Planning Section of San Francisco's Commonwealth Club was chaired by James Duval Phelan, a mayor and major downtown landowner; the club-sponsored Regional Plan Association of San Francisco was chaired by Frederick Dohrmann, Jr., the wealthy son of a successful retailer. See Scott, *The San Francisco Bay Area: A Metropolis in Perspective,* 2d ed. (Berkeley, Los Angeles, and London: University of California Press, 1985): 186–201.

For the general case of progressive reform, see Wiebe, *Businessmen and Reform*; Gabriel Kolko, *The Triumph of Conservatism: A Reinterpretation of American History, 1900–1916* (New York: Free Press of Glencoe, 1963); James Weinstein, *The Corporate Ideal in the Liberal State, 1900–1918* (Boston: Beacon Press, 1968).

8. The English garden city planner, Thomas Adams, quoted in CIH, *Second Annual Report* (1916): 198.

9. The exhibit also traveled around the state, while its illustrations served double duty in several CIH pamphlets. On Cheney, see CIH, *First Annual Report* (1915): 97; CIH, *Second Annual Report* (1916): 306; and Wood, "The California State Commission of Immigration and Housing," 225. See also chap. 428, California Statutes of 1915. A classic review of fallacious assumptions of value-free planners is Robert Goodman, *After the Planners* (New York: Simon and Schuster, 1971).

10. The CIH also instituted improvements in rural labor camps and made detailed urban housing surveys aimed at educating the public. Wood, "The California State Commission of Immigration and Housing"; CIH, *First Annual Report* (1915): 74, 80–84, 92; CIH, *Second Annual Report* (1916): 203, 268; CIH, *Ninth Annual Report* (1923): 69–70, 72, 74.

11. Byrnes, "Nurseries of Crime," 362.

12. In 1903, hotel runners (soliciting agents who boarded steamships, ferries, and passenger railroads to attract lodgers) had to be licensed at $10 per quarter; additionally, from 1903 to 1910, public dancing was not allowed between 1:00 and 6:00 A.M. *except* in hotels. San Francisco City Ordinances #826, 939, 1033. On the easing of the dancing restrictions in 1910, see "Lid Lifted from Tenderloin District: Dancing Allowed," *San Francisco Chronicle* (March 22, 1910), and the cartoon run on March 23, 1910, 3.

Note: Between 1856 and 1900, acts of the San Francisco Board of Supervisors were "orders"; from 1900 to 1906, "ordinances"; after the 1906 fire until the 1920s, "ordinances (new series)."

13. On red-light abatement and the municipal clinic, see Shumsky, "Vice Responds to Reform," 31–47, and Barbara Meil Hobson, *Uneasy Virtue: The Politics of Prostitution and the American Reform Tradition* (New York: Basic

Books, 1987): 148–149. On the 1917 moral crusade (and Lubin's quotation), see Central City Hospitality House, "Tenderloin Ethnographic Project," 13, 17–18; Gentry, *The Madams of San Francisco,* 219–225; and Brenda E. Pillors, "The Criminality of Prostitution in the U.S.: The Case of San Francisco, 1854–1919," (Ph.D. dissertation, University of California, Berkeley, 1984).

14. In Chicago, such recommendations came from the Council of Social Agencies. See Anderson, *The Hobo,* 275.

15. Elizabeth Anne Brown, "The Enforcement of Prohibition in San Francisco, California," (M.A. thesis in history, University of California, Berkeley, 1948): 9–11, 40–42, 50–55.

16. Girls Housing Council, "Where Is Home?" 29, 37. New York City eventually had eight major registries for women, although only a small percentage of the city's rooms were represented on the lists; Ford, *Slums and Housing,* 344–345. On registries for both men and women, see also Peel, "On the Margins," 814; Peel uses the term "regulation by inspection."

17. Boston's lodging house required an initial shower and another shower every seven nights; Kennaday, "New York's Hundred Lodging Houses," 490.

18. Veiller, *Housing Reform,* 89. For an early review of code reform, see Wood, *Recent Trends in American Housing,* 114–115. Building codes were so associated with Veiller and the National Housing Association that Wood and others have called them the "Veiller" school of thought.

19. The editor of the Sacramento *Record-Union* (November 16, 1876), quoted in Elmer Clarence Sandmeyer, *The Anti-Chinese Movement in California,* 63; see also 51, 63, 75–76. The state act of 1876 was America's first state lodging house sanitary law; its constitutionality was upheld in 1878.

20. On the use of the cubic air code after 1900, see SFHA, *Second Report* (1913): 24. For tax purposes, the city made no distinction between permanent and transient guests (as it does today) and used an equal gross revenues tax. On minor lighting, exit, and licensing ordinances, see Groth, "Forbidden Housing," 522–535, and San Francisco City Ordinances #102, 138, 303, 602, 913, 1493, 1677, and New Series #3361.

21. William Issel and Robert W. Cherny, *San Francisco, 1865–1932: Politics, Power, and Urban Development* (Berkeley, Los Angeles, and London: University of California Press, 1986); on Schmitz and his ouster in 1907, 139–164. The Board of Health empowerment is in Ordinance #501. In Sections 202 and 204 of the 1908 San Francisco Plumbing Code are rather lenient lodging house plumbing requirements: one water closet for every 25 people of each sex; the water closets did not have to be on the same floor as the tenants' rooms. After 1909, cubicle rooms were allowed only in steel frame or concrete frame buildings and not in buildings with masonry bearing walls with wooden floor joists (Sections 16, 190, and 191 of the 1909 San Francisco Building Laws, New Series Ordinances #1139 and 6286).

22. SFHA, *First Report* (1911): 7, 14. The California legislature was using

a draft of Veiller's *A Model Tenement House Law,* available in a published version in 1910 and intended for densely built cities like Boston and New York. In 1914, Veiller's office published *A Model Housing Law* for smaller or newer cities with more open-lot housing.

23. The clause remained in the California Statutes of 1915, chap. 572, the California State Tenement House Law; the quotation here is the entire text of Section 70, with emphasis added. Compare with Veiller, *Model Tenement House Law,* sect. 94. For other states' use of the Veiller models, see Wood, *Recent Trends in American Housing,* 114–119.

24. The 1913 act is California Statutes of 1913, chap. 395, State Hotel and Lodging House Act. It was neither very specific nor stringent in its requirements; see Groth, "Forbidden Housing," 523–535.

25. The trio of new statutes were California Statutes of 1917, chap. 736 (Hotel and Lodging House Act), 737 (Dwelling House Act), and 738 (Tenement House Act). The commission's boast is in CIH, *Fifth Annual Report* (1919): 35.

26. California Statutes of 1917, chap. 736, sects. 10 and 62, repeated in the 1923 State Housing Act.

27. California Statutes of 1917, chap. 736, sects. 33–36. New York also required one bathtub per 25 beds or one shower per 50 beds; Chicago Department of Public Welfare, "Fifty Cheap Lodging Houses," 70. On rag storage, see California Statutes of 1917, chap. 738, sects. 67 and 77, and chap. 736 (the hotel act), sects. 28 and 65.

28. California Statutes of 1917, chap. 736, sect. 65; see also Statutes of 1923, chap. 386, sect. 65.

29. The inspection forms are microfilmed in the 1920s documents in San Francisco's Department of Apartment and Hotel Inspection (DAHI). On inspections, see Wood, *Recent Trends in American Housing,* 118.

30. CIH, *Fifth Annual Report* (1919): 76. See also CIH, *Eleventh Annual Report* (1925): 18; and CIH, *Thirteenth Annual Report* (1927): 24.

31. The 1920s date is based on the earliest DAHI file, which records the requirement of additional plumbing at various hotels.

32. This example stands at 172–180 Sixth Street and was probably built for skilled workers; the Tenderloin has several other such buildings from the pre-1917 era.

33. Hoch and Slayton, *New Homeless and Old,* 64, 70, 101.

34. Veiller, *Housing Reform,* 30.

35. "Zone Plan for San Francisco," *The Architect and Engineer* 62, 3 (September 1920): 65–73, on 65.

36. On covenants in the elite west side district of St. Francis Woods, see Scott, *American City Planning,* 75; on the prefire mixtures in the Western Addition and downtown, see John P. Young, *San Francisco* (San Francisco: S. J. Clarke Publishing Co., 1912), 2:754; and Judd Kahn, *Imperial San Francisco:*

Politics and Planning in an American City, 1887–1906 (Lincoln: University of Nebraska Press, 1979): 3, 215–216. Zoning as promotion as well as protection is succinctly reviewed in Weiss, "Urban Land Developers and the Origins of Zoning Laws," 8–11.

37. The expert reformer is Frederick C. Howe, "The Municipal Real Estate Policies of German Cities," *Proceedings of the Third National Conference on City Planning* (1911): 15. Paul Scharrenberg, "The Housing Aspect of the City Planning Problem" [Address to the Commonwealth Club of California, San Francisco, June 16, 1917], *The Architect and Engineer* 50, 2 (August 1917): 66–68. Scharrenberg was secretary of the State Federation of Labor and by 1920, also a member of the San Francisco City Planning Commission. For Veiller, see *Protecting Residential Districts*, 11.

38. San Francisco, *Building Zone Ordinance* (Ordinance #5464), 1921 draft and 1927 revision, sect. 4. In the 1921 version, no housing was allowed in industrial zones; in the 1927 revisions, boardinghouses, lodging houses, and hotels were specifically added as allowed uses in industrial areas, indicating the continuing need for them in those areas of San Francisco.

39. From the 1890s through 1915, cleverly designed flats often mixed by developers into elite and middle-class districts of single-family houses; property owners who wished to build purposely designed rooming houses might have taken a similar visual cue.

40. Hamilton, *Promoting New Hotels*, 147.

41. On rooming house districts as zones of women's businesses, see Woods, "Social Betterment in a Lodging District," 967.

42. 195 Cal. 477, 234 P. 381 (1925), app. dismd., 273 U.S. 781 (1927). All quotations from *Miller v. Los Angeles* are from sect. 10.

43. 195 Cal. 477 (*Miller v. Los Angeles*), sect. 10.

44. *State ex rel. Beery v. Houghton*, 164 Minn. 146, 204 N.W. 569 (1925).

45. Jacqueline Tyrwhitt, *High Rise Apartments and Urban Form*, ACE Publications Research Report no. 5 (Athens: Center of Ekistics, 1968): 28.

46. 10 Minn Law R 48 (1925): 53, citing *Miller v. Los Angeles* (1925) and *Zahn v. Los Angeles* (1925).

47. The quotations from the *Euclid v. Ambler* decision are from 272 U.S. 365 (1926); see also 47 S. Ct. 114 and 71 L Ed 303 (1926).

48. Hoover was endorsing the reports of the 1932 conference on housing; Gries and Ford, eds., *Planning for Residential Districts*, xi.

49. Gries and Ford, eds., *Slums, Large-Scale Housing, and Decentralization*, 6; emphasis added. See also Joel Tarr, "From City to Suburb: The 'Moral' Influence of Transportation Technology," in Alexander B. Callow, Jr., ed., *American Urban History*, 2d rev. ed. (New York: Oxford University Press, 1973): 202–212; and Kenneth Jackson, *Crabgrass Frontier: The Suburbanization of the United States* (New York: Oxford University Press, 1985): 45–116.

50. On "making family life possible," Veiller, in Deforest and Veiller, *Tene-*

ment House Problem, 1:3. On "concern for wives and families," see Veiller, *Housing Reform,* 155. On the single lot house, Veiller, *Housing Reform,* 6, 30, where Veiller (revealing his weak understanding of the employment structures that kept people flocking to the cities) hopes that immigrants could continue peasant life in the United States.

51. CIH, "An A-B-C of Housing," 5.

52. Gould, quoted in Lubove, *The Progressives and the Slums,* 110-111. Wood, *Recent Trends in American Housing,* 41. See hotel limits in Veiller, *A Model Tenement House Law,* 54-55, and *Housing Reform,* 6.

53. Veiller, *Housing Reform,* 109-112.

54. The 1912 meeting was the National Conference of Charities and Correction, in Cleveland, which passed a statement on the right to a home. See Wood, *The Housing of the Unskilled Wage Earner,* 10. On New York definitions, see Lubove, *The Progressives and the Slums,* 18, 26; and Veiller, *Model Tenement House Law,* sect. 2.

55. The San Francisco zoning ordinance of 1921, Ordinance #5464, defined an apartment as "a residence for one family doing its own cooking on the premises." In 1957, the American Society of Planning Officials advised its members that the distinguishing factor between an apartment and a rooming house was "the absence of kitchen facilities for each rooming house resident"; ASPO, "Rooming Houses," 6. On the 1950 census, see U.S. Bureau of the Census, *U.S. Census of Housing, 1950,* vol. 1, General Characteristics, pt. 2 (Washington, D.C.: U.S. Government Printing Office, 1953): xvi; this was the first time the census office had used cooking as a definition to distinguish between rooming and apartment houses.

56. On risks, Federal Housing Administration, *Property Standards: Requirements for Mortgage Insurance under Title II of the National Housing Act, June 1, 1936,* Circular no. 2 (Washington, D.C.: U.S. Government Printing Office, 1936): 5.

57. FHA, *Property Standards,* 14-15, 17. On dwelling definition, 14. On the definition of "living unit," see Section 509. For San Francisco, the minimum number of rooms was set as three rooms and a bath; Pt. VI, Northern California District, 5. A later amendment technically included hotels in the definition, but other restrictions were not lifted. See Modernization Credit Plan, *Property Improvement Loans under Title I of the National Housing Act: Amendments of 1938,* Regulations effective February 4, 1938 (Washington, D.C.: Federal Housing Administration, 1938): 3.

58. FHA, *Property Standards,* 4-5. The guidelines did, however, allow up to 25 percent of a private dwelling to have rooming house or tourist house use, essentially allowing from about one to three boarders or roomers with a family; 17.

59. Jackson, *Crabgrass Frontier,* 196-219; *FHA Underwriting Manual* (Washington, D.C., 1939, typescript ed. 1934); Goodman, *After the Planners,*

56–59; Miles Colean, *The Impact of Government on Real Estate Finance in the United States* (New York: National Bureau of Economic Research, 1950). See also FHA, *Property Standards* (1936 ed.): 4–6.

60. The Los Angeles zoning law of 1955, for instance, specifically excluded hotels, boardinghouses, and lodging houses from the category of "dwelling." Concern over the ad hoc rooming house conversions prompted the American Society of Planning Officials to urge other cities to follow suit; ASPO, "Rooming Houses," 3–7, 10.

61. On the increase in tax benefits during the 1940s, see Jackson, *Crabgrass Frontier*, 293.

62. Johann Wolfgang von Goethe, *Opinions.*

63. Rose, "Interest in the Living Arrangements of the Urban Unattached," 486–498. Rose explained the interest before World War I as a function of labor migrations and Progressive Era concerns—municipal lodging houses, housing inspection, urban surveys that included transients and single people, and the proliferation of room registry organizations.

64. Ibid., 490. The peak of interest in Chicago seemed to be in the early 1920s, marked in part by the works of Nels Anderson and Harvey Zorbaugh. Rose attributed the decline of interest to a rise in political conservatism, a general decline in public concern about social problems, and immigration shutdowns that cut back the numbers of immigrant lodgers (and hence, social workers' concerns about their housing).

65. Deforest and Veiller, *Tenement House Problem,* 1:144.

66. Veiller, *Housing Reform,* 28. Investigation issues were also framed by conditions in New York City, where the tenement house department inspected apartments and the police inspected cheap hotels.

67. The exceptions, again, were in Chicago with Anderson's and Zorbaugh's work. A typical example of noninclusion is Wood's *The Housing of the Unskilled Wage Earner,* one of the best books on housing published immediately after World War I; it did not mention single people's housing at all.

68. Abbott, *The Tenements of Chicago,* 350. She expresses the same sentiment on 145 and 323.

69. The thesis was Wilson, "Chicago Families in Unfurnished Rooms," 25–50. Sampling based mostly on pathology also skews CSS, "Life in One Room."

70. Quoted in Hayner, "The Hotel," 69–70. Hayner also quotes a letter from the director of the Bureau of the Census stating that through 1920 no hotel study had been done.

71. U.S. Census definitions and categories for housing change from decade to decade. In 1890, the census made clear that a dwelling was anything from a "wigwam on the outskirts of a settlement, a hotel, a boarding house, a large tenement house," or a single-family house. From 1900 through 1920, dwellings were "where one or more persons regularly sleep," with no cooking requirement. The enumerators were to distinguish between "private families" and "economic families." In 1930, reflecting the mood of the previous decade,

the census shifted strongly and defined dwellings as only those places occupied by private families of one or more people. A "quasi-family" category was begun. Later census reports called the dwellings of quasi-families "group quarters." Changes associated with the first Census of Housing, in 1940, are reported in the text.

In 1950, "separation"—separate cooking equipment or a separate entrance—became a key criterion for identifying a dwelling unit. Furthermore, the minimum size of a lodging house went from more than 10 lodgers to 5 lodgers or more. In 1960, the new term "housing unit" replaced "dwelling unit," with the following definition:

A "housing unit" was "a house, an apartment or other groups of rooms, or a single room . . . occupied or intended for occupancy as separate living quarters, that is, when the occupants do not live and eat with any other persons in the structure and there is either (1) direct access from the outside or through a common hall, or (2) a kitchen or cooking equipment for the exclusive use of the occupants. (U.S. Bureau of the Census, *U.S. Census of Housing 1960, Metropolitan Housing Part I* [1963]: xvi.)

In hotels and rooming houses, a single room qualified as a housing unit "if occupied by a person whose usual residence is the hotel." In that same year, "group quarters" were defined as occupied quarters that do not qualify as housing units (usually institutions)—"nurses' homes, hospitals, rooming and boarding houses, military barracks, college dormitories, fraternity and sorority houses, convents, and monasteries."

The 1970 guidelines were essentially the same as those of 1960. In 1980, the staff split the "group quarters" category into two: (1) institutional group quarters are those that indicate custody or care, such as prisons or rest homes; and (2) noninstitutional group quarters, including boardinghouses and dormitories.

72. U.S. Bureau of the Census, *Fifteenth Census of the U.S., Census of Hotels, 1930* (Washington, D.C.: U.S. Government Printing Office, 1931).

73. John M. Gries and James Ford, gen. eds., *Publications of the President's Conference on Home Building and Home Ownership,* 11 vols. (Washington, D.C.: National Capitol Press, 1932). Single male lodgers living with families are mentioned in vol. 8, *Housing and the Community: Home Repair and Remodeling,* 158, 173.

74. In 1936, James Ford warned that the published data on single people were "surprisingly meagre"; Ford, *Slums and Housing,* 1:337, 344, 346, 349. For instance, in 1932, Edith Elmer Wood's article, "Housing in the U.S.," in the *Encyclopedia of the Social Sciences* contained no mention of single-room housing; she described the family houses built by the federal government during World War I but ignored the hotels and dormitory sections of those same projects.

75. On the 1933 SFHA survey, see Carl F. Gromme, "A Case Picture of Housing in a Slumless City," *Architect and Engineer of California* 117, 3 (June

1934): 35–38. In 1934, under the PWA's Civil Works Administration, surveyors conducted a 50-block survey in San Francisco. In 1936, California's State Emergency Relief Administration (SERA) surveyed half the city's living quarters; they included apartments and hotels, using the state's definition of hotels. The San Francisco Municipal Housing Survey, also of 1936 and a WPA project, used separate forms for "structures" (multifamily units and hotels) and "dwelling units" but carefully reported hotel conditions for each census district surveyed.

76. The beginning of the systematic excision can be seen in the office's in-house lists of buildings and conditions, where the staff did not give hotels building numbers as they did apartments. See, for instance, the "A" forms (or block lists) for Census Tract J-10, Block 757, in the survey manuscripts at the Bancroft Library, University of California. The seven pages about hotels are in SFHACC, *Real Property Survey, 1939*, 1:3, 26–27, 249–253.

77. The buried proportion is in Tables C and D under "Project Operations," 288–289, vol. 1. The one-third figure can be found by comparing data within the tables: precisely 32.5 percent of the substandard dwellings units and 31.9 percent of ill-housed people were in hotels. The survey's definition of a hotel excluded rooming houses, so the number of legally defined hotels would have been higher. Quotation on 1:27.

78. The bureau's instructions to census takers directed them to count only whole hotels or wings of hotels that were residential. They were not to include "cheap one-night lodging houses." Reports of one-room units were conflated with efficiency apartments and simple cabins or tents. In San Francisco, the remaining hotel units reported hardly equaled the figures for Chinatown alone. Compared to the notes for the 1900 and 1910 population censuses, these 1940 instructions seem to have been written by people much less familiar with American cities or hotel occupancy.

79. SFHACC, *Second Report* (1940): 8.

80. San Francisco City Planning Commission, *The Master Plan of San Francisco* (1945): 18. The areas in question were Chinatown, the Western Addition, and the South of Market.

81. See William Wheaton, Grace Milgram, and Margy Ellin Meyerson, *Urban Housing* (New York: Free Press, 1966); Rose's article is reprinted on 217–222.

82. Rose, "Interest in the Living Arrangements of the Urban Unattached," 493.

83. Wolfe, *Lodging House Problem,* 182. On correspondence, Wood, "The California State Commission of Immigration and Housing," 247.

CHAPTER NINE: PROHIBITION VERSUS PLURALISM

1. Of San Francisco's hotels standing in 1980, none in any rank with residential use was built after 1930; Scott Dowdee, "Final Run of San Francisco

Data," unpublished printouts used in Dowdee, "The Incidence of Change in the Residential Hotel Stock of San Francisco."

2. Gromme, "Case Picture of Housing in a Slumless City," 37–38. On 1939 data, see SFHACC, *Second Report*, 8.

3. "Ups and Downs of the Hotel Business for the Past 21 Years," *Hotel World Review: 75th Anniversary Edition* (New York: Ahrens Publishing Company, 1950): 38; Boomer, *Hotel Management*; McKowne, "Hotels in Wartime," 26. McKowne was the president of the Hotels Statler Company, the first company to build large new wartime hotels with an overt emphasis on convention and military trade.

4. CSS, "Life in One Room," 9; "Conversion of Dwellings for War Housing," *American City* (March 1942): 39; National Housing Agency, "Increase Housing Accommodations and Property Values to Serve War Workers" (Washington, D.C.: NHA pamphlet, 1942); Jane Marx, wartime rooming house resident on Russian Hill, interviewed in New York City, October 22, 1988.

5. Howard B. Myers, "Defense Migration and Labor Supply," *Journal of the American Statistical Association* 37, 217 (1942): 69–76. On young men, see Mary Skinner and Alice Scott Nutt, "Adolescents Away from Home," *Annals of the American Academy of Political and Social Science* 236 (November 1944): 51–59, quotation on 56. On racial districts, see Arnold Hirsh, *Making the Second Ghetto: Race and Housing in Chicago, 1940–1960* (New York: Cambridge University Press, 1983).

6. Cohn, "Architecture of Convention Hotels," 1–10. On rent controls, see Siefkin, *The City at the End of the Rainbow*. For an industry summary on conventions in hotels, see Donald E. Lundberg, *The Hotel and Restaurant Business* (Chicago: Institutions and Volume Feeding Magazine, 1970): 53ff.; on problems of conventions in older hotels, see "The Statler Idea in Hotel Planning and Equipment," *Architectural Forum* 27 (November 1917): 115.

7. *The Day the Earth Stood Still*, Julian Blaustein, producer (Twentieth Century Fox). Meyerowitz, "Holding Their Own," 192. On reduced ethnic matching, see Mostoller, "A Single Room," 191–216, and ASPO, "Rooming Houses," 1–5.

8. Maurice Groat, *Studies in the Economy of Downtown San Francisco* (San Francisco: Department of City Planning, 1963): 58–63; Paul F. Wendt, *The Dynamics of Central City Land Values: San Francisco and Oakland, 1950–1960* (UC Berkeley: Institute of Business and Economic Research, 1961): 24. On the 1970s, see Hartman, *The Transformation of San Francisco,* 2–3.

9. In the random sample of San Francisco hotel ownership, two generations of ownership was the usual maximum span of interest after 1940. The pattern of Tiburon inheritors selling South of Market property between 1942 and 1953 was notable (Tiburon is an elite suburb).

10. Cliff Ellis, "Visions of Urban Freeways, 1930–1970" (Ph.D. dissertation, City and Regional Planning, UC Berkeley, 1990). On poor housing conditions near the bridge, see SFHACC, *Real Property Survey, 1939,* 1:15. In the

census tract between Harrison and Berry streets, 55 percent of the buildings were listed in poor condition.

11. The Chicago study is Hayner, "The Hotel." The Hotel Eddy stood at 1430 Eddy Street, near Webster, in the Western Addition.

12. In many cities a legal loophole allowed rooming houses without parking until cities rewrote their zoning laws; ASPO, "Rooming Houses," 12.

13. On referral, Gazzolo, "Skid Row Gives Renewalists Rough, Tough, Relocation Problems," 327–336; Shapiro, *Community of the Alone,* 150.

14. Gazzolo, "Skid Row Gives Renewalists Rough, Tough, Relocation Problems."

15. William Graebner, *A History of Retirement: The Meaning and Function of an American Institution* (New Haven: Yale University Press, 1980): 215–234; Michael Barker, "California Retirement Communities" (Master's thesis, City Planning, UC Berkeley, 1965): 16, 135.

16. On California, Wolch and Gabriel, "Development and Decline of Service-Dependent Ghettos." The hotel owner is Harold Weingarten, interviewed in New York City on March 17, 1986. The actual date of influx depends on the state; in California, the key years were 1969 to 1974. See also Julian Wolpert and Eileen Wolpert, "The Relocation of Released Mental Hospital Patients into Residential Communities," *Policy Sciences* 7 (1976): 31–51.

17. Blackburn, "Single Room Occupancy in New York City," 2.1–2.2. On human residue, see Siegal, *Outposts of the Forgotten,* 192. Erickson and Eckert, "The Elderly Poor in Downtown San Diego Hotels," compares three different economic strata of the SRO market and the sometimes uneasy relations between them.

18. SFHACC, *Second Report* (1940): 12, 15–17; SFHACC, *Third Report* (1941): 9. In 1938, 73 percent of the clearance quota were demolished units; in 1940–41, 45 percent of the units were demolished.

19. Gries and Ford, *Slums, Large-Scale Housing, and Decentralization,* 1–2, 41; on cheap hotels as the prime example of blight, see 18. The wording of the distinction here comes from John Ihlder, "Rehabilitation of Blighted Areas: The Part of City Planning," *City Planning* 6 (April 1930): 106–118, on 106. While the National Housing Act of 1936 merged the terms "blight" and "slum," the FHA administrators distinguished them. See also U.S. Congress, 75th (1938) Public #412, chap. 896, 1st sess., S. 1685, sect. 2; and U.S. Congress, 75th (1938), Public #424, chap. 13, 3d sess., H.R. 8730.

20. San Francisco City Planning Commission, *The Master Plan of San Francisco,* 10. The same volume gives a long synopsis of the state's definition of blight. See also Philip V. I. Darling, "Some Notes on Blighted Areas," *Planners' Journal* 9, 1 (1943): 9–18.

21. On earlier concerns, Lawson Purdy, *The Districting of Cities,* Publication 38 (New York: National Housing Association, June 1917): 7–8; on San Francisco, see SFHACC, *Third Report* (1941): 7–8; on the Western Addition

compared with the outlying Marina district, see Scott, "Western Addition Re-development Study," 5, 7, 10; on dilapidation, see San Francisco Office of the Mayor, *Municipal Housing Survey of San Francisco* (Sacramento: State Emergency Relief Administration, 1935): 19, for Tract 1. A summary of standards of the period is Allan A. Twitchell, "A Yardstick of Housing Needs," *American City Magazine* (June 1945).

22. Scott, "Western Addition Redevelopment Study," 8.

23. On World War II dormitories in California, see Sally Carrighar, "Dormitories in Transition," *Architect and Engineer* 152, 2 (February 1943): 15–25. Under Title IV of the Housing Act of 1950, HHFA provided low-interest loans for student dormitories at colleges with G.I. bill impacts.

24. Revisions of 1937 to the National Housing Act set the structure for local authorities; see SFHACC, *Second Report* (1940): 12, 15–17; and "San Francisco Builds Low Rent Homes," *Architect and Engineer* 150, 1 (July 1942): 19–31.

25. This process in San Francisco is reviewed in San Francisco City Planning Commission, *The Master Plan of San Francisco*, 1–5.

26. The 1947 report is Scott, "Western Addition Redevelopment Study," 5–10, 25–28, 42–45. On "Negro removal," see Donald Canter, "How Negro Removal Became Black Renewal," *City* (October–November 1970): 55–59. For interpreting the professional dynamics of San Francisco planning in this period, I have relied on Greg Hise's interviews with Jack Kent (March 4, 1987) and James Redman McCarthy (March 11, 1987).

27. The activity of the agency was revived with the appointment of Justin Herman as director; Hartman, *Transformation of San Francisco*, 15–24.

28. On unit mix in the A-1 area, see "San Francisco Redevelopment Program: Summary of Project Data and Key Elements" (SFRA, January 1971): 18–19. On the waiting list and nonmention of hotels, San Francisco Inter-Agency Committee on Urban Renewal, "A Report on Housing in San Francisco" (San Francisco: The Committee, May 1967): 17. The thorough SFRACC study is E. M. Shaffran, "Relocation Survey Report: Western Addition A-2, Yerba Buena, and Hunters Point" (SFRA, 1967): VII-3.

29. FORD, *Slums and Housing*, 2:766–770. Ford felt the deficiencies in regard to single-room occupancy were "due primarily to the deflection of public interest and opinion from this problem to that of slum demolition and rehabilitation"; ibid., 1:337, 344–349.

30. Bauer and McEntire, "Relocation Study, Single Male Population, Sacramento's West End," 11–12, 14–15. A 1953 cover letter by Joseph T. Bill, executive director of the redevelopment agency, indicates agency support for the scheme. See also, *Journal of Housing* (October 1959): 324, and Bancroft Library, Catherine Bauer Wurster papers, Carton 6; McEntire, "Population and Employment Survey of Sacramento's West End."

31. "Tissue" and "scalpel" are from a 1960 issue of *Architectural Forum;*

"clearing" is Scott, "Western Addition Redevelopment Study," 3; "attractive new city," San Francisco City Planning Commission, *The Master Plan of San Francisco,* 7-a. On Norfolk, see Gazzolo, "Skid Row Gives Renewalists Rough, Tough Relocation Problems," 331, who quotes Lawrence M. Cox, executive director of the Norfolk Redevelopment Authority.

32. On San Diego, Mike Stepner, San Diego Planning Department, at the CGOPR conference. On invisibility, see Groth, "Non People."

33. Gazzolo, "Skid Row Gives Renewalists Rough, Tough Relocation Problems," 327, 334.

34. On area residents in the 1960s, see Schaffran, "Relocation Survey Report: South of Market Redevelopment Project," table 4; and Hartman, *Yerba Buena,* 92–98. On not keeping records, see San Francisco Department of City Planning, *Changes in the San Francisco Housing Inventory 1960–1966* (San Francisco, 1967): 11. On genuine SFRACC attempts, Peter Theodore interview (August 25, 1981).

35. For losses on New York's Upper West Side, see Shapiro, *Communities of the Alone.*

36. Samples of the pioneering literature are Elaine Frieden, "Social Differences and Their Consequences for Housing the Aged," *Journal of the American Institute of Planners* 26, 2 (1960): 119–124 (based on Boston surveys begun in 1957); Shapiro, "Single Room Occupancy: Community of the Alone," 24–33, and *Communities of the Alone* (1971); Carroll Kowal, "The case for Congregate Housing," mimeographed paper for the Office of Problem Housing, New York City Housing and Development Administration, 1971; Nathaniel Lichfield, "Relocation: The Impact on Housing Welfare," *Journal of the American Institute of Planners* 27, 3 (1961): 199–203; Chester W. Hartman, "The Limitations of Public Housing: Relocation Choices in a Working Class Community," *Journal of the American Institute of Planners* 24, 4 (1963): 283–296; Emanuel Gorland, "Relocation Inequities and Problems Emergent as a Result of the 1970 Uniform Relocation Act," *Journal of Housing* 3 (1972): 137–138.

37. Jane Jacobs, *The Death and Life of Great American Cities* (New York: Random House, 1961); Herbert Gans, *The Urban Villagers* (New York: Free Press of Glencoe, 1962); Martin Anderson, *The Federal Bulldozer: A Critical Analysis of Urban Renewal, 1949–1962* (Cambridge: MIT Press, 1964). Other classics among the renewal critiques are Raymond Vernon, *The Myth and Reality of our Urban Problems* (Cambridge: Harvard University Press, 1962); Scott Greer, *Urban Renewal and American Cities* (Indianapolis: Bobbs-Merrill Co., 1965); and John F. Bauman, *Public Housing, Race, and Renewal: Urban Planning in Philadelphia* (Philadelphia: Temple University Press, 1987).

38. A concise review of early debates between HUD and NAHRO is Byron Fielding, "Low Income, Single-Person Housing."

39. U.S., 91st Congress, PL 91-646, Approved January 2, 1971, "Uniform Relocation Assistance and Real Property Acquisition Policies Act of 1970," bill no. S1 (84 U.S. Stat. 1894), sects. 202, 204.

40. Hartman, *The Transformation of San Francisco,* 53–133, 205–209. TODCO was a successor organization to the original group, TOOR, Tenants and Owners in Opposition to Redevelopment.

41. Paul, *Rehabilitating Residential Hotels,* 15–16.

42. On 1970s losses, see J. Alter et al., "Homeless in America," in J. Erickson and C. Wilhelm, eds., *Housing the Homeless* (New Brunswick, N.J.: Center for Urban Policy Research, 1986): 3–16.

43. Eckert, *Unseen Elderly,* 58–59; Judith Spektor at the CGOPR conference; Hartman, *Development: How to Fight It.*

44. The examples of landlord abuse were collected at the CGOPR conference in 1981; from a meeting of Berkeley, California, hotel activists in 1983; Judith Spektor's interview of May 8, 1984; and Hartman, *Yerba Buena,* 105.

45. Trillin, "Some Thoughts on the International Hotel Controversy," 116–120; Grannan, "International Hotel"; Don Asher, "The hungry i," *San Francisco Examiner Image Magazine* (May 31, 1991): 12–23, 33.

46. U.S. Senate, *Single Room Occupancy: A Need for National Concern,* iii–iv.

47. See Coalition for the Homeless, *Crowded Out: Homelessness and the Elderly Poor in New York City* (New York: Coalition for the Homeless and the Gray Panthers of New York City, 1984); Peter Marcuse, "The Rise of Tenant Organization," in John Pynos, Robert Schaar, and Chester Hartman, eds., *Housing Urban America* (Chicago: Aldine, 1973).

48. William Fulton, "A Room of One's Own," *Planning* 51, 9 (1985): 18–22.

49. Dolbeare interview, March 11, 1987; Paul, *Rehabilitating Residential Hotels,* 5–9.

50. Franck, "Overview of Single Room Occupancy Housing," 252–253; Patricia King, "Help for the Homeless," *Newsweek* (April 11, 1988): 58–59.

51. On repair investments, Andy Raubeson, speaking at the CGOPR conference, and Judith Spektor interview (May 8, 1984); on inflation, Werner and Bryson, "A Guide to Preservation and Maintenance," pt. 1, 1003–1004.

52. "Problem hotel" is a pseudonym for "welfare hotels" with heavy public assistance. Siegal, *Outposts of the Forgotten,* 17, uses the term "open" hotels for those with no lobby surveillance; the term "street hotel" is used by West Coast hotel activists.

53. The street hotel description stems most from Siegal, *Outposts of the Forgotten;* Ehrlich, "St. Louis Downtown SRO Elderly," 8–11; Dorothy Place (Sacramento), Jan Tucker (Denver), Robert Ridgeway (Portland, Ore.), all at the CGOPR Conference; U.S. Senate, *Single Room Occupancy,* 43–46; Jim

Baumohl, interview on February 12, 1981, and from the hotel owners and residents' forum convened by Florence McDonald in Berkeley on February 26, 1981.

54. A long and excellent review of conditions in California is Pinsky, "Motel People." Courtland Milloy, "At a Seedy Motel in Memphis, A Dream Goes Unrealized," *Washington Post* (January 21, 1986): 1. On Westchester, see Kessler, "Down and Out in Suburbia," 306–313.

55. Cushing Dolbeare interview, March 11, 1987.

56. HUD's Madeline Hastings, quoted in Fulton, "A Room of One's Own," 19.

57. On FEMA, see Larry Maatz, "Quake Housing Money to Flow," *San Francisco Examiner* (February 24, 1990); Seth Rosenfeld, "Bay Area Wins More Quake Aid from U.S.," *San Francisco Examiner* (December 7, 1990).

58. Livingston, of San Francisco's Reality House West (the Cadillac Hotel), at CGOPR.

59. Judith Spektor interview, March 9, 1984.

60. On the positive potential of management roles, see the account of Cadillac Hotel manager Sarah Kearny in Amy Linn, "Tenderloin Mercies," California Living Magazine section, *San Francisco Sunday Examiner and Chronicle* (March 25, 1984): 11–15; on profitability, see Siegal, *Outposts of the Forgotten*, 70.

61. Paul, *Rehabilitating Residential Hotels*, 30.

62. Judith Spektor interview, March 9, 1984.

63. On Los Angeles, see Dave McCombs, "Two More SROs for Skid Row," *Los Angeles Downtown News* (January 1, 1990): 6. On San Francisco, see Andrew Ross, "Agnos Plans Six Hotels for Homeless," *San Francisco Examiner* (April 12, 1990). Gerald D. Adams, "S.F. Hotel to Convert to Homeless Housing," *San Francisco Examiner* (April 19, 1991): A-7. On Berkeley, see McCloud, "First in 40 Years." Howard Husock, "Boston, San Diego Show the Way," *New York Times* (January 21, 1989).

64. McCloud, "First in 40 Years," 29.

65. Davis Bushnell, "Too Soon for an Epitaph," *Boston Globe* (August 2, 1986): 37. Advertisement for El Cerrito Royale in El Cerrito, California, *San Francisco Examiner* (July 15, 1990). Frank James, "Elevating the High-Rise Life," *Chicago Tribune* (April 24, 1991): Sect. 5, 1, 5.

66. Kevin Sessums, "Wild about Perry," *Vanity Fair* (July 1992): 149–152; the producer of "Beverly Hills 90210" is Aaron Spelling.

67. A useful summary of both hotel and nonhotel experiments is Franck and Ahrentzen, *New Households, New Housing*.

68. Peter Drier, "American Housing Policy: Past, Present, and Future," Catherine Bauer Lecture (panel discussion), College of Environmental Design, University of California, Berkeley, April 21, 1993.

69. Jean T. Barrette, "Investing in Skid Row: An Interview with Alice Cal-

laghan," *Hemisphere* (November 1992): 19–20. *Hemisphere* is the in-flight magazine of United Airlines.

70. Peter Salons, "American Housing Policy: Past, Present, and Future," Catherine Bauer Lecture (panel discussion), College of Environmental Design, University of California, Berkeley, April 21, 1993.

71. Burki, "Housing the Low-Income Urban Elderly," 286; Marcuse, "Housing in Early City Planning," 153–177; Robert Goodman, "Excess Baggage: Professionalism and Alienation," in Goodman, *After the Planners* (New York: Simon and Schuster, 1971): 114–142.

72. Robert Venturi and Denise Scott Brown, "A Significance of A&P Parking Lots or Learning from Las Vegas," *Architectural Forum* (March 1968).

73. The HUD official is quoted in Stephens, *Loners, Losers, and Lovers,* 25.

INTERVIEWS

(All interviews are with the author unless otherwise noted.)

Jim Baumohl, Ph.D. candidate in Social Welfare, University of California, Berkeley, February 12 and March 15, 1981

Gray Brechin, architectural historian, San Francisco, January 12, 1982

Ramona Davies, former public health nurse, San Francisco, July 12, 1981

Cushing Dolbeare, Director, National Low Income Housing Coalition, interviewed in Berkeley, March 11, 1987

Jim Green, Director, Downtown Eastside Residents Association, Vancouver, British Columbia, March 25, 1992

Daniel Gregory, architectural historian, San Francisco, September 20, 1988

Richard Jewell, M.D., Psychiatric Director of the Tenderloin Clinic, San Francisco, November 14, 1980

Jack Kent, San Francisco Director of Planning, 1946–1948, interview with Greg Hise in Berkeley, March 4, 1987

Carroll Kowal, telephone interview in New York, May 7, 1984

Richard Livingston, Reality House West (Cadillac Hotel), San Francisco, July 13, 1979

James Redman McCarthy, San Francisco Director of Planning 1958–1966, telephone interview with Greg Hise in Sausalito, March 11, 1987

Steve Norman, Office of Housing Preservation and Development, New York City, March 19, 1986

Bradford Paul, North of Market Planning Coalition, San Francisco, February 26, 1981

Richard Penner, Cornell School of Hotel Administration, July 18, 1982

Hart Smith, San Francisco, January 27, 1988

Judith Spektor, Director, Mayor's Office for SRO Housing, New York City, interviews in San Francisco (June 11, 1981) and in New York (May 8, 1984)

Peter Theodore, Community Services Supervisor, San Francisco Redevelopment Agency, August 25, 1981

Robert Trobe, Deputy Commissioner for Housing Preservation and Development, New York City, December 12, 1985

Harold Weingarten, Director, Metropolitan Hotel Industry Stabilization Association, New York City, March 17, 1986

BOOKS AND ARTICLES

Abbott, Edith. *The Tenements of Chicago, 1908–1935.* Chicago: University of Chicago Press, 1936.

Allsop, Kenneth. *Hard Travellin': The Hobo and His History.* New York: New American Library, 1967.

Alpern, Andrew. *Apartments for the Affluent: A Historical Survey of Buildings in New York.* New York: McGraw-Hill, 1975.

American Society of Planning Officials. *Rooming Houses.* Planning Advisory Service Information Report No. 105. Chicago: ASPO, 1957.

Amory, Cleveland. *The Last Resorts: A Portrait of American Society at Play.* New York: Harper & Brothers, 1948.

Anderson, Nels. "Lodging Houses." In Edwin R. A. Seligman, ed., *Encyclopedia of the Social Sciences.* Vol. 5. New York: The Macmillan Co., 1937. Pp. 595–598.

———. *Men on the Move.* Chicago: University of Chicago Press, 1938.

———. *The Hobo: The Sociology of the Homeless Man.* Chicago: University of Chicago Press, Phoenix edition with autobiographical introduction by Anderson, 1961; first published in 1923.

Anderson, Peter. "Checking into an American Institution." *Boston Globe Magazine,* 4 August 1985.

Architectural Forum, Apartment Hotel Reference Number 41, 5 (November 1924).

Aronovici, Carol. *Housing Conditions in the City of Saint Paul.* Report to the Housing Commission of the St. Paul Association. St. Paul: Amherst H. Wilder Charity, 1917.

Averbach, Alvin. "San Francisco's South of Market District, 1850–1950: The Emergence of a Skid Row." *California Historical Society Quarterly* 52 (September 1973): 197–218.

Bacon, Albion Fellows. *Housing—Its Relation to Social Work.* National Housing Association Publication No. 48. NHA, ca. 1919.

Bahr, Howard M. *Skid Row.* New York: Oxford University Press, 1973.

Barrows, Robert G. "Beyond the Tenement: Patterns of American Urban Housing." *Journal of Urban History* 9 (1983): 395–420.

Barth, Gunther. *City People: The Rise of Modern City Culture in Nineteenth-Century America.* New York: Oxford University Press, 1980.

Bauer, Catherine, and Davis McEntire. *Relocation Study, Single Male Population, Sacramento's West End: Report Number 5.* Sacramento: Redevelopment Agency of the City of Sacramento, 1953.

Baxter, Ellen, and Kim Hooper. *Private Lives, Public Spaces: Homeless Adults on the Streets of New York.* New York: Community Service Society, 1981.

Beacon, David. "Home Is Where the Hotel Is: Personal Spaces," *Washington Home Magazine, Washington Post,* 1 September 1983. Pp. 16–19.

Beard, Miriam. "New York Squeezes into the 'Domestic Unit.'" *New York Times Magazine,* 7 November 1926. P. 4.

Beard, Rick, ed. *On Being Homeless: Historical Perspectives.* New York: Museum of the City of New York, 1987.

Benslyn, William. "Recent Developments in Apartment Housing in America." *Journal of the Royal Institute of British Architects,* vol. 32 (3d ser.) in two parts: 27 June 1925 and 18 July 1925. Pp. 504–519; 540–551.

Bernstein, Rachel A. "Boarding-House Keepers and Brothel Keepers in New York City, 1880–1910." Ph.D. dissertation, Rutgers University, 1984.

Blackburn, Anthony J. "Single Room Occupancy in New York City." Report prepared for the City of New York, Department of Housing Preservation and Development, January 1986.

Blackmar, Betsy. "Going to the Mountains: A Social History." In Alf Evers et al., *Resorts of the Catskills.* New York: St. Martin's Press, 1979. Pp. 71–98.

Bogue, Donald. *Skid Row in American Cities.* Chicago: Community and Family Study Center, University of Chicago, 1963.

Boomer, Lucius M. *Hotel Management: Principles and Practice.* 2d ed. New York: Harper & Brothers, 1931.

Boorstin, Daniel. "Palaces of the Public." In Daniel Boorstin, *The Americans: The National Experience.* New York: Random House, 1965. Pp. 134–147.

Borchert, James. *Alley Life in Washington: Family, Community, Religion, and Folklife in the City.* Urbana: University of Illinois Press, 1980.

Bowden, Martyn J. "The Dynamics of City Growth: An Historical Geography of the San Francisco Central District, 1850–1931." Ph.D. dissertation in geography, University of California, Berkeley, 1967.

Box-Car Bertha, as told to Benjamin L. Reitman. *Sister of the Road: The Autobiography of Box-Car Bertha.* New York: Macauley, 1937.

Breckinridge, Sophonisba P., and Edith Abbott. "Chicago's Housing Problem: Families in Furnished Rooms." *American Journal of Sociology* 16 (November 1910): 289–308.

———. "Housing Conditions in Chicago, III: Back of the Yards." *American Journal of Sociology* 16 (1911): 433–468.

Burki, Mary Ann. "Housing the Low-Income Urban Elderly: A Role for the Single Room Occupancy Hotel." Ph.D. dissertation in urban affairs, Portland State University, 1982.

———. "A Look at SRO Hotel Residents with Recommendations for Management and Design." In Karen A. Franck and Sherry Ahrentzen, eds., *New Households, New Housing*. Pp. 285–307.

Burnett, John. "Lodging Houses." In John Burnett, *A Social History of Housing*, 2d ed. London: Methuen, 1986. Pp. 61–64.

Butler, Thomas. "The Physiology of New York Boarding Houses." New York, 1857.

Byrnes, Thomas. "Nurseries of Crime." *North American Review* 149 (1889): 355–362.

Calhoun, Arthur W. *A Social History of the Family from Colonial Times to the Present*. 3 vols. Cleveland: Arthur H. Clark Co., 1919.

California State Legislature. *State Tenement House Act and State Hotel and Lodging House Act of California*. Sacramento: State Printing Office, 1917.

California State Relief Administration. *Transients in California*. Sacramento: State Printing Office, 1936.

Candee, Richard M. *Atlantic Heights: A World War I Shipbuilder's Community*. Portsmouth, Me.: Portsmouth Marine Society, 1985.

Carroll, Jane. "Home, Home on the Hill." *California Living Magazine, San Francisco Sunday Examiner and Chronicle*, 20 August 1983. Pp. 14, 16–17.

Cash, Robert Carroll. *Modern Type of Apartment Hotels Throughout the United States*. Chicago: Robert Carroll Cash, 1917.

Central City Hospitality House. "Final Report of the Tenderloin Ethnographic Research Project," ed. Ron Silliman. San Francisco: Hospitality House, 1978.

Chandler, Margaret. "The Social Organization of Workers in a Rooming House Area." Ph.D. dissertation, Committee on Human Development, University of Chicago, 1948.

Chicago Department of Public Welfare. "Fifty Cheap Lodging Houses." In *First Semi-Annual Report of the Department of Public Welfare of Chicago* (March 1915). Pp. 66–73.

Clemens, Samuel [Mark Twain]. "Those Blasted Children," 1864. Reprinted in Franklin Walker, ed., *The Washoe Giant in San Francisco*. San Francisco: George Fields, 1938. Pp. 18–23.

———. "'The Lick House Ball' and Other Fashion Reviews." In Franklin Walker, ed., *The Washoe Giant in San Francisco*. San Francisco: George Fields, 1938. Pp. 32–44.

Coalition for the Homeless. *Crowded Out: Homelessness and the Elderly Poor in New York City*. New York: Coalition for the Homeless and the Gray Panthers of New York City, 1984.

Cohen, Lillian. "Los Angeles Rooming-House Kaleidoscope." *American Sociological Review* 16, 3 (1951): 316–326.

Cohen, Lizabeth A. "Embellishing a Life of Labor: An Interpretation of the Material Culture of American Working-Class Homes, 1885–1915." *Journal of Material Culture* 3 (1980): 752–775.

Cohn, Amy Elizabeth. "The Architecture of Convention Hotels in the United States, 1940–1976." Ph.D. dissertation in fine arts, Boston University, 1976.

Cohn, Mark C., ed., *California Housing Handbook*. San Francisco: Pacific Coast Building Officials Conference, 1923.

Community Service Society of New York. "Life in One Room: A Study of the Rooming House Problem in the Borough of Manhattan." New York: CSS mimeographed report, 1940.

Condit, Carl W. "Hotels and Apartments." In Carl W. Condit, *The Chicago School of Architecture: A History of Commercial and Public Building in the Chicago Area, 1875–1925*. Chicago: University of Chicago Press, 1964. Pp. 148–159.

———. "Hotels and Apartments." In Carl W. Condit, *Chicago 1910–1929: Building, Planning, Urban Technology*. Chicago: University of Chicago Press, 1973. Pp. 151–166.

Cromley, Elizabeth. "The Development of the New York Apartment, 1860–1905." Ph.D. dissertation in art history, City University of New York, 1982.

———. *Alone Together: A History of New York's Early Apartments*. Ithaca: Cornell University Press, 1990.

David, Paul A., and Peter Solar. "A Bicentenary Contribution to the History of the Cost of Living in America." *Research in Economic History* 2 (1977): 1–80.

Davidson, Essie. "Organized Boarding Homes for Self-Supporting Women in Chicago." Ph.D. dissertation, University of Chicago, 1914.

Davis, Allen F. *Spearheads for Reform: The Social Settlements and the Progressive Movement, 1890–1914*. New York: Oxford University Press, 1967.

Dear, Michael, and Jennifer Wolch. *Landscapes of Despair: From Deinstitutionalization to Homelessness*. Princeton: Princeton University Press, 1987.

"Decline and Fall of Hotel Life." *Harper's Weekly* (vol. 1, May 2, 1857): 274.

Deforest, Robert W., and Lawrence Veiller. *The Tenement House Problem*. 2 vols. New York: Macmillan Co., 1903.

Devine, Edward T. "The Shiftless and Floating City Population," *Annals of the American Academy of Social and Political Science* 10 (1897): 147–164.

Dorsey, Leslie, and Janice Devine. *Fare Thee Well*. New York: Crown Publishers, 1964.

Dowdee, Scott. "The Incidence of Change in the Residential Hotel Stock of San Francisco, 1975–1980: A Report to the San Francisco Department of City Planning." M.A. Professional Report, Department of City and Regional Planning, University of California, Berkeley, 1980.

Dreiser, Theodore. *Sister Carrie*. New York: Doubleday, Page & Co., 1900.

Eckert, J. Kevin. "Dislocation and Relocation of the Urban Elderly: Social Networks as Mediators of Relocation Stress." *Human Organization* 42, 1 (1983): 39–45.

————. *The Unseen Elderly: A Study of Marginally Subsistent Hotel Dwellers.* San Diego: Campanile Press, 1980.

Eckert, J. Kevin, and R. E. Dunkle. "Need for Services by the Elderly Experiencing Urban Change." *The Gerontologist* 24, 3 (1984): 257–260.

Eckert, J. Kevin, and Marie Haug. "The Impact of Forced Residential Relocation on the Health of the Elderly Hotel Dweller." *Journal of Gerontology* 39 (1984): 753–755.

Ehrenreich, Barbara, and Deirdre English. *Complaints and Disorders: The Sexual Politics of Sickness.* Old Westbury, N.Y.: Feminist Press, 1973.

Erickson, Rosemary J., and J. Kevin Eckert. "The Elderly Poor in Downtown San Diego Hotels." *The Gerontologist* 17, 5 (October 1977): 440–446.

Evers, Alf, Elizabeth Cromley, Betsy Blackmar, and Neil Harris. *Resorts of the Catskills.* New York: St. Martin's Press, 1979.

"The Experiences of a Boarding House Keeper," *American Magazine* (November 1922): 134.

Fayès, Harriet. "The Housing of Single Women." *Municipal Affairs* 3 (1899): 95–107.

Fergusson, Mary S. "Boarding Homes and Clubs for Working Women." *U.S. Department of Labor Bulletin,* no. 15. Washington, D.C.: Government Printing Office, March 1898. Pp. 141–195.

Fielding, Byron. "Low Income, Single-Person Housing: What's Happening as a Result of the 'Congregate Housing' Provisions of the 1970 Act?" *Journal of Housing* 29, 3 (1972): 133–136.

Flagg, Ernest. "The Planning of Apartment Houses and Tenements." *Architectural Review* 5 (August 1903).

Follett, Jean. "Hotel Pelham: A New Building Type for America." *American Art Journal* 15, 4 (Autumn 1983): 58–73.

Ford, James. *Slums and Housing: History, Conditions, Policy with Special Reference to New York City.* Cambridge: Harvard University Press, 1936.

Ford, Simeon. *A Few Remarks.* New York: Doubleday, Page, & Co., 1903.

Franck, Karen A. "Overview of Single Room Occupancy Housing." In Karen A. Franck and Sherry Ahrentzen, eds., *New Households, New Housing.* Pp. 245–262.

————. "The Single Room Occupancy Hotel: A Rediscovered Housing Type for Single People." In Karen A. Franck and Sherry Ahrentzen, eds., *New Households, New Housing.* Pp. 308–330.

Franck, Karen A., and Sherry Ahrentzen, eds. *New Households, New Housing.* New York: Van Nostrand Reinhold, 1989.

Fretz, Franklin K. "The Furnished Room Problem in Philadelphia." Ph.D. dissertation, University of Pennsylvania, 1912.

Gazzolo, Dorothy, ed. "Skid Row Gives Renewalists Rough, Tough Relocation Problems." *Journal of Housing* 18, 8 (August–September 1961): 327–336.

Gentry, Curt. *The Madams of San Francisco: An Irreverent History of the City by the Golden Gate.* Garden City, N.Y.: Doubleday and Co., 1964.

Gilman, Charlotte Perkins. "The Passing of the Home in Great American Cities." *Cosmopolitan* 38 (April 1905): 135–143.

———. [Mrs. Bradley Gilman]. "A Possible Solution of the Domestic Service Problem." *Good Housekeeping* 32 (1901): 271–277.

Girls Housing Council of San Francisco. "Where Is Home? A Study of the Conditions for Non-Family Girls in San Francisco." Mimeographed report [in the San Francisco State University library], 1927.

Glassberg, David. "The Design of Reform: The Public Bath Movement in America." *American Studies* 20, 2 (Fall 1979): 5–21.

Godfrey, Brian. *Neighborhoods in Transition: The Making of San Francisco's Ethnic and Nonconformist Communities.* University of California Publications in Geography, vol. 27. Berkeley: University of California Press, 1988.

Goldberger, Paul. "Seeking the Ideal." *New York Times Magazine,* 23 September 1984. Pp. 52, 55, 59–60.

Grannan, Caroline. "International Hotel: The Sorry History of a Hole in the Ground." *This World* magazine, *Sunday San Francisco Chronicle and Examiner,* 25 May 1986. Pp. 9–11.

Grier, Katherine C. "Hotels as Model Interiors." In Katherine C. Grier, *Culture and Comfort: People, Parlors and Upholstery, 1850–1930.* Amherst: University of Massachusetts Press, 1988. Pp. 29–38.

Gries, John M., and James Ford, eds. *Planning for Residential Districts.* The President's Conference on Home Building and Home Ownership. Vol. 1. Washington, D.C.: National Capital Press, 1932.

———. *Slums, Large-Scale Housing, and Decentralization.* The President's Conference on Home Building and Home Ownership. Vol. 3. Washington, D.C.: National Capital Press, 1932.

———. *Housing and the Community: House Repair and Remodeling.* The President's Conference on Home Building and Home Ownership. Vol. 8. Washington, D.C.: National Capital Press, 1932.

Groth, Paul. "Building Form, Social Class, and Micro-Morphology," Working Paper Series, Center for Environmental Design Research, University of California, Berkeley, 1986.

———. "Forbidden Housing: The Evolution and Exclusion of Hotels, Boarding Houses, Rooming Houses, and Lodging Houses in American Cities, 1880–1930." Ph.D. dissertation, Department of Geography, University of California, Berkeley, 1983.

———. "'Marketplace' Vernacular Design: The Case of Downtown Rooming Houses." In Camille Wells, ed., *Perspectives in Vernacular Architecture* 2

(1986). Columbia: University of Missouri Press for the Vernacular Architecture Forum. Pp. 179–191.

———. "Non People: A Case Study of Public Architects and Impaired Social Vision." In Russ Ellis and Dana Cuff, eds., *Architects' People*. New York: Oxford University Press, 1989. Pp. 213–237.

Hamilton, W. I. *Promoting New Hotels: When Does It Pay?* New York: Harper and Brothers, 1930.

Hancock, John. "The Apartment House in Urban America." In Anthony D. King, ed., *Buildings and Society*. London: Routledge and Kegan Paul, 1980. Pp. 151–189.

Harney, Robert F. "Boarding and Belonging: Thoughts on Sojourner Institutions." *Urban History Review* 2, 78 (1978): 8–37.

Hartman, Chester. *Yerba Buena: Land Grab and Community Resistance in San Francisco*. Berkeley: National Housing and Economic Development Law Project, 1974.

———. "Housing Struggles and Housing Form." In Sam Davis, ed., *The Form of Housing*. New York: Van Nostrand Reinhold, 1977.

———. *The Transformation of San Francisco*. Totowa, N.J.: Rowman & Allanheld, 1984.

Hayden, Dolores. *The Grand Domestic Revolution: A History of Feminist Designs for American Homes, Neighborhoods, and Cities*. Cambridge: MIT Press, 1981.

Hayner, Norman S. "Auto Camps in the Evergreen Playground." *Social Forces* (December 1930): 256–266.

———. "The Auto Camp as a New Type of Hotel." *Sociology and Social Research* (March–April 1931): 365–372.

———. "The Hotel: The Sociology of Hotel Life." Ph.D. dissertation in sociology, University of Chicago, 1923.

———. *Hotel Life*. Chapel Hill: University of North Carolina Press, 1936.

Hepburn, Andrew. *Great Resorts of North America*. Garden City, N.Y.: Doubleday & Co., 1965.

Herrick, Christine Terhune. "Cooperative Housekeeping." *Munsey's Magazine* 31 (1904): 186–188.

Hines, Thomas S. "The Paradox of 'Progressive' Architecture: Urban Planning and Public Building in Tom Johnson's Cleveland." *American Quarterly* 25, 4 (1973): 426–448.

Hoch, Charles, and A. Cibulskis. "Planning for the Homeless." Paper presented at conference "Housing Research and Policy in an Era of Fiscal Authority," Amsterdam, June 1985.

Hoch, Charles, and Robert A. Slayton. *New Homeless and Old: Community and the Skid Row Hotel*. Philadelphia: Temple University Press, 1989.

Hoch, Charles, and Diane T. Spicer. "SROs, An Endangered Species: Single Room Occupancy Hotels in Chicago." Chicago: Community Emergency

Shelter Organization and Jewish Council on Urban Affairs, December 1985.

"The Holmes Wall Bed." *Pacific Coast Architect* (Published in Portland, Ore.) 3, 4 (July 1912): 454.

Horwitz, R. P. "Architecture and Culture: The Meaning of the Lowell Boarding House." *American Quarterly* 25 (1973): 64–82.

"Hotel Life as It Is and Was." *Chambers Journal* 21 (7th ser., June 20, 1931): 441–451.

Hotel Planning and Outfitting: Commercial, Residential, Recreational. Chicago and New York: Albert Pick-Barth Companies, 1928.

Howells, William Dean. *The Hazard of New Fortunes.* New York: Signet Classics of New American Library, 1965; first published in 1889.

Hunt, Milton B. "The Housing of Non-Family Groups of Men in Chicago." *American Journal of Sociology* 16 (1910): 145–170.

Ihlder, John. "What Are the Best Types of Wage-Earners Houses?" *Housing Problems in America: Proceedings of the Second National Conference on Housing.* Cambridge: Harvard University Press, 1912. Pp. 85–94.

Irvine, Alexander. "A Bunk-House and Some Bunk-House Men." *McClure's Magazine* (August 1908).

Jackson, Kenneth T. "The Bowery: From Residential Street to Skid Row." In Rick Beard, ed., *On Being Homeless: Historical Perspectives.* New York: Museum of the City of New York, 1987. Pp. 68–79.

Johnson, Fred R. "The Lodging House Problem in Minneapolis." Undergraduate honors thesis in economics, University of Minnesota, 1910.

Kasinitz, P. "Gentrification and Homelessness: The Single Room Occupant and the Inner City Revival." *Urban and Social Change Review* 17, 1 (1984): 9–14.

Kennaday, Paul. "New York's Hundred Lodging Houses." *Charities* 13, 21 (February 18, 1905): 486–492.

Kessler, Brad. "Down and Out in Suburbia [residential motels]." *The Nation* (September 25, 1989): 306–312.

Kettleborough, Charles. "Inspection of Hotels and Public Lodging Houses." *American Political Science Review* 7 (1913): 93–96.

Keyssar, Alex. *Out of Work: The First Century of Unemployment in Massachusetts.* Cambridge: Cambridge University Press, 1986.

Kilham, Walter H. "Housing the Single Worker." *Architectural Forum*, 28, 4 (April 1918): 161–167.

King, Doris E. "The First-Class Hotel and the Age of the Common Man." *Journal of Southern History* 23 (May 1957): 173–175, 178–179.

Knowles, Jane Boyle. "Luxury Hotels in American Cities, 1810–1860." Philadelphia: University of Pennsylvania, 1972.

Kowal, Carroll. "Housing Needs of Single Persons: Will Federal Programs Meet Them?" *Journal of Housing* 6 (1976): 277–280.

Kozol, Jonathan. *Rachel and Her Children: Homeless Families in America.* New York: Crown Publishers, 1988.

Krag, Laurine Marion. "How I Made a Boarding House Successful," *The Ladies' Home Journal* (April 1906): 34.

Laffan, William M. "Caravansaries of San Francisco." *Overland Monthly* 5 (August 1870): 176–181.

Lalley, M., et al. "Older Women in Single Room Occupant (SRO) Hotels: A Seattle Profile." *The Gerontologist* 19, 1 (1979): 67–73.

Lewis, Oscar, and Carroll D. Hall. *Bonanza Inn: America's First Luxury Hotel.* New York: Alfred A. Knopf, 1939.

Lewis, Sinclair. *Work of Art.* Garden City, N.Y.: Doubleday, Doran & Company, 1935.

Limerick, Jeffrey, Nancy Ferguson, and Richard Oliver. *America's Grand Resort Hotels.* New York: Pantheon Books, 1979.

Liu, John K. C. "San Francisco Chinatown Residential Hotels." San Francisco: Chinatown Neighborhood Improvement Resource Center, 1980.

Lubove, Roy. *The Progressives and the Slums: Tenement House Reform in New York City, 1890–1917.* Pittsburgh: University of Pittsburgh Press, 1962.

Martin, Edgar W. "Boarding and Lodging." In Edgar W. Martin, *The Standard of Living in 1860: American Consumption Levels on the Eve of the Civil War.* Chicago: University of Chicago Press, 1942. Pp. 148–180.

Martin, Marsha. "Homeless Women: An Historical Perspective." In Rick Beard, ed., *On Being Homeless.* Pp. 32–41.

Mazzi, Francis J. "City from Frontier: Symbols of Urban Development in Nineteenth-Century San Francisco." Ph.D. dissertation in history, University of Southern California, 1974.

McCloud, John. "First in 40 Years: A New Northern California SRO." *New York Times,* 10 March 1991.

McEntire, Davis. "Population and Employment Survey of Sacramento's West End." Typescript manuscript [available in the Bancroft Library]. Sacramento: Redevelopment Agency of the City of Sacramento, 1952.

McGlone, Robert E. "Suffer the Children: The Emergence of Modern Middle-Class Family Life in America, 1820–1870." Ph.D. dissertation, University of California, Los Angeles, 1971.

McKowne, Frank A. "Hotels in Wartime." *Hotel Management* (July 1942): 26.

Meyerowitz, Joanne J. "Holding Their Own: Working Women Apart from Family in Chicago." Ph.D. dissertation in history, Stanford University, 1983.

———. "Sexuality in the Furnished Room Districts: Working Class Women, 1890–1930." Paper presented at the Organization of American Historians annual meeting, April 1986.

Minkler, M., and Beverly Ovrebo. "SROs: The Vanishing Hotels for Low Income Elders." *Generations* 9 (1985): 40–42.

"Model Lodging Houses for New York." *The Review of Reviews* (January 1897): 59–61.

Modell, John, and Tamara K. Hareven. "Urbanization and the Malleable Household: An Examination of Boarding and Lodging in American Families." *Journal of Marriage and the Family* 35 (1975): 467–479.

Monkkenon, Eric, ed. *Walking to Work: Tramps in America, 1794–1935.* Lincoln: University of Nebraska Press, 1984.

Monroe, Day. *Chicago Families: A Study of Unpublished Census Data.* Social Science Studies, no. 22. Chicago: University of Chicago Press, 1932.

"Most Lodging Houses Are Perilous Firetraps." *Safety Engineering* 27, 1 (January 1914): 1–8.

Mostoller, Michael. "A Single Room: Housing for the Low-Income Single Person." In Eugenie Ladner Birch, ed., *The Unsheltered Woman: Women and Housing in the '80s* New Brunswick: Center for Urban Policy Research, 1985. Pp. 191–216.

———. "The Design of a Single Room with Furniture for a Residential Hotel." In Karen A. Franck and Sherry Ahrentzen, eds., *New Households, New Housing.* Pp. 263–284.

———. "A Refuge from the Street." *Metropolis* (March 1989): 54–58ff.

Moudon, Anne Vernez. *Built for Change: Neighborhood Architecture in San Francisco.* Cambridge: MIT Press, 1986.

"The Murphy Bed." *Pacific Coast Architect* 3, 2 (July 1912): 455–456.

Nee, Victor G., and Brett deBary Nee. *Longtime Californ': A Documentary Study of an American Chinatown.* New York: Pantheon Books, 1972.

Newman, Gerald S., ed. *The Homeless Man on Skid Row.* Chicago: Chicago Tenants Relocation Bureau, 1961.

Nienburg, Bertha. *The Woman Home-Maker in the City.* Washington, D.C.: U.S. Bureau of the Census, 1923.

Norris, Frank. *Vandover and the Brute.* New York: Doubleday and Co., 1914.

Nylander, Towne Joseph. "The Casual Laborer of California." Master's thesis, University of California, Berkeley, 1922.

O. Henry [William Sydney Porter]. "Between Rounds." In *The Four Million and Other Stories.* New York: Airmont, 1963; first published in 1906.

Olmstead, Roger R., and Nancy Olmstead et al. *The Yerba Buena Center: Report on Historical Cultural Resources.* San Francisco: San Francisco Redevelopment Agency, 1979.

"Our Family Hotels: Their Rapid Increase in Ten Years: Five Millions Invested in the Buildings: Rooming and Boarding Houses Galore: Cost of Maintenance: Other Details." *San Francisco Chronicle*, Sunday, 31 July 1892, p. 12.

"Over the Draughting Board, Opinions Official and Unofficial." *Architectural Record* 13 (January 1903): 89–91.

Park, Robert E. "The City: Suggestions for the Investigation of Human Behavior in the City Environment." *American Journal of Sociology* 20, 5 (March 1915): 577–612.

Paul, Bradford. *Rehabilitating Residential Hotels.* Information Sheet Number 31. Washington, D.C.: National Trust for Historic Preservation, 1981.

Peel, Mark. "On the Margins: Lodgers and Boarders in Boston, 1860–1900." *Journal of American History* 72, 4 (1986): 813–834.

Penner, Richard H. *Hotel Design and Development: An Introduction and Bibliography.* Exchange Bibliography #1399. Monticello, Ill.: Council of Planning Librarians, 1977.

Perelman, S. J. "Nathanael West." In S. J. Perelman, *The Last Laugh.* New York: Simon and Schuster, 1981.

Philpott, Thomas Lee. *The Slum and the Ghetto: Neighborhood Deterioration and Middle-Class Reform, Chicago, 1880–1930.* New York: Oxford University Press, 1978.

Pinsky, Mark I. "Motel People: A New Class of Homeless on Horizon." *Los Angeles Times,* 27 March 1985. Pp. 1, 3, 24–25.

Plunz, Richard. *A History of Housing in New York City: Dwelling Type and Social Change in the American Metropolis.* New York: Columbia University Press, 1990.

Reitman, Benjamin L. *Sister of the Road: The Autobiography of Box-Car Bertha.* New York: Macauley, 1937.

Richardson, Dorothy. *The Long Day: The Story of a New York Working Girl* (first published in 1905). In William O'Neill, ed., *Women at Work.* Chicago: Quadrangle Books, 1972. Pp. 1–270.

Riis, Jacob. *How the Other Half Lives: Studies Among the Tenements of New York.* New York: Dover Publications, 1971; first published in 1890.

Robbins, Raymond. "What Constitutes a Model Municipal Lodging House." *Proceedings of the National Conference of Charities and Corrections,* 1904.

Rollinson, Paul A. "Prisoners of Space: The Impact of Urban Revitalization upon the Elderly 'Single Room Occupancy' (SRO) Population." Paper given at the meeting of the Association of American Geographers, 1986.

———. "The Story of Edward: The Everyday Geography of Elderly Single Room Occupancy (SRO) Tenants." *Journal of Contemporary Ethnography* 19, 2 (1990): 188–206.

Rose, Arnold M. "Living Arrangements of Unattached Persons." *American Sociological Review* 12 (1947): 429–435.

———. "Interest in the Living Arrangements of the Urban Unattached." *American Journal of Sociology* 53 (1948): 483–493.

Sala, George Augustus. "American Hotels and American Food." *Temple Bar Magazine* 2 (July 1861): 345–356.

———. "The Philosophy of Grand Hotels." *Belgravia Magazine* 10 (2d ser.; March 1873): 137–144.

———. *America Revisited.* 6th ed. London: Vizetelly and Co., 1886; first published in 1879.

San Francisco City Planning Commission. *The Master Plan of San Francisco: The Redevelopment of Blighted Areas: Report on Conditions Indicative of Blight and Redevelopment Policies.* San Francisco: Planning Commission, 1945.

San Francisco Housing Association. *First Report.* San Francisco: SFHA, 1911.
———. *Second Report.* San Francisco: SFHA, 1913.
San Francisco, Housing Authority of the City and County of San Francisco. *Real Property Survey, 1939.* 3 vols. San Francisco: City and County of San Francisco, 1940.
Schneider, John C. "Skid Row as an Urban Neighborhood, 1880–1960." In Jon Erickson and Charles Wilhelm, eds., *Housing the Homeless.* New Brunswick: Rutgers Center for Urban Policy Research, 1986. Pp. 167–189.
Scott, Mel. "Western Addition District: An Exploration of the Possibilities of Re-planning and Rebuilding One of San Francisco's Largest Blighted Districts." San Francisco: Department of City Planning, December 1947.
Sexton, Randolph Williams. *American Apartment Houses, Hotels, and Apartment Hotels of Today.* New York: Architectural Book Publishing Co., 1929.
Shapiro, Joan. *Communities of the Alone: Working with Single Room Occupants in the City.* New York: Association Press, 1971.
———. "Reciprocal Dependence Between Single-Room Occupancy Managers and Tenants." *Social Work* 15, 3 (June 1970).
———. "Single-Room Occupancy: Community of the Alone." *Social Work* 11 (1966): 24–33.
Shumsky, Neil. "Tar Flat and Nob Hill: A Social History of San Francisco in the 1870s." Ph.D. dissertation in history, University of California, Berkeley, 1972.
———. "Vice Responds to Reform: San Francisco, 1910–1914." *Journal of Urban History* 7 (1980): 31–47.
Siefkin, David. *The City at the End of the Rainbow: San Francisco and Its Grand Hotels.* New York: G. P. Putnam's Sons, 1976.
Siegal, Harvey A. *Outposts of the Forgotten: Socially Terminal People in Slum Hotels and SRO Tenements.* New Brunswick, N.J.: Transaction Books, 1978.
Solenberger, Alice W. *One Thousand Homeless Men.* New York: Russell Sage Foundation, 1911.
Spradley, James P. *You Owe Yourself a Drunk: An Ethnography of Urban Nomads.* Boston: Little, Brown and Co., 1970.
St. Louis Institute of Applied Gerontology. *The Invisible Elderly.* Papers and discussion presented at the First National Conference, "The Invisible Elderly," held in St. Louis, August 1975. Washington, D.C.: The National Council on the Aging, Inc., 1976.
Statler, E. M. "The Race for the Guest." *Nation's Business* (June 1928).
Stephens, Joyce B. *Loners, Losers, and Lovers: Elderly Tenants in a Slum Hotel.* Seattle: University of Washington Press, 1976.
Stern, Jane, and Michael Stern. "Cafeteria." *New Yorker* (August 1, 1988): 37–54.
Stern, Robert A. M. "With Rhetoric: The New York Apartment House." *Via 4: Culture and Social Vision.* Philadelphia: University of Pennsylvania School of Design, 1980. Pp. 78–111.

Stern, Robert A. M., Gregory Gilmartin, and John Massengale. "Palaces for the People." *New York 1900: Metropolitan Architecture and Urbanism, 1890–1915*. New York: Rizzoli, 1983. Pp. 252–305.

Stone, Ursala. "Hospitality, Hotels, and Lodging Houses." In Edwin R. A. Seligman, ed., *Encyclopedia of the Social Sciences*. Vol. 4. New York: The Macmillan Co., 1937. Pp. 472–477.

Stutz, F. P. "Adjustment and Mobility of Elderly Poor Amid Downtown Renewal." *Geographical Review* 66, 4 (1976): 391–400.

Swanson, Charles G. "Social Background of the Lower West Side of New York City." Ph.D. dissertation, at New York University, n.d. (before 1936).

Taylor, C. Stanley. "Efficiency Planning and Equipment." *Architectural Forum,* Apartment Hotel Reference Number 41, 5 (November 1924): 253–258.

"Ten Cent Lodgings." *San Francisco Chronicle,* 5 October 1890. P. 9.

Thompson, Kay. *Eloise*. New York: Simon and Schuster, 1955.

"To Cook or Not to Cook: Where Law Evasion Leads." *Housing Betterment* 16, 1 (1927): 68–82.

Trillin, Calvin. "U.S. Journal: San Francisco: 'Some Thoughts on the International Hotel Controversy.'" *New Yorker* (December 19, 1977): 116–120.

Trollope, Anthony. *North America*. New York: Harper & Brothers, 1862.

Tygiel, Jules Everett. "Workingmen in San Francisco: 1880–1901." Ph.D. dissertation in history, University of California, Los Angeles, 1977.

U.S. Bureau of the Census. *Fifteenth Census of the U.S., Census of Hotels, 1930.* Washington, D.C.: U.S. Government Printing Office, 1931.

U.S. Bureau of Labor. "Boarding Homes, Aids for Working Women." In *Working Women in Large Cities*. Report of the Commissioner of Labor. Washington, D.C.: U.S. Government Printing Office, 1888.

———. *Housing of the Working People in the United States by Employers,* by G. W. W. Hanger. Extension Bulletin No. 54 (1904).

U.S. Senate, Special Committee on Aging. *Single Room Occupancy: A Need for National Concern*. Information Paper, June 1978.

"Unique Workingmen's Hotel for San Diego." *Architect and Engineer of California* 34, 1 (August 1913): 80–82.

University of California, the Heller Committee for Research in Social Economics. "Cost of Living Studies II: How Workers Spend a Living Wage." *University of California Publications in Economics* 5, 3. Berkeley: University of California Press, 1929.

———. *The Dependent Aged in San Francisco*. University of California Publications in Economics 5, 1. Berkeley: University of California Press, 1928.

"Ups and Downs of the Hotel Business for the Past 21 Years." *Hotel World Review: 75th Anniversary Edition*. New York: Ahrens Publishing Company, 1950.

Van Antwerp, Harriet. "Study of Boarding Homes for Employed Women and Girls." St. Louis: Community Council, 1923.

Van Orman, Richard A. *A Room for the Night: Hotels of the Old West.* Bloomington: Indiana University Press, 1966.

Vance, James E., Jr. *This Scene of Man: The Role and Structure of the City in the Geography of Western Civilization.* New York: Harper & Row, 1977.

Veiller, Lawrence. "The Housing Problem in American Cities." *Annals of the American Academy of Political and Social Science* 25 (1905): 248–272.

———. *A Model Housing Law.* New York: Russell Sage Foundation, 1914.

———. *A Model Tenement House Law.* New York: Russell Sage Foundation, 1910.

———. *Housing Reform: A Handbook for Practical Use in American Cities.* New York: Charities Publication Committee, 1910.

———. *Protecting Residential Districts.* Publication No. 26. New York: National Housing Association, 1914.

Wallace, Samuel E. *Skid Row as a Way of Life.* Totowa, N.J.: Bedminster Press, 1965.

Ward, David. "The Victorian Slum: An Enduring Myth." *Annals of the Association of American Geographers* 66 (1976): 323–336.

Warren, James S. "What the Typical Apartment Hotel 'Looks Like.'" *Hotel Management* 18 (November 1930): 406–409.

Weiner, Lynn. "Sisters of the Road: Women Transients and Tramps." In Eric Monkkenon, ed., *Walking to Work.* Pp. 171–188.

Weiss, Marc. *The Rise of the Community Builders: The American Real Estate Industry and Urban Land Planning.* New York: Columbia University Press, 1987.

———. "Urban Land Developers and the Origins of Zoning Laws: The Case of Berkeley." *Berkeley Planning Journal* 3 (1986): 7–25.

Werner, Frances E., and David B. Bryson. "A Guide to the Preservation and Maintenance of Single Room Occupancy (SRO) Housing." *The Clearinghouse Review.* National Clearinghouse for Legal Services (April 1982): 999–1009; (May 1982): 1–25.

Westfall, Carroll William. "The Golden Age of Chicago Apartments." *Inland Architect* (November 1980): 18–26.

Wharton, Edith. *The Custom of the Country.* New York: Scribner's Sons, 1913.

———. *The House of Mirth.* New York: Charles Scribner's Sons, 1952; first published in 1905.

White, Edmund. *A Boy's Own Story.* New York: Plume Books of the New American Library, 1982.

Whitman, Walt. "Wicked Architecture." *Life Illustrated* (July 19, 1856), reprinted in Emory Holloway and Ralph Adimari, comps., *New York Dissected: A Sheaf of Recently Discovered Newspaper Articles by the Author of Leaves of Grass.* New York: Rufus Rockwell Wilson, 1936. Pp. 92–98.

Wiebe, Robert H. *Businessmen and Reform: A Study of the Progressive Movement.* Cambridge: Harvard University Press, 1962.

Williamson, Jefferson. *The American Hotel: An Anecdotal History.* New York: Alfred A. Knopf, 1930.

Willy, John. "Hotels." *Architect and Engineer of California* 22, 3 (September 1935): 17–19.

Wilson, Evelyn Heacox. "Chicago Families in Furnished Rooms." M.A. thesis, School of Social Service Administration, University of Chicago, 1929.

Wilson, Robert S. *Community Planning for Homeless Men and Boys: The Experience of Sixteen Cities in the Winter of 1930–1931.* New York: Family Welfare Association of America, 1931.

Wolch, Jennifer R. "Residential Location of the Service Dependent Poor." *Annals of the Association of American Geographers* 70, 3 (1980): 330–334.

Wolch, Jennifer R., and Stuart A. Gabriel. "Development and Decline of Service-Dependent Ghettos." *Urban Geography* 5, 2 (1984): 111–129.

Wolfe, Albert Benedict. *The Lodging House Problem in Boston.* Boston: Houghton Mifflin and Co., 1906.

Wood, Edith Elmer. *The Housing of the Unskilled Wage Earner.* New York: Macmillan, 1919.

———. *Recent Trends in American Housing.* New York: Macmillan, 1931.

Wood, Samuel Edgerton. "The California State Commission of Immigration and Housing, A Study of Administrative Organization and the Growth of Function." Ph.D. dissertation in political science, University of California, Berkeley, 1942.

Woods, Eleanor H. "Social Betterment in a Lodging District." *Charities and the Commons* 19 (1907): 962–968.

Woods, Robert A. "The Myriad Tenantry of Furnished Rooms." *Charities and the Commons* (November 2, 1907): 955–956.

Yip, Christopher Lee. "San Francisco's Chinatown: An Architectural and Urban History." Ph.D. dissertation in architecture history, University of California, Berkeley, 1985.

Zeisloft, E. Idell, ed. *The New Metropolis: Memorable Events from 1600 to 1900: From the Island of Man-hat-ta to Greater New York at the Close of the Nineteenth Century.* New York: D. Appleton and Co., 1899.

Zorbaugh, Harvey Warren. "The Dweller in Furnished Rooms." *Papers and Proceedings of the American Sociological Society* 20 (1925): 85–86.

———. *Gold Coast and Slum: A Sociological Study of Chicago's Near North Side.* Chicago: University of Chicago Press, 1929.

Salvation Army, 150–151

Salvation Army Evangeline Residence, San Francisco, 102, 99

San Augustine, Texas, 180

San Diego, 282. See also Baltic Inn; Golden West Hotel

San Francisco Bay Area, 291, 253. See also Alameda; Berkeley; Claremont Hotel; Hotel Del Monte; Oakland; Tubbs Hotel

San Francisco city development, 19, 123

trade and manufacturing, 17–18, 134, 137, 182, 269

San Francisco districts. See Barbary Coast; Chinatown; Civic Center; Manilatown; Nob Hill; North Beach; Potrero Hill; South of Market; Telegraph Hill; Tenderloin; Third and Howard; Union Square; Waterfront; Western Addition

San Francisco hotels

lodging houses (see Bonanza House; Central Hotel; Denver House; International Hotel; Portland Hotel; Reno Hotel)

midpriced rank hotels (see Berkshire Hotel; Delmonico Hotel; Hotel Cecil; Hotel Victoria)

palace rank hotels (see Canterbury Hotel; Fairmont Hotel; Hotel Bellevue; Hotel Whitcomb; Huntington Hotel; Lick House;

Mark Hopkins Hotel; Palace Hotel; Saint Francis Hotel; Sir Francis Drake Hotel)

recent SROs, 9, 294, 299

rooming houses (see Clayton Hotel; Delta Hotel; Grand Central Hotel; Hotel Eddy; National Hotel; Sierra House)

total room supply, x, 19, 24, 305, 25, 181

San Francisco reformers and housing officials, 191, 236

City Planning Commission, 261, 277, 278

early codes and reports, 100, 229, 241–242, 257–261

Housing Association: original, 208, 236, 258; second, 260–261

Housing Authority, 192

Redevelopment Agency (SFRA), 279

Renewal Agency and TOOR, 285

Scientific management, 204

Seattle, 63

Separation of spaces and groups, 70, 213–214, 244–245, 255. See also New city; Single-use districts; Social stratification; Specialization of buildings and neighborhood

Servant problem, 28, 62

Settlement houses, 207

Sexual immorality, 216, 219

Shahn, Ben, 231

Shanghaiing, 140

Sheraton Washington, Washington, D.C., 2

Showers, municipal lodging houses, 240

Sierra House, San Francisco, 15, 172, 15

Single family houses, 251–253, 269, 304, 307, 18, 123

Single laborers' zones: definition, 151–152, 156, 228. See also Barbary Coast; Bowery; Chicago; Chinatown; Douglas Street; Gateway District; Lodging houses, building types; Lodging houses, general issues; Third and Howard

Single people

as housing residents, 14, 46, 86, 90, 137, 212, 300, 302

as seen by housing experts, 91, 211–213, 257–258

and public housing programs, 259, 277–280

Single Room Occupancy hotels. See SRO hotels

Single-use districts, 251, 253, 256

Single workers' districts, 151–163, 194, 280–281, 193, 272

and reformers, 193, 272, 282, 282

See also Bowery; Gateway District; Main Stem; Norfolk, Virginia; Third and Howard

Sir Francis Drake Hotel, San Francisco, 43

Sisson Hotel, Chicago, 65

Siting of hotels, 47–50, 191, 194, 27, 41, 42, 69, 82, 194

Designer:	Nola Burger
Compositor:	G & S Typesetters, Inc.
Text:	10/16 Sabon
Display:	Copperplate
Printer:	Malloy Lithographing, Inc.
Binder:	John H. Dekker & Sons